Herders, Warriors,
and Traders

African Modernization and Development Series
Paul Lovejoy, Series Editor

Herders, Warriors, and Traders

Pastoralism in Africa

EDITED BY

John G. Galaty and Pierre Bonte

Westview Press

BOULDER • SAN FRANCISCO • OXFORD

African Modernization and Development Series

Copyright © 1991 by Westview Press, Inc.

Published in 1991 in the United States of America by Westview Press, Inc., 5500 Central Avenue, Boulder, Colorado 80301-2847, and in the United Kingdom by Westview Press, 36 Lonsdale Road, Summertown, Oxford OX2 7EW

A CIP catalog record for this book is available from the Library of Congress.
ISBN 0-8133-8067-7

Printed and bound in the United States of America

10   9   8   7   6   5   4   3   2   1

To the memories of

Suzanne Bernus
and
Harold K. Schneider,

friends of African pastoralists

Contents

Figures and Plates

Preface

African pastoralists have been devastated by over twenty years of drought, famine, and dislocation. Images of starving children in the Sahel, lines of refugees in Ethiopia, and dying cattle in the Sudan are familiar to all of us. Why this calamity should have happened, and should continue to happen, is a question addressed by a generation of researchers in anthropology, economics, geography, ecology, and history who have studied African pastoralism in the context of environmental instability, political strife, and social collapse.

International aid agencies, aware of the humanitarian expectations held by a sympathetic public, have invested heavily in the African arid zone since the trans-African drought of the early 1970s. This has, directly or indirectly, stimulated research on all aspects of pastoralism. The effort itself has become world-wide, with scholars from throughout the world carrying out research and exchanging insights concerning the current and historical realities of pastoral communities in Africa.

In the late 1970s, several research and communication networks were created for academics and development personnel involved with pastoralist societies. The Overseas Development Institute in London formed a "Pastoral Network," which publishes the *Pastoral Network Papers*. At the Maison des Sciences de l'Homme in Paris, the "Equipe écologie et anthropologie des sociétés pastorales" produced for over a decade until 1989 the journal *Production pastorale et societé*. And at McGill University in Montreal, the "Commission on Nomadic Peoples," of the International Union of Anthropological and Ethnological Sciences, has published *Nomadic Peoples* for over a decade; in 1990, the Scandinavian Institute for African Studies in Uppsala took over its sponsorship. The two editors of this book have participated in the groups located in Paris and Montreal and acknowledge the benefits gained from those organizations and the scholars affiliated with them.

In the wake of decolonization, the naive and frustrated developmentalism which ensued, and the complex catastrophes subsequently experienced on the African continent, scholars have increasingly taken cognizance of social and political factors constraining pastoral societies and have become aware of the importance of the indigenous knowledge, goals and interpretations of pastoralists for both scholarship and policy development. National governments and development agencies have tended to view pastoralists in purely economic terms, as livestock producers and resource managers, rather than as human agents within the context of culture and political economy, active within multi-leveled political structures that shape economic and social life at local, regional and national levels. Too often the dialectics between economic practice and social value and between pastoralists and the state have been ignored, as have the regional contexts of ethnic and economic reciprocity and competition and the historical precedents for current responses to drought, social change, and state power.

This volume juxtaposes anthropological and historical perspectives on the political economy of African pastoralists, emphasizing dynamic factors in the emergence and current realities of livestock-based societies in Africa. African social science and historiography have tended to look outward from cities and states, a view that marginalizes pastoralists, the quintessential rural dwellers. This book presents a "pastoralist perspective" that focuses on the interstices, on the rangeland communities, trade routes and social networks which have so influenced the states and markets which lie between them. But the arid and semi-arid African savanna not only links regions of sedentary life but is one of the largest zones of human occupation in the world, with its own economic and political fabric.

Contributors to this book represent several disciplines but share a keen sense of the social dimensions of political economy and a scepticism for romantic notions of nomadic life. The book emphasizes the economic variation and diversity found in livestock-keeping societies by considering the linkages between pastoralism and cultivation, hunting, foraging and trade. Given that several economic forms can and are pursued within any given ecological setting in Africa, pastoralism represents a political and ideological as well as an economic practice. Pastoralism is a "commitment," predicated on cultural assumptions embedded within diverse political, economic, religious, and military institutions, which in given regions may cut across distinct communities.

We have attempted to construct the conceptual basis for an understanding of African pastoralists as part of the larger social and historical experience of the regions they inhabit. Key topics include the emergence and evolution of pastoralism in Africa, the interplay of ecology and political history, the expansion of pastoral societies and their influence on the formation of African trade, markets and states, the diversity in pastoral social and political institutions, the colonial experience, and current pastoralist conditions, responses and prospects. The chapters are addressed both to scholars and policymakers, who will continue to have material effect on future developments among pastoralists, who despite crisis and calamity, persist in making the African arid and semi-arid zones their home.

The editors wish to acknowledge with appreciation the help and support of institutions and individuals who contributed to the production of this volume: the Centre Nationale de Recherche Scientifique of France for supporting a workshop where many of the papers were initially presented and discussed; the Social Sciences and Humanities Research Council of Canada and the Fonds pour le Formation des Chercheurs et l'Aide à la Recherche of Quebec for support and travel during the preparation of the volume; Pierre Bigras, Salina Cheserem, Lisa Edelsward, Josée Lavoie and Eric Worby for invaluable editorial assistance at various stages of the project; and Diane Mann, for patient and competent help in computerizing and printing the manuscript. We also acknowledge the *American Ethnologist* and the *Journal of African History* for permission to reprint the chapters by J. and J. Comaroff (*American Ethnologist*, Vol. 17, No. 2, May 1990:195-216) and D. Johnson (*Journal of African History*, Vol. 30, 1989:463-486) originally prepared for this volume and since published in the indicated journals. If not otherwise noted, photographs were taken by J. Galaty.

John G. Galaty
Pierre Bonte

About the Contributors

Pierre Bonte, who studied anthropology at the University of Paris, has carried out extensive field research over a fifteen-year period among the Tuareg of Niger and the Moors of Mauritania. He has served as *Conseiller* for the anthropology section of the Centre Nationale de Recherche Scientifique in France, was a founding member of the "Equipe écologie et anthropologie des sociétés pastorales," and is a member of the Laboratoire d'Anthropologie Sociale at the College de France.

Jean Comaroff is a professor of anthropology at the University of Chicago. She received her Ph.D. at the London School of Economics (1974), has done extensive fieldwork in Botswana, South Africa and Great Britain, and has previously held research posts at the University College of Swansea (Wales) and the University of Manchester. She is the author of *Body of Power, Spirit of Resistance* (1985), a study of the culture and history of a South African people, and of numerous essays in medical, cultural and historical anthropology.

John L. Comaroff is a professor of anthropology and sociology at the University of Chicago. He received his Ph.D. at the London School of Economics (1973), has done extensive fieldwork in Botswana and South Africa, and has previously taught at the University College of Swansea (Wales) and the University of Manchester. He is the author, co-author and editor of several books and papers on the Tswana, comparative African studies and political, legal and historical anthropology.

Edouard Conte studied anthropology at Cambridge University and the University of Paris and has pursued long-term field research in the Chad basin. He has been affiliated with the Laboratoire d'Anthropologie Sociale at the College de France in Paris, the Frobenius Institute in Frankfurt, and the CEDEJ in Cairo.

John G. Galaty pursued studies of anthropology at the University of Chicago and has carried out anthropological research among the Maasai of Kenya and Tanzania. An associate professor at McGill University, he has served as secretary to the Commission on Nomadic Peoples and associate dean of McGill's Faculty of Graduate Studies and Research. He is currently director of McGill's Centre for Society, Technology and Development and heads a team research project on agrarian and pastoral systems.

Douglas H. Johnson carried out archival and field research on Nuer history in the Sudan in 1972 and 1974-1976. After completing his Ph.D. in history at the University of California at Los Angeles, he served as Assistant Director for Archives in the Juba Regional Ministry for Culture and Information in 1980-1983, continuing research with a Fulbright-Hayes research grant in 1982. He is a research fellow at the Queen Elizabeth House Centre for Commonwealth Studies at Oxford and works with the World Food Programme in Operation Lifeline Sudan.

Abdel Wedoud Ould Cheikh is director of the Institut Mauritanien de Recherche Scientifique and has carried out extensive historical and field research on societies of Mauritania, including the Moors. He received his doctorate from the University of Paris.

Neal Sobania carried out field research in Kenya and Ethiopia on the regional history of the Lake Turkana basin. He pursued a Ph.D. in history at the School of Oriental and African Studies in London and presently serves as assistant professor of history and director of international exchanges at Hope College, Michigan.

David Turton has carried out anthropological field research among the Mursi of southwestern Ethiopia. He pursued his doctoral studies at the London School of Economics and has taught in the Department of Social Anthropology at the University of Manchester. He has served as editor of the journal *Man* and on the Africa (North) Field Committee of Oxfam (U.K.).

Edwin Wilmsen has carried out archaeological research on the pre-history of native North America and southern Africa, including the ethnohistory of San-speaking communities of the Kalahari. He has served as professor of anthropology in the African Studies Center at Boston University and research fellow at the Max Planck Institute in the Federal Republic of Germany.

PART ONE

INTRODUCTION

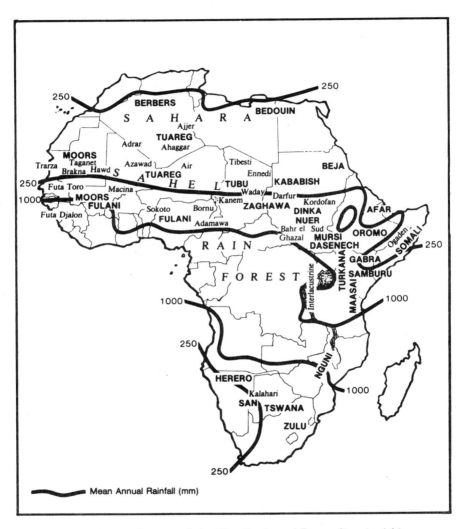

FIGURE 1.1 Climatic Zones and the Distribution of Pastoralists in Africa

1

Introduction

Pierre Bonte
and John G. Galaty

Pastoralism is the dominant way of life throughout the drier regions of the African continent that receive less than 1,000 mm of rain per year: horizontally across the Sahara and the Sahel from the Atlantic Ocean to the Horn of Africa, and vertically down the Rift Valley from eastern Africa and the Intralacustrine plateau to southern Africa (See Figure 1.1). Domestic animals fail to thrive and pastoralism diminishes in importance only in the tsetse-infested belt of wetter forest, from the thick forests along the West African coast through the rainforests of the Zaire basin and the woodlands of central Africa to the Indian Ocean. Elsewhere, pastoralists inhabit remote, rural areas, out of sight of urban centers and foreign eyes. Only during crises is the attention of the world briefly alerted to the plight of these citizens of Africa's deserts, savannas and rangelands, when emaciated animals, desperately being driven to market, die near roads and when herders settle in famine camps or flock to urban peripheries to seek menial employment. But when rains come and pastures are renewed, pastoralism resumes its pace across the vast arid zone made habitable only through the economy of herding.

Images of gaunt herders experiencing double catastrophies of drought

3

and famine reinforce distorted notions of the non-viability of a pastoral economy or of the failure of pastoral Africa to share the continent's expectations of and aspirations for development. Scholars have too often contributed to popular misconceptions by describing African pastoralists in univocal terms, not so much wrong as inadequately nuanced. Accounts often suggest that herding societies:

- Form self-sufficient and autononous rather than complex, interacting communities;
- Practice strictly subsistence-oriented rather than flexible production strategies articulated with markets;
- Are irrationally motivated towards unfettered livestock accumulation rather than rationally facing compromises between security and economic growth;
- Participate in static rather than dynamic systems of social life;
- Are ecologically limited to, rather than seeking out for the benefit of the domestic animals, the resources of the arid zone;
- Are intrinsically expansionist rather than expanding situationally to achieve political or economic ends;
- Are insensitive to environmental constraints rather than managing a fragile environment under difficult circumstances; and
- Are marginal to the African experience rather than having played central roles in its political and economic history.

Together, these generalizations constitute a romantically archaic pastiche of the pastoralist which ignores the social, political and ecological contexts so necessary for understanding complex currents of African history and the historical context crucial for interpreting African social and economic processes.

This book brings together currents of scholarship that, linking social and historical perspectives, provide more complex but more convincing images of African pastoralism. Pastoralism in Africa does not constitute a single phenomenon and certainly does not represent a distinct mode of production, but reflects the diverse cultural and historical settings and political-economic circumstances found throughout the continent.[1] We find wide continental variation in the scale and degree of stratification of societies and polities dependent on pastoralism, and in the way in which livestock-keepers participate in complex regional systems of political economy. The value and significance of domestic animals in the African economy is quite central to understanding the role of pastoralists and pastoral systems in the African experience, and a certain similarity is apparent between societies as varied as the Fulbe, Maasai, or Herero, Tuareg, Tutsi or Tubu, given that their forms of thought and action are permeated by cultural assumptions and symbolic codes regarding the meaning and utility of livestock and the material exigencies of herding.[2] But, beyond pastoralism proper, elements of animal husbandry are woven together with other cultural strands to form the social fabric proper to the Sahel, the Horn of Africa, or the Rift Valley of East Africa.

To encourage comparison across diverse situations, chapters are arranged thematically to demonstrate similarities across different geographical regions. These themes are: the cultural and economic rationale of herding and the value attributed to domestic animals; political aspects of dry-land ecology and social responses to drought and famine; regional systems of trade, exchange, ethnic interaction, and conflict; the implications of pastoral mobility, warfare and expansion for ethnic emergence; and regional economic differentiation, social stratification and inequality. Each key theme encompasses a body of myths, misconceptions, simplifications, and overgeneralizations about pastoralists that pervade our popular and academic vision of Africa. The book refutes or puts into context these thematic myths: of an irrational African "cattle complex"; of either (paradoxically) the ecological determination or ecological insensitivity of pastoral systems; of closed, self-regulating pastoral subsistence systems; of the intrinsically expansionist nature of pastoralism; and of the inherently egalitarian nature of pastoral systems.

Superceding these myths, we aim to present in this volume a multi-faceted and complex paradigm for interpreting the African pastoral experience, which includes dynamic responses to regional power systems, trade and exchange networks and ethnic processes, the interplay of symbolic and economic value, and the dialectics of culture and political economy. We offer a reinterpretation of African pastoralism that emphasizes the importance of pastoral diversity, the regional context for the political and economic pursuit of animal husbandry, and the value of combining historical and anthropological perspectives. A final chapter on "The Current Realities of African Pastoralism" applies the insights gained from the case studies in presenting current experiences in the larger national and international contexts within which pastoral communities pursue cycles of mobility, husbandry and domestic life. In this conclusion, we consider the local influence of the post-colonial state, of national boundaries often dividing pastoral groups, the impact of national and international markets, the role of internationally supported development assistance programs, and conflicts of an ethnic, nationalist and global nature. We intend to show how African pastoralists have been, and remain, both subject to larger forces of influence and agents of their own histories, shapers of their own futures, and significant factors in African history and contemporary life.

Singular Myths and Diverse Realities

Despite the diverse forms pastoralism takes in Africa, we tend to "think about" pastoralists in terms of a "pure" or specialized type. Associated with the quintessential "pure" African pastoralist are a number of "myths", by which we mean complexes of signs and assumptions woven into narratives, often more inadequate than untrue, that reflect limited but often insightful visions of reality, often couched in allegorical form (Clifford 1986). The myth of subsistence, that pastoralists live solely on pastoral produce and manage herds strictly for subsistence rather than sale, contains the allegory of the virtue of precommoditization; the myth of the "cattle complex", which proposes that domestic animals are objects of cultural and religious rather than economic value, contains an anti-utilitarian allegory; and the myth of the "pastorale", by which herding seen as a "natural" rather than a social process, entailing minimal labor, scant effort and little judgement, betrays an allegory of aboriginal harmony. The reality is not simply the opposite of the myth, although domestic animals are often marketed, agricultural produce is in fact frequently consumed by pastoralists, animal husbandry is actually a highly strategic, labor intensive process, and animals clearly are perceived (in part) in economic terms by herders, and these facts do not completely elude allegorical form. The pastoral reality does involve, however, a dialectic between circumstances and practices and the myths, symbols, and allegories that are intrinsic to pastoral sensibility and identity. Rather than opposing myth with reality, we aim to situate both ideas and practices, which underlie pastoral production, labor and value (the subject matter of the three myths just addressed), in the context of current knowledge about diversity in the African pastoral experience.

The Pastoral Continuum: From Specialization to Diversification

Most communities in the African arid and semi-arid zone that are involved in specialized animal *production* are not necessarily committed to exclusive *consumption* of pastoral products. Indeed, most livestock-keeping peoples in Africa are in a strict sense agro-pastoralists, combining animal husbandry with crop production and - in many cases - with bee-keeping, foraging, hunting and/or fishing. Further, specialists in pastoral production invariably seek a more diversified diet through exchange with cultivating neighbours. Along a pastoral-agricultural "continuum", most rural communities pursue a diversified form of production, combining livestock and crops but adjusting the emphasis given to one or the other according to climate, soil conditions, capital, resources and labor. But the existence of a behavioral continuum should not lead us to ignore the fact that, as cultural and economic systems, specialized pastoralism and agro-pastoralism can differ dramatically.

Specialized pastoralism is associated with entire groups, such as the Maasai, Boran or Gabra of East Africa, or with fractions of groups, such as among Fulbe or Tuareg of West Africa, or even with herder status-groups within larger agro-pastoral societies, such as the Intralacustrine Bahima. Specialized systems usually are found in relatively dry, sparsely populated areas, where cultivation may be tenuous or impossible and animals require greater per capita pasture area for sustenance. While "stocking rates" are usually lower in these regions of pastoral specialization, the size of herds managed is far greater than in wetter agro-pastoral areas, as are the average animal holdings of families and individuals.[3] Notwithstanding wide variation, over time and between families of a given community, it may be useful to identify three levels of per capita holdings which correspond to three points on the pastoral continuum. The cattle holdings of specialized herders such as Maasai or Fulani often vary from ten to twenty cattle per person, richer agro-pastoralists such as the Dassanetch average around three to four cattle per capita (reported by Turton in this volume), while most agro-pastoralists, such as the Nuer, Mursi or Gogo, average only a single animal per person. However, agro-pastoralism tends to take place under conditions of richer soil and higher rainfall favorable to higher human and animal population densities than are possible in drier lands. The total number of livestock held by agro-pastoralists is far greater but animals contribute proportionately less to their subsistence and exercise less overall influence on their economic life than do livestock held by more specialized pastoralists (Galaty 1988; Sandford 1985).

The Labor Factor in Animal Husbandry

Based on casual observation, a myth of the idle pastoralist has been propagated that assumes animal production and reproduction is essentially a "natural" process which requires little social labor.[4] It follows from this assumption that pastoralists could diversify their production without decline in the productivity of their animal husbandry. But in fact, the productivity of pastoral labor significantly increases with specialization, since economies of scale are achieved through using fewer herders for larger herds over greater expanses of pasture. There may be a certain "elasticity" in the labor requirements of pastoralism, since one herder is needed for one head or fifty. Still, labor represents the major constraining factor in virtually all systems of pastoral production in Africa, given the wide range of different work tasks required, the need for additional workers to tend subherds grouped according to species or by age (cattle versus goats and sheep, or cattle and sheep versus camels and goats, or by milking versus dry herds, or calves versus matures), and the necessity of continuous herd movement, especially in the dry season (Sperling 1987; Swift 1977).[5] In this volume, Sobania in particular shows that herd growth is constrained by limits on the availability of labor. Wilmsen, however, writing of Southern Africa, points out that there is a definite limit to the demand by Tswana for San herding labor, but this occurs in the quite unique Kalahari setting where the absence of predators and limited availability of water provides for a sort of feral grazing.

Most rural African production is based on domestic, family labor. The need for pastoral labor may represent one reason herding communities practice higher degrees of polygyny, which is aimed at achieving growth of the family as a social and economic unit. But, given that the amount of labor available varies as the family steadily grows in size and then decreases as members establish their own homes (through the developmental cycle of the domestic group) and that the labor available in richer families may be inadequate to tend for their greater animal wealth, labor will often be sought from other less well-endowed families, from the kin group, from the neighborhood, from other societies, such as from the San in southern Africa, or from political dependents or even slaves in the West African Sahel. As well as "sloughing off" excess population following drought and animal loss, pastoral populations also assimilate when needed supplies of additional labor.[6]

Although it may appear that rural producers simply shift along a behavioral continuum of specialized to agro-pastoralism according to circumstances, agro-pastoralists and specialized pastoralists differ quite fundamentally in their allocation of labor than the notion of contingency would imply. Among what we might call "casual" agro-pastoralists, such as the Turkana, sporadic rain-fed or river-bank agriculture is often practiced by women, with fields modestly prepared and haphazardly planted but given little attention. More committed agro-pastoralists, for whom agriculture is economically dominant, may experience severe deficits of labor when workers are simultaneously needed in both herding and agriculture, especially during the late dry-season/early wet-season "bottleneck" when labor demands may be felt simultaneously for harvesting, for preparing fields for planting, and for moving herds to distant pasture and water. Such constraints on labor often lead groups or individiuals to specialize in either herding or agriculture within families, between different segments or communities within a single society. For instance, the Pokot are divided between lowland pastures and highland farms, with kinship and exchange links between the two communities, while the Intralacustrine Hutu and Tutsi of Rwanda, discussed in this volume by Bonte, represent strata within a single society specialized in cultivation and herding. While agro-pastoralists experience severe labor constraints and fail to benefit from the economies of scale achieved by more specialized herders, they do gain ecological insurance by diversifying their use of resources and avidly exploit the advantage of being able to invest the value generated through cultivation in the form of added livestock.

Livestock Value and Ideology

No myth has been more repeated and less understood than Herskovits' notion of the "cattle complex", which proposed that the pastoral populations of Eastern Africa shared a common commitment to the acquisition and accumulation of cattle, valued for cultural and religious rather than economic reasons (Herskovits 1926). Today, it is well understood that domestic livestock serve a variety of economic functions, in particular as subsistence goods for specialized pastoral communities such as the Maasai, who even today essentially pursue milking (rather than beef) enterprises. But livestock are also clearly seen as marketable commodities and clearly serve certain functions of "capital", as reliable stores of value, as media for exchange, and objects of investment.[7] This is even more true for agro-pastoralists than for pastoralists, since the former invest returns from cash crops in livestock, and it holds as well for salaried workers and urban dwellers, who, as absentee herdowners, find cash too liquid and banks too inflationary.

Ironically, the notion of pastoral economic "irrationality" continues to have currency in the discourse of development, where the notion is used to justify development interventions which would increase pastoral market participation. But Herskovits' essential insight, although often misused by the critics of pastoralists, remains sound, that livestock - in particular cattle - are, in Mauss' (1954) sense, "total social facts," signifying well-being and abundance, providing fertile objects for metaphorical thought and expression, and representing religious symbols, emblems of divinity and vehicles for sacrifice. Based on a reconsideration of the notion of value, Bonte develops in this volume the link between the institution of kingship and the value attributed to cattle among Intralacustrine societies.[8] Since rural African societies often cohere less through force and formal structure and more through social networks, livestock exchange, in particular in bridewealth, serves to create and strengthen social ties.[9] The social significance of livestock exchange is developed in virtually every contribution to this volume. Herskovits' notion of a "cattle complex", then, accurately depicts the pervasive ideology of livestock value in much of Africa, among both specialized and agro-pastoral communities, but must be supplemented - as it is in the Comaroff's excellent discussion in this volume of the value of cattle among the Tswana - by awareness of how both material and symbolic value is attributed to domestic animals, whose cultural utility is often expressed in condensed religious form.

The History and Political Ecology of Pastoralism

Pastoralism has been viewed as more subject to environmental constraint than foraging and agricultural adaptations, which span many natural habitats. In this sense, pastoralism represents a neolithic adaptation to aridity, in biotic terms a method of extracting protein from otherwise unpalatable cellulose of grasses and shrubs through the secondary use of the products of domestic ruminants (Dyson-Hudson 1980). But pastoral ecology is political as well as natural, since the definition and use of rangeland resources depend on local institutions of ownership and labor, on networks of trade and exchange, and on the definition of ethnicity and the establishment of social boundaries.

Pastoralism generally sustains population densities greater than those of foraging but less than those of cultivation. The pursuit of animal domestication was once thought, within the historical materialist perspective, to represent a transitional stage between the hunting of animals and the domestication of crops.[10] This myth has been put to rest through the archaeological study of the neolithic coevolution of animal and plant domestication in central and southwest Asia. While aridity most likely played a role in the secondary diffusion of livestock throughout Africa (which ironically may have occurred prior to the spread of agriculture), the somewhat contradictory myth of the nomad as the "father of the desert" has been used to explain the dessication of the Saharan/Sahelian zone, a viewpoint far from academic which influences national and international development policy towards pastoralists throughout the arid zones of Africa.[11]

Ecology and Pastoral Prehistory in Africa

The first pastoralists in Africa were apparently relatively sedentary Saharan fisher-foragers, who sought to diversify a declining resource base through the adoption of domestic animals. Neolithic pastoralism appears somewhat earlier in the Saharan "Sudanese" tradition than in the Nile Valley or the Maghreb traditions that were strongly influenced by the neolithic pastoral tradition of the western Mediterranean (Guilaine 1976). Sheep and goats, originally from the Near East[12], appeared in Cyrenaica around 4,800 B.C. (McBurney 1967) and contributed to the later expansion of Sudanic peoples from 4,000-5,000 B.C. (Ehret 1982). The first cattle[13] were humpless long-horns, represented in numerous Saharan cave paintings between 4,000 and 3,200 B.C., which were partially supplanted during the second millenium B.C. in West Africa by humpless short-horns. Approximately 2,000 years later, the humped zebu (See Plate 1.1) arrived through the Horn of Africa which, after interbreeding with preceding species, has come to constitute the preponderant African bovine (Epstein 1971; Clutton-Brock 1987).

The progressive southward movement of pastoralism in West Africa appears to have been associated with growing dessication. Sedentary herders appear in Mauritania around the fourth millenium B.C. (Hugot 1974; Holl 1986), perhaps representing ancestral Fulbe, and domestic animals were present in the Sahel and northern Ghana by the beginning of the second millenium B.C. (Smith 1976; Carter and Slight 1972) and shortly thereafter in northern Nigeria (Shaw 1981). With the arrival of the horse in the Sahara in the second millenium B.C., a new phase of equestrian pastoralism emerged among Libyan Berbers which was subsequently to influence all Saharan pastoral cultures.

Cattle and ovicaprin pastoralism, spreading southward from the Sudan, was combined with fishing and plains hunting near Lake Turkana from 1,000-3,000 B.C. Evidence for several pastoral neolithic cultures further south in East Africa proper is abundant for the period beginning 1,000 B.C. (Bower and Nelson 1978; Robertshaw and Collett 1983b), with sheep and cattle pastoralism combined with hunting-foraging in both forest and savanna sites (Gifford *et al.* 1980). It is debated whether grain cultivation occurred in conjunction with the "savanna pastoral neolithic" (associated with early Southern Cushites and Southern Nilotes) or whether it only arose with the later arrival of iron-age Bantu farmers. The latter, combining cattle, sheep, grain cultivation, and metallurgy, appeared 2,000 years ago in East Africa (Ambrose 1984; Robertshaw and Collett 1983a, 1983b), in southern Africa several centuries later (Shrire 1980). However, Wilmsen recounts in this volume that livestock may have been acquired prior to the Bantu arrival in southern Africa by Khoisan-speakers, who would then have represented the region's first herders. In East Africa, increased pastoral specialization, reflecting greater mobility and dispersion of settlements, is associated with the beginning of the pastoral iron-age around 600 A.D. (Bower & Nelson 1978). Paradoxically, specialized herding was furthered by the spread of agriculture, that made possible the development of a more integrated regional economy involving complementary exchange, described for the Maasai by Galaty, for southern Ethiopia by Turton, and for northern Kenya by Sobania.

The camelid was introduced around the third millenium B.C. to the Horn of Africa from Arabia, where it had been domesticated (Digard 1990:109), then, beginning in the sixth-seventh centuries B.C., diffused slowly through North Africa into a Sahara already characterized by extreme aridity. In North Africa, where it was found by the Romans

(Demougeot 1960), this one-humped dromedary was primarily used for military and agricultural purposes and proved a remarkable instrument for the penetration of the Sahara by Moors, Tubu and Arabs and by the Somali and Gabra (See Plate 1.2) in the Horn of Africa. The camel made possible the establishment of stable trans-Saharan caravan links between the Mediterranean, Saharan and sub-Saharan worlds from the fourth century. These routes were further developed beginning in the eighth century, when they facilitated the expansion of Islam and the founding of a succession of Sudanic empires.

The spread of pastoralism throughout Africa has been associated in the archaeological record with increasing dessication, especially of the Sahara and Sahelian regions. However, although animal husbandry has indeed provided African communities with the means of thriving in otherwise uninhabitable lands, the widespread efflorescence of pastoral culture cannot be adequately explained as a simple response to aridity. In fact, due to their value and the advantages they offer, livestock - together with social relations and technical knowledge involved in their husbandry - rapidly diffused into regions unconstrained by extreme aridity, where pastoralism was often combined with other subsistence activities: foraging, fishing, agriculture. At the same time, pastoralism played a key role in the refiguration of regional economic and social systems, described in this volume by Galaty for East Africa, through stimulating forms of ethnic economic specialization, social differentiation based on ownership or control of livestock, and diverse systems of mixed farming and pastoro-foraging. The diffusion of livestock represented a cultural and historical as well as a technical process which acted on and shaped as well as responded to an arid-land ecology.

The Political Ecology of African Pastoralism

From the viewpont of rangeland and savanna ecology, the broad correspondence between pastoral and ecological regimes suggests that herding systems have evolved as adaptations to differing degrees of aridity (See Figure 1.1). Very dry, desert-like regions receiving under 10-12" (250-300 mm) rainfall each year are primarily exploited by camel pastoralists, with population densities of under one person per sq km: the Moors, Tubu and Tuareg of the Sahara, the Kababish Arabs of the Sudan, the Beja and Afar of the Red Sea coast hinterland, and the Somali, Rendille and Gabra of the Horn of Africa and its interior. The semi-arid open grassland and savanna woodland regions of the Sahel, the East African corridor and the periphery of the Kalahari, that receive from 10-20" (250-500 mm) of yearly rainfall, are generally exploited by cattle pastoralists (See Plate 1.3): specialized herders, such as the Fulani of the

Sahel and the Maasai, Samburu, Borana, and Turkana of East Africa, with population densities of one to three persons per sq km, and dry-land agropastoralists, such as the Barabaig and Gogo of East Africa and the Tswana and Herero of southern Africa, with population densities rising to between four and eight per sq km. In regions receiving over 40" (1000 mm) of rainfall per year, animal husbandry rapidly diminishes in importance, due to the proliferation of animal parasitic diseases, lack of palatable and nutritious forage and agricultural intensification (Galaty 1988). Camel (or, to be more precise, dromedary) and cattle pastoralism represent two quite distinct technical systems associated, respectively, with arid and semi-arid settings (Bonte 1975b); camels serve primarily for mounted transport and carrying burdens as well as for subsistence (Gauthier-Pitters and Dagg 1981), cattle for milk and secondarily meat production but in some agropastoral systems for traction. Cultural and ideological emphasis placed on these large domestic species often obscures the universal presence of sheep and goats across most environmental conditions and their economic importance as a ready medium of exchange and a ready source of meat and sometimes milk. Together with donkeys, widely used for transport and occasionally for subsistence, these secondary species provide uniformity across continental systems of animal husbandry dominated by cattle or camels.

Pastoralism represents a socio-technical rather than a "natural" subsistence system, which requires political, economic and cultural investment in land, social relations, regional security, animal capital, and labor, and competence in animal behavior, environmental knowledge, and the skills and tastes of animal husbandry. Dryland ecology serves primarily as a *negative* determinant of pastoralism, most domestic livestock being excluded from tsetse-infested forest, camels from regions which are too wet (over 350 mm annual rainfall), cattle from regions which are too dry (under 250 mm annual rainfall)(Dahl and Hjort 197:246). Where their husbandry is not prevented, species are chosen for economic, cultural and historical as well as for ecological reasons. For instance, camels could survive and thrive in many areas occupied by cattle-keeping Samburu, but only recently were adopted by Samburu in small numbers, herded in the same manner as cattle (Sperling 1985a). And due to Saharan dessication, Tuareg now often herd camels far south into the Sahel, in proximity to cattle, while, due to pressure from cultivators, cattle keepers increasingly penetrate lands previously given over to camels.[14] In the Intralacustrine region Tutsi herded cattle in regions well-suited to agriculture, which now predominates, and, through the nineteenth century, Maasai pastoralism monopolized use of the lush Uasin Gishu plateau. Today, although scattered dry-land and riverine cultivation is increasingly practiced in semi-arid rangelands, in an apparent adoption of agro-pastoralism among previously specialized Maasai or Fulani herders. However, these activities are often initiated by non-pastoralists, intermarried with or invited to do so by pastoralists, who aim to diversify community or household production while both maintaining a pattern of pastoral labor allocation and a sense of cultural honor.

Pastoralists are sensitive to ecological variations in space and time, and divide and move herds to better exploit available pastures and marshall the energies of human and herd. Johnson describes the herd movements of Nuer and Dinka through seasonal cycles and periodic catastrophes of rain, drought and flood, and how the exchanges of milk, grain and fish help make more secure the overall food economy within a regional subsistence system. The importance to herders in the Southern Sudan of *toic*, patches of hilly grass amidst lowland floodlands, should be contrasted to the significance of *b'la* depressions in the Chadic steppe, sites of water catchment and irrigation, recounted by Conte. In Eastern Africa, areas of seepage and swamp, at the foot of escarpments and hills or along water courses, provide critical dry-season and drought forage for domestic animals. The availability of dry forage is the critical pastoral constraint in riverine regions of the southern Sudan or the Omo River, where floods may bring famine, but the occurrence of adequate sources of water, in wells, oases or boreholes, often represents the critical limiting factor in the Sahara or the Botswana rangelands.

The contributions to this volume do not grant ecological factors theoretical primacy, but note and analyze in detail the historical interplay between environmental and climatic variation and pastoral practice. Knowledge of the physical environment alone cannot account for the dynamics of pastoral systems, but ecology is the subject of much pastoral interest and concern. Pastoral systems, imprinted by culture and shaped by history, serve aims and motives beyond the secondary extraction of protein from vegetal biomass through the mediation of domestic ungulates. Among these aims are establishing social relations, exercising or evading political control, and creating or expanding wealth. African pastoralism occurs within a *political* ecology (Bennett 1984, 1988), of local power, state influence, markets, ideological commitments and ethnic values, as well as of arid-land resources.

Pastoralists in Regional Systems

Pastoralists have been associated with closed social and economic systems, in part due to their necessarily autonomous cycles of herd movement, their historical reliance on non-marketed pastoral foods, their often exclusive occupation of rangeland territory, and a certain ethnic pride, arrogance and exclusivity. The contributions to this volume put each of these stereotypes into question, or, rather, put each image into social and historical context, generating a more dynamic model of pastoralists participating in open regional systems.

Subsistence and Networks of Exchange

All herding communities in Africa depend for their subsistence in part on the products of their animals, the more specialized among them relying quite heavily on milk and meat, especially in the wet season when, even today, many families reduce their consumption of non-pastoral produce to a minimum. Further, most pastoralists define their most valued foods in pastoral terms and explain away their consumption of grains or foraged foods as incidental or anomalous, no matter how vital these are to the family diet. However, that said, virtually no pastoral society has succeeded in attaining a strictly pastoral diet without periodically entering into trade or exchange with neighbors for dietary supplements, usually in the form of millet, sorghum or maize. Regional networks of exchange are not only evoked in times of crisis, but represent stable forms of linkage between communities that enjoy different and complementary forms of production, between them exploiting the variation in ecological setting and natural resources (Little 1983, 1985).

Sobania in this volume notes the trade links which existed in the Lake Turkana region in the nineteenth century: Turkana traded small-stock to the Dassanetch for millet and tobacco, and sometimes for clay pots, coffee and cloth, while Samburu received millet in exchange for livestock; these relations were strengthened through the establishment of bond partnerships. Among agro-pastoral Mursi, Turton describes how southerners who cultivate exchange their produce with northerners, who have more pastoral involvement. Johnson makes the insightful claim that the economic viability of the Nuer and the Dinka of the Sudan depends on their participation in a "common economy", based not on exclusive occupation of resources but on the maintenance of "regular access to alternate resources", itself a social process. Informants noted that "people go where the food is", and that it is "scarcity and not sufficiency that makes people generous". For the complex social setting of Kanem in the Lake Chad basin, Conte describes how variation in climate and environment stimulated complementarity between camel pastoralists and cattle-keepers, with nomadic hunters playing a key role in preserving an often fragile agro-pastoral system in the face of stress. In Mauritania, a principal issue in the regional political order was the control by the nomadic Moorish population of former slave cultivators and of trade with riverine cereal cultivators. In some regions of Africa, colonial administrations defined pastoral districts as "closed", cutting off herders from social and economic ties with their neighbors; this made pastoralists necessarily more autonomous and gave them the appearance of "timeless" self-sufficiency.

Commercial Trade

The notion that pastoralists resist the commercial sale of animals is so often repeated that it appears a truism, and yet it is essentially false. Livestock owners often engage in trade on their own terms, as an adjunct to their system of livestock production. While they are careful to retain a rich, core breeding herd, differentiated across species, breeds and reproductive types, they invariably participate in livestock marketing, either to acquire cash (for taxes, food, amenities or fees) or to procure other livestock for breeding or fattening through exchange or purchase with revenues from animal sales (Simpson and Evangelou 1984). Today, livestock represents the richest economic resource on the African continent, with pastoralists feeding African cities teeming with people. At the same time, livestock represents one of the continent's greatest sources of foreign exchange, with live animals and meat being exported, primarily to the Middle East. Nonetheless, livestock are only "semi-commercialized," since animals continue to represent subsistence goods, stores of value and sources of investment for rural areas lacking in financial institutions or access to stable currency.

Pastoral participation in trade is not new, as contributions to this volume attest. Wilmsen presents evidence for long-distance trade in the Kalahari around 800 A.D. and for San participation in Zimbabwe trading networks between the eleventh and fifteenth centuries. In the nineteenth century, San were involved in the Portuguese maritime trade in trophies, which led to the appropriation of their livestock in part through the establishment by the Tswana of a monopoly over European trade (Wilmsen 1989a). Regional exports of cattle from the Kalahari began in the early 1890s with the construction of the railroad to South Africa, and today Botswana uniquely in Africa enjoys preferential status in livestock exports to the European Economic Community (EEC), which has stimulated attempts to consolidate and monopolize rights in rangeland, control of water sources and ownership of cattle (Worby 1988; Hitchcock 1990).[15]

Livestock and animal trophies have always been favored commodities sold by savanna dwellers to the outside world, often through caravan trade. Sobania refers to participation in the nineteeth century Somali caravan trade by the Boran, who exchanged livestock, ostrich feathers, ivory, rhino horn, gum and camphor for brass and copper wire, iron, cowries and tobacco. Control of the salt trade was central to the involvement of nomadic populations in Saharan caravans (See Plate 1.4), through which salt, cloth, copper, livestock, paper and luxury foods were traded southward for gold, cereals, ivory and slaves (Lovejoy 1986).[16] In most cases, the local procurement of livestock was critical to the subsistence of long-distance caravans, which, as food "on the hoof" could accompany mobile traders. This trade often stimulated profound social and economic shifts in the conditions of rangeland pastoralism, through, for example, concentrating livestock wealth in Southern Africa and strengthening the role of nomads in the formation of the Sudanic states.

Mutable Ethnicity and the Common Economy
    Emerging out of the colonial mandate to establish social control in the sparsely-populated arid lands was the perception that pastoralists formed mutually hostile groups, divided by linguistic, cultural and ethnic differences, in conflict over pasture and indulging in reciprocal raiding. While not denying the reality of pastoral conflict, to be further discussed below, the contributions to this volume convey a surprisingly different image of inter-group relations and ethnic processes. Turton cites Waller's (1985) vision of nineteenth century East Africa, "socially fluid, highly adaptable, capable of absorbing outsiders easily". Sobania, in documenting the movement of people between relatively stable economic "niches" in East Africa, speaks of "mutable ethnicity" regarding strategic shifts in subsistence activity and movement between communities as conditions warrant. Other authors have noted the "blurred" ethnic boundaries between Fulani and Hausa.
    It is important, however, to distinguish between economic, residential and ethnic identity. In response to environmental shifts and stress, individuals and families move along the continuum of subsistence practice, giving greater emphasis to cultivation when herds diminish, or to hunting and foraging when grains fail. Destitute herders move to sites of greater food abundance, often along lines established through prior friendships, bond partnerships or marital exchange, sometimes across ethnic lines. Fertile river valleys and lakes, such as occupied by the Dassanetch of the lower Omo, by the Chamus of Baringo, or by the people of the Lake Chad basin, have always provided haven for destitute herders. But the tendency is strong for pastoralists to return to their home areas and revert to their previous subsistence pattern when stress or catastrophe passes. The reemergence of these cultural commitments signifies the quite different structural principles underlying specialized pastoralism, agro-pastoralism and peasant farming that underlie the continuum of contingent behavior and response. We now realize how prevalent multi-ethnic and multi-lingual settlements must have been,

given contemporary cases such as the Ariaal, who straddle Samburu and Rendille, and reports, such as Johnson's in this volume, of ethnically intermingled homesteads in the southern Sudan, in which Dinka settled, marrying Nuer, claiming, "If we had no flood, we would not take our daughters to the Lou". In mixed residences, albeit temporary, individuals gain behavioral and linguistic competence in the cultural codes of other ethnic communities without ethnic boundaries - ultimately a matter of symbols - being obscured.   Given long-term residential change, individuals (especially children) may in the second generation be perceived as "ethnically assimilated" when residence is combined with both cultural competence and socio-economic commitment. But when two languages - or economic values and cultural practices - begin to merge, the "ethnic category" itself becomes mutable. African pastoralists participate in these three distinct processes, of shifting residence, economy and ethnicity. Paradoxically, they have combined tenacious cultural and economic commitment with pragmatic flexibility, both asserting cultural, economic or ethnic "purity" (an indigenous notion, at least for Maasai and Fulani) and practicing economic, residential and ethnic opportunism.

Mobility, Conflict and Expansion

Does pastoralism inevitably entail "predatory expansion", disrupting the stable development of sedentary agriculture, regional trade and urbanization, such as Perry Anderson (1974) asserted for Central Asia? Such views hold that endemic conflict and expansionism among pastoralists stems from the exigencies of herding or from the ethos or cultural character shaped by herding. Colonial administrations, acting on such assumptions, sought to separate pastoral groups, but in trying to prevent conflict also inhibited interchange and exchange between them. Similarly, the notion that pastoralism is "non-progressive" has influenced the development of national and international policies toward nomadic, arid-land dwellers, for socialist and market-oriented countries alike, that promote sedentarization, which, when carried out, tends to undermine the livestock economy through inhibiting mobility.

Processual Models of Pastoral Conflict and Expansion

It is important to distinguish between *mobility*, some form of nomadic, semi-nomadic or migratory movement of human and herd being intrinsic to pastoral systems, *expansion*, which involves change in the domain controlled, and *conflict*, which is a political process reflecting clashes of interests between groups. The three processes are quite different, although they may be associated in practice. Most forms of pastoral movement involves the exercise of established rights over definite pastures; most expansion, like immigration, is an ongoing peaceful process, reflecting underlying shifts in the balance of resources, but also between human aspirations and circumstances; and most conflict within or between groups does not involve expansion. Several contributions to this volume consider questions of pastoralist expansion and conflict, not only in relation to pastoral mobility but in terms of regional economic and ethnic dynamics. Livestock raiding, for example, ubiquitous among herding communities of the world, represents in the African setting not simply a mode of controlled conflict - although personal aggression and defense may be part of this sort of community drama - but also a means of redistribution, between richer and poorer regions and from more to less wealthy families and individuals. Similarly, expansion, rather than exemplifying conflict and predation, represents a process of redistributing human and animal populations across resources, the spread of novel cultural and economic forms, the experience of ethnic assimilation and change, and the emergence and realignment of regional political systems. Images of conflict and scenarios of expansion often sum up more complex histories of movement and longer-term transformations of political and economic relationships, which are recounted through allegories of predation.[17]

In developing a processual model of social fluidity and movement in African pastoralism, three issues have been considered by anthropologists and historians. One is whether movement involves the spread of an existing economic practice, ethnic group or political system or its transformation. The second, a subsidiary of the first, concerns the linkage over time between expansion and group emergence or identity. The third concerns whether particular social institutions stimulate, encourage or facilitate expansion, or to the contrary whether they can be seen as developing out of the expansion process. In pursuing these questions, we will review some of the key African pastoral cases.

Social Transformation through Expansion

The classic cases of pastoral expansion are "segmentary", where non-cyclical migration leads to the emergence or "hiving off" of pastoral units identical to a parent group. Turton, in this volume, distinguishes between several types of movement, the "breakaway" from a parent body (Type A) and the gradual occupation of territory, through which the geographical location of a territorial or ethnic boundary shifts (Type C), both of which may serve to replicate or extend the existing social and economic system. The dramatic, long-term movement of the Fulbe across the Sahelian corridor has been associated with "pastoral drift" (Stenning 1959), with herding mobility providing both motive and means for expansion. The Fulbe migratory group involves a territorial dimension, access to new pastures being sought through perpetual migration, and a lineage dimension, whereby lineages are continuously reconstructed as a function of changing neighborhood relations (Dupire 1970). Galaty describes how spiralling "orbits" of pastoralism, involving the appropriation of critical swamp, water or dry-season pasture sources, have been involved in the long-term Maasai expansion. The herding process frequently involves the penetration of peripheral pastures by herders, with reinforcements marshalled when the incursion is resisted; this leads either to judicious withdrawal or the *de facto* encorporation of the area into the group's pastoral domain. This movement may involve a "trek" to distant pastures (which resembles Turton's Type A movement). The expansion process may be seen to represent a mode of demographic and economic redistribution, of animals across regional resources and human communities, or (to reverse the customary pattern of thinking) of people across available animal and territorial resources.

However, expansion is a political as well as a demographic process, especially when large-scale warfare and movement stimulates the emergence of new political forms. The Fulbe-led Jihad in West Africa resulted in the formation of Sahelian states from Futa Toro to Sokoto, while the Sharr Buba war, discussed in this volume by Ould Cheikh, involved the consolidation of the Moorish social hierarchy in favour of the aristocratic Arab warriors, rather than their Marabout cleric opponents, and the emergence of powerful Emirs. On the basis of a social hierarchy similar to that of the Moors, the Tuareg consolidated through expansion a form of political organization involving the integration of pastoral/agricultural sectors through exchange within a regional economic system of diversified yet complementary parts.[18] Access to agricultural provisions within the more pastoral Iwellemmedan Kel Denneg confederation in Niger was ensured through the establishment of military control over cultivators and the institutionalization of slavery at their political periphery (Brock 1984). Centralized polities proliferated throughout southern Africa as a result of the great nineteenth century *Mfecane* migrations by Nguni-speaking peoples such as the Ngoni and Ndebele (from South Africa into Zimbabwe, Zambia, Malawi and southern Tanzania), stimulated by the wars of Shaka, the Zulu King (Were and Ogutu 1978; Edgerton 1987).

Expansion, Identity and Group Formation

Expansion can influence identity in at least three ways, through the assimilation of people to an expanding group, through the assimilation of an expanding people to the group encountered, and through the emergence of new groups. Rather than just a "particle" flow of people through space, the Maasai expansion may in part represent a cultural "wave phenomenon" through preexisting groups, as "being Maasai" became coterminous with being assimilated to a new form of pastoralism (Galaty 1982a; Lamphear 1985). In the case of the Fulbe, pastoral expansion had at least two quite different results, one, in their domination and assimilation of Hausa-speakers, the other in their loss of identity within the Sahelo-Sudanese states they founded or conquered during the eighteenth and nineteenth centuries, including the ethnic assimilation of sedentarized "Cattle Fulani" within Hausa and Bornu states. This end was avoided by some Fulani only through continuing nomadism, which resulted in their marginalization within the Jihad states they had formed. The Oromo expansion, which began in the sixteenth century, moved from the southern Ethiopian lowlands into the highlands, during which tribes and states were assimilated to Oromo language and culture, with many Oromo in turn being assimilated to Coptic Christianity, non-pastoral pursuits, and sedentary and often urban life (H. Lewis 1966; Hultin 1975). These are examples of Turton's Type B expansion, the gradual infiltration of a group across an ethnic boundary.

Turton has suggested that the northern Mursi - in an example with wider applicability - do not exist and then expand but are expansion. That is, the process of expansion precipitates the formation of new groups at the frontier, whose identities are defined in contradistinction to parental groups and to groups encountered. Conflict and warfare often represent not simply the process of territorial advance but a retrospective ritual legislation of it, signalled through peacemaking ceremonies. Similarly, following the formation of a centralized Emirate in the wake of the Moorish expansion in Mauritania, pastoral tribes were also conceived as Emirates and "created" as such.

The Institutional Basis for Expansion

In contrast to the belief that pastoral mobility in itself offers an expansionary advantage, links between expansion and characteristic social or religious institutions of expanding groups have been posited. Sahlins (1964) suggested that the Nuer segmentary lineage system represented a mechanism of "predatory expansion", the Nuer coming to represent a positive social mutation out of a larger Dinka entity (*cf.* Newcomer 1972; Southall 1976; Kelly 1986); in Turton's terms, Nuer are "Dinka in expansion". The great Oromo expansion has been seen as resulting from the exigencies of the Gada generation-grading system, which called for each new group to conquer a new territory, and the kinship system, which restricted access to cattle for bridewealth for young men of marriageable age, thus stimulating them to seek livestock abroad (Hultin

1975). With similar motivations, Maasai expansion involved "deadly jousts" between groups aggregated in age-set villages, followed by less restrained age-set clashes and ultimately to the occupation of territory, appropriation of livestock, and the dispersion or assimilation of defeated communities. These cases demonstrate that the social institutions most characteristic of pastoral societies served to precipitate or to organize expansionary movement. But it is difficult to say whether given institutions favored expansionary movement, whether expansion encouraged the emergence and refinement of given institutions, or whether those institutions simply served as vehicles for expansionary processes whose determinants lay elsewhere.

Apropos of this problem of analysis is the relation between Islam and expansion in the West African arid zone. Commerce and Islam have been proposed as the two principle motives for this expansion. Ould Cheikh notes the role of Islam in the formation of the vast but ephemeral Almoravid Dynasty in the eleventh century, that was both supported by and had great impact on the camel herding tribes of the Sahara. In the Horn of Africa, Somali and Afar expansion was associated with the spread of Islam, the former moving northward toward Djibouti, into the Ogaden and southwestward deep into Kenya, where they dislodged Oromo pastoralists who had preceded them. Certainly Islam offered a political ideology and, in the form of the Jihad, a set of motives for expansion. But it was primarily through factors of commerce, state formation and expansion that Islam was dispersed across the Saharan and Sahelian regions.

The Pastoral Factor in Expansion

Pastoralists move to seek pasture but it is a misnomer to equate nomadism and mobility with conflict and expansion. It is true that many instances of societal expansion in Africa are associated with pastoral or agro-pastoral peoples, since well-developed livestock economies gain significantly in having mobile subsistence. Historically, conflict often has involved inter-group livestock raiding, and successful expansion invariably entailed confiscation of domestic animals and appropriation of pastoral territory.

However the warlike and predatory image of pastoralists derives from the the myth of the nomad. When one studies within the same cultural context the operation of internal violence, in feuds, vendettas, raids, and razzias, it appears that sedentary more than nomadic communities suffer more from the unfolding of unchecked cycles of violence (Edgerton 1971; Black-Michaud 1975). Further, cultivators also carry out similar processes of incremental drift, with pioneer fields established in interstitial or neutral ground, followed by population increase, claims consolidated by conflict and peace-making. Indeed, the planting of fields often ratifies expansion identified here as "pastoral" but actually involving agro-pastoralists such as the Nuer, Mursi, or Ngoni.

Expansion is not an intrinsically pastoral trait but represents a complex social process in which herders and cultivators are equally involved. At the micro-level of political economy, pastoral migration in the more permanent form of expansion helps reestablish the three-way balance between human communities, animal populations, and local pastoral resources. However, at another level, expansion may involve highly intentional, institutionally-defined, and dramatically enacted process involving external "triggering" factors, such as Islamic ideology, the aim of controlling trade, the process of state formation, threats to control of regional resources, the development of new social and technological forms, or the onset of colonialism. We have recounted here only a few examples of the processes expansion might entail, such as the role of mobility in the transformation of society, the link between expansion and ethnic emergence, and the association between social organization and expansion. In migration, expansion and conflict, the herding factor may be significant not due to its "predatory" nature but because of the particularly dynamic combination of social and economic factors present in pastoral societies.

The Pastoral Politics of Segmentation and Stratification

In ethnographic studies of nomadic and semi-nomadic herding communities in Africa, including Nuer, Fulbe, Baggara, Turkana, Borana, Somali, pastoral polities have been seen as intrinsically egalitarian and "acephalous", literally "headless", or without centralized authority. Schneider (1979) suggested that there were political entailments to the fact that livestock wealth - being self-reproducing and mobile - cannot be monopolized, for in the absence of any other factor of production which can be centrally controlled, pastoralism will make possible, indeed will stimulate diffusion of wealth and thus decentralization of power. This argument is most applicable to East Africa, where most pastoralists are organized in relatively discrete herding sections, in which community leadership is exercised through local councils or age-groups. However, these conditions do not obtain where pastoral communities are situated within wider systems of political centralization and social stratification, where they merely represent social segments - either dominant or subordinate - or specialist groups. This volume illustrates the diversity of political experience in pastoral Africa and should dispel any myth that associates pastoralism with a certain form of political culture or organization, whether hierarchical or egalitarian, centralized or decentralized.

Yet, an egalitarian ethic is strongly asserted by many pastoralists, Maasai, for instance, maintaining the intrinsic worth, the freedom of action, and the right to express public opinion of any herd owner. The notion of the "peace of the Boran" asserts the importance of achieving internal harmony through avoiding resentment or domination in human relations. Since animal husbandry, involving family ownership of livestock, virtually requires decentralized judgements about very local herd movements, pastoralism instills in its very nature a high degree of assertiveness, independence and autonomy (Edgerton 1971). However, even the most assertively egalitarian pastoralists - such as the Maasai or Fulani - harbor notions of the superiority of livestock ownership and husbandry over other metiers and indulge themselves in discourse regarding the inferiority of non-pastoralists, laborers, and women (Galaty 1982). In effect, attributes of value, including strength, courage, restraint, animal wealth, and honor, on which the equal worth of pastoralists is based, are predicated on the existence of symbolic "others" who exemplify the negation of pastoral value and esteem. In many African pastoral societies, one finds endogamous caste groups, artisans, blacksmiths, hunters, fishermen, and even bards and diviners, who are marked by notions of pollution and inequality and viewed ambivalently. In such cases, it appears that internal egalitarianism is acquired at the price of external hierarchy.

Elsewhere, unequal statuses are codified as "estates" within a stratified social system. Among the Tswana, discussed by the Commaroffs and referred to by Wilmsen, persons are distinguished by their propinquity to the chief, with aristocratic collateral lines benefiting from higher status than commoners, laborers, and "serfs" of lower status; around the chief's capital, estates are geographically situated in concentric circles formed by adjacent arable land, more distant pastures and remote cattle posts (Worby 1984:63; 1988). In the Intralacustrine cases presented by Bonte, "aristocratic" Tutsi or Hima, associated with a symbolic monopoly on cattle, were attributed honor and labor by Hutu agricultural commoners and Twa forager/serfs within an ideology of intrinsic "ethnic" difference, despite a common Bantu language and culture (Maquet 1961). In Kanem, described here by Conte as an ethnically complex region that includes Teda-Daza and Arabic-speaking pastoralists, Chadic-speaking pastoralists and agro-pastoralists and Nilo-Saharan speakers of diverse occupation, three social cleavages occur: the first between cattle-owning "people-of-the-spear" attributed "noble descent" and the inferior "people-of-the-bow", the hunters and smiths; the second between freemen and slaves; and the third between masters and dependents. In the Sahara, Tuareg pastoralists have asserted social and economic rights over oasis cultivators, while Moorish nomads controlled former slave cultivators and other tributaries and slaves. In effect, the economic integration, within a regional political order, of pastoralism, cultivation and other economic specializations occurs through a system of virtual "estates", economic status groups inflected by ethnic and linguistic differences. Such a system represents a form of "complementary" agro-pastoro-foraging, with circulation of goods and the investment of value occuring through trade, tribute and exchange between groups, rather between communities or sectors within a single diversified yet integrated local or domestic economy.[19]

Such pervasive systems of social hierarchy were often, but not always, associated with highly centralized systems organized around a distinctive leader, for example, a powerful Tswana chief, a Tutsi King, or a Moorish Emir. These polities came to resemble "States" when military, economic and legal control was systematically exercised in the extraction of tributary revenues which when redistributed strengthened in turn the ties of commoners to the Chiefs, Kings or Emirs who held a symbolic monopoly on land, cattle or other royal prerogatives. This centralization of power, despite the presence of mobile livestock capital, often rested on control of agricultural resources (such as in the cases of the Tswana, the Tutsi, or in Kanem) or was associated with long-distance trade (as in the case of the Moors or the Tuareg Kel Gress) (Bonte 1975b). What is striking is how frequently chiefly or kingly authority, and its ritual and ideological link to divinity, was mediated by an intrinsic link to cattle, considered both as evidence and emblem of power, wealth and grace.

Far from exemplifying egalitarianism, pastoralism seems rather to heighten any particular political propensity, with cattle, that above all represent objects of generalized wealth, tokens of capital accumulation and exchange, and propitious symbols for reciprocity and sacrifice, serving to magnify statuses of every sort, of ordinary herders claiming equality or of aristocrats claiming superiority. However, egalitarian or stratified orders, acephalous or centralized polities, all bear the specific imprint of regional systems of political culture, proper to the western Sahara, to the Intralacustrine area, to highland Ethiopia, or to eastern or southern Africa, and thus they transcend the influence of the pastoral dynamics that had often been central to their original establishment and growth.

Conclusion: African Pastoralism in Dynamic Perspective

We have highlighted here those myths of *Value, Nature, Autonomy, Predation and Egalitarianism* in pastoral societies which the contributions that follow implicitly criticize, supplement, or put into perspective. In these "myths", both ideological and scientific, pastoralism has been depicted: (a) as an irrational, if not lackadaisical, process of unbridled herd accumulation predicated on cultural rather than economic (read "rational") value; (b) as a "natural" adaptation to the arid lands, currently explicable as a set of micro-ecological subsistence strategies; (c) as an ethnically and economically closed system of autonomous subsistence production; (d) as entraining "predatory" conflict and inevitable territorial expansion; and (e) as inevitably egalitarian in ethos, associated with non-stratified, acephalous systems of political organization (or disorganization). These popular beliefs, seen as commonsense by many government administrators and professional development personnel and often by the general public, have been lent support by academic research that too often has failed to place the complex realities of pastoralism in realistic perspective. Pastoralists in effect represent that fraction of the rural peasantry which specializes in animal husbandry, but do so both as social beings who invest their practices with intention, meaning and value and as lively participants in larger systems of regional political economy. As careful social and historical analysis shows, pastoralists are neither autonomous, though their lives are shaped by the exigencies of local community and small-scale institutions, nor dependent, although they are often subject to larger-scale political structures. They both propogate and manipulate the discourse and ideology of pastoral value, that represents a conceptual framework for their culturally rational pursuit of pastoral strategies rather than a set of blind and irrational edicts of tradition.

Pastoralists more often than not combine animal husbandry with agriculture, and in both agro- and specialized pastoralism engage in a labor intensive process in which men and women of all age levels participate. Pastoralism, like other forms of African rural economy, is a domestic process, but households and neighborhoods are part of larger polities through which resources, security and exchange are ensured. These larger political structures may take the form of relatively decentralized pastoral sections or of tribes, emirates, incipient states, or simply districts. Although African pastoralists produce for their own subsistence, they also participate in systems of local and regional economic networks, of exchange, tribute or trade. Through these networks, people move, socially and physically, to form friendships or partnerships, to change residence or to marry, and these movements have implications for processes of ethnic assimilation and change. Pastoralists do not exclusively inhabit arid lands, for livestock keeping has spread to virtually every part of the African continent where not prevented by environmental conditions. And while they have intimate knowledge of pasture ecology, and respond to micro-variation in resource quantity and quality, pastoralists are at the same time engaged in the wider politics of life, making decisions based on an entire gamut of social, cultural and economic aims and conditions. Intense pride is frequent in the pastoral character, with egalitarian ideology seen to obtain primarily between pastoralists, with non-pastoralists frequently deemed of lesser honor and quality. And if pastoralism has been associated with conflict and expansion, the qualities of mobility and individual aggressivity usually serve the functions of military conflict and expansion as means rather than causes. The latter we find in wider regional processes, historically specific experiences, and the cultural needs and motives embedded in social forms.

Given this model of African pastoral dynamics, based on a synthesis of anthropological and historical understanding, what is its import for understanding the predicaments and opportunities facing Africa's herders today? One objective of this book is to provide background, through analysis of social and historical processes regarding key case studies, for the assessment of pastoralist development policies and programs. The substantive contributions which follow shed light on pastoral "myths", not untruths but complex realities which should supersede the simpler and less nuanced views mentioned above. The relevance of this knowledge to our understanding of contemporary forces of change - through drought and famine, markets and migration, war and development - will constitute the subject of the final chapter of this volume, on "The Current Realities of African Pastoralists".

Notes

1. The idea that there exists a "pastoral mode of production" has had few if any defenders (*pace* Asad 1979), despite the fact that certain authors have sought to apply Marxist mode-of-production analysis to African pastoral societies; on this question, see Rigby (1985:15 sq.).

2. The social, economic and cultural values attributed to domestic animals tend in particular to render those symbolic codes of pastoralists more uniform which express their social identity and their relations with non-pastoral neighbors. Evans-Pritchard's description of the Nuer as "people of cattle" (1940) is echoed by Dupire's description of the nomadic Wodaabe Fulani (1962). The norms, practices, and values of pastoral behavior constitute among the Wodaabe a *mbodangaaku* complex, essential to Fulani identity and social cohesion (Bonfiglioli 1988). Pastoral values are also often used to express notions of social hierarchy within a given group, such as the aristocratic Royalty among the Interlacustrine societies, or, on the ideological and political level, between neighboring societies, such as between the Nuer and the Dinka.

3. For elaboration of structural differences between specialized and agro-pastoral systems, and comparison of degrees of livestock density and per capita holdings based on aggregate national statistics, see Galaty and Johnson (1990).

4. This myth is deeply rooted in the history of ideas. Pastoralism was long considered, from an evolutionist perspective, to have represented the first stage of civilization, prior to the appearance of agriculture. This myth has been perpetuated in the nomadic-sedentary opposition, which connotes a series of stereotypes: herders are predators, thieves, parasites who refuse to work, etc. Good examples of the influence of these stereotypes on scientific thought is the opposition, established in the history and ethnology of Africa under French and British colonization, for North Africa between sedentary "Berbers" and nomadic "Arabs" (or the nomadic mentality in general), by which the invasion of the Maghreb by Arab Bedouins was assigned a negative role, for East Africa between pastoralists (especially Maasai) monopolizing valuable land and diligent farmers.

5. When in the 1950s the study of the developmental cycle of domestic groups was developed (Goody 1958), the question of the social and demographic regulation of the labor force within the family and of the pastoral means of production was pursued as a problem of the reciprocal adaptation of human and herd populations. At that time, the International African Institute in London supported a series of studies among the Fulbe (Hopen 1958; Stenning 1959; Dupire 1962), pursued in part from this perspective, and convened an influential seminar on the topic (1952).

6. The relation between "Dorobo" hunters and pastoralists in East Africa is especially interesting in this regard, the former providing haven for destitute pastoralists following drought and supplying pastoral labor in times of abundance; for the Samburu-Dorobo relation, see Spencer (1973); for Okiek-Maasai relations, see Kratz (1981, 1986). For similar movement of people between pastoral and agropastoral communities, see Sobania and Johnson in this volume.

7. The fact of investment in livestock raises more general questions regarding its role as "capital." First, the accumulation of value in the form of animals - both mobile and convertible goods - in numerous societies, as well as in the history of our own economic and political institutions, has provided the semantic and material referent for wealth or capital (Benveniste 1969; Bader 1978). Second is the notion of a sort of "pastoral capitalism," which attributes to pastoral management the capitalist virtue of maximizing the particular object of livestock (Barth 1967; Goldschmidt 1972; Schneider 1979), in contrast to land and labor, which serve as primary values in most societies studied by anthropologists.

8. In this case, analysis of the value of livestock is based on a critique of the Marxist theory of value, in which there simultaneously exists a "natural" concept of value and one we might qualify as "anthropological", regarding fetishism and exchange value. The notion of value envisaged, outside of its normal useage, is close to that employed by Dumont as a holistic "totalizing" category, through which social experience is symbolically and practically organized. For further development of this approach, see Bonte (1981b, 1984).

9. It is difficult, despite Kelly's contribution to the problem (1985), to interpret the importance of cattle among the Nuer, their historical differentiation from their Dinka neighbors, and segmentary character of their social organization, to the quantitative importance of bridewealth to the Nuer. Attempts to interpret the social functions of bridewealth as a mode of economic regulation obeying laws of capitalist exchange also appear questionable (Goldschmidt 1974). In fact, it would appear that the amount given in bridewealth does not depend on the importance of or the degree of specialization in pastoral production, since it is lower among the highly specialized Maasai than among the agropastoral Nuer or Jie. It is important to interpret the circulation of animals at marriage within the larger totality of livestock exchanges out of which the system of social organization is woven.

10. This thesis, which had certain Biblical precedents, was put forward throughout the nineteenth century by evolutionists intent on defining a unique evolutionary sequence for the history of human society; introduced by A. Smith, the thesis was codified by G. Klemm and further developed by Morgan and Engels.

11. In recent years, viewpoints have polarized over the communal nature of pastoral production, with communal appropriation of pastures being seen as an obstacle to any "rational" form of rangeland development (Hardin and Baden 1977). Before the consequences of widespread drought in Africa led some developmentalists to radically question their perspective, this ideas was quite influential in the design of programs of rangeland development financed by the World Bank and many bilateral aid agencies in th 1960s and 1970s; in some countries (*e.g.* Kenya), it remains influential today.

12. Sheep and goats were originally domesticated around the beginning of the seventh millenium B.C., the former in the mountains of the Middle-East, the latter more specifically in Iran; they subsequently spread to Western Europe along the Mediterranean coast, to Africa and to East Asia (Digard 1990:107-108).

13. Cattle-proper (*Bos taurus*) were apparently domesticated independently in Eastern Europe and the Middle-East around the seventh millenium B.C., the zebu (*B. indicus*) originating in India around the same time (Digard 1990:105-106).

14. In fact, the Tuareg also practice cattle husbandry but camels are associated with aristocratic values within the society; nobles practice camel herding while religious leaders and vassels are more associated with cattle herding.

15. For further elaboration of Botswana's "Tribal Grazing Land Policy" (TGLP), see our discussion in the final chapter of this volume.

16. It would be impossible to understand the history of the southern Saharan pastoral societies without reference to regional and international exchange. Herders were involved in the large-scale transcontinental commerce through providing animal transport, guides and military escorts for caravans, by which they were also able to "tap" local wealth through extracting tribute or through pillage. More importantly, regional exchange networks tended to favor, in Mauritania, for example, the commercial specialization of only a part of the pastoral society, who, as in the central Sudan, participated in the development of regional production in the Hausa cities (Lovejoy 1986). The importance of the

slave trade stems in part from the fact that it was involved in two trading systems, both regional and continental (Lovejoy 1083).

17. These images are often imprinted on pastoral societies themselves, who tend to interpret their own histories in terms perpetual movement, either conflictual or in the form of human and herd migration. In this context, "pastoral aristocracies" in Interlacustrine Kingdoms consider themselves as "foreigners" and "conquerors" of the local populations living from agriculture or hunting. In this regard, the "Hamitic Hypothesis", which from its diffusionist and quasi-racist perspective attributed any elaborated political form to the influence of Middle Eastern civilizations, could call for support upon local oral traditions. Historical and archaeological evidence shows that the reality is much more complex. It is intriguing to ask whether this almost universal aspect of the history of pastoral peoples is not a manifestation of the symbolic value attributed to domestic animals, concerning their original relation with human beings expressed in myth, as well as the mobility inherent in representations of their systems of production.

18. In the Kel Gress confederation, established to the south, the salt trade provided the basis for hierarchical relations, which oscillated between the perpetuation in power of a "pastoral aristocracy", supported by the cultivating Ighawelen Tuareg and Hausa, and the creation of a centralized state (Bonte 1975b).

19. In virtually all these cases, a hierarchy is formed based on the superior value of livestock and pastoral labor. Agriculture is, in all West African pastoral societies, associated with slavery and servility. Even in the Interlacustrine Kingdoms, cultivation is excluded from both symbolic and concrete relations of power.

PART TWO

CATTLE AND CULTURE: DOMESTIC ANIMALS AS VALUE AND SIGN

2

"How Beasts Lost Their Legs": Cattle in Tswana Economy and Society

*Jean Comaroff
and John L. Comaroff*

*Kgomo modimo wa mogae, modimo wa nko e metse;
kgono le otlanya ditshaba, o bolaile banna ba le bantsi.*

*Beast, god of the home, god with the damp nose;
beast that makes the chiefdoms fight, you have killed many people.*
Tswana song[1]

Introduction

Ever since the dawn of modern social theory, as we all know, efforts have been made to address the rival claims of material and conceptual forces in shaping human society. The place of cattle in Africa is especially interesting in this respect. On the one hand, their significance, even in such obviously *social* processes as marriage exchange, has been explained in entirely economistic terms (*e.g.* Gray 1960; Goldschmidt 1974; *cf.* Schneider 1964), this being taken in some quarters as general confirmation of the force of materialist approaches to African ethnography. On the other hand, anthropologists have also followed the

Dinka insight that "the people are put together, as a bull is put together" - that livestock are first and foremost metaphors of social community, signifiers of the human condition (Lienhardt 1961:23). Yet long ago Evans-Pritchard 1940) noted that cattle provided the meeting ground of ecology and symbolic value; that their prominence in indigenous consciousness and social life went well beyond the purely utilitarian.[2] Not only was it by means of beasts that social identities and relations were represented (*Ibid.*:18, 89). In the "bovine idiom" and "cattle clock" of the Nuer (*Ibid.*:19, 101) lay a bridge between material conditions and collective meaning, between practical activity and its cultural construction. *The Nuer* might have succeeded, finally, in crossing that bridge "in one direction only". But Evans-Pritchard leaves little doubt that cattle here were objects *at once* economic and symbolic.

We shall attempt to build on this insight and, in looking afresh at the role of cattle in another African society, return to Marx - the Marx of *Capital* and, especially, of the commodity. As we understand it, the latter was held to derive its significance under capitalism from (a) the way in which it links processes of production and exchange, (b) the fact that it is alike a concrete product and the embodiment of an order of meanings and relations; and (c) its capacity, through its circulation, to reproduce a total social system. Our interest here, however, is not primarily in the commodity as a *specific* historical form. Instead, we take Marx's account as a general model for examining relations among people and goods; as the basis, that is, for exploring the production and representation of value in all societies (Turner n.d.). Of course, Marx himself did not hold that commodities exist only in the capitalist world. They might be found anywhere. But their salience, he stressed, varied greatly across space and time: indeed, this variation was itself taken to be critical in shaping the historical character of different social systems. One obvious corollary follows: that the transformation of any society should be revealed by the changing relations of persons to objects within it.

This conception of the commodity, we believe, lays out the terms for examining the place of cattle in precolonial African societies, and for tracing the effects upon those societies of incorporation into a global order of markets and money. Taking one exemplary case, we argue that, among the Tshidi Barolong, a Tswana people, beasts were like commodities. But they were like them only in the precise sense outlined above: as the medium of transformation, in a *total* economy of signs and practices, between a material economy of things and a moral economy of persons. Further, we shall demonstrate that the changing salience of livestock here can only be fully grasped with reference to that total economy and its encounter with the forces of colonialism - a critical aspect of which was played out in the relationship between cattle and cash. At the same time, we do not wish to imply that animals meant the same thing, or played the same role, among all African pastoralists - or even among all Tswana. Quite the opposite. Recall how, in discussing the rise of capitalism, Marx set out to establish the manner in which the general principles of political economy had taken on their particular historical shape in modern Europe. In similar vein, it may be shown that, while livestock in Africa share a number of formal properties and potentialities, these have been variously put to work in different social contexts.

The Centrality of Cattle

It is sometimes said, in comparing the peoples of southern Africa, that Nguni speakers attached "more" significance to their herds than did the Sotho-Tswana (*e.g.* Sansom 1974:150). Such things are difficult to measure, of course, but the centrality of beasts in Tswana economy, culture, and society has been noted for as long as there is a documentary record. For example, Barrow (1806:393f), among their earliest European visitors, wrote that "One great source from which they draw support is their cattle," of which they had a "very considerable" number. Nor did he intend this to refer purely to material subsistence, adding quickly "...whose flesh, however, they eat but sparingly." Two of his early observations were to be repeated many times by those who followed after him (*e.g.*, Lichtenstein [1807] 1973:66, 77-81; Burchell 1824,2:386; Moffat 1842:250): that a man's wealth was counted in livestock; and that the division of labor placed women securely in cultivation, gathering and domestic tasks, while men devoted themselves to herding, hunting and tanning. Burchell (1824,2:347) went on to expand upon the first observation, the association of cattle with wealth and power:

> ...from the possession of property [specifically cattle], the distinction of men into richer and poorer classes has followed as a natural consequence. Those who have riches, have also, it seems, power; and the word *kosi* [denotes] either a chief or a rich man.

By contrast, "...a *muchunka* or a *mollala* (a poor-man, or servant) had no need of cattle, as he had only to mind his duty in attending those of his superior" (*Ibid.*:348). Another early visitor, John Campbell (1822,2:206), a missionary with an eye for telling detail, added a further insight: that there appeared to be a direct symbolic identity between man and beast. When a woman bore twins, one of the children was put to death; when a cow had a pair of calves, one was killed or driven away. Similarly, a man was expected to place a reed on the fence around his homestead to signal either the death of a beast or the mortal illness of a member of his household.

Later missionaries were to remark again on the Tswana tendency to draw their cattle into their symbolic practices. A rich source of omens and auguries (J.T. Brown 1926:92), beasts were the medium of domestic sacrifices. They were also the focus of such rituals as male initiation, through which adolescent boys were made over into social adults (J. Comaroff 1985:Chap.4). As Brown (*Ibid.*) put it, the place of livestock in Tswana life was "not accounted for by the fact that they form[ed] the wealth of the people". As in many other African societies that allegedly share (or once shared) the "cattle complex",[3] pastoralism was always distinctly secondary to cultivation in its contribution to brute subsistence. Ultimately, the significance of animals flowed from another source: that, "in a strict sense [they were] not a private, but a social possession" (J.T. Brown 1926:92). By this, Brown did not mean merely that their ownership was collective. We might gloss his use of "social possession" to imply, after Mauss (1954:1), that they were a "total social phenomenon" - *i.e.* things that contained all "the threads of which the social fabric is woven."

We shall not simply be concerned here only with drawing out these threads, however. As Kuper (1982:11) has pointed out, "one could pile up endless examples" of the centrality of cattle in ritual and bridewealth, of their celebration in idiom and song, and of their salience as political currency. Kuper himself suggests that the exchange of women for beasts is *the* central social transaction among Southern Bantu-speaking peoples.[4] It is

> ...related both to the more general set of exchanges between the male domain of pastoral production and the female domain of agriculture, and to the series of exchanges of goods and services (basically the gift of fertility and the return of part of the product) between superiors and inferiors (*Ibid.*:18).

This summarizes nicely the role of cattle, at least in times past, as (i) the mediating link between production and exchange, and (ii) a means of forging sociopolitical ties. But, in order to account for that role - and for why it was beasts, in particular, that assumed it - it is necessary to show how animals actually entered into the making of persons and things, relations and statuses. In short, we seek to explain how they took on the character of total social phenomenon; how their unique capacity to store and transform value enabled Tshidi to sustain a viable social world; and how the fundamental changes brought about by the colonial encounter came to threaten that world - with some rather unexpected consequences. Such matters, thought can only be addressed by situating relations among people and objects, historically within the division of labor of which they were part. We enter the Tshidi *morafe*, their political community in the first half of the nineteenth century.[5]

Town, Chief, and Identity in a Hierarchical Polity

In the early nineteenth century, the Tshidi lived on the Molopo plain, along the present South African-Botswana border. The peoples who would soon come to know themselves as "the (southern) Tswana", or "Bechuana", existed in a field of complex regional relations. Their inherently dynamic polities were increasingly affected by commerce with the Cape Colony, and by the shockwaves that spread across the subcontinent in the wake of the rise of the Zulu state. In the early 1800s, European visitors recorded striking variations among these polities. At one extreme was the Tshidi chiefdom, *ca.* 1824, described by the Rev. Robert Mossat (1842:388) as a large, highly centralized city-state under a ruler who wielded great power and monopolized external trade; settlements of similar scale, some of them bigger than Cape Town, were also observed elsewhere among the Rolong and Tlhaping (*e.g.* Barrow 1806:404; Burchell 1824,2:511). At the other extreme were a number of small, acephalous communities dotted over the landscape. These were made up of single, autonomous villages, some of which had, until recently, been part of sizeable chiefdoms (Barrow 1806:412; Smith 1939,1:240f). As this suggests, social fragmentation was an ever-present possibility in Southern Tswana politics and loomed large in the Tshidi imagination; counteracting its threat, we shall see, was integrally tied to the potential of cattle to build enduring social bonds. At the same time, The Tshiti world, with its elaborate capital town, was centered upon an hereditary chiefship, in which were vested mechanisms of control at once ritual, political, and economic (*cf.* Shapera 1938; Okihiro 1976: Chap.2). Radiating outward from the office was an administrative hierarchy made up of nesting residential units (households, agnatic segments, and wards), each with a position of authority at its head. Such units usually had agnatic cores and their headship devolved according to genealogical seniority, although rank was often the object of contention. Despite the stress on agnation, however, the Tshidi lacked segmentary lineages (*e.g.* Campbell 1822,1:314-6). Despite the stress on agnation, however, the Tshidi lacked segmentary lineages. Descent groups did not coincide with administrative divisions, and their members only engaged in common action when they also belonged to the same ward. Apart from defining relative rank - and, with it, access to property and position - these groups had little collective identity. This was due, in part, to the fact that Tshidi practiced cousin marriage - including unions between close agnates, a form of endogamy which, as we have shown elsewhere (Comaroff and Comaroff 1981), prevented the emergence of large corporations. It also individuated households as units of property and production, marital alliance and social management, and created a field of overlapping social ties, in which people were related in many different, often ambiguous, ways.

The features of this world to be stressed here may be subsumed into two oppositions. The first was between its center, embodied in the court and person of the chief, and its periphery of households made up of female-centered houses (see below). The chiefship was located, spatially and symbolically, at the hub of the town (*motse*), which itself stood in stark contrast to *naga*, the wild (*cf.* Campbell 1813:187). The settlement was visible evidence of the triumph of the social over rank nature. But it was a triumph that had to be protected by a vigilant ruler, who had to ensure that the town remained intact, its households held together within the administrative hierarchy. As a Setswana proverb put it, *motse olwapeng*, "the town [polity] is [rooted] in the domestic courtyard" (Brown 1926:201). At the same time, the relationship between center and periphery was, potentially at least, an antagonistic one. While centralized domicile was prescribed, and was enforced where possible, families had their fields outside the settlement; and they took to them for the agricultural season once the sovereign gave the word, usually after he had them plow his gardens in the wake of the first rains (Willoughby 1928:226).[6] Tshidi showed some resentment toward this arrangement, however. They spoke of the benefits of remaining where nobody could demand their tributary labor, or delay them from cultivating their crops. And so households were wont to scatter wherever a chief lost the power to keep them at the capital (Philip 1828:133). In sum, while the prevailing structure of authority favoured centralization, the individuation of households, encouraged by existing marriage practices, gave rise to centrifugal forces at the heart of the polity.

The second opposition involved agnation and matrilaterality, about which much has been written (*e.g.* Comaroff and Roberts 1981). For now, it is enough to note that agnation, the cultural idiom of political and economic status, was associated with rivalry and conflict; matrilaterality, with moral solidarity and social complementarity[7]. The former grew out of bonds among men, and tied their households into the administrative hierarchy and the public domain; the latter had its roots in relations through women, and evoked the privacy of the house[8] and its confines (Phillip 1828,2:132; Soloman 1855:42). Although they might share common concerns and often cooperated, patrikin were held nonetheless to have inimical interests in property and position; it was a lamentable -

but understandable - fact of life that they should try constantly to "eat" one another by means both mystical and material (Burchell 1824,2:272; Lichtenstein 1973:66ff). The inherently political content of their relations was marked in kin terminology: it was impossible to refer to an agnate without ranking him relative to oneself in the positional order. By contrast, matrilaterals were always unranked, this being an expression of the fact that "a man and his *bomalome* (mother's brother's people) never fought," never practiced sorcery, and never found themselves in completion with each other. Each, to be sure, was the other's prime social resource.

Agnatic politics, along with the ambiguous social bonds created by endogamous marriage, then, gave the Tshidi world the appearance of being highly negotiable: a fluid, dynamic universe in which practical efforts to construct identity, rank and relations were the stuff of social action (see MacKenzie 1871:410). These processes, in turn, integrated households into the hierarchical polity - at least for as long as the centripetal forces around the chiefship could hold them there and prevent them from asserting their autonomy. It is against this background that the social division of labor is to be understood.

Gender, Generation and the Division of Labor

As early observers among the Tswana noted, precolonial productive arrangements were based primarily on differences of gender and generation. Women and their daughters cultivated crops, gathered the fruits of the wild and took care of the domestic hearth. Men, by contrast, engaged in leather work, tool-making, and public deliberations assisting in the fields mainly in times of unusually heavy toil. Their major sphere of control was the pastoral economy, and they drew on the labor of their young sons, impoverished clients or subjugated Sarwa to herd their animals. They also hunted, especially in periods of scarcity. But unlike females, adult males did not contribute much to the routine material reproduction of the household. They busied themselves instead with the various forms of exchange that created and recreated the social world. And, in so doing, they transformed the yield of women's fecundity - the grain to feed their dependants and retainers, the sons to tend their stock, the daughters to marry off in alliances - into both political currency and more enduring communal values.

This bald summary of the allocation of productive tasks, to which we shall add further detail in a moment, wili be readily familiar. It evokes a very common pattern in southern and eastern Africa (Kuper 1982:11). Yet to understand how it was elaborated into a *social* division of labor we need to look briefly at the meaning ascribed by Tshidi to human activity itself; in particular, at their conception of work and fabrication. The vernacular term *go dira* (or *diha*) meant "to make," "do" or "cause to happen," and referred to a wide range of actions upon the world, from tilling the soil to the performance of ritual. *Tiro*, the act of fabrication (Brown 1931:308), yielded positive value in the form of persons, things and relations.[9] Its converse was sorcery which negated constructive labour, undid people and destroyed social wealth (*cf.* Munn 1986 for a similar conception of sorcery in a Melanesian context).

For Tshidi, work was not an abstract quality or a thing to be exchanged. It simply could not exist in the form of a commodity, as alienable "labor power." Even the energies of a serf were only available to his master by virtue of a total bond of interdependence. They could not be given over to another person unless the relationship itself was transferred. Work, rather, was the creative process inherent in all human existence, and was expressed in the making of self and others in the course of everyday life (Alverson 1978:132). Yet, because people were not all the same, not all *tiro* was alike. Above all, however, male and female "work" were fundamentally different - and unequal.

The precise character of the difference flowed from the cultural construction of gender and its place in the Tshidi world. Women, associated with cultivation and reproduction in the domestic sphere, were uncertain mediators of nature. Their bodies were the source of the most prized value of all - human life -yet that very faculty imperilled the polity. For their fecundity generated heat (*bothitho*), a destructive force that threatened such things as rainmaking and initiation rites, ancestral veneration and deliberations at the chiefly court, land and cattle - all quintessentially male concerns (Schapera 1938:28; Willoughby 1909:234). Not only did their bodies require confinement, but females were denied a role in the collective world shaped through exchange; by the transaction, often, of the value created by their own productive and reproductive labor (Kinsman 1983). Debarred from contact with beasts, they were "jural minors" who had to be represented by men in the public domain.

The formal subordination of women was marked in many ways. For example, in the conjugal process, the process that reproduced the social division of labor itself (Comaroff and Roberts 1981), they were acted upon: unlike men, who married (*nyala*), they *were* married (*nyalwa*). By convention (*ka mekgwa*), moreover, women were portrayed as being unable to extend their personal influence in time and space. Their restricted power of movement, and of inducing movement in others, was captured in the very term that labelled them. The "original" meaning of the word for woman, *mosadi* (from *sala*, "stay"), Sandilands (1953:333) offers, was "the-one-who-remains-at-home." This is not to imply that wives and mothers were totally impotent in Tshidi society at the time. There is clear evidence that they wielded (sometimes considerable) influence behind the scenes in both the court and the domestic compound (see Philip 1828,2:133 for a notable Tlhaping case); in addition, royal women exercised a measure of authority over their commoner sisters through the system of age regiments (Schapera 1938:74). But, in the formal calculus of institutional power, the marginality of females was conspicuous. The point was made with great symbolic force by the place of the chief's mother - *mohumagadi*, the mother of the people - in the political architecture of the capital. Not only did her homestead stand at the edge of the chiefly court (*kgotla*) as periphery to center. It was also a house of asylum, a private, behind-the-scenes refuge for those sentenced in the public domain for crimes other than homicide (Schapera *Ibid.*).

In contrast, males were intrinsically stable and "cool" (*tshididi*). The latter quality was especially significant, since it was required for effective action in the public sector. Salutations at the royal meeting place underlined this. They called for "*Pula!*" ("Let it rain!") and implored "*A go nne tshididi!*" ("Let it be cool!", Brown 1926:156; Solomon 1855:47). Furthermore, the term *go hodisa* ("to cool") also meant "to heal," a male skill which tempered the heat of illness and pollution (Willoughby 1928:363). As players in the public domain, men could make alliances through women, and make subordinates or clients of their rivals. In so doing, as we said earlier, they forged the social connections and status relations that shaped the hierarchical polity, a community which also embraced the invisible realm of spirit forces. Participation in these processes - and they covered a wide spectrum from flamboyantly open conflicts to secretive transactions of patronage and debt - impelled men to act potently upon the world, to engage in acts of competitive self-construction that implied "eating" or "being eaten" by others. Of course, given the fluidities of that world, such processes of social management and self construction were unceasing. As we shall see, they also had a material expression in political economy: dominating other men and controlling the capacities of women amounted, finally, to the social production of a workforce and a following.

The differences between male and female "work" were most apparent perhaps in everyday productive processes, the routine activities that created persons while persons created themselves. Let us explore these activities further.

Gender and Production

Agriculture, augmented by gathering, yielded the bulk of everyday subsistence, while pastoralism, along with hunting, provided largely for the ritual diet and for extra domestic exchange. The contrast between them, as we would expect, followed the cultural logic of gender difference. Thus females, corn, and bush foods were the very opposite of males, stock, and game. While the former involved an uncertain hold over nature, ever threatening to fail, the latter were the epitome of forceful mastery of the environment. The fact that cultivation was regarded as an inherently risky business was entirely consistent with the prevailing image of women; as predictable was the notion that pastoralism was an activity far more controlled. Even though they were liable to be lost through sickness, predation and war, beasts were held to afford security in the face of crop failure and, while meat was reserved for special occasions, milk was the most reliable component of the daily diet. In times of drought men coordinated their hunting efforts to provide game in plenty (Burchell 1824,2:320; Livingstone 1858:28).

These associations went yet further, extending to the status of male and female products in the Tshidi scheme of values. Cattle, the essence of dependability, were largely self-reproducing, and were mobile in the face of drought and danger; they permitted the stable storage, exchange, and seemingly spontaneous growth of wealth (Burchell 1828,2:272, 347); and they supplied dung, *boloko* the substance used to make the durable surfaces that set off domestic space from its surrounds. Their hides and bone furnished the stuff from which most lasting personal possessions were made. The hunt, too, yielded lasting material objects and trade goods - plumes, skins, and ivory - as well as consumables. On the other hand, grain was vulnerable to the climate, and at least in the nineteenth century (Grove 1989), frequent crop failure promised to wipe out seed altogether; it had to be arduously threshed before it was cooked, and often rotted in storage; and it had little exchange value, being worth no more than the clay pot in which it was carried (Schapera 1938:242). In addition, while cows yielded milk as a finished product, the agricultural counterpart, corn beer, had to be prepared by women in a delicate operation that was easily spoiled, especially by their own polluting heat. In fact, the entire arable cycle was metaphorically linked to procreation and, tacitly, to the ever-present danger of miscarriage. For instance, *tlhaka* denoted "seed" or "grain" and "fetus," and *tlhakanèla dikobò* ("to plant", "fuse under the blanket") implied both sexual intercourse and the act of impregnating the land. Similarly, the term for "reap" (*go sega*) was used for cutting the umbilicus in childbirth. And where the harvest failed, it was usually attributed to the planting of an aborted fetus, an act of sorcery which "spoiled" the ground and prevented the rain from falling (Schapera 1971(a):107).

But the social basis of the division of labor was most clearly marked in death. As Willoughby (1928:57) reports, a "patriarch" was buried inside the cattle byre "so that he may hear the tramp of the cattle as they go out to graze in the morning and return for safety at sundown," and his corpse was shown an ox bone and a milk bowl before being placed beside some dry cow dung in its grave. His wife was interred under the threshing floor "that she may hear the thud of the flails, threshing out each new crop"; she was shown a pestle, a winnowing fan and domestic utensils, and was sprinkled with corn (*Ibid.*:40). Where men became *badimo*, spirits who received regular sacrifice and continued to be central to affairs of the living, women lost their identities, being subsumed into an agnatic ancestor cult (Willoughby 1928:330). Ironically, they were sealed into their state of spiritual anonymity under a surface of the very *boloko*, the cow dung, that was made by their labor into the permanent planes of the domestic homestead.

As all this suggests, cultivation and pastoralism were not simply opposed and complementary domains of production, just as women and men were not simply opposed and complementary social beings. It is true that females held fields in their own right, had their own granaries, and exercised some control over the use of their harvest. Yet even as producers they were anything but independent, their "works" being regularly appropriated by adult males in one or another capacity. The general point, again, was underscored in Tshidi poetics and myth. Frequent cosmogonic reference was made to the notion that the social world had its origins in the domestication, by men, of raw female fecundity; the theme being most cogently enacted in initiation rites, when males seized the capacity to generate fully social beings and communal institutions by symbolically recapitulating childbirth (Willoughby 1909; J. Comaroff 1985:85ff). More practically, the fruits of female labor were appropriated in two distinct ways. First, they were harnessed to the creation - and cyclical recreation - of the polity and of the chiefship itself. And, second, they subsidized everyday male sociopolitical activity, providing a material base for interhousehold transactions.

The link between female productive activity and the (re)creation of the polity hinged on the centralized controls exercised over the agricultural cycle. Specifically, the chief regulated that cycle, allowing it to begin when he "gave out the seed time" (Willoughby 1928:226f; see also Campbell 1822,2:154). This form of control empowered the ruler to extract tributary labor before people dispersed, thereby providing him with surpluses for later redistribution, a prerogative that shored up his legitimacy (Schapera 1943:184). But it also expressed a more subtle tenet of Tshidi political culture. Like work, time here was not an abstract thing, a resource that existed apart from events and actions. In the absence of activity, there literally was no time. Not surprisingly, the Setswana term *lobaka*, "[a period of] time" also translated as "space" (Comaroff and Comaroff n.d.). In this context, then, the chiefly act of dispensing seed time, which was closely tied to his ability to bring rain, was seen actually to enable the productive season; for it set in motion the insemination of the land and the gestation of the crop. It also called into being the entire social calendar and, with it, the order which gave meaning and material form to the social world. In this respect, the two sides of centralized regulation of female labor - the regeneration of the polity and the production of a redistributable surplus - were interdependent. Together they transformed human energy into a vital political economy.

The same theme was taken one step further later on in the agricultural cycle. Once the grain had begun to ripen, the most elaborate rite of the year was performed. *Go loma thôtse*, the "tasting of the gourd," tied the maturation of the crop to the renewal of the social community (Willoughby 1928:226f). Females brought their first fruits to the court, where they were ceremonially eaten by male royals, after which a pulp of their leaves was carefully rubbed onto the body of every citizen, man and woman alike, in strict rank order (Holub 1881,1:329; Schapera 1971 (b):156). Between these periodic rites, of course, political fortunes rose and fell. Hence *go loma thôtse* gave annual reckoning of the state of power relations at the same time as it marked out afresh the enduring structure of the chiefdom. And so the yield of women's labor was absorbed into the body politic via its center, providing the material and symbolic substance of an hierarchical order whose living form was imprinted on the skin of all subjects.

This, in turn, throws light on the second aspect of the appropriation of female "work," namely, its subsidy of everyday male activity in the public domain. Once the polity was defined, its centralized structures annually renewed, so too was the *lobaka*, the space-time, in which agnatic politics might proceed. But for any man to participate - and, as noted before, there was little alternative but to do so - the ability to feed himself and his retainers was a basic requirement. Otherwise he had to work for others, and so lost the autonomy to act on his own account. In short, access to the yield of female labor was *the* basic provision - in both senses of that term - for entry into the political arena as a free person.[10] This was most routinely captured, in the iconography of goods, by corn beer, a beverage manufactured by wives from their surplus grain. The very essence of hospitality, it was the refreshment which a husband could serve to his allies and clients, enhancing his status in the process (Schapera 1943:201). In its passage from her private backyard to his public frontyard, this product of her work flowed into, and fed, the sphere of male exchange: and she lost control over its use.

But perhaps the most palpable expression of the same point came after the harvest, when a woman's garden had been denuded of its corn, its broken stalks signalling the end of the arable season. At that stage, her husband's stock were led into the field, to eat what was left of her toil; the toil which ensured that, for another year, his household was provided for, thus allowing him to pursue his social career - and, as we shall see, to deploy his herd to the full in doing so. As this implies, it was the encompassment of agriculture by pastoralism that held the key to the social division of labor and, therefore, to the role of beasts themselves.

Pastoralism, Property, and Social Identity

Tshidi herds were comprised of cattle, goats and somewhat fewer sheep. Both precolonial and modern observers (*e.g.* Schapera 1953:23) have had difficulty in assessing the size of individual and collective holdings among Tswana: beasts were widely dispersed under various forms of patronage, and any display of stock wealth was believed to invite plunder and ritual attack (Schapera 1938:24; Matthews n.d.). Moreover, post-colonial history has shown that the total animal population tends to fluctuate quite considerably over time, long-term cycles of depletion by disease and drought being followed by spontaneous recovery. But the documentary record does confirm the presence of large herds in the early nineteenth century, and gives evidence of visible inequalities in their distribution.

If the products of cultivation and gathering fueled physical subsistence, cattle were the media through which men shaped their social biographies. This flowed from the fact that, for Tshidi, they were the supreme form of property. Even late into the colonial period, they were spoken of as the only heritable wealth of real worth (Mathews n.d.; Schapera 1934:14). It is, of course, very widely the case that persons objectify themselves in things, goods either produced or circulated; that, by investing their identities in matter, they seek to project their being through space and time, enhancing their value as they are united with qualities outside of themselves (Munn 1977). However, goods differ in their culturally recognized capacity to embody value and meaning. The English word "property" is interesting in this respect. It implies both the intrinsic character of a thing ("properties") and a particular relationship to it ("possession"). And it marks a subclass of articles that may serve as vehicles of individual or collective status. Similarly, the Setswana term *khumó* ("wealth object", from *huma*, "be [become] rich" *humisa*, "make rich") connotes the ability to enhance wealth as well as the quality of possession. Only beasts combined both of these features; only they, among wealth objects, could congeal, store and increase value, holding it in stable form in a world of flux; only they could take on, and represent, the identity of their owners.

The capacity of the beast to carry social identity, both individual and collective, was most vividly marked in two sets of conventional practices. The first involved the "cattle linkage" of siblings and bridewealth; the second arose out of inheritance.

When children were young, their fathers "cattle linked" (*go rulaganya bana*) full siblings into mixed pairs (Smith 1939,1:345). Once tied to a particular sister, the brother was obliged to look after her and to represent her, and she was to cook and care for him, especially before he married. The defining feature of the link was that the brother was the recipient of the sister's bridewealth (*bogadi*), which was to be used to support her in times of want and, if necessary, to enable his own marriage (*cf.* Schapera 1938:143). In practice, it was rarely put to this last use; the conjugal process here was not a major context for the exchange of goods, *bogadi* being relatively low and rarely paid until many years had passed (J.L. Comaroff 1980). But the cultural stress on this arrangement was itself a statement of the moral and material significance of the brother-sister bond. This relationship would, in time, mature into a set of privileged matrilateral ties, ties that set men apart as individuals in relation to their agnates. Inasmuch as his sister's bridewealth was instrumental in creating these bonds, it derived from the transfer of *her* productive and reproductive powers for a return that gave the man the *symbolic* capital with which to marry - to be endowed with food and children, and so to enter the arena of agnatic politics as a free actor. Until then, a bachelor was described as a "locust," a hapless parasite. Only through marriage could he enter into the public domain as a fully social being. Not coincidentally, the *bogadi* that placed a male between two women, a sister and a wife, and enabled his very manhood, translated literally as "womanhood" (Brown 1926:61). In sum, *go rulaganya bana* and *bogadi*, the two major forms of cattle exchange through women, established males as actors in the public domain. And it marked out the special matrilateral ties, the bonds that distinguished a man and gave him his prime social resource, an exclusive reservoir of support in the hostile world of agnatic politics (Comaroff and Roberts 1981:50f).

If *go rulaganya bana* and *bogadi* were an essential part of the making of male identity, inheritance placed men in the social field. The devolution of property was a gradual process, cattle being passed on to children, and distributed among houses, throughout the lifetime of their father. By convention, the ideal estate had little left at death, but this residue, known as *boswa*, had great significance. Apart from all else, its passage gave public recognition to the naming of a senior heir, often a matter of contention. This son was known as *moja boswa*, the "eater" of *boswa*, the stress on "eating" as a sign of political preeminence again being noteworthy (*cf.* Schapera 1938:230f). So, too, was the fact that the transfer was closely linked to the renewal of the social order at large. For the domestic unit, which divided after the death of its founder, gave birth to the families that formed the core of the local agnatic segment, the grouping which tied households into the administrative hierarchy. Yet it was at this very moment that its members were most likely to disband, often amidst conflict over rank. For Tshidi, *boswa* represented the integrity of the fragmenting group as it became a local segment and took up its place in the wider polity. The heir received these animals so that he might "look after" (*go disa*, "herd") its members--a generalized metaphor for sustaining their unity. In purely economic terms, *boswa* was insufficient unto the task. But this was a *symbolic* herd which defined a bounded, if still fragile, social grouping. In "consuming" it, the heir assumed legitimate control over the people and property in the segment. If anyone was to preempt his status, they would have to "eat" him. As this suggests, inheritance turned the passage of cattle into two social facts: it provided the next generation with the core of their own estates, the material bases of their careers; and it situated individuals and households within the political field.

As this implies, beasts built social identities, individual and collective, and they gave men the basis to engage as actors in the public arena. But they did not make all males alike. Quite the contrary, in Tshidi culture the innate qualities of cattle - like the fetishized commodity - were an alibi for distinctions of rank, gender and social power. The varying ability to control them as property, to impose a personal stamp on them and put them in circulation, was *the* major mode of distinguishing persons and statuses (Burchell 1824,2:247f). Indeed, among Southern Bantu-speakers in general, livestock fostered the growth and expression of great discrepancies in wealth (Lichterstein 1973:76f; Solomon 1855:42). In the same way as capital, they served both as standards of value and as a means of accumulating and transforming it into other kinds of wealth in the political economy at large (*cf.* Sansom 1974:153).

From Division of Labor to Political Economy

In collective representations of the polity, the chief was described as its supreme "herdsman" (*modisa*). This metaphor ran to the heart of the Tshidi conception of political economy. In contrast to other citizens, as Mackenzie (1871:368) tells us, a Tswana sovereign could graze his animals anywhere, the relevance of this being illuminated by the fact that the vernacular term for "government" was *puso*, which betokened both "regime" and "dominion," the area over which a chief's authority extended (J.L. Comaroff n.d.). This realm was not bounded by a fixed, continuous line, but by the furthest ring of water holes to which he could lay claim for his pasture -either against other chiefs and/or by virtue of having the servants to tend his herds over such a distance. The Tshidi sovereign might not have been a shepherd-king, but his domain was, in the final analysis, a range.

The chief controlled the largest herd in the community (Burchell 1824,2:272, 347). This was assured by the prerogatives of his office, among them the right to retain a portion of fines levied at his court and, in extreme cases, to seize the livestock of a man who consistently flouted his authority; to keep strays (*matimela*); to receive tribute on special occasions; and to barter other gifts for beasts (Lichtenstein 1930,2:414; Campbell 1822,2:194; *cf.* Schapera 1938:64ff). Significant, too, were the spoils of raiding, the desire to increase the royal fund at the expense of neighbors being a major motive in the mobilization of male age regiments. In fact, the names of these regiments - *Mathibakgomo*, "those who brought back cattle"; *Majakgoma*, "those who 'eat' cattle"; and so on - often equated male vigor with the capture of herds (Breutz 1956:164). In principle, Tshidi distinguished sharply between animals belonging to the chiefship and those possessed by the office holder; in practice, it was hard to separate the two. But there was nothing ambiguous about the part they played in the exercise of power. Not only did they sustain the people who actually husbanded them, the royal servants who performed a wide range of productive and political tasks for the ruler. They could also be given away in return for support and submission. Such distributions took various forms: outright transfers to loyal followers, sometimes along with appointment to newly-created headmanships; long-term loans (*mahisa*), in which the recipient might use the milk of the cows and keep a heifer, and reciprocate by giving their owner "support in public life" (*cf.* Schapera 1938:214); payments to specialists, such as rainmakers, who, in assuring communal wellbeing (*pula*; also "rain"), reinforced the legitimacy of the chief; sacrifices to the ancestors to ensure their protection; and the despatch of gifts to neighboring rulers.

As everywhere in precolonial southern Africa, then, "cattle [were] converted into fealty and political support" (Sansom 1974:163). And they had this capacity precisely because they bore the imprint, a part of the essence, of their owner. For a man to hold a beast that belonged (or had once belonged) to the ruler was to have the presence of the man himself in his midst. To succour that beast was to honor the chief and, by extension, the chiefship and polity embodied in him; to hurt it was to strike against him, and to risk the sanction that might follow. Cattle, in sum, naturalized sovereign authority and gave it an ineffable quality (Burchell 1824,2:272, 347). But this did not mean that rulers were all-powerful here. Quite the contrary, they had constantly to ward off the efforts of their most influential agnates to reduce their legitimacy, even to remove them (Moffat 1842:389; J.L. Comaroff 1973). Nonetheless, the chief*ship* remained above negotiation. And, as long as he occupied the office, the holder personified it. Just as the commodity bore, in both its physical existence and its circulation, the set of relations involved in its production, so the Tshidi beast carried with it the relations of authority and inequality that shaped the political economy.

Although the chief stood at the apex of the polity, it was not only for him that cattle were the currency of power. The accumulation of a large herd also gave others the opportunity to initiate ties of alliance and patronage. But this was effectively confined to those already with access to high rank and, usually, office. For most ordinary townsmen, cattle were acquired mainly through inheritance, bridewealth, and natural increase, and, except in rare circumstances, it was impossible to build up a sizeable estate in one generation. Burchell (1824,2:348), in fact, observed early on that the social order was constructed in such a way as to prevent the "poor" from rising above their station. The extension of *mahisa* loans, the major vehicle by which men might come to control others, was only open to those with substantial and, more importantly, growing herds - supported, as noted before, by food-producing wives.

For the affluent, however, *mahisa* did offer a direct medium for transforming wealth in cattle into wealth in people. But it had two quite different faces. Where these loans were made to free men of lower status they were usually part of wider processes of social management; of "eating" others through lengthy (and often very subtle) series of transactions. In itself, each loan made a limited material difference, unless it came at a time of particular misfortune. It only added marginally to the recipient's herd, and did little for his economic fortunes. Similarly, while it gave some political advantage to the patron, who might expect generalized support in return, it was not really a basis to demand any more. Only when the client had been "consumed," and was no longer an independent person, could he actually be made to give of his labor and other services. This first form of *mahisa*, in other words, was just one element in the longer term negotiation of power relations. On the other hand, loans to *balala* (or *batlhanka*; "serfs", lit., "those laid low"), who had no access to the means of production, nurtured a more enduring relationship of servitude; that of an underclass in perennial subordination. Here the stock contributed directly to the survival of their holders, who were excluded from the politico-jural process and forced to live outside the settlement, either at hunting camps or at the cattleposts of their patrons, from where they regularly sent skins, honey, and milk to the town (Kinsman n.d.:14; MacKenzie 1871:368; Lichtenstein 1973:76). This underclass comprised former captives in war, families or small communities of Sarwa and Kgalagadi, and free citizens who had been "eaten" and had lost their herds entirely. Together with young boys, these serfs made up the bulk of the pastoral workforce, swelling the surpluses that made possible the social activities of the wealthy. They were also sometimes called on, by their masters, to augment female agricultural labor. The fact that impoverished Southern Tswana were used in this way adds an interesting footnote to the cultural basis of gender and production here. In Tshidi imagery, to "be eaten", and hence "laid low," was to be feminized. Such men, in short, had become fit to do women's "work." The same did not apply to Sarwa and Kgalagadi vassals, who were held to be innately "wild"; to be, literally, "*bushmen*". Being incapable of leading a domestic life, they were debarred from the fundamental rights of civilized beings, namely, living in a settlement or acquiring stock (Burchell 1824,2:348).

The production and exchange of cattle, then, sustained a structure of inequality, an entire system of distinction. Built on class, gender and rank, it was this structure that gave characteristic form to Tshidi economy and society. For citizens of the chiefdom, beasts were both the medium through which men achieved their relative standing and the social means of producing a labor force. They roused human beings to intense affect and activity, from political intrigue to praise poetry, sorcery to warfare. Persons of rank, those who were "strong" enough to consume others, were thought actually to attract animals; that is, to draw them by being sought out as the recipients of chiefly favor and ancestral blessing, as would-be affinal allies and holders of office. As this suggests, cattle wealth was seen to reflect an inherent ability to mobilize people, and to extend the self by generating support and radiating a personal presence. This form of wealth, in other words, had the tautological quality of all political currency: it was taken to be an expression of the very power that it served to create.

For their part, Tshidi, like other Tswana, glossed the supremely creative quality of cattle by calling them as "gods with wet noses" (*cf.* Alverson 1978:124f). They were pliable symbolic media, similar enough to human beings - yet different enough among themselves - to express a range of personal identities, common values, and states of relationship. As Lienhardt (1961:23) said of the Dinka, people were put together like livestock and could, by the same token, be rearranged through the appropriate manipulation of their bovine alters; the same principle being invoked in, among other things, Tshidi healing rites (J. Comaroff 1974; *cf.* Schapera 1953:59f). Along with their ability to embody particular identities, beasts were also the living products of a stratified order. Thus they could only be owned by male citizens, whose stamp they bore; they had to be kept apart from mature females, to whom they had an innate antipathy; and, being the essence of social value, they were not fit possessions for beings themselves not fully socialized (women, children and subject peoples; MacKenzie 1871:499; Campbell 1822,2:254). As a focus of everyday activity, cattle were the epitome of social and symbolic capital; the capital, to paraphrase our opening statement, that linked a material economy of things to a moral economy of persons, and so constructed a total economy of signs and practices.

From the Past to the Present

The first sustained effort to colonize the Tshidi world was made by the Methodist mission.[11] This was the thin edge of a European wedge, and it inserted itself into the fissures of their social system, opening the way for more pervasive external forces (Comaroff and Comaroff 1989, n.d.). Ironically, the impact of the evangelists was less in the sphere of the sacred than in that of production and exchange. The nonconformists introduced a worldview framed in terms of a moral economy, a free market of the spirit, in which Africans were to be cut loose from "tribal" entanglements and set on the path to individual self-construction (J. Comaroff 1985:129f). This implied a notion of person and property drawn from the industrial capitalist culture of early nineteenth century Europe. Founded on the private family estate and the ideal of material and spiritual accumulation, it entailed a division of labor that placed agriculture in male hands and confined women to the domain of the domestic household. And, most crucially, it assumed participation in a global market economy, one that would clasp the black convert in the civilizing embrace of Christian Europe. As Livingstone (1858:34) put it:

> Sending the Gospel to the Heathen...[must include more than] a man going about with a bible under his arm. The promotion of commerce ought to be specially attended to, as this, more speedily than anything else, diminishes the sense of isolation which heathenism engenders...[I

wish] to promote the preparation of the raw materials of European
manufactures in Africa, for by that means we may not only put a stop
to the slave trade, but introduce the negro family into the body of
corporate nations...

Above all, it was commodity production and trade that would recreate
the black person and community: only when the 'raw material' of African
agriculture became an item of exchange within the colonial system - a
system at once moral and material - might the native Christian take his
proper place in a new order of imperial relations. The vital medium of
this transformation was to be money. Methodist ideology focused from
the start on its "talents" as both a means and measure of self-
improvement (J. Comaroff 1985:133).

At the outset, nonconformist values were clearly at odds with Tshidi
social and cultural forms, and presented a bewildering array of
attractions and disincentives. The evangelists sensed early that the path
to the spirit was through practical innovation, and they lost no time in
introducing the plow and irrigation to all who would try them (Comaroff
and Comaroff 1989, n.d.). Initially, it was those excluded from the
spheres of power and prestige who identified with Christianity. But the
impact of the church was soon felt further afield. The plow permitted
large acreages to be brought under cultivation, and regular surpluses to
be produced. Urged on by the mission's Benthamite faith in trade, Tshidi
began to direct these surpluses to colonial merchants rather than to
indigenous relations of exchange (*cf.* Bundy 1979:39; Ranger 1978:109).
The practical innovations brought by the Protestants were to have a
profound effect upon the division of labor and the engendered bases of
production. Plows required beasts for draught, and women were
forbidden to handle them. Men, therefore, were drawn into agriculture;
in any case, where grain was sold, they were quick to assert control over
the wealth yielded in the process. And so, previously discrete domains
of activity, of male and female "work", began to intersect and merge - one
consequence being that women were relegated to the devalued tasks of
tending and reaping (Holub 1881,1:339; Kinsman 1983). What is more,
sexual distinctions were increasingly subsumed into relations of class.
Since only those with access to sufficient oxen could use the plow
effectively in this semi-arid environment, differences in cattle wealth were
introduced into the domain of cultivation. Those who owned stock
began to withdraw them from loans and other forms of patronage
arrangements, sought to increase their arable holdings, and put ever more
of their crops on the market; women, in fact, could no longer be sure of
any control over the harvest, even for purposes of subsistence. As
Shillington (1982:102) has pointed out of the nearby Batlhaping, this led

to a cycle of dispossession as powerful pastoralists seized the most fertile land, gradually depriving other members of the community. For the first time, too, starvation became rife in many chiefdoms, and rulers found it necessary to limit the sale of produce (J. Comaroff 1985:146). Among the Tshidi, this was most visible at the centers of mission influence, where money had become a pervasive medium of exchange (Holub 1881,2:113).

The 'mineral revolution' in the late nineteenth century ushered South Africa into the age of industrial capitalism. This, and the coming of the colonial state, brought radically new material conditions to bear on peoples like the Tshidi. The annexation of British Bechuanaland to the Cape Colony in 1896 led to the imposition of taxes and to systematic attempts to coerce men into the labor market; these attempts being abetted both by the practical and ideological changes initiated by the mission and by the rinderpest pandemic of the mid-1890s (Comaroff and Comaroff 1989; Shillington 1985:16f, 112). Overrule also had a direct effect on the internal political economy. By putting an end to war and raiding, it severed the ruling cadres from their major external source of power - namely, serfs and cattle (J.L. Comaroff 1987:80). In addition, royals had their trade monopolies undercut by white merchants, who bought and sold grain and stock to the disadvantage of local producers. Under these new conditions, chiefs were reduced from recipients of tribute and fines - paid in beasts - to collectors, on behalf of the state, of taxes levied in money. The bases of a centralized Tshidi polity were gradually being eroded, although the elite still enjoyed greater wealth and self-determination than the rest. Faced with the need for cash, men of the rank and file were increasingly compelled to sell their cattle. Tshidi had long traded animals sporadically, it is true, but they were reluctant to do so except when in dire need (Schapera 1933:648). Now they had little alternative, for it was stock that yielded the highest returns; and, in any case, most had little else to sell. These without herds were forced into the labor market very rapidly (Schapera 1947:134). Others, however, also found themselves being drawn, slowly yet inexorably, toward the same fate. For a cycle of impoverishment had been set in motion. Restricted by government decree to the contracted borders of its arid territory, the Tshidi community became increasingly polarized. Only those wealthy in beasts were able to ensure sizeable grain surpluses and withstand ecological risk. Further, like other African peasants, Southern Tswana had to compete on ever less favorable terms with white producers (*cf.* Bundy 1977), who came to dominate the market and demand a growing black workforce. The capacity of Tshidi farmers faltered and erosion, overcrowding and manpower shortage took their toll on crops and herds. Growing rates of male migration drew the chiefdom into the subcontinental political economy as a reservoir of labor, and ensured that money became the prime medium of exchange. Yet wages were kept below the level at which they might support a worker and his family. The majority of the population thus gradually became a "peasantariat" (Parson 1984), trapped in an inescapable combination of wage labor and farming, neither of which was sufficient to meet their subsistence needs (Palmer and Parsons 1977; Murray 1981). As the Tshidi became more deeply imbricated in the regional political economy, relations of production and the sexual division of labor among them underwent yet further change (J.L. Comaroff 1987:81). Most men became wage workers of some sort while women, debarred from joining their husbands in the cities, became the heads of households made up of the very young and the aged. To survive, they had either to enter the restricted local labor market or to eke out a living on ever more barren, infertile land. Agriculture fell back on female shoulders; a devalued and highly precarious activity once more, it was now synonymous with the productive uncertainty of the feminized rural reserves. Men and women had become complementary fractions of an underclass dependent upon the regulatory mechanisms of an increasingly assertive capitalist state. A new center of power controlled the space, time, and movement of all Tshidi; all, that is, save a small petty bourgeoisie which earned its comfortable income from trade, salaries, and commercial farming on large holdings accumulated in the late nineteenth century.

By the time we first did fieldwork in the Tshidi chiefdom in 1969, only twenty percent of families had any rights in cattle.[12] Among stock holders, less than .01 percent (all senior royals and educated entrepreneurs) had more than 500 head; the vast majority owned no more than a handful. "Money has eaten our beasts" (*madi a jele dikgomo*), ordinary people would say. Those who still had cattle also husbanded what remained of the values they used to carry - those expressed in the politics of agnatic rank. But agnation, which had formerly woven domestic units into the body politic, was now eclipsed by the social and material forces that bound the community as a whole to the South African state (cf. J. Comaroff 1985:160f; *cf.* Schapera 1947; Shillington 1985; Arrighi 1979). Except for the elite few, marriage had also been disengaged from the pursuit of political alliance (J.L. Comaroff 1987). Domestic histories collected in 1970 suggested that, over the previous twenty-five years, only half of all unions had involved the exchange of cattle. Here, as elsewhere among the dispossessed of the earth, the overall marriage rate had declined sharply. Domestic histories collected in 1970 suggested that, over the previous twenty-five years, only half of all unions had involved the exchange of cattle, and *go rulaganya bana* was rarely practised any longer (*cf.* Murray 1980:107f). Where bridewealth was transferred, it had come increasingly to feature cash, although, significantly, it was still spoken of in terms of a given number of beasts, a matter to which we shall return below. Caught in a web of poverty and dependence, most people had only their labor power to offer, and their depressed wages rendered them more or less impotent in a world dominated by money (Comaroff and Comaroff 1987).

Not surprisingly, Tshidi have fashioned an elaborate symbolic discourse on the subject of money itself. The term for it, *madi*, an Anglicism, is a homonym for "blood," an irony which is put to cogent rhetorical use. Just as blood is seen as a source of life-giving motion within the body, so money seems to suggest the circulation of essential vitality in the social world (J. Comaroff 1985:174f). But, where bodily health is a function of the temperateness and fluidity of blood, illness and debilitation, both physical and social, bespeak its overheated, sluggish flow. Money as we might expect, is "hot." Like a corrosive acid, it "burns" the pockets of those who try to hold on to it; like the unpredictable, dangerous fire of female fertility, it is explicitly opposed to the cool stability associated with cattle and male political control. "*Madi* runs through your pockets and leaves you hungry. Cattle always return to make you fat," we were often told (*cf.* Ferguson 1985:662). The point, rather, is that virtually all Tshidi, now at the mercy of the capricious coin, exist in the state of subordination formerly associated with femaleness. For these people, men and women alike, the beast remains a symbol of economic and cultural self-sufficiency. It represents the freedom from the labor market of which many Tswana dream (*cf.* Alverson 1978:123; Peters 1983). That dream, typically, hinges upon turning cash earnings into a herd, thereby to break out of the cycle of migration and want. The dream is seldom realized, however. Rich men, the miniscule middle class under *apartheid*, may invest in animals and still negotiate rights in people through them. But, for others, such transactions have become the stuff of an idealized, bygone age. While the market price of cattle has fluctuated greatly this century, their real cost has risen steadily "relative to the earnings from migrant labor" (Roe 1980:40), making them ever more difficult to buy. Consequently, for most Tshidi, cattle are, today, the tragic icon of a vanished world of self-determination; a mythic society in which men were men, in which women did not struggle alone in the rural wastelands, in which the control of social vitality was ultimately ensured by the goodly beast. Modern migrants offer a cynical commentary on the irony of their predicament, their world turned upside down. They describe themselves as "women", "tinned fish", and, above all, "draught oxen". Reduced to less than fully social beings, it is they who are now the animate source of value for others (Comaroff and Comaroff 1987:200). In spite of all this, or perhaps because of it, the "bovine mystique" (Ferguson 1985) is perpetuated. In Tshidi eyes, livestock remain the ideal medium for the storage of wealthy being much more resilient to dissipation than is money.

And notwithstanding the practical difficulties of doing so, many still speak in various ways of converting cash back into cattle, of casting off their state of dependency. Given the inroads made into their world by commerce and commodities, not to mention their brute poverty, this preoccupation is not hard to fathom. Neither is the fact that coins circulate among them as symbolically charged currency. Or, that much of their ritual activity focuses on the manipulation of money in an attempt to bring it under control (J. Comaroff 1985:236). For the majority, as we have said, the most salient feature of cash is its sheer velocity and elusiveness. This, and its association with the dark and distant forces which dictate the rhythms of modern life, merely reiterates the contrast with beasts; with their manifest, dependable powers of increase and their resistance to the voracious demands of everyday need. Cattle, Tshidi say, are their "Barclays Bank".[13] They are not alone in speaking thus. The same sardonic imagery appears widely among Central and Southern African pastoralists (*cf.* Alverson 1978:124; Fielder 1973:351).

Certain important transactions within the community - among them, marriage, and court fines, patronage loans and payments to healers - are still reckoned by everyone in terms of cattle. But, much of the times, these are "cattle without legs" (*dikgomo tse di tlhokang maoto*), the phrase used by Tshidi for tokens of (ostensibly) fixed cash value. Sansom (1976:144) has noted that, among Pedi, "signal transactions" of this kind are characteristic of bridewealth, initiation, fines, and damages; that is, of prestations and compensations involving changes of status. In signalling such transitions, nominal animal currency also distinguishes this *form* of exchange from ordinary market dealings. The monetary worth of a token beast is generally not frozen for all time. But it is always for lower than the going commercial price. The discontinuity is further underlined by the fact that nominal values are spoken of in pounds sterling an archaic currency (Sansom 1976:145).[14]

Tshidi "cattle without legs" carry similar signal value. They too mark transactions that stress the enduring quality of persons and relations. In the early 1970s, a nominal beast was worth six pounds - ludicrously below prevailing market price, as Tshidi themselves readily pointed out. But it is precisely in this discrepancy that the significance of any symbolic currency lies. In an expanding universe, in which little seems to escape being equated with or reduced to money, "legless" livestock are a salient anachronism. By denying the universalizing rationality of commerce - its colonizing "modernity" - these "cows" inscribe the work of local social practices in the cultural capital of *"setswana"* ("Tswana Ways"). And, by restricting their conversion to a cash equivalent they put such practices beyond the purview of the coin. The relations built with token animals are thereby distinguished as special and, as important, stable; in this respect, they are set off from the uncertain world of *sekgoa*, things "European". An expansion of the opposition between the beast and the banknote, these legless animals stand as a line of defence against the erosion of what most Tshidi take to be their distinctive social wealth. They represent an effort to make cattle serve again as the guarantor of value in a world of flux, as an "enclave" that resists dissolution to the promiscuous terms of the market (*cf.* Ferguson 1988:494). After all, *madi ga a na mong*, money has no owner.

Money and Cattle

This returns us to the issue with which we began. Marx (1967:82) saw money as a "special commodity", a sort of "social hieroglyph". Being a "natural object with strange properties", it serves at once as a measure of value and a standard of price for all other commodities (*Ibid.*:94, 106). Much the same can be said of beasts among the Tshidi. They, too, may be currency and capital simultaneously; they, too, have the unusual ability to make commensurable different forms of value, and to convert one form into another. It is this capacity - to equate and transform, to give worth and meaning - that quite literally animates both cattle and cash. And makes them objects of fetishism; objects, that is, which seem to have a logic all of their own, able to do things, to forge relations, and to increase of their own accord - without ever disclosing the forces that fabricate *them* Fetishism, of course, was essential to Marx's notion of the "strange properties" of the commodity; of its role in mediating production and consumption, power and meaning. Ironically, perhaps, it is just this, the fetishism of things, that is most conspicuously absent from recent anthropological accounts of the nature of objects in other cultures.

Thus Appadurai (1986), to take one noteworthy case, defines the commodity merely as an "object in motion", and seeks the "social life of things" primarily in exchange. His approach has many virtues. For one thing, it does away with the misleading opposition between gifts and commodition (Gregory 1982); similarly, it has no place for facile dichotomies between use and exchange value (Taussig 1980; *cf.* Ferguson 1988). And it encourages us to explore the ways in which "the capitalist mode of commoditization... interact[s] with myriad other indigenous social forms of commoditization" (Appadurai 1986:16). On the other hand, in treating all goods as though they were like objects in Maussian gift exchange, (surplus) value is generated, appropriated, and naturalized; through which, by means of *some* objects, particular forms of consciousness and inequality are shaped and reproduced. Goods may indeed come to signify "regimes of value", as he says (Mauss 1954:4). But both cattle and money are *particular* sorts of goods, with a peculiar aptitude for abstracting and congealing wealth, for making and breaking meaningful associations, and for permitting some human beings to live off the backs of others. And all this without ever disclosing quite how or why any of it should, or does, happen.

While they are alike in these respects, cattle and money are dissimilar in important ways as well; this being the consequence of their situation, respectively, in very different economies of signs and meanings, very different cultures of production and exchange. Thus beasts might have facilitated the abstraction and transaction of value among precolonial and colonial Tshidi; and, notionally at least, they still have the potential to do so. But they had nowhere near the capacity of cash in capitalist societies to free goods and services from their contexts and make them commensurable. Conversely, the coin does not have the same capacity as the cow, symbolic or substantial, to embody a biography, let alone to bear within it an entire grammar of social relations. Southern Tswana are themselves wont to note the contrast, especially when they compare the world of the workplace with life beyond its purview. Not only do they remark that "money has no owner". They also add, wryly, that "one can eat cattle but not cash".

As they have learned, however money *can* eat cattle. In a world increasingly dominated by the commodity, little remains irreducible to a cash equivalent; little escapes the indiscriminate melting-pot of the market. We have seen how, as the South African political economy engulfed the Tshidi, it undermined not only their order of values, but also their ability to make a living without resort to wage labor. Time, work, sexual and ritual "services" - all things once embodied and conveyed through animals - have been variously reified, commoditized, given a price. No wonder that the tyranny of money is most plainly and painfully visible, to Tshidi, in the peremptoriness with which it has eaten away at their herds and the social fabric once knitted together by them.

Perhaps this is why Southern Tswana continue to make such a great imaginative investment in livestock, marking them out as the media with which to hold the line against the ravages of the market. By struggling to prevent the goodly beast from becoming mere beastly goods, they seek to limit the Midas touch of money, to resist the implosive effects of commerce and commodities within their world. Herein lies the significance of the "bovine mystique" for black migrant laborers all over southern Africa (Ferguson 1985, 1988) - and, in particular, the salience of legless cattle among the Tshidi. Symbolic currencies of this sort are tokens of the attempt to dam the corrosive flow of cash, to force it to bear the imprint of human relations. Africa offers many examples of such currencies, and of the effort to decommoditize the coin,[15] especially in those transactions, like bridewealth, which build enduring social ties. Indeed, in the space between old and new commodities, hybrid beasts - like the nominal "cows" of the Pedi and Tshidi - have been born; beasts that challenge the uncompromising logic of a monetary economy. THe impact of cash may be everywhere to hand, and it may have converted much into its own terms. But not everything. Many Africans still cherish the ideal of reversing this process, and strive hard to do so. The Tshidi are not alone in hoping that their labors may yet yield cattle *with* legs, cattle with which to rebuild a durable world.

Notes

1. This song was recorded by Schapera (1934:14). We have modified his translation slightly, using the term "chiefdom" for "tribe", and have modernized the Setswana orthography.
2. Evans-Pritchard was not alone in this observation. Others before him (*e.g.* Casalis 1861; Hunter 1936; Schapera and Goodwin 1937) had also noted the pervasive significance of cattle in African social and cultural life.
3. As is well-known, the concept was introduced by Herskovits (1926), and, states Mair (1985:743), has been misused ever since. For brief but useful comment, with reference to southern Africa, see Kuper (1982:10f).
4. Kuper's generalization is perhaps too sweeping. While bovine bridewealth was indeed crucial to cattle-keepers, some predominantly agricultural peoples exchanged other things; the Lovedu, for example, gave ceremonial hoes for wives until the end of the nineteenth century, when they switched to livestock (Krige 1981:149). Among all Southern Bantu-speakers, moreover, the role of animals in marriage prestations has undergone complex transformation during the twentieth century. Of course, beasts played, and continue to play, a rather different part in the social lives of such non-Bantu-speaking pastoralists as the Herero.
5. Given limitations of space, we cannot hope to include an adequately detailed account of precolonial economy and society here. In summarizing their most salient features, we take for granted our earlier writings on the subject. The same applies to our sources; they are annotated and evaluated elsewhere (*e.g.* J.L. Comaroff 1973; J. Comaroff 1985; Comaroff and Comaroff n.d.).
6. Although he never worked among Rolong, Rev. Willoughby, a missionary-ethnographer, clearly intended his observations to apply to *all* Tswana, unless otherwise specified; in his writings, in fact, he was always careful to record variations in cultural practices. Willoughby was well-qualified to make such

comparative statements, since he knew almost as much about the Rolong and Tlhaping as he did about the Kwena, Kgatla, and Ngwato, of whom he had direct experience. Like Livingstone before him, he first made acquaintance with the "Bechuana" through his brethren in the south before going on to take up his own mission. What is more, he remained an active member of their circle, visited them often, and read their extensive accounts of "native life". Later he became head of Tiger Kloof Native Institution, a school near Vryburg on the borders of Rolong territory.

7. Gulbrandsen (1987:239f; see also 1986) has criticized us for, among other things, making too much of the opposition between agnation and matrilaterality. He also believes that we overstress the competitive quality of agnation. It is difficult to know how to react to these criticisms, however. Firstly, they are based on ethnographic findings among a different Tswana people (the Ngwaketse) at a different period in time (the mid-1970's), notwithstanding our efforts to contextualize our own accounts as carefully as possible. Secondly, they characterize our descriptions of the Tshidi sociocultural order in a somewhat oversimplified manner, so that what is being taken to task is often not exactly what we intended. Thirdly, we have ourselves taken pains to analyze the contradictions in Tshidi views of agnation, and to account for the ambiguities surrounding their cultural categories and oppositions. We stand by those analyses. Further than this, it would take a lengthy response to address all the minutiae of Gulbrandsen's case, which clearly would be inappropriate here.

8. A house consisted of a wife and her children. In a polygamous household, the unity of the different houses was stressed: each had its own fields and share of the family estate. Most significantly, its children were differentiated from their half-siblings by their ties to their matrilateral kin. Elsewhere (*e.g.* Comaroff & Roberts 1981; J. Comaroff 1985), we have provided detailed analyses of the house as an "atom" of sociocultural structure.

9. We have discussed the Southern Tswana conception of *tiro* more fully elsewhere, albeit for different purposes (1987; n.d.). Here we merely summarize its main features.

10. It was not only the productive labor of a wife that subsidized a man's political enterprises, of course. His wife also bore him children - just as his mother had given him his matrikin, his most steadfast supporters - through whom to make alliances and gain control over other people.

11. This discussion draws from our current research on nonconformist evangelism among the Southern Tswana between 1820 and 1920. In addition to ethnohistorical materials collected in the late 1960s and mid-1970s, we have made extensive use of the archives of the London Missionary Society and Wesleyan Methodist Missionary Society (see Comaroff and Comaroff n.d.).

12. Tshidi who live in Barolong (or the Barolong Farms) in southern Botswana have, with few exceptions, long ceased to keep cattle in large numbers. This small community, known as the "granary of Botswana", has been given over almost entirely to cultivation, most of it for the market. Although it falls within the greater orbit of the South African political economy, Barolong has not been subjected to the oppressive controls of the *apartheid* state, and has retained much greater productive autonomy. The handful of wealthy farmers who do have

sizable herds tend now to run them on commercial ranches provided for under Botswana's national Tribal Grazing Land Policy.

13. The subsidiary of a British company, Barclays is one of the oldest banks in South Africa, and has branches in virtually every city and small town - as it once did throughout much of the empire. For black South Africans, it has long been a powerful symbol of white wealth.

14. South Africa had changed its currency from sterling to rands some years before we did our first fieldwork among the Tshidi.

15. For an especially striking example, see Hutchinson's (1988) excellent analysis of modern Nuerland.

3

"To Increase Cows, God Created the King": The Function of Cattle in Intralacustrine Societies[1]

Pierre Bonte

The region of Central Africa delimited by the great lakes - including Lake Victoria and Lake Tanganyika - is occupied by a group of societies who share a common system of cultural features, symbolic representations and practices regarding political power: the institution of sacred kingship. There are some forty Intralacustrine societies characterized by sacred kingships, some already powerful states at the time of the colonial scramble, such as Buganda, Burundi, and Rwanda, while others could at best be considered local chieftainships (See Figure 3.1). In spite of a diversity of political institutions, their common identity has been recognized both in scholarly works preceding the end of the colonial era (Troubworst, d'Hertefelt, and Scherer 1962; de Heusch 1966) and in the more recent work of local historians (Mworoha 1977; Bujumbura Conference 1982). While all these societies share a hierarchical system of values differentiating pastoralism and agriculture, in full-fledged pastoral aristocracies cattle are distinctly associated with kingship (See Plate 3.1).

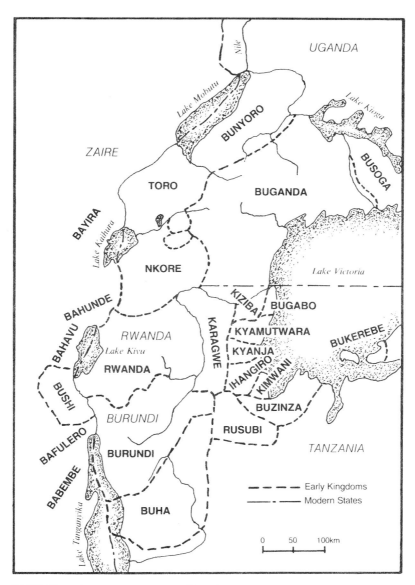

FIGURE 3.1 The Intralacustrine Kingdoms

This chapter will concentrate on the significance of pastoralism for the system of social stratification found in these societies. Both features have given rise to a variety of interpretations we shall briefly review. We aim to demonstrate that the social and political relations based on the ownership of cattle can only be understood in terms of the symbolic and ideological representations of sacred kingship. These representations themselves are based on a unique symbolic construction of gender relations that operates within the political context of sacred kingship to define the organization of the family and the distinction between "herders" and "cultivators".

From Hamitic Conquest to African Feudalism

For some time the association between livestock and royal power and the prevailing hierarchy of pastoralism and agriculture was considered to be the end result of conquest of sedentary agricultural peoples by Hamitic or Cushitic pastoral nomads (Pagès 1933). These diffusionist hypotheses, which stated that ancient African civilization was introduced from the Nile Valley, were often blatantly racist. They assumed that people of negroid stock were incapable of conceiving the idea of the state. Other authors, and more specifically authors from these African societies (Karugire 1971; Mworoha 1977), have attacked these hypotheses and denounced their ideological underpinnings. In a manner perhaps more insidious, the same idea can be found in analyses which emphasize ethnic and "caste" structures, even in the face of substantial contrary evidence, such as the lack of any such notions in Bunyoro cultural representations. Most often such interpretations rest upon the notion of a quasi-natural superiority of pastoral societies, quite independent of any demonstrable tendency on their part towards military conquest.

Towards the end of the 1950s, other hypotheses were put forward (Maquet 1954, 1961; Beattie 1964; Steinhart 1967; and Goody 1971 for a review) on the nature and the function of cattle in Intralacustrine societies[2]. It was proposed that these societies were structured along feudal principles, livestock serving a function homologous to that of land in the European fief, as the cornerstone of bondage. The debate rapidly exhausted itself in the search for similarities and differences between "African feudalism" and its European counterpart (Beattie 1964). The discussion did however have the advantage of demonstrating the autochthonous nature of these political systems and their degree of independent development. However, the limits of the approach were also quickly demonstrated, notably its failure to account for aspects of social organization not associated with "relations of cattle." Furthermore, instead of excluding interpretations centered on notions of conquest, ethnicity and caste, the feudal hypothesis often perpetuated them.

A number of authors adopted a critical perspective regarding the "premise of inequality," a notion introduced by Maquet (1954). They considered it not as a structural feature of these societies but as the conceptual and material result of colonialism;[3] they also questioned the idea of relations of domination between these groups, as well as the very existence of an objective pastoral/agricultural hierarchy. Karugire is very clear on this subject:

> The economic relations between the Bairu and the Bahima were based on mutual exchange of the goods produced by each other and their occupations were made mutually exclusive by environmental conditions rather than by ethnic superiority or inferiority (Karugire 1971:41).

Doornbos (1978:17) reached similar conclusions with regard to Nkore, noting the Nkore society gave a contradictory picture of itself: "while one suggests a pattern of coexistence and symbiosis between two separate communities, the other conveys a picture of basic inequality and subordination between them." For the author this second picture stems from a "superstructure" (*Ibid*.:37) of rank and political status. In the economic sphere the two groups are seen as largely autonomous, engaging only in limited exchange.

Chrétien's (1974) analysis, although it deals with the highly stratified society of Burundi, goes beyond previous critiques of the models of domination applied to these societies. At every level, exchange and reciprocity are present. The concept of rank seems more appropriate than the concepts of caste and feudalism, which are linked to myths of racial or ethnic superiority and which legitimized the intensification of economic exploitation under colonialism. In a comparative study along similar lines, Mworoha examined social stratification in Burundi, as well as across the other kingdoms. The power of the king stands at the apex of a ranked society and constitutes "government by an aristocracy controlling a vast hierarchical network of power" with the backing of "all forms of solidarity and royalty" (1977:208).

Thus, side by side with old issues, such as the internal or external (*i.e.*, conquest) origin of this differentiation, or the issue of ethnicity, new questions arise. Is sacred kingship merely a system of religious representations or is it a specific form of the state? Is the social order organized around the ranked stratification of status groups or is it organized around antagonistic classes? A few hypotheses will be put forward in an attempt both to deal with and go beyond the inherent limitations of these alternatives. One cannot identify the sacred kingship in each case as a centralized political structure, in effect, a State. To the contrary, what is necessary to explain is how under certain circumstances ritual and the system of religious representations developed into state-like political institutions, with new forms of social and political hierarchy.

Cows and the Kingdom

The distinction between the sacred kingship as a system of representations and a concept of political organization, on the one hand, and the forms of the state which have developed within Intralacustrine societies, on the other hand, draws attention to the anteriority of a religious and political dimension. Given that various points of view are opposed on this subject, certain retaining the notion of anteriority (Mworoha 1977), others denying it (Karugire 1971; Beattie 1971:104), it is difficult to see in this religious dimension the simple legitimation of an earlier political and economic order. The institution of the sacred kingship is based on founding myths, justifying the fact that the king, genealogically related to mythical dynasties, appears both as founder and restorer of the natural order. Kingship is thus conceived as a truly ritualized function. The king is not assimilated to the numerous ritual specialists who otherwise participate in the institutional organization of the kingdom. He is but one element constituting the system of kingship as a whole. In this vast ritual process, organized at times on a dynastic scale - as in Rwanda where it involves the succession of four sovereigns with distinct and complementary features - we can identify several clear sequences. In certain cases these sequences were codified according to precise and secret rules known only to a few ritual specialists who subdivided this knowledge among themselves so that none of them would be able to monopolize and thus draw power from it[4].

One ritual series takes place between the death and subsequent funeral of a king. During this time there is a period of grief appropriate to the collapse of the natural and social order. In Nkore this is rendered by the saying "heaven has fallen." All activities, especially of a sexual and reproductive nature must cease. The death of the king throws society into a state of complete disorder, returning it to primordial chaos until the crowning of the next king. This highlights the relation between the function of kingship, especially as related to the king's physical integrity and strength, and the surrounding world order. That order is restored through the rituals surrounding the ascent to the throne of a new monarch, which constitutes a true *rite de passage* for the individual vested with the sacred dimension of the royal office. As a Rwandan dynastic poem emphasized (Kagame 1951:53),

> (The king) is a man before his crowning but once named he becomes separated from the ordinary nobility, from which he stands apart. The sovereign knows no rival: he is unique.

Before the king can perform any of the symbolic acts which constitute an important part of his duties - cultivating, smithing, making fire, hunting, leading his people in war, *etc.* - and before he receives any of the royal *regalia*, especially the royal drum, he must go through a series of rituals designed to ensure his purification.

The prosperity of the kingdom, the fertility of humanity, animals and crops, all depend upon the repeated performance of ritual activities. The importance of agriculture is expressed by the preeminence of rites related to cultivation. In Rwanda, for example, there are rites related to first-fruits, during which the king fertilizes a sample of fresh cut sorghum. In Burundi, the *Muganuro* is the ritual opening of the agricultural cycle. In other parts of this region the main rituals are associated with the harvest. Elsewhere, other complex and elaborate rituals (*e.g.*, "the path of the drinking-trough" in Rwanda) are associated with pastoralism. They express symbolically the notion of renewal by linking kingship to cattle through the idiom of pastoralism.

The sacred kingship appears therefore primarily as a ritual function. Ritual activities are essential for the pursuit of human activities, for the maintenance of the natural and social orders. The specific authority of the king stems from his ritualized roles and from his association with the sacred kingship rather than simply from his identification as a specialist in ritual activities. It is the royal office which makes kings, providing them with a unique character left undisturbed by their individual deaths. The founding myths of royal families, dynastic genealogies and cults devoted to deceased kings, all contribute to the perpetuation of the royal office by reference to the primordial time of the creation of the world. Thus, if the death of a king suspends the world order for the period of mourning, it can also be perceived as a necessary regeneration after the period of steady decline caused by the aging and illnesses that affected the king's vital energy and jeopardized the efficiency of royal rites[5].

One needs to pose the question as to why these royal rituals are necessary. At the core of the sacred kingship lies a concept of the sacred expressed through representations of the supernatural that are apparently shared by all Intralacustrine peoples. The supernatural power associated with kingship is also linked to an founding principle of fertility which assumes the aspect of God the Creator. It is this power which confers its sacred character on the royal office (Mworoha 1977:291):

> The king was seen as an agent of mysterious forces which uphold the social and natural order. The kings did not create the monarchy, the monarchy took them.

In Rwanda this power is called *imaana*:

This term refers to a powerful quality, a dynamic principle of life and fecundity that the ancient Rwandans sought to appropriate through ritual techniques. In some cosmological stories this same power is conceived of in terms of a conscious entity and will which could be qualified as divine. However, since the term *imaana* does not specifically designate an individual being that should be honored and implored, but rather a diffuse fluid that has to be tapped, there are no specific cults directed at this anthropomorphic hypostasis.... The quality of *imaana* is associated with a wide category of objects and persons through which ancient Rwandans thought they could benefit from its effects.... But, according to the conceptions of the Rwanda it is the sovereign who is the supreme detainer of the fecunding *imaana* fluid; royal ritual therefore is a compendium of the techniques used to direct its beneficial effects upon the whole country (Coupez and d'Hertefelt 1964:460).

This power is neither good nor bad, but is always potentially dangerous. Beattie, in reference to the proximal notion of *mahano* in Bunyoro, notes that "the concept involves both the idea of pollution and at the same time a notion of something like baraka or blessing" (1968:439). Royal rituals not only tap this power for the benefit of the whole kingdom and its inhabitants but also neutralize its dangerous aspects. Everything in the king's daily life underlines this peculiar character of the royal person. The king is kept in isolation, eats alone, wears unusual clothing, etc. Constant purification rituals revolve around his person. The realm is ever threatened by the king's aging and illness. Channeling the benevolent aspects of the power embodied in the king is not a given; this must be ritually organized and great care must be exercised to exclude aspects of pollution and danger from his person and activities[6].

The efficacy of this ritual "tapping" of power, and its culturally imperative character, is expressed in the idea that the king "owns" the kingdom, his subjects and their worldly possessions. This notion of "ownership", while it does convey a political dimension when a state has emerged from the institution of sacred kingship, does not have a juro-legal or even economic nature. Rather it is of the order of qualities, of essential attributes, reflected in the consubstantial relationship between the royal office and other social statuses, most specifically with pastoral activity. The coding of nutritional behaviour, for instance, underscores these relations. In Rwanda, as in Nkore and other kingdoms, the king's nutrition emphasizes liquid foods, agricultural products being consumed only in this form (*i.e.* as sorghum and honey beer), along with milk drawn from ritually pure and sacred cows. The consumption of this milk by the king is held as "being the best thing" for the kingdom. These same principles also come into play to distinguish "pastoralists" from "agriculturalists". Thus, under the royal office, consumption of food, productive activities, and sexuality, all appear linked to the office and its ritual efficacy; but they are also perceived, through a consubstantial relationship, as contributing to the reproduction of the link to the sacred originally initiated under the kingship.

Intralacustrine societies are also organized according to a hierarchy of social functions (royalty, pastoralism, agriculture). That reference is made to "functions" rather than "activities" implies that they are non-exclusive in material character, that is, "pastoralists" can also pursue agricultural occupations and "agriculturalists" generally own cattle. This character is justified by representations that attribute qualitative traits of heterogeneity and hierarchy to social groups; these hierarchical relations vary from one society to another.

Among the Bunyoro, royal office is associated with a geographically diffuse and demographically important clan, distinct from "pastoralist" and "agriculturalist" clans. These latter are little differentiated from one another and of a completely different origin. In Nkore, the Bahinda clan is strongly linked to the Bahima who are geographically and ethnically distinct from the Bairu. The Batutsi-Bahutu opposition is also evident in the southern kingdoms. In Rwanda the royal clan is considered to be Batutsi but in Burundi it can be Bahutu. Thus the relative specificity of the royal office and its relation to the category "pastoralists" cannot be explained in terms of this hierarchical social categorization. Our hypothesis is that the royal office cannot be deduced, as has often been suggested, from social hierarchy and that it is not the values revolving around pastoral activities and cattle which justify their association with the royal office; it is rather the institution of kingship which determines both the specific qualities attributed to cattle and the hierarchy of social statuses.

Cattle intimately share the power associated with royal office. For instance in Rwanda the king "owns" all the cattle in the same manner as he "owns" the entire kingdom. The concept of *imaana*, the founding principle of kingship, applies not only to the king but also to the dominant bull of any given herd. A whole series of specific dietary rules underlines the narrow consubstantial relation between the king and cattle[7]. On an equal footing with the royal drum, the bull shares the power associated with the royal office and stands out as a dynastic standard. The *Mahabura* bulls of Burundi constantly accompany the king; others named *Semasaka* were at the center of the festivals surrounding the sowing season, their urine mixed in the ritually prepared sorghum porridge eaten by the king (Mworoha 1977). In Rwanda the king owned the "bulls of the reign" that belonged to three separate herds (the "respectables," the "dynastics," and the "rooted") whose descent and succession paralleled succession to the throne. These bulls were kept in regional capitals which they left only in order to participate in royal rituals (Coupez et d'Hertefelt 1964:306). They insured the fecundity of the royal cattle and were symbols of the king's own strength and reproductive power. They held power over the realm alongside the king, who was responsible for earth and humankind. During periods of warfare, these bulls, just as the king, kept in a state of readiness, were never allowed to sleep; their massive strength was contained but was always ready to be called upon (Coupez et d'Hertefelt 1964:347). When the king or any other Tutsi died the head bull of the herd was sacrificed and the funeral preparations of the body were carried out in its skin (Ibid.:361). In Nkore the king is even considered as a metonym of the bull.

These latter representations strongly encourage sexual differentiation. In Nkore the kingdom is inversely associated with cows (Elam 1973). In Rwanda the analysis of one of the most important rituals for the periodic renewal of the royal office, the "royal path to the drinking-trough," sheds light on its other characteristics. The ritual is organized around the cyclical dynastic system of naming implemented by the "herder-king" who presides over an important part of this ritual. Each king rules in association with the preceding herder-king, whose smoked remains are not buried but are thought to sojourn within the sacred half of the living king[8]. These rituals involve, therefore, a ritualized spatial representation of the kingdom. They require the sacrifice of bulls, the making of dynastic drums (each of whose heart is that of a bull), and ritual drinking-troughs. Cows and the pastoral activities revolving around the king's herds supply a ritualized representation of the kingdom, the fecundity of which is his ultimate responsibility, just as that of the herd is the ultimate responsibility of the bull. The king also "owns" cows deemed sacred, which manifest the ambiguous good and evil character of all objects invested with royal power. In Rwanda possession of long-horned *Inyambo* cows were a royal prerogative, but neither the king nor the Tutsis could drink of their milk because the cows were originally from Bunyoro and might have caused the death of the preceding ruler; drinking their milk might destroy the cosmic order upon which the present rule rested. The same logic applies in Burundi where the sterile cow (*save*) and the he-goat (*Rusasu*), another polluted animal, were associated with the king's ritual enthronement.

The value of cattle and of pastoralism relates to their privileged association with the royal office and its supernatural attributes. It is not because one is a pastoralist that one has a privileged position in the social hierarchy; rather, it is because one is in a privileged position with regard to sacred kingship that one owns livestock and can be a pastoralist. Thus, in the Nkore Kingdom, where the association between pastoralism and royal office is the closest and where the distinction between Bahima "pastoralists" and Bairu "agriculturalists" takes the form of an ethnic cleavage, the royal office-pastoralist association results in the equation of control over livestock with participation in royal office.

> There are numerous examples in Nkore history of people who were born Bairu, distinguished themselves in the service of the *Omugabe*, acquired cattle in the process, married Bahima women and whose descendants became Bahima in the course of two or three generations (Karugire 1971:56).

Such processes are in partial contradiction with a history represented in terms of conquest, as well as of ethnic if not overtly racial oppositions. Before we examine the problem of the nature of social stratification in this region we must analyze more precisely the association between pastoralism and royal office by taking into account the structure of political relationships revolving around cattle.

The Political Function of Relations through Cattle

The ethnological literature dealing with Intralacustrine societies has identified cattle as the basis for generating relations of subordination and domination and of social stratification conceived in terms of castes, feudal relations, etc. We have already mentioned the problems raised by these interpretations, to which we now return.

The facts which served a starting point for these theoretical interpretations were generated from the observation of the contractual bond relation between pastoralists and agriculturalists known as *ubuhake* in Rwanda and *bugabire* in Burundi. These are personal relationships (but not private since they can involve domestic groups) between an owner of cattle (*shebuja*, the patron) and the person soliciting cattle and protection (*umugarugu* in Rwanda or *mugabire* in Burundi). The relation is initiated by the client. If the pastoralist who is sought out as patron agrees, he loans the the client one or more cows that remain his property. The client has the usufruct of the livestock, namely the milk and, more importantly, the calves. In return he is obliged to render a steady stream of gifts and to respond to his patron's demand for services. This dependency is underlined in the sayings used to describe the situation: *Kwabake inkike*, "building the fence," or *gufata igehe*, "losing one's time." The relation can be severed but then the client faces the possibility of losing the cattle gained (d'Hertefelt 1962). The other side of the livestock relationship is the protection afforded by the patron over the client's worldly possessions, the provision of juridical services, etc. In this sense the relationship has a definite political twist and we may talk of bondage or caste stratification.

Vidal has shown that these generalizations about bond partnerships do not in fact correspond to social reality. In Rwanda, in spite of the fact that the *ubuhake* is considerably developed, it is of recent origin and never developed into a system extending to the whole of social relations:

> The structure of the pastoral clientele was not generalized to all members of society and involved more family groups than individuals. The theoretical liberty of choice was considerably restrained in reality. The theoretically free choice of *Shebuja* patrons was in reality greatly limited. In the end, the network formed by *ubuhake* bonds was not the major determinant of the system of livestock exchange, and the Tutsi were not able to prevent the Hutus from acquiring their own cows (Botte *et al.* 1969:392).

In fact, the institution is closely associated with the development of the Rwanda state in the middle of the nineteenth century and is linked to the implementation of a new power structure involving land tenure and political subordination. For Vidal, cattle relations appear more as an ideological manifestation of this new structure rather than its basis.

> Cattle symbolized the fundamental ambiguity of this social formation: it embodied the ideological primacy of the relationship linking man to man, as an instrument of political domination and simultaneously marked the objective difference between those - Hutu and Tutsi - which feudalism had privileged and those it had disowned. Fetishized, the possession of cattle represented success for every Rwandan. "Nothing is superior to cattle", says a proverb (Vidal, 1974:73).

Thus the development of the political role of cattle must be seen in the light of the evolution of Intralacustrine politics. It is impossible to generalize about the role of cattle from isolated observations within this evolutionary process. But can we, as Vidal does by focusing his analysis on land tenure, reduce the role of cattle to that of a mask which hides relations of subordination, while at the same time continuing to conceptualize the political situation as feudal? Such an approach neglects the meaning attributed to cattle and pastoral activities by virtue of their association with the royal office. Before returning to the analysis from this perspective, we wish to make two more comments.

On the one hand, the pastoral relations described above cannot be totally distinguished from other social relations which are grounded in the exchange of cattle in other sectors; these forms of circulation correspond to the "universe of cattle" among neighboring societies, such as that of the Maasai.[9] In the Nkore Kingdom, where differentiation between the specialized Bahima "herders" and Bairu "agriculturalists" is most prominent, these relations are highly elaborated (Lukyn-Williams 1938). *Omukwato* is the name given to a cow used as collateral for a debt until it has produced a heifer to be used in repayment; *mpanano* is the gift of a cow designed to create a relationship of intimate friendship, in the same way as *engaburano*; *akuhonha* is the cow given as payment for a service. Likewise, in Rwanda, the *inka y 'ineza* cow creates a reciprocal non-hierarchical contractual social relation between parties; the *inka y 'inyiturano* cow leads to a bloodwealth relationship with precisely defined rules of behaviour between the parties (Dusengeyezu 1978). Everywhere, cattle intervene in bridewealth arrangements. It is impossible to analyze the hierarchical and political nature of relations generated by cattle without situating them in the overall body of social relations created through their exchange, even if the circulation of livestock does not have in every instance the same importance as it does in neighboring societies for which we have described the effects of cattle fetishism.

On the other hand, the vocabulary of these political relations places us in another semantic field located on the border of pastoral activities, which joins the notions of power and those of circulation and exchange (Chrétien 1974). In Burundi the term *bugabire* is derived from the root *kugaba* which means "to give freely," "to own in full," but also "to distribute," "to dominate," "to rule." In the same way the root *gusaba* means both "to ask," "to pray," but also "to pay hommage," "to be subject of." In Bunyoro the *mukama* is often called *Mwebinge*, "the one to call on while in need," or again *Agutamba*, "the medicine that cures from poverty" (Beattie 1971). Similarly the Nkore king holds the title *mugaba*, "the giver," and more specifically "the giver of cattle." God himself is often referred to as *Rugaba*, "the giver."

In the context of Intralacustrine states and of the social and political hierarchies constituted through sacred kingship, we are justified in asking if the development of contractual relations of *bagabire* or *ubuhake* are not related to a more general model of political domination that associates the pastoral pursuit with kingship. I have already shown in the second part of this study the tight overlapping of the royal function and pastoralism on the ritual and symbolic plane. I will attempt now to reconstruct this model, not in a chronological perspective - too many facts escape us to warrant an attempt in this direction - but rather through a logical procedure, which, although it cannot provide the key to historical reconstruction, may nonetheless help to generate certain rules about when sacred kingship leads to the formation of complex states. I will try to demonstrate how the capacity of such a model to account for the resulting system of political organization supports the hypothesis I put forward at the beginning of this chapter. The notion of the sacred kingship is not simply an ideology legitimating and organizing the power of royalty; rather, it serves as the veritable matrix, by which political relations within these Intralacustrine societies - through the ritual functions which it defines - are constituted, both conceptually and practically.

One might be tempted to interpret the royal function in terms of reciprocity, as Chrétien did in the paper quoted above (1974): the king gives not only cattle but also prosperity and fertility, and in return he receives goods and services. These "terms of exchange" are in fact of a greatly heterogeneous and hierarchical nature, although the royal function remains determinant, "unique", as says Kagame; it alone establishes the commensurability of these terms. The king is the "giver" *par excellence*, since he "owns" everything and is the source of all social wealth. But since by definition he also always gives more than he receives, a consubstantial participation in supernatural power, channeled in a creative manner, is associated with the royal office. Moreover, by giving cattle he gives something invested above all with the value of supernatural kingship.

In Burundi, *bagabire* bond partnerships, which concern the king and his personal links with members of the dominant social group, are called *batongore* (Mwosoha 1977). This relation is essentially an exchange of goods in return for services and political protection that foregoes its contractual and contingent character. A relation of political clientage is established between the king and the wealthiest cattle owners who thereby accept a degree of royal control over their herds. Once the specificity of this relation is recognized we are warranted in asking, according to a logical rather than a chronological mode of inquiry, whether in the case of Burundi the royal *batongore* does not represent the more general form and the secular *bagabire* the more particular.

We can compare the Burundian *batongore* with the central Nkore social relation of *okutoija*, which operated in a social environment totally different from that of Burundi. The *okutoija* relationship, which centres on the person of the *mugabe*, supports the emergence of client relations between the king and Bahima pastoralists. It is in his role as "owner" of all the cattle in the kingdom that the king receives gifts; royal power rests essentially on identification with the supernatural, in accord with what could be labelled "symbolic consent" or a shared worldview.

Decisions carried weight because they were ordained in the name of high authority, even if this authority was highly symbolic and only partly involved direct control over subordinates. The coherence of the political community depended critically on maintaining this myth (Doornbos 1978:60).

Okutoija is the visible expression of the "gift" made by the king of what he rightfully "owns" but it is also a visible form of the authority relationship which is its consequence. In Nkore, where the political apparatus of the state is institutionally weak, the *mugabe* creates a direct political relationship with territorial chiefs - *bakungu* -by delegating certain powers through the distribution of large herds (Roscoe 1923). Thus by the incremental delegation of his symbolic and material rights over cattle, the king builds the political framework of Nkore society.

As in the case of the Burundian *batongore*, the Nkore *okutoija* relationship appears in a society where the apparatus of the State is already developed. One still might be inclined to see this as a primordial form, without implying any evolutionary connotations such as the idea of an archaic social form of the Nkore state. Each of the Intralacustrine states is characterized by a distinct political and institutional evolution. In Nkore the relation between cattle and the royal office seems to involve more immediate notions of consubstantiality, redistribution of cattle by the king, and authority relations which result. The case of Bunyoro, where pastoralism is only a secondary economic activity, sheds a different light on the same process. Here, in a ritual known as "drinking the milk", political and ritual powers are delegated to provincial chiefs on whom the administration of the kingdom rests. The close albeit symbolic association between this ritual and pastoralism underlines the fact that the giving of milk also represents a delegation and a sharing of the power (*mahano*) vested in royalty (Beattie 1971).

There is a marked difference between these "elementary" forms, which materially and/or symbolically underline relations of authority and delegation of power, and secondary forms, which imply contractual cattle relations such as those observed in Burundi and, in particular, Rwanda, linked to the emergence of new political relationships and land rights that lend new significance to the delegation of rights in cattle. This is what Rwabukumba and Mudandagizi (1974:19) express in different terms:

> In the last third of the nineteenth century these personal relations multiplied. But this new stage was preceded by the emergence of a landed aristocracy closely linked to the royal court and welded together by fealty. Already a cleavage separated this minority from the masses, not only because it did not participate in production and attributed to itself a large proportion of the cattle but also because in the areas where it lived it assumed control of the land.

If cattle have retained here certain representations associating them with the supernatural power of royalty while at the same time accounting for the more personalized and contractual relations of authority and domination, they also simultaneously fulfill other functions pertaining to the evolution of the state in the direction of greater differentiation and complexity of political and administrative structure. But even in the form already described, cattle, which through hierarchical exchange make relations of authority more apparent, are not associated exclusively with royal office. Other kinds of goods and services, particularly apparent during the course of ritual activities, imply that royal office is associated with other social functions - and groups - in the same way it was associated with pastoral activities and "herders".

In Bunyoro the *mukama* maintained close relations with certain *bajwara kondo* (crown wearer) chiefs who possessed the sort of ritual power (*mahano*), ordinarily associated with royalty, retained on a hereditary basis by certain groups. "Banyoro express this by saying that crown wearers like the king himself possessed an exceptional degree of *mahano*" (Beattie 1971:20). In circumstances related to the political development of the sacred kingship, ritual specialists take on a similar importance due to their association with royal power. On a more general level multiple relations are concretely and symbolically established through ritual practices which involve the royal office and specific social groups. The king very often receives the first fruits of agricultural produce, as well as annually renewing the fertility of the soil through the performance of specified rites. During his enthronement, or simply on a periodic basis, he performs rituals related to hunting, to smithing, etc. In Burundi, he in turn receives (from certain groups) an important ritual produce, honey. From others he receives his royal garments or steel artifacts, and still others participate in the royal hunts (Mworoha 1977). Beattie (1971) has listed the specific function fulfilled by different clans in Bunyoro. Among these is the supplying of wives to the king. In theory, the *mukama* of Bunyoro remained the husband of all the women of the kingdom. In fact, he was given women enslaved through war or chose them personally without paying bridewealth (Beattie 1971). More often than not the suppliers of royal brides are specific groups who thus play a particular political role, if only because royal mothers and wives play an important ritual role. This justified the importance of clanship in the development of the political and administrative apparatus of the state.

Nonetheless, cattle remain of paramount importance in constituting relations of political domination due to their privileged association with the royal office. The idea of a king who is both owner and provider, who is legitimized by a mythical charter of the founding of the kingdom and whose power is validated through ritual, justifies return gifts in the form of goods and services. In a number of cases these gifts are of a symbolic nature: ritual objects, first fruits of the harvest, etc. In other cases we encounter more elaborate systems of prestation necessitated by the political and administrative apparatus, even including actual exploitation between rulers and ruled. In cases where contractual and personal livestock relations are more developed, the highly symbolic and political nature of cattle makes visible these relations of exploitation, even when they merely represent a way to obtain services (military, economic, political, etc.) or agricultural produce.

Herders and Farmers

It is necessary to distinguish between, on the one hand, social groups whose names connote the differentiation between pastoral and agricultural activities ("herders" and "farmers" sometimes considered as different ethnic groups) and, on the other hand, the physical distribution of herding and farming in the society. We can begin by asking ourselves a few questions regarding the actual place of agriculture in the societies for which we have so far considered only the political and symbolic role of cattle associated with royalty. A few words about the ecology of the Intralacustrine zone are first necessary.

Where there is a relatively favorable rainfall pattern averaging more than 1000 mm and in mountainous areas with rich soils, the diversity of ecological zones favors a diversity of productive activities, especially agriculture[10]. Agriculture is everywhere possible and in most cases provides higher returns than pastoralism, if we analyze simple, rather than simplistic, criteria such as the number of persons that can be sustained on a given unit of land by one or another of these activities. Under these conditions the social and economic reasons for pastoralism must be explained. Although the primacy of pastoralism remains constant, given the hierarchy of social functions, the importance of pastoral produce in the diet varies considerably from one Intralacustrine society to another. In Bunyoro, and even more so in Buganda, the contribution of pastoralism to material production remains very limited. In the kingdom of Nkore, pastoralism and agriculture are activities controlled by groups who perceive themselves as ethnically distinct and who live in separate geographical areas of the kingdom: some of these areas could be exploited by "agriculturalists" but are reserved for "pastoralists". In this instance, herding contributes a significant portion of total production. In Rwanda and Burundi, under ecological circumstances that are even more favorable for supporting high population densities, micro-level differentiation highlights the opposition between highlands and marshland/riverine areas; the consequences of this differentiation are similar to those in Nkore, which experienced the emergence of localized pastoral territories.

Within all these societies, agricultural production occupies an important place; it is often economically dominant. This is expressed in representations and practices associated with the sacred kingship. Even in a state such as Nkore where the hierarchy of offices is laid down as an ethnic division, the rituals related to the royal enthronement grant importance to agriculture. In Burundi the main ritual offices, and no doubt the kingship itself, were occupied by Hutu "agriculturalists". In Burundi as in Rwanda, Hutu kingdoms, led by a King responsible for fertility and reproduction, possessor of the drum and executor of the necessary rituals for the good of the kingdom, have played an essential role in the history of the region. Given the present state of archeological and historical knowledge, we cannot say much more but it is likely that agriculture (along with the pastoral features previously noted) has played a major role in the processes leading to the constitution of sacred kingship.

We have noted the privileged association between pastoralism and royal office and have shown that cattle underpinned a model of political domination that assumed different forms according to the nature of various Intralacustrine states. We will now proceed to examine from the same perspective the hierarchy of pastoral and agricultural functions, of "herders" and "farmers".

As observed in the case of Nkore, it is not because one has cattle that one is in a dominant political situation but rather the reverse; even in a society where the ethnicity provides the idiom of social distinction, it is possible for an individual to move from "agriculturalist" to "pastoralist". The difference between Bahima "pastoralists" and Bairu "agriculturalists" is defined in terms of access or non-access to cattle but it is not a quantitative difference, a simple unequal distribution of livestock as means of production:

> The value placed by Bahima on the control of cattle made it extremely difficult, if not in practice impossible, for Bairu through exchange of products of labour to submit realistic claims on cattle ownership (Doornbos 1978:41).

Particular values are attributed to cattle which correspond to their association with supernatural aspects of royalty. Because this difference is of a qualitative nature, it can be conceived as cultural: agricultural and pastoral products are neither homogeneous nor commensurable.

The value attributed to livestock gives rise to distinct and often exclusive behaviors and practices. This is true of dietary practices.

Among the Bahima the mixing of milk and agricultural products is held to be dangerous for herds, except if these products are transformed into a liquid form metaphorically associated with milk. In the same way there is a radical and exclusive opposition between Bahima cattle conceived of as a "good" *par excellence* and Bairu goats, which are considered to be "bad". Monopolized by "pastoralists" based on qualitative criteria, cattle further enhance the separation of "herders" and "farmers" through social exchange. Without cattle, Bairu men cannot marry Bahima women. Bahima men, on the other hand, can easily take Bairu women as concubines and the children of these unions constitute a specific social category named *abambari*. Social differentiation thus acquires a demographic and genetic dimension and, if we keep in mind that dietary habits within the two groups are radically different, it becomes easy to understand the distinction as ethnic and even racial,[11] although archaeological data suggests this differentiation is local.[12] Twenty years ago Posnansky (1966) was among the first to propose that these hierarchical structures could be the result of internal differentiation related to and accentuated by distinct matrimonial and dietary practices. His conclusion was based on archaeological research at sites associated with the legendary Bacwezi kings:

> The strongly marked physical differences between Bairu and Bahima (are) due to nutritional and social factors rather than necessarily inferring a folk movement from the Horn of Africa (*Ibid.*:6).

Similarly, Nkore values related to the possession of cattle have modeled the natural environment and determined a production process organized along a rather rigid division of labor. Bahima and Bairu occupied separate areas, the former controlling drier areas which could nevertheless have been used by agriculturalists. Indeed, given the political evolution of colonial rule, agriculturalists have tended since then to occupy these areas.

Although the situation is different in other kingdoms, the same mechanisms tend to generate and reproduce the distinction between "herders" and "farmers". In Bunyoro, where agricultural production accounts for the major part of total productive output, cattle nonetheless retain a similar value but the Bahima and Bairu distinction loses its rigid and exclusive hierarchical features; anyone owning cattle becomes a *muhuma*. In Burundi and especially in Rwanda cattle relations structure a complex hierarchical network which is impossible to understand if not examined in association with political, administrative, judicial and other relations. The opposition between Tutsi and Hutu is in fact between "herders" and "farmers" but does not imply the same ecological and technical division of labor. Conversely in Karagwa we find in the Bahima "herder" and Banyambo "farmer" opposition a situation comparable to the one in Nkore (Katoke 1975).

We have seen how cattle can be the basis of social stratification, in multiple forms, but always positing a difference of rank between "pastoralists" and "agriculturalists." The political role of cattle and its effect on the stratification of social groups is partially predicated on the notion that the political order is responsible for the distribution of cattle among social groups[13]: "to increase cows, god created the king." Concretely the system of political relations based on cattle enhances the reproduction of stratification:

> Nkore society was a class society in which the possession of cattle counted for much. The class system was an open one but it was a class system all the same in which the Bairu were of lower social standing than the Bahima. Nkore's governing class was drawn from the wealthy section of the Bahima and the criterion for belonging to that class was wealth in cattle (Karugire 1971:66).

Hierarchy and the Representation of Gender

It is not sufficient, however, simply to acknowledge the association of cattle with the function of royalty in order to understand how these societies operate. In fact, this association results from the property, attributed to cattle in Intralacustrine societies, of generating social relations. Moreover, this property is inscribed in the hierarchical vision of the distinction between the sexes. Cattle are attributed a similar property in neighboring non-stratified pastoral or agropastoral societies (for example, different Nilotic societies or among the Maasai) where they similarly support hierarchical relations of masculinity, agnation, etc. In the Intralacustrine societies, however, these relations take on a new dimension. Here, the images of Bull-Kings and of Cow-Kingdoms are not only metaphorical; they express and define relations of political authority and domination and legitimate political power related to the fecundity and prosperity which the kingship ensures. Moreover, the same images and principles of classification can be found in other domains of social life, such as familial and domestic organization. We will develop this line of enquiry by referring to Elam's excellent study on the Bahima of Nkore.

> The central idea which runs like a red thread though Hima culture and way of life is embodied in the separation from cattle of wives whose mission is to bear children (Elam 1973:XV).

In a social group where life depends on cattle, Hima women are excluded from all pastoral activities. A cluster of symbolic rites and representations justify this exclusion in terms of the association of female sexuality with danger for cattle. The first ritual which excludes a girl from her father's herds is held as soon as her first teeth appear. Exclusion is even stricter after menarche. During menstruation women must not drink cow's milk; they consume butter, meat, beer or vegetables obtained from Bairu agriculturalists (Elam 1973:58). Should they contravene these rules, their cows would become sterile. It is only after bridewealth is transferred that a woman and her children may drink milk from her father's herds. This is why pre-marital virginity is important; if it were not respected the girl's father's cattle would be in danger. Upon arrival at her husband's camp, the woman must be purified immediately after the first milk is drawn. The milk or butter of certain sacred cows will always remain forbidden. Finally, she will never be allowed to milk cows, to cross the *kraal* in the presence of the herd, or to protect the herd by sounding the alarm or killing a menacing dog or hyena (Lukyn-Williams 1938).

Although the Bahima have a tendency to pose this issue in terms of the competition between cows and their calves, on the one hand, and between women and their children, on the other, this is not the basis for these representations and practices. In fact it can be argued that women play the role attributed to cattle in neighbouring egalitarian pastoral societies, of ensuring the production and reproduction of social relations. In the case of affinal relations this role is readily visible. It is not the bridewealth payment (which is small) that generates an alliance but rather the woman herself who establishes it between the two domestic groups involved.[14]

> In her role as a spouse, particularly as a child-bearer the Hima woman links her husband's family with that of her father... In her role as a lover she enables her husband to form and strengthen links with men in many other families (Elam 1973:158).

The role of linkage is clearly visible in the manipulation of the sexuality of married women in order to generate or reinforce social relations. The so-called sexual freedom enjoyed by the Bahima women, which has been noted by some authors (Lukyn-Williams 1938), does not take into account the rights of control exercised by men over both women and their sexuality[15]. Thus, within her husband's family, a wife cannot refuse sexual intercourse with her husband's father, his brothers or even with sons from another wife. This situation reinforces patriarchal authority and enables the head of the household, who is the sole owner of the herd, to better control his sons' labor. Within the residential group, sexual relations with the wives of co-residents are desirable and serve to enhance unity and cooperation. In the same way that social solidarity in neighboring groups was based upon the exchange of cattle and upon the sharing of common rights in them (Bonte 1978a), among the Bahima (although to a less exclusive degree) the sharing of reciprocal rights to the married women of a domestic and residential group serves the same purpose. "The solidarity of men ... is supported by their reciprocal rights over the other's wives" (Elam 1973:185).

In the last instance the status of women, their exclusion from cattle, and the rights exercised over them by men exist because of their relation to cattle and because of the symbolic interpretation of pastoral categories. They cannot milk cows and the fact that a man draws milk for a woman legitimates the sexual demands he can make on her. The container given to a woman for milking, which a man holds between his thighs, is similar to the female's vagina and milk to semen. This sexual symbolism, opposing the jar of milk to the spear, the latter associated with the phallus, is central and present in representations of the sacred kingship. The category of sexuality is thus amenable to a paradigmatic treatment generating models of stratification at different levels of social organization. Through the juxtaposition of gender distinctions and cattle and livestock categories, as in the symbolic opposition King-as-Bull versus Kingdom-as-Cow, the categories of cattle and gender contribute to the organization of the field of social practices, in the domestic as well as the political sphere.

The Nkore domestic unit is patrilineal and even strongly patriarchal; the head of the household has exclusive rights over livestock and absolute authority over the members of his family. Matricentric organization, which in neighboring egalitarian pastoral societies duplicates the rule of patrilineal descent and grants women an intermediary role in the transmission of livestock, is non-existent here. The *aka* is a residential unit that includes the married sons of the head of the family and their children. The household head can delegate certain rights to his sons (just as the king delegates to his subjects) but he can also take them back and has the right to disinherit his sons, inheritance normally being shared among them. Sons do not have the possibility of leaving their father before he dies; the exclusion of women from pastoral labor means that all available male labor must be used. Control over and use of female sexuality reinforce the unity of domestic and residential groups.

The exclusion of women from pastoral activities contributes to the emergence of a new structure of authority. There is a shared element in the power exercised by both the king and the head of a household, both of whom are called *mukama* in Nyoro. All the cattle in the kingdom are "owned" by the king who in order to ensure their prosperity, "delegates" this right to household heads.[16] Beattie (1957) notes that in Nyoro the title of the household head, *Mukama*, signifies "master" of goods and people; in this context inheritance appears more as a transfer of authority than a transfer of property. In Nyoro, where rights in land are more important than those in livestock, the son who is chosen to exercise those rights replaces his father, gaining the same material and symbolic prerogatives. For this it is necessary that cattle circulation be hierarchical, even if other modes of exchange continue to exist and even if within certain limits cows are replaced by women in order to generate collective solidarities.

Conclusion

It would thus appear that social, political, and sexual systems are hierarchically structured according to principles identical to those we have seen at work within the political and symbolic complex of the sacred kingship, as well as within the family unit. These principles are established above all by reference to the possession or non-possession of cattle. The exclusion of women from any contact with cattle is best conceived in these global terms among the Bahima of Nkore. Not only are Bahima women excluded from and considered dangerous to cattle, as are Bairu agriculturalists (and Bairu goats), but during their menstrual periods they are directly identified with "agriculturalists", being forbidden to drink milk and being required to consume only agricultural products.

Much more would have to be said in order to understand the effects of this ordering of sexual categories on the organization of the sacred kingship[17] I cannot develop this aspect of the analysis further, my aim being only to illustrate the place occupied by cattle within the political model of the Intralacustrine royal kingship. The royal function is essentially of a ritual nature, royal rituals being seen as indispensable to a social and natural order capable of establishing a hierarchy on a social and political plane. The hierarchical transmission of cattle, on which the establishment of social (men and women, "herders" and "farmers") and political (rulers and ruled) hierarchies is based, follows the principles constitutive of the sacred kingship. But cattle and pastoral activity - in contrast to agriculture, forging, hunting, etc. - the pursuit of which depends as well on the exercise of royal ritual, have particular properties which resemble those found among their pastoral or agropastoral neighbors. It is no longer the generalized exchange of cattle which provides the course for social life but the relations between cattle and royalty. In that sense, I have tried to show that one can identify a logically prior model of political subordination and social stratification in Intralacustrine societies, founded on the dedication to political ends of the supernatural power over cattle attributed to royalty, a model developed within systems of sacred kingship and elaborated in the more complex states found in that region of Africa.

Our goal was to demonstrate the basis on which these complex societies have emerged, and to develop the association between the concept of sacred kingship and livestock. This association generates multiple forms of stratification. Some are directly political and based on hierarchical circulation of livestock, others are of a social nature, implying both symbolic and material "possession" and distribution of livestock between dominant and dominated social groups: "herders" and "farmers", men and women. These developments occurred because of the parallel evolution of domestic organization and gender relations, which added a fundamental dimension to the model of subordination and stratification which emerged with sacred kingship.

In states such as Rwanda it is sometimes difficult to recognize those processes which we have identified in the Nkore literature. However, it is likely that they have occurred in an analogous way even if they have resulted in different institutional and political systems, for the centrality of livestock remains. We will consider the famous bovine-armies of Rwanda as one example of this continuity (Kagame 1961:4). In Rwanda every man is part of a *ingabo* army and depends on the king through the intermediary of an army chief. At the beginning of each new reign an army was formed by the children of client Tutsi who had not yet been incorporated into a standing army. Around this nucleus of warriors devoted to the king (*intore*) groups were incorporated from standing armies. Each standing army was composed of warriors and herders responsible for the herding of cattle belonging to the chief, cattle belonging to pastoralists and their clients, and cattle entrusted to them by the king. Through this military and administrative system, which probably emerged late in history, not only men but also cattle were placed in a direct relation to the king. "All the cattle owned by the Rwandan were assigned to a specific army" (d'Hertefelt 1962:66). Cattle, as we can see again in this example, were used throughout the history of these Intralacustrine kingdoms as a means not only to think about but also through which to build political systems.

Notes

1. Rwandan dynastic poem (Kagame 1947:47). This paper was translated by Pierre Bigras, a graduate student in the Department of Anthropology, McGill University.

2. Although the question had been previously posed, it was not given much attention prior to the above quoted works. Trouwborst mentions that one of the goals of Belgium ethnographer, G. Smets, during his 1935 fieldwork in Burundi was to verify the hypotheses of feudal organization within these societies (Bujumbara conference 1981:283-94).

3. Conceptually this is achieved by generating an inegalitarian and hierarchical representations of colonized peoples, which conform to those in the colonizers' own society. Concretely it is achieved by using pre-existing social relations assigned new and different meanings to generate local hierarchies that enable the colonizer to achieve control over the peasantry. In reality, this often results from changes in rules concerning land tenure.

4. The best example of this is the *ubwiru* code of Rwanda, which was described and analyzed by Coupez and d'Hertefelt (1964). The code includes some 18 yira which describe in detail the different ritual activities related to the Royal Office.

5. The idea that suicide - or even ritual killing - of the king is necessary and warranted when he is weakened by age or disease, or even when his son is old enough to replace him, occurs in most of these societies. Whether or not it is actually practiced matters little since its existence as a generalized representation can be assimilated to a kind of "royal sacrifice"; other representations attest more directly to the king's being "sacrificed" in order to save the kingdom (Bonte and Becquemont, forthcoming).

6. When its benevolent powers are not channeled through ritual, the drum itself, symbol of the permanency of the royal office and endowed with the same power, can also be a source of potential danger; or, again, the rituals can be aimed at capturing the drum's dangerous and polluting effects. In Rwanda, the *abiiru* guardians of the ritual code could fabricate an impure ritual drum by making the "heart" of the instrument from the lungs of a physically imperfect bull. This impure drum is left at the frontier to be captured by enemies to whom it would bring bad luck. "Like ritual purity, impurity constitutes a magical force which can be activated to obtain a desired result" (Loupez et d'Hertefelt 1964:355).

7. We have already noted that the king can consume food only in a liquid form (*i.e.* sorghum, banana or honey beers) that is assimilated to milk, considered the food *par excellence*. However, the king cannot totally consume the contents of a container of milk, or any other drink that he is offered, without becoming responsible for a shortage of livestock.

8. The territory is divided into equal parts by the Nyabarongo river, the pattern of royal residence alternating between those two halves of the kingdom.

9. We have elsewhere identified in apparently egalitarian societies - which do not have the institution of sacred kingship - the fetishized effects of cattle on social relations at the community level that are constituted on a ritual and

territorial basis (Bonte, 1975, 1978, 1979, 1984). Livestock, by circulating between men on various occasions - in the form of bridewealth transfers, gifts and loans under specific or non-specific circumstances, *etc.* - and by circulating between men and the divine during ritual sacrifice, is endowed with the faculty of generating social relations; with its dietary and economic uses being assumed, this social faculty remains its central value.

10. Chrétien (1983) gives a bibliographic and thematic exposé on the history of the African Intralacustrine region which includes geographical data, a review of the history of human occupation and information on the origin of cultigens and the evolution of land tenure.

11. For example in the colonial literature, references speak of the great "hamitic" Tutsi and of the "negroid" Hutu.

12. This theory enables us to account for a whole series of other traits, such as the existence of a common language, of a frequently unified clan system, *etc.*, left unexplained by proponents of an ethnic distinction.

13. "At the bottom of this lay the consideration that the possession and retention of cattle ... would have been impossible without some form of government" (Karugire 1971:206).

14. "Hima bridewealth is sometimes lower than that of the Samburu. It is generally lower than that of the Gogo not to mention the Turkana and the Nuer. So also is the size of the units assembling and receiving the Hima bridewealth. Although marriage is viewed during the ceremonies as an alliance between territorial clans the actual bond is forged mainly between the bride and the groom's households in each of which there is also a senior man. This is due to the absence among the Hima of lineage groups bigger than the household of a single cattle-owner so that such a household is the effective unit in the context of establishing affinity" (Elam 1973:143).

15. "Whereas men have rights to impose lovers on their wives, to seek for themselves the love of a large number of married women other than their wives, and to forbid their wives to associate with any particular individual, the limited sexual freedom of women is essentially a by-product of men's rights over them" (Elam, 1973:176).

16. Household heads in Nyoro are the exclusive owners of the family herd. This contrasts with neighbouring egalitarian pastoral societies in which cattle constantly circulate. In these latter societies usufruct rights over cattle are allocated to women at the time of marriage; their sons in turn will inherit rights to this part of the herd at the time of their own marriage. In certain cases, such as the Dassanetch, an old man whose sons are married no longer has rights over cattle (Almagor 1978).

17. Other effects underline in a complementary way the fundamental ambiguity of women's roles: *e.g.* the ritual and political role of the Queen-Mother and of the group supplying royal brides.

PART THREE

EXCHANGE, ECOLOGY AND THE "COMMON ECONOMY"

4

Political Ecology in the Upper Nile:
The Twentieth Century Expansion of
the Pastoral "Common Economy"

Douglas H. Johnson

The environment of the clay plains of the Upper Nile region in the Sudan is peculiarly harsh, imposing considerable restraints on its inhabitants, who almost all survive through mixed cultivation and herding. The combination of erratic flooding, "unreliable rainfall and uncompromising soil" has forced the development of a mainly pastoral economy, which has been well established throughout the region for at least a millennium (Mefit-Babtie Srl. 1983:34). The standard ethnographies and ecological studies of the region have all emphasized the interdependence of cultivation and animal husbandry within local economies, and the variations in local environments which produce different balances of agro-pastoral activity (Evans-Pritchard 1940; JIT 1954; Mefit-Babtie Srl. 1983; Howell, Lock and Cobb 1988). What emerges even more clearly from a historical study of the region is that the economies of the various ethnic and political groups contained within it are linked together and form a wider regional system which enables each to survive the limitations of its specific area. They have been linked through a variety of networks of exchange; some based on kinship obligations, some on direct trade. Through these networks the peoples of the region have at times been able to gain regular access to the resources of areas at some distance from themselves, crossing political and ethnic boundaries to do so. Survival of peoples as well as individuals depends on maintaining such access in a number of ways. It is therefore not possible to discuss the local economies of the Nuer without reference to the local economies of the Dinka, nor is it possible to understand the survival of the Dinka without reference to their economic relations with the Nuer (Johnson 1986a, 1986b, 1988a, 1988b).

The scholarly image and understanding of the Nilotic pastoralists of the Sudan is based primarily on Evans-Pritchard's study of the Nuer, which was produced from fieldwork undertaken between 1930-1936. His work has become the point of reference for all comparative studies of pastoralists within the region - and rightly so. It is important, therefore, to test some of his conclusions through an analysis of historical data, comparing the time in which he worked with both earlier and later periods in this century.

Evans-Pritchard emphasized the precariousness of agriculture among the Nuer, pointing out that each year he visited them there was a narrow margin between sufficiency and famine. The ecology required a mixed economy of horticulture, fishing and pastoralism, but with the greatest emphasis placed on pastoralism. Prior to the introduction of rinderpest in the nineteenth century, he proposed, pastoralism had been a more viable activity, and the Nuer were in the habit of making good their stock losses through raiding the Dinka. Seasonal scarcity and recurrent famines produced a high interdependence between members of the same village and cattle camp, and the constant threat of scarcity encouraged a "common economy" of "mutual assistance and common consumption of food" within these groups. While both the nature of pastoralism itself and the erratic distribution of water in the region required establishing economic and political relations beyond the village, the low technology of the Nuer, their meager food supply and scanty trade restricted social relations: "social ties are narrowed, as it were, and the people of village and camp are drawn closer together, in a moral sense, for they are in consequence highly interdependent and their activities tend to be joint undertakings" (Evans-Pritchard 1940:81-93).

Evans-Pritchard's identification of a common economy based on the mutual sharing of food supplies is extremely important, not just for understanding relations between Nuer communities, but for understanding the relations which exist between all the Nilotic communities (Shilluk, Dinka, Nuer and Anuak) living in the uncertain environment of the Upper Nile. Yet his assertion that it is precisely this mutual assistance which narrows social ties not only limits the operation of such a common economy specifically to the Nuer, but reinforces his presentation of the Nuer as isolated from their neighbors through a combination of ecology and political hostility. It is our contention here that Evans-Pritchard's conclusions were influenced by his observation of a particular configuration of flooding and epidemics, whose destructive effects were exacerbated by the nature of colonial intervention at the time, affecting especially patterns of settlement and land use. We will compare this period (1929-1936) with other periods of extreme flooding, one immediately prior to colonial subjugation (1916-1918) and one following the end of colonial rule (1961 and after). By analyzing the response of the Gaawar and Lou Nuer, their Ngok, Ghol and Nyareweng Dinka neighbors, and the Luac, Thoi and Rut Dinka who live interspersed among them, we will show how some of the social interdependence which food scarcity promoted within Nuer communities can also be seen to operate at a wider level. In addition to that we will suggest that the historical pattern of flooding in the region has been a significant factor in the expansion of the Nilotic common economy throughout the twentieth century.[1]

Topography and Hydrology:
Patterns in Flooding, Herding and Planting[2]

The Upper Nile plains are intersected by two main tributaries of the White Nile: the Bahr al-Jabal, which is fed by the East African lakes; and the Sobat, which draws its water from the Ethiopian plateau and the Pibor river system. Because of this there are a number of independent causes of flooding. Ethiopian rains, East African rains, and local rains all produce differences in the Bahr al-Jabal and Sobat flood patterns. Thus there are local variations in flooding and susceptibility to economic disruption and famine. There is no strict ethnic or political equation with geography as the Nuer and Dinka, especially, each occupy a number of areas which vary in vulnerability to floods and have different productive capacities. This is the ecological basis for wider regional ties.[3]

The region's weather alternates between a wet season (April-November) when the rivers rise, the rains fall, and the land is flooded, and a dry season (December-April) when the rivers drop, the rains cease and the floods recede. Most of the soils are clay, virtually impervious to water at the height of the rains, but there are some outcrops of sandier soil, slightly elevated above the plains, where woodland can be found, permanent villages built and cultivation undertaken. The combination of soil types and slight elevation produce four main vegetation areas: permanent swamp (mostly along the Bahr al-Jabal and Bahr al-Zaraf), river-flooded grasslands (the dry season pastures, or *toic*, along the rivers), rain-flooded grasslands, and relatively flood free land which supports woodlands, grasslands or cultivation (see Figures 4.1a & 4.1b).

92

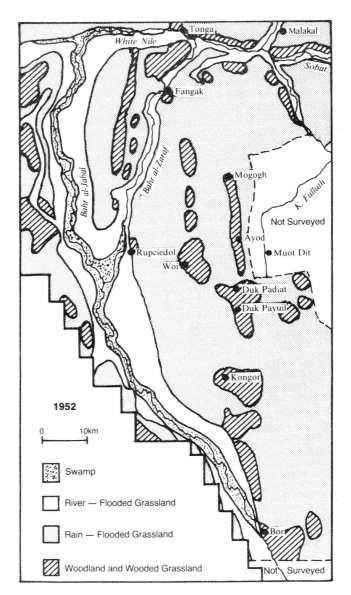

FIGURE 4.1a Main Vegetation Areas in the Upper Nile, 1952
(based on Mefit-Babtie 1983).

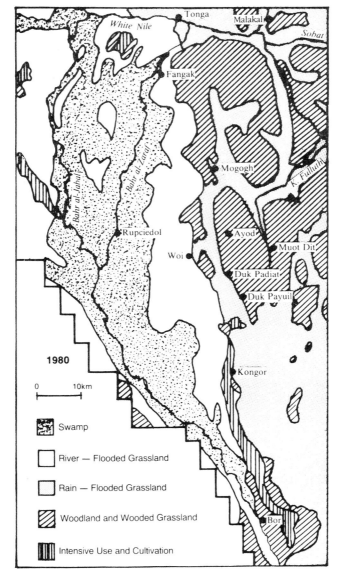

FIGURE 4.1b Main Vegetation Areas in the Upper Nile, 1980
(based on Mefit-Babtie (1983)

The transhumant life of the Nilotic pastoralists is so well known that it need only be summarized here. Two crops of sorghum (three among some Nuer) are sown during the rains: once at the beginning in fields close to the permanent villages along the elevated ridges, and once at the end as the water recedes, exposing lower-lying moist soil. During the dry season cattle are moved away from the villages in stages, following the water as it dries up and exposes new pastures, until they come to rest on the *toic* of the riverine marshes. With the onset of the rains there is a more rapid retreat to the ridges as the low-lying countryside quickly fills with water. The transhumant activities in both seasons are therefore crucially influenced by the location and extent of water.

The extent of wet season flooding and the distribution of dry season water depend on three factors. (1) The Bahr al-Jabal is the source of most of the river-flooded areas; the level of river-flooding in any year depends more on the inflow from the East African lakes than on local rainfall, but it is also affected by the course of local channels through the swamp. In the past, shifts in blockages within the swamp have altered the patterns of local flooding (*i.e.* blockages along the lower Bahr al-Jabal have perhaps re-channelled water through the Bahr al Zaraf) (Johnson 1988a). (2) The banks of the Sobat are both steep and high enough to prevent much direct overflow from the river to the surrounding plains, but when in flood the Sobat does back up into the major *khors* (seasonal watercourses), which also collect water from local precipitation. A high Sobat can keep the *khors* filled long into the dry season; thus providing a source of inland water. (3) The area affected by river-flood is relatively small and is most important for the grazing and water it offers in the late dry season. Most of the land surface of the Upper Nile plains is subject to rain-flooding, when rain seeps only very slowly through the heavy clay soil, forming large pools of standing water on top. In most years these dry up rapidly during the dry season. In some years heavy rains can combine with an overspill from the Pibor, causing a "creeping flow", a slowly flowing flood up to two feet or more in depth, moving from south to north along the eastern plains adding to the standing water already created by the local rains.

It is the timing and level of the different types of floods which influence agricultural and pastoral schedules and the selection of areas to be exploited in any given year. Heavy late rains and high "creeping flow" can destroy the second crop which is planted on lower land, as well as keep early pastures under water long after grazing around the villages has been exhausted. A high minimum flow of the Bahr al-Jabal (i.e. a high level when the river is at its lowest point during the depth of the dry season) can mean that riverine pastures remain under water and inaccessible throughout most of the dry season. For this reason those living closest to the river prefer drought to flood years, as in the former they still have access to (reduced) pasture and water. The lack of inland water becomes a particular problem the further east one goes from the Bahr al-Jabal. It is for this reason that the inland *khors* become extremely important in years of sustained high Sobat levels, allowing groups to congregate around the pools in the *khors* rather than go to the rivers. In some years high rivers and heavy rains combine to produce widespread devastation and dislocation, but only in exceptional circumstances have there been long term alterations to flooding patterns and water availability.

The pattern of flooding limits the reliability of cultivation areas. The most stable cultivations are found along those parts of the Sobat and White Nile where flooding is most restricted, due to a combination of deep banks and high ridges. These areas include the Shilluk and the northern Dinka along the White Nile; the land between the mouths of the Khors Atar and Fulluth where the Rueng, Thoi and Luac Dinka are now settled; both banks of the lower Sobat around Abwong, occupied mainly by the Ngok Dinka; and the area immediately around and to the north of present-day Nasir, occupied by the Gaajok section of the Eastern Jikany Nuer. In the far north-east corner of the Upper Nile plains, separated from the White Nile by a broad stretch of waterless country, the Meban very frequently produce abundant grain, which is just as frequently exported out of their country by Arab, Dinka and Nuer neighbors in such quantities as to cause repeated hardship.

South of the Sobat and White Nile the pockets of cultivable land become smaller, more scattered, and more subject to flooding. The Duk ridge - a series of sandy knolls now occupied by the Gaawar Nuer from Mogogh to south of Ayod, the Ghol Dinka at Duk Padiat and the Nyareweng Dinka at Duk Payuil - was frequently productive throughout the first half of the century, as were the Bar Gaawar settlements around Woi. By far the most productive land south of the Duk ridge was in the area of Kongor among the Twic-Lith, the largest division of the Twic Dinka. The area of Kongor is dark soil, but it lies on a depression, subject to much flooding. The area of permanent habitations and cultivation is in fact "an island won from the marsh and protected by banks round all the villages" offering some security from the seasonal floods (R.T. Johnston 1934). These low mud embankments are a distinctive feature of Twic Dinka villages, not found to the same extent elsewhere in the region.

Areas of relatively stable productivity are situated next to areas of chronic shortages. The southern Shilluk, living on over-cultivated and narrow ridges around Tonga, are frequently subject to food shortages and sometimes have to rely on the Lak Nuer, who are not constant over-producers and have other demands upon them from the Gaawar and the Thiang. The Lou Nuer are subject to rain flooding but also to extremes of aridity throughout most of their territory during the dry season, which can force them to rely on grain from their Eastern Jikany, Gaawar and Dinka neighbors. The Twic-Lith of Kongor have frequently been productive, but to the south the smaller Twic-Fakerr and Twic-Ajuong sections and all of the Bor Dinka live in areas chronically vulnerable to rain and river flooding which historically have had low productivity. "Sufficiency", then, is relative. An area need not produce an absolute surplus, enough for its own needs with some left over, to be called on by others. Demands will be made when one area produces more grain than another, whether the amount is enough to feed the local population or not. By the middle of this century the Upper Nile plains as a whole probably produced enough grain for its own needs (JIT 1954 I:357). It was the erratic distribution of grain which caused local famines. We will see below just how important access to the main growing areas of the region has been, not only for those habitually short of grain, but for those who can normally provide for themselves.

Access to grazing and water has been no less problematic. Good grazing is dependent as much on sufficient drinking water as on abundant nutritious grass. Some areas of reasonable cultivable land have only limited pastures, such as the northern end of the Zaraf island (Lak Nuer), the area between the Khors Atar and Fulluth, or around Abwong (Dinka). Peoples living in these areas must seek access to the more extensive river-flooded pastures along the east banks of the Bahr al-Jabal and the Bahr al-Zaraf. The east bank of the upper Zaraf is particularly sought after, especially by peoples living along the Duk ridge and lower Zaraf valley. The Dinka living south of the Duk ridge go mainly to the Bahr al-Jabal.

Inland grazing along the eastern plains presents other problems because of the uneven distribution of water. The Lou Nuer country

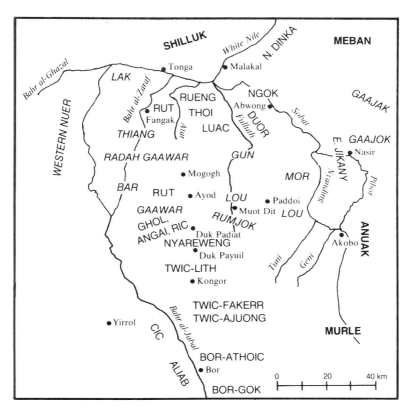

FIGURE 4.2 Settlement in the Upper Nile Region of the Sudan

between the Khor Fulluth and the Pibor river contains some of the best grazing land in the region, especially around Paddoi, Muot Dit, the upper Fulluth, and along Khor Geni where water can usually be found. The eastern plains are not affected by the height of the Jabal floods, where a sustained high river can keep riverine pastures under water even during the dry season. A high Sobat, on the other hand, can keep the *khors* backed up, making it unnecessary for people to move their herds to the river. There are, however, large tracts of good grasslands which usually have insufficient water in the dry season and which cannot be used. These are found especially to the east of the Ghol, Nyareweng, Twic and Bor Dinka. They can be used in exceptionally wet years, and were so used in parts of each of the three periods under study here. However, a high Bahr al-Jabal, which makes the riverine pastures inaccessible, will not necessarily coincide with high rainfall which might make these eastern lands usable.

In any year the variations and combinations of river and rainfall levels produce a changing and unstable mosaic of accessible pastures, available water and safe cultivations. Conditions can change to such an extent that successive years present different patterns of lands available for use. The economic viability of local communities is determined not so much by occupation and possession of land and water resources, as by regular access to alternate resources. By looking at the three periods of most extreme variations in flooding this century we will be able to see just what strategies pastoralists employed to maintain access to these alternatives.

1929-1936: Natural Catastrophes and Political Subjugation[4]

The political independence of the Nuer came to an end in the 1920s, following a series of military campaigns intended to bring them under closer administrative control. These campaigns were concluded in 1929 by a new policy of tribal segregation, whereby security was to be improved through the separation of the Nuer from the Dinka in the central Upper Nile area (Johnson 1979, 1980, 1982). Evans-Pritchard first visited the Nuer when these policies were being implemented, and he last visited them only shortly before the policies were reversed. His field observations, therefore, reflected the special circumstances of this early period of subjugation.

The settlement patterns and seasonal movements of the Gaawar and Lou were severely restricted by government actions throughout 1929-1936. Large numbers of Dinka formerly settled among the Gaawar or along the Khor Fulluth near the Lou were forcibly moved south to become part of new political amalgamations within the Ghol and Nyareweng Dinka. A "No-Man's Land" was fixed with the Gaawar and Lou on one side and the Ghol and Nyareweng on the other. Resettlement, repatriation and restrictions on movement broke, for the time being, ties between Nuer and Dinka groups which had been in the making for some three-quarters of a century (Johnson 1982:198-201). This coincided with and contributed to a massive regional rinderpest epidemic and outbreaks of other cattle diseases. Further dislocation and hardship was caused by a series of floods and a severe locust plague. The strain placed on the networks of the common economy in the region simultaneously by the government and the environment, and the effect this had on Evans-Pritchard's observations, will be described in detail in this section.

At the beginning of the 1928-1929 dry season (November-April) both the Gaawar and Lou were ordered to evacuate their southernmost territory and concentrate in areas well away from the border of the new No-Man's Land. The Mor Lou were concentrated on the Sobat, the Gun Lou inland around Muot Dit, and the Bar Gaawar on the northern end of the Duk ridge and in the already crowded and precariously settled woodland of Rupciedol. Armed government patrols traversed most parts of Nuer country throughout 1929 enforcing this order. A small band of Angai Dinka living among the Gaawar had already been relocated to Duk Payuil, and in the 1929-1930 dry season the Luac Dinka living along the Kohr Fulluth were expelled from their homes and sent south.

The Bahr al-Jabal was low that year, the rains unexceptional if uneven, and crops among the Lou and the Dinka of northern Bor District (who were soon to receive an influx of other Dinka) were sufficient. But by the end of 1929, rinderpest broke out among the Gaawar and the Dinka of the Duk Padiat/Duk Payuil area. It spread throughout the Upper Nile Province until July 1931, reducing herds by up to fifty percent in some districts. The Dinka of Bor District (from Duk Padiat to Bor) lost nearly 25,000 head of cattle out of an estimated total cattle population of 40-67,000. The Nuer, forcibly concentrated as they were by government order, were not able to segregate and disperse their herds as they usually did when an epidemic struck. In fact the Gaawar, among whom the disease first appeared, were reported to be segregating their herds only towards the end of the epidemic. Some Dinka were forced by government orders to move into, rather than away from, the heart of the epidemic. The Luac Dinka arrived at one of the hardest hit areas in time to lose most of their cattle.

There was a resurgence of rinderpest at Duk Padiat in mid-1932 from infected Gaawar cattle, extracted by the government and paid to the

Dinka in compensation for earlier Gaawar raids. Further outbreaks occurred in 1934 among the Bor, Twic, Nyareweng and Ghol Dinka, and the Gaajok Nuer on the mouth of the Nyanding. In 1935-1936 sections of the Bor, Nyareweng, Twic-Fakerr, southern Shilluk, western Nuer and Aliab Dinka were hit, and particularly heavy losses occurred among the Eastern Jikany. There were fewer losses over-all than in 1929-1931, and the Gaawar and Lou, who suffered greatly in the earlier epidemic, were unaffected. But the net effect of the outbreaks of 1929-31, 1932, 1934 and 1935-1936 was that nearly every herd in the region was struck at one time or another by rinderpest during this eight year period.

Other cattle diseases also spread at this time. Contagious Bovine Pleuropneumonia (CBPP) increased partly because of the wetter conditions caused by widespread flooding during 1932-1934. Trypanosomiasis also spread as game, fleeing the floods, came into closer contact with cattle (R.T. Johnston 1934). Herds in Bor District suffered from CBPP throughout 1932, and it developed in the rest of the province in 1933, following the 1932 flood. The southern Lou in particular seemed to become inflected in 1933 and 1935 after outbreaks among the Gaawar and in Bor District. Incoming Luac Dinka cattle brought it to Duk Padiat in 1932 and, as with rinderpest, infected Gaawar compensation cattle sent to the Dinka brought more CBPP in 1931. The Ghol and Nyareweng Dinka thus experienced an influx of diseased cattle in 1930-1932 which they otherwise would have been spared.

Crop production was uneven throughout 1930-1932 and became particularly parlous with the onset of the 1932-1934 floods. The rains of 1930 were exceptionally light and the harvest correspondingly poor, with the Ghol, Nyareweng and Bor Dinka all facing famine. Only the Twic-Lith around Kongor reported average crops. The land on which the Luac and Duor Dinka had formerly settled was good cultivable land. On their departure the Ngok Dinka immediately occupied it, but the total area under cultivation along the Khor Fulluth dropped with the loss of Luac labor. This reduced the grain reserve on which the Lou and Gaawar normally drew in times of shortage. Locusts appeared in Nasir and Kongor just as the 1931 crop was being sown. They spread south and southwest and infested the entire province for the rest of the year. Bor District and Yirrol, across the river (on whom the Bor frequently relied for grain), were hardest hit.

The difficulties of 1931 were further aggravated by the variability of river and rain. Early 1931 continued exceptionally dry and both the southern Shilluk and their Lak Nuer neighbors across the river suffered severe reductions in already limited pastures. The rains were delayed until the first week of July and then merged with an exceptionally high

Bahr al-Jabal flood at the end of the year, damaging many crops throughout Bor District. The Bor and Ghol Dinka were saved from starvation in 1931 only by the rinderpest epidemic which, while depleting their herds, gave them a temporary excess of meat from dead animals.

There was enough grain harvested in 1931 in Bor District, especially around Kongor, to feed large numbers of people. The Twic-Lith supplied grain to some Nuer, the Ghol and the Bor-Gok as late as July. After that the Bor-Gok turned to the Aliab Dinka of Yirrol. But the Ngok Dinka and the Jikany Nuer on the Sobat, and the Mor Lou east of Paddoi all lost substantial amounts of early maize and the first sorghum crop to locusts. The southern Shilluk, already in a precarious state at the beginning of the year, were afflicted by their worst famine in living memory. They sold off large numbers of cattle to buy grain. The Nuer, who had lost cattle to rinderpest, came to Malakal to buy them.

The high floods which occurred in 1932-1934, reaching their peak in the 1933-1934 wet season, resulted from a combination of high rivers and heavy late rains. The destructiveness of their impact varied. In late 1932 crops around Akobo on the Pibor were flooded out; only a restricted area around the two Duks in Bor District remained dry; and the triangle between Khor Atar, the Zaraf mouth and Fangak was submerged. Late rains and almost unprecedented floods along the Zaraf the next year destroyed the crops of the Lak, Thiang and southern Shilluk and forced the Gaawar out of most of their settlements. Despite a lower Bahr al-Jabal at the end of 1934 the Gaawar and Thiang again suffered high floods, and even the Sobat flooded cultivation north of Nasir. Throughout these repeated assaults it was the newly arrived immigrants who suffered the most: the Gaawar who had been evicted from their homes along the duk ridge, and the Luac Dinka settled in the now flooded regions outside Duks Padiat and Payuil.

Late rains and sustained high floods in 1932-1934 meant that not only were crops destroyed but harvests were delayed. The backing up of the *khors* throughout the region compensated for this to some extent by opening up some normally arid lands for both cultivation and grazing, as well as bringing fish further inland. For a while this altered, and in some cases reversed, the patterns of exchanges between communities within the region.

Grain was harvested late in January 1932 in many parts of the region because late receding floods in 1932 had delayed the planting of the second crop. This offered some relief in a normally hungry time. The Bor Dinka began to run out of grain by April but were supplied from the Duk ridge. The riverine pastures of the Bahr al-Jabal continued to be submerged by the high river, but the extreme wetness of the year meant that the Bor-Gok and Bor-Athoic were able to move to normally dry lands far to the east of Bor where they not only grazed their animals but cultivated some crops. Late rains further north caused considerable hunger among the Lou and Zaraf Nuer when planting was delayed. The first harvest of the Ghol Dinka, on the other hand, was plentiful and neighboring Nuer were able to get some grain from Duk Padiat. At the end of 1933 heavy rains and almost unprecedented high floods washed away the crops of the Gaawar, Lak, Thiang and southern Shilluk. This flood is remembered as *Nyoc Thoini*, the flood of the heglig nuts, because the Zaraf Nuer were reduced to eating heglig fruit when their crops were destroyed. But even in the flood area there were variable effects. One patch of the northern Lak remained fairly dry. Around Fangak the crops were spared by the flood, while the cattle starved when their pastures were covered by water.

The grain-import figures for 1933-1934 indicate that these two years were particularly hungry ones for the Zaraf Nuer and southern Shilluk, while local grain supplies generally improved for the Dinka of Bor District. At the end of 1933 the northern Dinka, Lou and Eastern Jikany all had good harvests, while the Ngok were suffering from hunger and had to go to the Lou and Jikany for food, the reverse of previous patterns. Most of the grain harvested on the Sobat seems to have been consumed locally in 1933, and more grain had to be imported by the government, again the reverse of recent trends where there had been an annual export of grain in 1930-1932 and again 1934-1935 (SDIT 1954:Table 49). The ample supplies of the northern Dinka brought many Nuer, and even Meban, to the White Nile well into the 1934 dry season, exchanging tobacco for grain.

The beginning of 1934 seemed to bode better as the Bahr al-Jabal began to drop to safer levels, but the rains failed in August, when they should have been at their height, and a province-wide grain shortage that month affected even normally productive areas like Abwong and Nasir. The overall cultivation area among peoples such as the Gaawar was reduced by famine-induced weakness and lack of seedgrain. Even grazing suffered, for hunger inhibited the people's movements, and in the area between Fangak and the White Nile cattle grazed in a much restricted area. Then, at the end of the year there was a resumption of heavy flooding along the Bahr al-Zaraf (despite a continued drop in the Jabal), and the Thiang and Gaawar again lost crops.

The floods of 1932-1934 directly affected government plans to separate the Nuer and Dinka. The Dinka among the Gaawar - the Rut and Thoi communities and individual Angai families, a total of about 1200 persons - had resisted government orders and refused to budge. The Rut and

Thoi, stood to lose their old riverine pastures along the Bahr al-Zaraf, where they grazed by special arrangement with the Gaawar (JIT 1954 I:292), if they moved south and had to share the less attractive Bahr al-Jabal pastures of the Ghol and Nyareweng. They had been ordered to move to Bor District after the 1931 harvest, but by December 1932 floods had so restricted potential settlement lands that there was no room for the new immigrants. Plans for their repatriation were permanently abandoned.

The Luac Dinka from the Fulluth were an even more pathetic case. About a thousand had been forced to move to join the Nyareweng. Once in Bor District they lost most of their cattle and crops to epidemics and floods. By the dry season of 1933 many had begun to drift back to their old homes, some of which had been taken over by the Ngok. In April 1933 even those Luac who had accepted the idea of moving south wanted to return home and petitioned the government to do so. The Lou District Commissioner had always opposed their move, as they contributed significantly to the grain production of his district, so permission was granted.

Before 1932 some 4000 Lou of the Rumjok section had been forced to move out of their territory adjacent to the Nyareweng Dinka. This area was comparatively well watered, suitable for both permanent villages and inland grazing. Prior to the evacuation order half of the Rumjok there used to graze east of the Khor Fulluth, while the Nyareweng used the pastures to the west. The other half of the Rumjok went further east, towards the Khors Geni and Tuni, closer to the Anuak and Murle. There had been no conflict over grazing between the Rumjok and Nyareweng. In fact, some Nyareweng continued to graze their cattle in Lou camps as late as June 1933, and the Rumjok had frequently protected Nyareweng cattle in the past from Gaawar and even Mor Lou raiders (Johnson 1982:197).

The attempted evacuation of the southern Rumjok area meant that other Lou further inland had to be moved to make way for the newcomers, Lou use of Gaawar and Anuak pastures increased, and a large tract of extremely good grazing land became unused. The Nyareweng, being smaller in number than the Lou, had no need for and did not use the evacuated land. Quite naturally the Rumjok began to return, against government orders. By the end of 1931 they were reported to be "begging most abjectly" to stay in their old territory. Since by this time the Luac Dinka were beginning to return to their old homes, the idea of keeping the old Rumjok territory free for eventual Dinka occupation was no longer valid. After paying a token fee to the Nyareweng (in July 1932) for permission to remain, the Rumjok were allowed to return.

The pattern of flooding along the Bahr al-Zaraf during this time indicates a temporary shift in the channels through the swamps, intruding the area of the swamp into new lands. Rupciedol, one of the few elevated woodlands in the area, became overcrowded in 1930 when the government expelled many Bar Gaawar from the Duk Ridge. From 1930 to 1935 the Gaawar along the Bahr al-Zaraf were forced to live "a precarious amphibious existence". It is no wonder that the No-Man's Land was repeatedly breached. As early as the 1932 dry season small bands of Gaawar, Lou and Dinka were found living or camping in the areas the Gaawar had been forced to evacuate. The high 1932 flood made it impossible to fix and patrol a tribal boundary there, so the government conceded to the Gaawar the right to graze and fish in their old pastures in the No-Man's Land. But by the end of the 1933-1934 dry season floods had forced even more Gaawar to return to their old permanent settlements on the Duk ridge. In 1935, even as the Bahr al-Jabal dropped dramatically, the government abolished the No-Man's Land, and the Gaawar returned to the ridge in time to sow their crops and reap an ample harvest for the first time since 1929.

The two years of 1935-1936 showed remarkable fluctuations in the fortunes of the different areas of the region. The late heavy rains of 1934 which had destroyed the crops of the Zaraf Nuer also damaged many of the cultivations of the Nyareweng, Twic-Fakerr, Twic-Ajuong and Bor-Athoic Dinka, leaving only the Twic-Lith and Bor-Gok with any grain reserves. While the Lak and Thiang recovered in the 1935 harvests, the rains between Duk Padiat and Bor were too light, leaving only the Twic-Lith and one section of the Bor-Gok with good harvests. Very few Nyareweng harvested any crops at all and most scattered abroad looking for food throughout June-November. By contrast the Eastern Jikany had a massive harvest and the entire Sobat valley exported 636 tonnes of grain in 1935, its highest grain export figure for the period 1930-1944 (SDIT 1954:Table 49).

The year 1936 looked as if it might maintain this trend. Kongor continued to supply grain to Dinka to the north and south and even to government famine relief projects elsewhere, until by June all the Twic-Lith grain also was exhausted. The Bor Dinka had to sell cattle to buy grain. But the 1936 harvest brought a brief reverse. There were good harvests again along the Zaraf and Sobat, and among the Nyareweng, while crops failed from Kongor to Bor. Throughout 1936-1937 there were heavy imports of grain into Bor, while the Aliab and Cic Dinka across the river exported it in large amounts. Many Bor and Twic crossed the river to buy grain while others went to the Nyareweng for food. With the complete abolition of the No Man's Land, parties of Dinka women from throughout Bor District travelled to the Nuer to get food. Other Dinka sold hides of cattle killed in renewed rinderpest outbreaks to buy imported grain in the Bor market. By the end of 1937 the situation was again altered. All Dinka crops north of Kongor were washed out by the rains, but there was no shortage around Kongor itself.

We may now summarize this year-by-year, almost month-by-month, account. Throughout much of the period 1929-1936 the Gaawar and Lou Nuer were artificially restricted in both their permanent settlements and their seasonal movements. Large sections of each tribe were prohibited from visiting or fully using their normal dry-season pastures. Restrictions on their movements inhibited their normal precautionary measures against the spread of animal diseases - such as the separation and segregation of herds - and this may have contributed to the severity and spread of the 1929-1932 rinderpest epidemics, as well as the resurgence of rinderpest in a number of areas throughout 1934-1936. The climatic conditions of the period, including a succession of high rivers in 1931-1934, favored the further spread of CBPP and trypanosomiasis, so that cattle continued to be endangered by disease over a wide area throughout the period. The government's dual policy of concentrating Nuer settlements and relocating large numbers of Dinka had an adverse effect on the region's agriculture, taking large tracts of land out of cultivation precisely at a time when extreme inundation and locust plagues further reduced grain yields. The artificial separation of peoples inhibited their ability to make full use of scattered areas of grain supplies. Only a few Nuer were able to get grain from the Nyareweng, Ghol and Twic at Kongor, and even fewer Dinka could apply to the Nuer. It was only in 1936-1937 that free movement between Dinka and Gaawar and Lou Nuer was resumed. Before that time even contacts between normally adjacent Nuer (such as the Gun Lou and Bar Gaawar) were reduced through relocation. The government did make new sources available to some pastoralists through the cattle and grain markets at Malakal and Bor, but such centers were not opened up in the areas where the older ties of mutual assistance were most severely restricted.

Evans-Pritchard's description of Nuer society and ecology clearly reflects the dislocation the Nuer suffered during this time. He visited the Lou at Muot Dit and Abwong, and the Jikany at Nasir and Khor Nyanding in 1930-1931, and returned to the Eastern Jikany and western Nuer in 1935-1936. He witnessed the rinderpest epidemics of 1930-1931 and 1935-1936, which occurred in different places in Nuer land, but made no observations among the Zaraf Nuer or along the Nuer-Dinka border. Drought or excess of water caused considerable damage to crops each year he visited the country (though he did not visit the same places each time). Locusts also caused "immediate and wholesale destruction." He observed the Lou gaining access to Ngok Dinka agricultural land and produce, and also exchanges of cattle for grain between the Lou and Eastern Jikany (who, we will remember, regularly produced a greater supply of grain than the Lou during this period), but he did not believe that such exchanges between major political groups had at any time been extensive, and he did not observe any major trading activity. Being nowhere near the Dinka border he did not witness such exchanges between Nuer and Dinka as continued despite the imposition of the No-Man's Land. His impressions of a meagre food supply and shrinking social ties were quite accurate, but not necessarily for the reasons he gave (Evans-Pritchard 1940:50, 57, 69-70, 78, 81-93). The Nuer food supply had been reduced by an unusual combination of high floods, locusts and cattle epidemics, while Nuer access to a wider food supply had simultaneously contracted due to government restrictions on their movements and contacts with other peoples. We will now turn to the floods of 1916-1918 to see how far the conclusions based on observations in 1929-1936 can be applied to earlier periods.

1916-18: The White and Red Floods.[5]

The floods of 1916-1918, which occurred before colonial rule was fully established, were the greatest to afflict the peoples of the region in the first half of this century. They were produced by a combination of extremely high rivers, heavy rains and "creeping flow". In the aftermath of the floods the networks of reciprocal exchange between Nuer and Dinka grew, even though this was a time when there was marked hostility between specific Nuer and Dinka communities, exacerbated in part by environmental problems. The very extremity of the environmental problem forced the Nuer and Dinka to attempt to overcome their hostility if both were to survive.

The floods came in two waves. The Gaawar gave them two distinct names: *Pibor*, the White Water, a frothy flood which came from the river, and *Pilual*, the Red Water, which seemed to come up from out of the ground. Among the Lou and Twic they are seen as the same flood, coming twice. The main source of the floods was the East African lakes which rose from mid-1915 to 1918 and then rapidly dropped to more normal levels. This by itself would have affected only the Bahr al-Jabal and Zaraf valley, but throughout 1916-1918 the Sobat, fed by heavy Ethiopian rains, also rose to its highest recorded level in the first half of this century (Hurst 1920:30-32. JIT 1954 I:30). There seems also to have been consistently heavy rain throughout much of the Jonglei region during these years, producing a high "creeping flow" in the Murle and Lou country. What was different about *Pilual* was not just its height and expanse, which were extraordinary, but its duration, because it did not recede after the first dry season as most floods did.

The Zaraf valley is especially vulnerable to floods. The Gaawar see much of their recent history as having been dominated by floods, forcing them from the west bank of the Bahr al-Jabal during the first quarter of the nineteenth century, across the southern end of the Zaraf island, and on to the Duk ridge by the 1890s where they settled in relative ease until 1916 (Johnson 1982:185). During the wet season of 1916 the river rose, reaching its height in September. October was a period of heavy rains covering the area from Bor and Kongor to the Murle country on the Pibor river with water. The Twic fled east to relatively drier ground. Among the Gaawar the wooded area of Rupciedol, usually a safe refuge from floods, was overwhelmed, and everyone there had to flee with their cattle to the Duk ridge between December 1916 and March 1917. Even Lou Nuer country was reported to be almost completely under water. The heavy rains produced a strong "creeping flow" that year which, because the *khors* flowing into the Sobat were already backed up with water from the higher river, did not readily drain away.

The flood did not recede until the late dry season (March-June) of 1917; thus delaying the commencement of a government military patrol in Lou and Gaawar country until March. Even then, while the Duk ridge was dry, there were large pools of water to the east and west of it, and the area between the Bahr al-Zaraf and Woi remained flooded and swampy. Both the Twic and Gaawar were able to return to some of their pastures; the people of Rupciedol cultivated around their homes; Lou country was dry enough to move about in, with many Lou moving early to Khor Tuni to secure the exceptionally good fishing there (Bacon 1917). Very heavy local rains began in April, the high 1916 levels of the East African lakes began to make themselves felt along the Bahr al-Jabal in 1917, and the river rose dramatically in May that year. The new flood (*Pilual* to the Nuer, *Amol Thit* to the Twic) hit the Gaawar in August-September, just as the crops planted after the previous flood were ready to be harvested. Rupciedol was again washed out and the Duk ridge remained one of the few places of refuge.

Pilual did not recede that subsequent dry season. Water covered a vast area, from Bor to Malakal and from Kongor to the Pibor river. The highest discharges of the Sobat and the White Nile for the first half of this century were reached within a month of each other, February and March 1918. But not all areas within the region were equally affected.

The Luac and other Dinka living along the Khor Fulluth, an area more subject to Sobat river inundation, were relatively safe. It was the outlying Dinka communities who were forced by the Zaraf flood to come to the higher wooded ground along the left bank of the Fulluth. Murle country was flooded in 1917 (B.A. Lewis n.d.), and it was probably these waters which reached Paddoi the same year (JIT 1948:99). The Lou were reported in 1918 to be dying of starvation and fleeing to the Jikany, but modern Lou accounts of their flight stress that they were fleeing the consequences of the government invasion in April 1917 - the early planting season - when troops burned villages (where grain was stored) and seized cattle. That Lou country was not as heavily flooded in 1918 as in 1916 and 1917 is further indicated by the fact that in the same year the Murle, in whose country "creeping flow" originates, had a drought (B.A. Lewis n.d.). The Lou appear to have suffered less from floods than the Gaawar.

The area of the greatest flood-borne distress ran parallel to the Bahr al-Jabal from Bor up past the Duk ridge. Many of the southern-most Dinka were said to have been forced into the treetops (R.T. Johnston 1934). The Twic around Kongor raised embankments along the *toic* and around each homestead, but the flood topped the embankments, and heavy rains destroyed the protected cultivations inside them. People once again fled east. After two years there was no sorghum left and people lived off fish and the water lotus, a traditional famine food. By the end of 1918, when the flood waters began to recede, the entire sorghum crop of the Dinka of Bor District failed.

The Gaawar were the hardest hit of all Nuer (JIT 1954 I:212). The Duk ridge was crowded with refugees from Rupciedol, and even the area around Mogogh was partially washed out. The sorghum harvest of 1917 had been destroyed by the onrush of *Pilual* and people could cultivate only small plots around their huts. Some groups of young men still went out into the flooded pastures to build embankments around the surviving outcrops of land, raising them further with palm trunks and mud. These became new camps where young men, instead of tending cattle, fished and hunted hippos. But no one else went to the *toic* for three years. At the end of this time the Gaawar, too, were surviving mainly on fish and water lotus.

Cattle suffered both during and after the flood. In western Nuer and around Fangak brief outbreaks of rinderpest and other cattle diseases followed *Pilual* (Winder 1946-47). Some Luac Dinka lost cattle to the flood waters, but they quickly replaced them with cattle obtained from the Ngok Dinka on the Sobat or from the cattle market in Malakal. The Gaawar, too, lost large numbers of animals, but not to water or disease. Many Gaawar cattle were sent east to safety with the Lou Nuer. Those that were kept behind were slaughtered for meat. The Twic did not then have access to Lou protection and thus had to keep their animals with them. As was to happen in Bor District after the 1932 flood, many Twic animals suffered from the excessively damp and unhealthy conditions and were soon attacked by a lung disease, probably CBPP.

With the end of the flood and the return to a more normal distribution of water in the 1918-19 dry season, the Dinka and Nuer living along the Bahr al-Jabal and Bahr al-Zaraf had to revive their cultivations and regenerate their herds. There was a general grain shortage with the reduction of cultivation areas and crop yields during the flood, and the most immediate need was seed grain. The government did bring some grain for famine relief to the river ports after 1918, but the Nuer got very little of it - in fact a good portion of Bar Gaawar tribute to the government throughout 1923-1926 was actually paid in grain (Coriat 1991a). The Gaawar had long been in the habit of approaching the more reliable grain producing areas in times of their own scarcity, so they now took cattle to exchange for grain with the Lak and Thiang Nuer, and the Luac Dinka of the Khor Fulluth. Such exchanges, often following marriage lines, had been going on with some sections of the Luac Dinka since at least the turn of the century. Prior to *Pilual* there had not been the same range of exchanges between the Gaawar and the Ghol and Twic Dinka. In fact from 1908 through 1914 there had been considerable hostility and raiding between them. By the end of the first decade of the twentieth century, however, the Gaawar were being approached by all of the southern Dinka in times of need. For a short time before 1913 the Bar Gaawar specifically limited their exchanges with the southern Dinka, refusing grain and insisting that the Dinka bring girls for marriage if they wanted cattle. The Gaawar paid a lower rate to the Dinka than was customary among the Nuer, but higher than most Dinka could afford among themselves, so there was an economic incentive for intermarriage on both sides.

The result of all this was that by the time of *Pilual* the southern Dinka were used to marrying their daughters to the Nuer in times of need, in spite of intermittent periods of conflict, and there were already a number of Dinka women living among the Nuer in marriages mutually recognized by both peoples. When the Twic needed sorghum to eat, seed grain to plant, or cattle to replace those lost in the flood, they went to those places where such things could be found in greater abundance than in their own land: south to the Bor Dinka and north and east to the Gaawar and Lou. When going to their Nuer in-laws they were given grain free, "for it is scarcity and not sufficiency that makes people generous," as Evans-Pritchard so perceptively remarked, "...since everybody is thereby insured against hunger. He who is in need today receives help from him who may be in like need tomorrow" (Evans-Pritchard 1940:85). The Twic did not confine themselves exclusively to existing Nuer relatives. After *Pilual* they approached anybody for grain, and they began to marry their daughters much more frequently to the Lou, since Lou herds had suffered the least.

The Dinka also had recourse to another system of exchange, one which Evans-Pritchard, writing from the vantage point of post-conquest Nuer, dismissed as limited and unimportant (Evans-Pritchard 1940:87-88). This was the ivory-cattle-firearms trade between Ethiopia and the Nilotic peoples, carried on through the mediation of the Eastern Jikany from c. 1910 to 1930 (Johnson 1986a). The main items of exchange were ivory, cattle and guns but also included metalware, tobacco and grain. Following *Pilual*, until the trade was restricted by military action in 1928-1930, the Gaajak and the southern Dinka traded freely in cattle and ivory. The Twic took ivory directly to the Gaajak to trade for cattle, which they then drove home. Gaajak came to the Twic, buying ivory for cash, and the Twic used this money to buy more cattle in the new markets at Kongor and Bor.

Pilual was followed by a seven-year period of low rivers (1920-1926). At the same time the environment around the Duk ridge deteriorated; the ridge itself became excessively dry and the nearby pastures produced unpalatable grass. The Jamogh-Bar Gaawar began to move south and south-west in search of better pastures and homestead sites, encroaching on Dinka territory. This move was resisted by the Ghol Dinka as well as by some smaller Gaawar sections already living among them. The incipient confrontation was avoided by government mediation between the Gaawar and Dinka in 1925, mediation which both Gaawar and Dinka leaders welcomed and abided by (Winder 1946-1947; Coriat 1991a, 1991b).

Despite this tension along the southern Gaawar frontier, there was remarkably little cattle-raiding between Nuer and Dinka following *Pilual*. Instead, what we see - and this quite clearly - is an expansion of the networks of reciprocity between Nuer and Dinka: reciprocity based mainly, but not exclusively, on marriage ties, expressed most often in exchanges of cattle, but allowing access to grain resources as well. This network was different in quality from the trading activity based on ivory and guns which operated in the Upper Nile at the same time. Both types of exchange between Nuer and Dinka expanded in the aftermath of flood. Both types of exchange were subsequently restricted by government intervention in the early 1930s. The reciprocal network survived this brief period of artificial isolation, but the ivory-cattle-gun trade contracted severely with government restrictions.

Pibor and *Pilual* were the most destructive floods of the early twentieth century in the Upper Nile region. They forced all peoples to contract their movements and settlements and narrow their social ties, as one might expect from Evans-Pritchard's analysis of Nuer economy. But the recovery from the floods was accomplished by expanding an existing network of cross-community ties. It was as if the balance could be restored only by equal movement in the opposite direction. Later government action inhibited the scope of this type of counter-active expansion in 1929-1936. As we will see in the next section, though, ties established to recover from *Pilual* assumed even greater importance during the aftermath of the great floods of the 1960s.

1961 and After[6]

The flood which is called *Pawer* by the Dinka began in 1961 and, unlike all previous remembered floods, it has never fully subsided. Survivors of *Pilual* are unanimous in declaring that the 1916-1918 floods were lower, shorter, and less destructive than the most recent floods. There were four years of progressively higher floods, beginning in 1961 and peaking in 1964, again related to the rise in the East African lake levels. Since that time the river discharges have remained high. They are almost double the previous fifty year average at the beginning of the swamp in the south, and one-and-a-half times the previous average at the tail of the swamp near Malakal in the north. The area of the permanent swamp and seasonal floodplain has increased by two-and-a-half times, the swamp having increased the most, and the seasonal floodplain is now one-and-a-half times its size thirty years ago. This massive alteration in water distribution has lasted for nearly a quarter of a century and has caused considerable changes in settlement and grazing patterns among the Upper Nile pastoralists.

The most noticeable changes have been in settlement. The Dinka living along the Fulluth were once again beyond the reach of the highest waters. They did, however, have to evacuate some of their pastures. The Zaraf Nuer (especially the Thiang) then came, escaping their own flood. When the floods left the Fulluth area the Nuer, unable to return to their old homes which were still submerged, stayed. Luac grazing has thus been reduced by Nuer occupation. The Gaawar have lost all their westernmost settlements along with many of their old pastures. Rupciedol and many other places are once again under water and abandoned. The Twic-Lith of Kongor were, as in 1916-1918, temporarily flooded out from behind their low protective embankments by the combination of flood and rain. Human and livestock populations are now restricted to a smaller space and cover the high lands more densely and uniformly in some areas than thirty years ago. But the floods and the simultaneous reduction of pastures were a further impetus to Dinka movement out of Bor District and permanent settlement among the Lou.

Following the high floods of 1948-49 (*Amol Alier*), many Dinka from Bor District moved to the Lou, where some 2000 were listed as unassimilated settlers in 1955 (Population Census Office III 1962:165).[7] There has been no reliable census of the area since then, but Nuer and Dinka testimony is unanimous in stating that Dinka settlement among the Lou greatly increased after *Pawer*. This influx of population into the Lou area, however, may be a factor in the continuing eastward movement of Nuer settlements. Throughout the 1970s and early 1980s the Nuer steadily moved into Anuak territory around Akobo, an area previous given over mainly to cultivation.

There were great stock losses during Pawer, greater than those remembered during *Pilual*. Not only were animals killed in the flood, but a number of diseases, such as rinderpest, broke out afterwards, in marked contrast to the remembered aftermath of many previous floods. Veterinary services in the rural areas declined at this time because of the intensification of the civil war in the late 1960s. This, plus increased raiding during the war, reduced the livestock population throughout the region so that it is now scarcely higher than the minimum estimate of thirty years ago. In the aftermath of the flood, stock levels have remained low. The flood caused massive deforestation around Kongor, on a far greater scale than *Pilual*, and after 1972 animals were regularly sold to raise money to import building materials from Bor, Mongalla and even Juba.

People tried to regenerate their reduced herds in a number of ways. The settlement of Twic and other Dinka among the Lou led to a number of marriages there, with the Dinka keeping their cattle with the Lou. Other Twic men resorted to the old method of marrying their daughters to the Lou in order to bring cattle back to Twic country. Those Dinka already with marriage ties to the Lou and Gaawar also received cattle from the Nuer. When their sons married, they got cattle from the Nuer to help make up the bridewealth; when their Nuer granddaughters married, cattle also came back to the Dinka grandparental home. The fact that the eastern edge of the seasonal *toic* has now moved further inland seems to have had a countervailing effect on Lou movements. The Gaawar *toic* is closer to the Lou than it was throughout the first half of this century, and more Lou than before appear to have negotiated the use of that *toic* for part of the dry season, bringing more cattle through the Duk ridge and adjacent territories.

Since the 1960s an increasing number of men have gone into migrant labor, mainly in the northern Sudan, but also in other parts of the Middle East. They returned with money which was used to buy cattle in Malakal and Bor, as well as in numerous smaller local markets. Many

Twic also bought cattle from the Lou. After the end of the first Sudanese civil war in 1972 the demand for meat in the growing regional capital of Juba rose, most of it being supplied by the Bor Dinka until 1982, with the proceeds of sales in Juba going back to buy cattle in other markets where prices were lower.

The most novel development in the aftermath of *Pawer* was the expansion of the dried fish trade. A number of persons who lost cattle in the flood turned to fishing to live, just as the market demand for dried fish in the southern Sudan increased. Many Dinka and Nuer began catching, drying, and transporting fish to Juba and Zaïre, where it became a major item in Sudanese-Zaïre trade. The money accumulated in this trade returned to the Upper Nile region to buy cattle. Like so many other promising efforts in the southern Sudan, this trade suffered from the outbreak of the second civil war.

Conclusion

The Upper Nile plains of the Sudan have often been presented in anthropological literature as a uniform zone of unvarying ecological relationships, inhabited by sharply defined ethnic groups locked in enduring hostile opposition.[8] The historical study of changing ecological and social relationships - the "political ecology" of the region - reveals a far more complex picture. Underlying ethnic, linguistic and political differentiation is a dynamic response to changes in the environment. There are subtle, but significant, variations in local ecologies that in turn influence the balance between pastoral and agricultural activity throughout the region. Individual as well as community survival depends on being able to shift the balance when environmental circumstances change. This has encouraged the development of a common economy linking various ethnic and political groups - however tenuously - together.

The physical characteristics of this region have remained essentially the same for centuries (Johnson 1988b), and as long as pastoralists have occupied it there has been an enduring pattern of vulnerability to a regular succession of floods. The succession of natural catastrophes within the region is a constant fact of life. Times of major natural disaster are part of the collective living memory of the Nilotic peoples; I collected information on *Pilual* in 1981-82 from survivors of that flood who could compare it with their direct experience of *Pawer* and with their parents' accounts of the great floods of 1878 and 1890s. Rarely, however, is a catastrophe universal, as we have seen in both the high floods of 1916-1918 and 1961-1964. There are usually reserve areas of cattle and crops on which others draw, even if the margin of surplus is narrow, and even if it is a surplus only in relative terms. The peoples living along the Zaraf valley and the Duk ridge are periodically forced to rely on peoples of the Sobat hinterland for grain and cattle. In turn the peoples of the Sobat hinterland are periodically forced to rely on some of the more secure agricultural areas of the Sobat valley and the White Nile.

Raiding for both cattle and grain, especially throughout the nineteenth century, was one way in which these reserves were tapped. It was also a way which degraded the reserve areas, principally by depopulating them. While raiding was more common in the nineteenth century than in the twentieth, it is an exaggeration to suggest that raiding was the principal economic link between the Nuer and Dinka. The Nuer and Dinka communities of the Upper Nile region are currently linked in a variety of networks of reciprocity whose construction began in the nineteenth century.

We should recognize that people go where the food is, that in this region lines of kinship follow and strengthen lines of feeding. Social ties, eventually leading to kinship links, were, and still are, the main way in which the Nilotic peoples survive and recover from the natural catastrophes which are endemic to their region. The greater the extent of the disaster, the greater the expansion of the social network during the period of recovery - except in the 1930s when government policies interfered with the social network. Certain facets of the modern economy - trade and migrant labor - have been open to the Nilotes in varying degrees for most of this century, but they have not yet fully supplanted the networks of reciprocity.

The very regularity of the appearance of floods, and their erratic behavior when they do appear, influences human settlement to the point where there are few strict political or ethnic boundaries in the region. As Elsammani and Elamin (1978:8) noted about southern Dinka settlements after *Pawer*, individuals from various political groups often settle within the territory of another group. "This has resulted in continuous fusion, and even distribution of human settlements over space", they observed. "It follows that any spot potentially suitable for settlement is occupied, which is one of the factors accounting for the continuous spread of human settlements over the high lands." Evans-Pritchard earlier recorded a similar mixture of immigrant Nuer and Dinka settling in territories of dominant Nuer Groups. We have seen from this study that settlement constantly crosses ethnic boundaries, especially recently when numbers of Dinka were forced by floods to settle among and marry into the Nuer. One Twic elder specifically linked this pattern of Twic marrying out to the occurrence of floods, saying, "if we had no flood, we would not take our daughters to Lou" (EHJP-12). Yet floods have been a part of the region far longer than pastoralist settlement. There has never been an ideal time when communities could remain self-contained and flood free. It is because of the floods that "Nuer expansion" is part of an older and more general eastward pastoralist movement and still continues (Johnson 1986b).

The current anthropological understanding of the region is derived mainly from Evans-Pritchard's study of the Nuer, which was undertaken within the 1929-1936 period. We have seen that this was a period of an unusual concurrence of floods, cattle disease and locusts, as well as a period of exceptional disruption of ties amongst the Nuer and between Nuer and Dinka through forced resettlement and segregation. We have confirmed, through contemporary documents, Evans-Pritchard's observations. The Nuer during this period were restricted by their ecology, and their social ties and economic options were limited. Evans-Pritchard was unable, however, to compare the impressions of his own time with the record of any earlier time. We are able to compare his with earlier and later periods,[9] and we have seen a pattern in the response to natural disasters carrying through most of this century.

Had the Nilotic peoples lived in the small, narrowly self-defined units in which they appeared to live when Evans-Pritchard observed them in the early 1930s, their options and resources would most certainly have been severely limited. However, the reconstruction of their local economies which followed *Pilual* and *Pawer* indicates that a broader system of interdependence than that described by Evans-Pritchard operates throughout the region. Much of the common economy which he suggests as exclusive to the Nuer can be seen to extend to and include other peoples as well. The ties may lie submerged, to be activated as circumstances require, but this is precisely the strategy for survival which Evans-Pritchard accurately identified among the Nuer themselves. Neither the Nuer nor their Nilotic neighbors may be able to control their environment, but their own responses to environmental change have neither been static nor cyclical. Equilibrium with nature is achieved only through dynamic responses by each community, responses which progressively alter their own internal composition and their social and economic relations with their neighbors.

Notes

1. The data for this chapter were derived mainly from sources found in the Upper Nile region: interviews collected in 1975-76 and 1981-82, and local government documents collected and deposited in Juba in 1981-83 when I was employed as Assistant Director for Archives in the Regional Ministry of Culture and Information in Juba. I am extremely grateful to Dr. P.P. Howell for his

extensive comments on an earlier draft of this paper and for the additional information he provided. I do not wish here to become involved in the complexities of the Nuer-Dinka debate in anthropology. The interests of the principal participants in that debate have been mainly theoretical. None have been able to familiarize themselves with a comprehensive range of historical sources (both oral and documentary). Whatever their contribution to the refinement of anthropological discourse, all have inevitably misunderstood, and unintentionally misrepresented, the history and ecology of the Upper Nile region; therefore, they cannot be reliably used as a starting point for a historical study of ecological change. I feel that no useful purpose would be served by charting either my disagreements or agreements with the points raised by previous authors and have confined my used of secondary materials to those based on fieldwork or local historical research.

2. Except where specifically noted this section is based on Winder (1946-1947), JIT (1948, 1954), and Howell, Lock and Cobb (1988).

3. See Johnson 1986b, 1988a, & 1988b.

4. Except where specifically cited this section is based mainly on materials now deposited in the Southern Records Office, Juba [SRO]. These are: the Upper Nile Province Monthly Diaries and the Bor District Monthly Reports in files BD 57.C.1 and BD 57.D.1; the Nuer Settlement and Nuer-Dinka Intertribal files UNP 66-B.10, UNP 66.B.11, BD 66.B.1/3 and BD 66.B.3. A number of taped interviews in the Ecology and History of Jonglei Province [EHJP] series have also been used. These interviews were undertaken by Philip Diu Deng and myself in April 1981 and May 1982, financed by a Fulbright-Hayes senior research grant. Those used in the paper are: EHJP-1, Rut, Thoi and Luac Dinka elders; EHJP-2, Lueth Ayong & Malok Lam (Luac Dinka Chiefs); EHJP-3, Luac Dinka elders; EHJP-4, Ruot Rom, Cuol Macar & Gai Thung (Gaawar Nuer Chiefs); EHJP-5, Ruot Diu (Bar Gaawar - *Pilual* age-set); EHJP-6, Cuol Cany Bul, Pok Tuot & Jal Wang (Gaawar Nuer - *Pilual* age-set); EHJP-7 & 8, Kulang Majok (Bar Gaawar - *Pilual* age-set); EHJP-11, Family of Moinkwer Mabur (Ghol Dinka); EHJP-12, Twic Dinka elders. The table in JIT (1954:239) has also been used.

5. Except where specifically stated this section is based on: interviews EHJP-1 to 8, 11-12; Winder (1946-7); and contemporary corroboration of some points in "Report on Lau Patrol 1917:: and "Diary of Political Officer 'C' column Lau Patrol 1917" (both in SRO UNP SCR15.10), and *Sudan Intelligence Reports*: 268 (Nov. 1916), 3; 283 (Feb.1918), 3; 291 (Oct. 1918), 3.; and 292 (Nov. 1918), 2.

6. This section is based mainly on Howell, Lock and Cobb (1988), JSERT (1976), Elsammani & Elamin (1978), Payne & Alamin (1977), and interviews EHJP-2, 3, 5, 12.

7. The 1955/56 census gave a figure of 1842 Bor Dinka, but this must be taken as a minimum estimate rather than a precise count.

8. See especially Sahlins (1961:322-44) and Kelly (1985). Neither is based on comprehensive archival or field research. Sahlins constructs his theory from no more evidence than can be selectively taken from Evans-Pritchard. Kelly has read more widely, but still not systematically. He does use some colonial primary sources, but only those which randomly found their way to Britain. As a result

he presents a distorted and false picture of Nilotic history, demography, bridewealth exchanges, and ecological relationships.

9. I have examined the colonial context of Nuer history in greater detail (especially the events of the 1920s and 1930s) and have discussed the relationship of that context to the Nuer ethnography in Johnson (1979, 1981, 1982a, 1982b, 1985, 1986a, and 1986c). A fuller treatment will be found in Johnson (forthcoming).

5

Feasts, Famines and Friends: Nineteenth Century Exchange and Ethnicity in the Eastern Lake Turkana Region[1]

Neal Sobania

Introduction

Nineteenth century East Africa was characterized by small-scale societies with fluid boundaries and highly adaptable populations. Throughout the region these societies were continuously reshaped as necessity or choice dictated. Individuals, families, and groups shifted between a variety of economic modes, adopted new subsistence patterns and social structures to maintain themselves and became economically and linguistically assimilated into new social formations.[2] Nowhere is this better illustrated than in the oral traditions that describe the disasters that swept across East Africa in the last two decades of the nineteenth century. The dominant themes in the traditions of the peoples of northern Kenya concerning these years focus upon their struggles to remain within the pastoral economy and the reshaping of their communities as people were dispersed in the wake of this series of disasters. These traditions graphically illustrate the complex networks of social and economic ties that linked individuals across the region, and the period offers an unusual opportunity to examine the strategies governing social relations between individuals and groups.

The importance of such networks in our understanding of the history of East Africa has recently been indicated by several writers (Johnson and Anderson 1988), yet there has been little attempt to examine the manner in which such networks were constructed and maintained in the nineteenth century. This chapter offers a description of these processes among the peoples of the Eastern Lake Turkana basin in the last decades of the nineteenth century. The first part of the chapter gives a general picture of the social and ecological environment of the region. The next section considers the networks of trade and exchange that operated across the region, while the third section examines the bond relationships that linked individuals within certain societies and permitted links to be constructed between societies. An awareness of the operation of social bonds of this type allows us to gain greater insights into the pre-colonial social history of the region, and suggests that ethnicity was a mutable, and not fixed, notion. The final section considers the impact of the late-nineteenth century disasters and the subsequent intrusion of colonialism upon the economic and social networks of the region.

The Social and Economic Environment

The three epidemics that swept across the region initially destroyed the cattle herds and then decimated the human population. The first half of the 1880s was dominated by the outbreak of contagious bovine pleuro-pneumonia, the second half by the panzootic of rinderpest. And as people were reacting to the ensuing famine and dislocation, the 1890s saw an outbreak of smallpox and an associated period of widespread drought. The magnitude of the resulting crises necessitated people utilizing the full range of social networks designed to manage such times of ecological stress. At the community level these networks of exchange and reciprocal obligation provided needed trade goods and the loan and transfer of stock and labor. As a defence against severe adversity the networks included points of social contact that had been purposefully developed across societal boundaries. From an examination of these networks one can see clearly the pathways taken by individuals and groups who shifted in times of crisis, not merely from one locale to another but from one society to another.

From the semi-arid desert to scattered highland forests and from the dry savanna plains to perennial grasslands, East Africa provided a mosaic of ecological zones. These zones formed the basis of a series of overlapping regional systems in which clusters of complementary subsistence modes were each adapted to prevailing environmental conditions. The system that will be examined here is that of the Eastern Lake Turkana basin (*cf.* Waller 1985; See Figure 5.1). In a similar way, however, the area west of Lake Turkana including the northeast and the

120

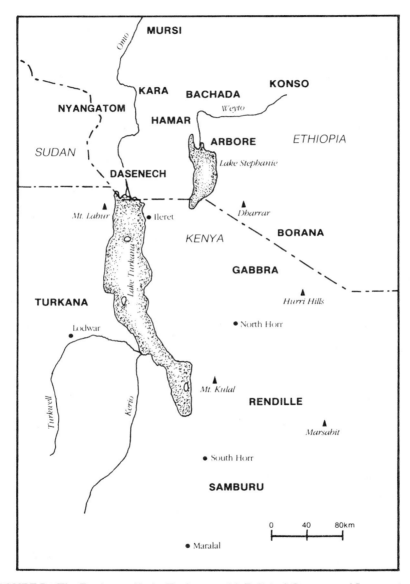

FIGURE 5.1 The Regions of Lake Turkana, with Political Groups and International Boundaries

southern lands of present day Uganda and Sudan, respectively, comprised another system, and the Central Rift Valley stretching from modern Kenya in the north to Tanzania in the south yet another. Each of these systems was defined by the contemporary focus of their ethnic components. For example, through much of the nineteenth century the Dassanetch at the northern end of Lake Turkana were part of the eastern Lake Turkana system, together with the Arbore near Lake Stephanie part of highland system to the northeast, and with the Turkana part of a system west of the lake (See Plate 5.1). Each system is thus one particular way of defining a region in order to make more comprehensible the complex relationships in which each society was involved. In summary, these regional systems of East Africa each contained a number of ethnic communities that sustained themselves by following different economic modes in diversely overlapping ecological zones. Yet, as this examination of the eastern Lake Turkana system will show, the strategies of the various societies that made up these regional systems formed an economically interrelated whole.

The matrix of economic modes in the eastern Lake Turkana region included cattle pastoralism, camel pastoralism, agro-pastoralism, and hunting-gathering. For every individual in the lake basin, these four economic modes represented subsistence options. It might be argued that the most basic option to maintain was that of hunting-gathering (including fishing); however, as an alternative its status ranked well below those of the stock options. Indeed, the vast majority of individuals in this regional system had an economic and emotional commitment to herding.

At the best of times the cattle-herding Samburu were among the region's most productive pastoralists. As compared to their camel-herding neighbours, the Rendille, they were capable of generating stock increases in excess of their human population growth.[3] Like the Samburu, the agro-pastoralist Dassanetch had a similar productive capacity, yet for both the availability of labor represented a limiting factor. The potential for growth within their herds was sufficient to ensure that as the herd developed particular beasts were recognized as belonging to individual members of the household. Among the Samburu a son built up a herd with the animals alloted to him from the family herd. A Dassanetch son's herd grew from a nucleus of one or two heifers which he received at birth. By the time of marriage the sons in both societies had rights in ownership in enough stock to constitute an independent herd. Whereas the Samburu continued to delay the separation of the household herd as long as the father remained alive, among the Dassanetch the household unit was subdivided at marriage and each son established his own independent home (Almagor 1978:66-

72).

The Dassanetch pattern, which combined pastoralism with agriculture, included a further set of possibilities beyond the productive growth potential of only cattle keeping. This extra capacity was built into their grain production. Occupying the unique environmental niche at the north end of Lake Turkana, the Omo River and its delta, and the northern margins of the lake, enabled them to practice flood-retreat agriculture to grow millet. The garden plots along the Omo River were limited and subject to special rules of allocation (Almagor 1978:43-45). Easily accessible, and among the first to dry out, these plots were brought into production first and heralded an end to the yearly cycle of dry-season food shortages. The flats beyond the river and along the lakeshore were less reliable and less convenient, but still suitable for planting. In contrast to the gardens along the Omo, however, these lakeside plots were considerably more numerous and could be planted by anyone. Here, supply always exceeded demand. Again, the only factor which limited growth in this economy was the shortage of labor. Perhaps its greatest value was as a built-in economic reserve. As employed by the Dassanetch, the production of grain served in times of need both as an alternative source of food with which to supplement shortfalls in milk yield and through trade as a means to acquire stock.

The subsistence option of camel herding as practiced by the Rendille had built-in limitations that made it the region's most difficult subsistence option to sustain. Constraints on the fertility of camels, with long gestation periods, low birth rates and rain-linked ovulation cycles, resulted in a production level that barely kept up with the human population. Today, the Rendille, as the inheritors of this economy, delay marriage and are largely monogamous in order to control population size. In the past, to further control human birth rates, they also practiced customs such as abortion, the expulsion of young unmarried mothers and the killing of unpropitiously-born children. Of greater consequence, however, were the rules of inheritance which bequeathed the entire camel herd to the eldest son of the original owner in order to prevent its being divided into uneconomic portions. The practice of shared beasts and occasionally prescribed gifts of stock, as for example at circumcision, enabled some younger men to persevere in the camel economy, but for those too poor to extablish an independent existence, and for those herdsmen reduced to poverty by misfortune, the path was generally one of emigration.[4]

Despite the commitment to herding in the Easten Lake Turkana system, and the specialized adaptations made by the various societies of the region, pastoral production as the mainstay of a socio-economic existence has always been a risky business. In order to survive as a pastoralist it was necessary to contend with a variety of natural and man-made circumstances which could threaten the existence of the family, and, in extreme cases, that of the society as a whole. The unpredictability of the renewal of vegetation and water necessary for herd survival was one such circumstance. The ability to compensate for loss caused by raiders or disease, either of which could overnight deplete or eliminate a viable herd, was another. And the necessity of providing an adequate labor force, its size and strength subject to variation in human fertility and to human diseases, also needed to be addressed. Necessity thus dictated that each herdsman manipulate the use of his stock in order to limit the effects of these unknowns.

For every pastoralist, livestock served two crucial roles. On the one hand, it provided the basis for subsistence and, on the other, served as the means by which social relationships were formed and maintained: "pathways of stock exchange are usually analogous to pathways of social interactions" (Carr 1977:9). Every pastoralist was the center of a unique cluster of personal relationships entirely different from that of every other man. Birth established the agnatic members of this cluster, marriage extended it to a particular group (or groups) of affines, and throughout life the deliberate creation of bond partnerships expanded the network.

Given the unpredictable growth of vegetation upon which herds fed, the family, as the elementary production unit, was also subject to an irregular food supply. In response to this uncertainty, there occurred a broad sharing of personnel and productive property between domestic groups. Loans of labor in the form of unmarried sons to assist in herding, the dispersal of herds or certain beasts to other herdsmen to create viable herds or promote better management and the gift or loan of animals for support in times of need, whether economic or ritual, were all aspects of such sharing. Agnates were one source for such assistance.

Other pathways of stock exchange and social relations centered on marriage. The transfer of bridewealth opened an entirely new range of potential individuals within the wife's kinship group to whom the husband-herdsman could turn for the sharing of herding labor, for the loan of beasts for feasts or ritual slaughter and for sharing in times of famine, disaster or other difficulties.[5] Furthermore, polygamy was preferred by all the pastoralists of this area. If a man prospered, that is, his herds multiplied, he was likely to take additional wives and further expand the range of potential assistance.

Bond partnerships were exceptionally valuable for expanding an individual's line of social and economic cooperation. Deliberately selected, they filled gaps in a herdsman's range of relationships that were not met through ties of kinship or marriage. Formed at various times in an individual's life, they varied in strength of obligation and duration.

Bond partnerships thus provided support and cooperation in the same way as did ties with agnates and affines, and were especially useful for rallying support in disputes and in opening new fields for establishing further economic or social relationships.

The individuals in a herdsman's cluster of relationships were all potential sources of assistance when he needed help and they were the people whom he helped when called upon to do so. With each new relationship the herdsman established reciprocal rights to claim gifts of domestic animals in a conscious translation of social relationships into stock. Since all rights were reciprocal, an individual without stock became isolated from potential pathways of cooperation and mutual insurance in times of hardship, and had therefore to survive outside the pastoral economy. Notions of poverty related not to an individual's ability to survive physically but to the possession of a number of livestock insufficient for him to live as a herdsman.[6] Self-sufficiency based exclusively on livestock was often the professed norm of pastoralists. Few herdsmen, however, had this capability. Cultivation, foraging, and to an extent, hunting, were employed to meet economic needs. Through trade a herdsman obtained those commodities he required but could not produce himself. Bond partnerships were another source. An individual's existence in the community at times required that he seek out and nurture social support and cooperation.

Regional Networks of Trade in the Nineteenth Century

In the nineteenth century the peoples of the Eastern Lake Turkana system herded their stock in what would later become a frontier region between Emperor Menelik's Ethiopian Empire and the British East Africa Protectorate. Today the Dassanetch are found to the north and east of Lake Turkana; the Borana and Gabbra are to their east and both north and south of the modern-day boundary between Ethiopia and Kenya; and the Rendille and Samburu are well south of that border area at the southeastern end of the lake. However, from at least the middle of the nineteenth century until the years between the 1880s and the 1920s saw a reordering of the grazing areas into the pattern we find today, the cattle-herding Samburu and the camel-herding Rendille dominated the region east of Lake Turkana, especially that area which they called "Wato" at the northeastern end of the lake. To the north and east of Wato were the Boran-speaking populations. Still free of the constricting influences which the coming decades would herald, by the 1880s they had not yet pushed out to the plains below the escarpment that until then marked the southern extent of their wet-season grazing. Further, through the mid-nineteenth century Dassanetchland was far more extensive than today, stretching from the Mount Labur region on the lake's western shore northeastwards around to the eastern shore. Potentially productive land was so extensive that the Dassanetch made parcels available along the lake shore and river courses for cultivation by destitute refugees from neighboring Hamar, Arbore and Turkana.

Several other smaller societies who combined millet cultivation with herding along the Omo River in the mid-nineteenth century were the Nyangatom, the Kara, the Mursi, the Murle, the Gomba, the Bogudo and Morgundji,[7] while the Hamar and Bachada were among the peoples occupying the foothills which run to the northeast and ultimately lead to the Ethiopian highland plateau. To their east, along an indistinct boundary which separated them from the pastoral Oromo, were the Arbore and Konso. The former, who followed an economic adaptation similar to that of the Dassanetch, lived immediately north of Lake Stefanie; the latter lived further up the Weyto River where it turns westward. As in the Omo region, the wide range of climate and natural resources in the Wato region led each society to adopt different combinations and varying degrees of pastoralism, agriculture, hunting, gathering and fishing. But in contrast to the Dassanetch, these other societies were sharply constrained in where they could plant by their access to only limited stretches of river bank. And whereas the seasonal Weyto River assisted the Arbore, much as the Omo did the Dassanetch, the crops planted by the Hamar had to rely on local rainfall only.[8]

Between all these societies, often with neighboring groups as intermediaries, there passed diverse agricultural and livestock products and well-made articles for use in the household, for decoration and for war. Central to this pattern of trade was millet cultivation, and the role played by the chief "manufacturers" of the region, the Konso and the Bachada.

Trade in the region resulted from the complementary needs of societies that lived in proximity to each other and exploited different natural and human resources. The Dassanetch looked chiefly to the Kara, the Hamar and the Arbore for exchange. In turn, they and many others, including the pastoral Turkana, Samburu and Rendille to the south, who know nothing of cultivation themselves, sought out Dassanetch millet and also traded for tobacco and small stock. The Dassanetch sought to acquire products fashioned of iron, such as spears, axes, bells and ornaments, woven cloth, clay pots and coffee. There were two principal trade networks through which they obtained these items. Both generally carried the same goods and both were oriented in the direction of the Ethiopian highlands.

South of Lake Chamo, on terraced hillsides above the Weyto River, the Konso grew coffee, grain, tobacco and cotton. Weavers crafted cotton yarn into cloth of various weights and designs. Blacksmiths forged spear points, knives, axe blades and hoes, as well as leg irons, bracelets and other decorative pieces. As a rule, however, the Konso did not venture very far with their wares, and never to the Omo River or Lake Turkana. Instead, markets were held in the highlands to which people like the Arbore came. And although there never emerged a class of "traders" among any of the peoples of this region, perhaps due to the personalized nature of the exchanges that were entered into (see below), it was through such middlemen that the production of the Konso farmers and craftsmen spread through southern Ethiopia (des Avanchers 1859; 161-62; Smith 1897:230; Kluckholm 1962:411, 415-16; Abir 1970:132-34).

The Arbore were particularly well suited for the enterprise of linking the Konso and the Dassanetch. Arbore society was divided into two named segments, Ulde and Marle. Although the Ulde segment claimed descent from the Boran, and the Marle descent from the Dassanetch, the Arbore managed to maintain relationships with both communities, who were themselves deadly enemies.[9] The Arbore therefore were able to cross through Boran country of the Konso and to return to their own lands to the Dassanetch.[10]

In addition to the cloth the Arbore obtained from the Konso, they exchanged coffee, ironware, clay vessels and several types of beads with the Dassanetch. Smaller objects of ornamentation made from iron, such as rings for earrings, chains and bracelets, were fashioned locally by the Arbore themselves. In addition to iron ore, they had access to pot-clay and to a kind of soft stone used for working into beads. In exchange, the Arbore received millet, either as seed grain or to supplement their own, some of which they traded to the Boran, and small stock, hides and skins. The last three items, and also honey, were among those things they bartered with the Konso.[11]

A second exchange network reached the lake area through the Hamar and Kara peoples from the Bachada, who at that time lived in the mountains above the Kara. The Kara generally traded with the Dassanetch sections along the west bank of the Omo while the Hamar traded with the Dassanetch sections on the east bank. Although the Kara now speak a dialect of the language they share with the Hamar and Bachada, they do not view themselves as historically related to these communities. Rather, through a more ancient "Kara" group, they link themselves to the Arbore and the Dassanetch. In the nineteenth century the Kara and Hamar served as brokers between the Dassanetch and the Bachada, as well as providing articles of their own manufacture.[12]

Especially important to the Dassanetch from this network was the ironware forged by the blacksmiths of the Bachada and others beyond them to the north. Having no smiths of their own, the Dassanetch were entirely dependent on others to provide these wares (von Hohnel

1894,II:165). These northern blacksmiths therefore provided everything from spears and axes to leg irons and bells for oxen.[13] The supply of metal goods would seem to have been adequate, since, when von Hohnel visited the region in 1888, he found the iron, copper and brass he carried to be "worthless" and of "little value" for trade. On the other hand, some objects, such as the iron bells placed around the neck of livestock remained relatively scarce and were passed on through specific rules of inheritance (von Hohnel 1894,II:161; Almagor 1972a:89n).

Two other necessities of life, coffee and clay pots, also had to be obtained by trade. Coffee was used widely for ritual occasions, and clay pots, coiled by the Bachada, Hamar and more recently the Kara, were used for cooking and carrying water. The Dassanetch held these vessels in high esteem but due to a lack of clay locally they were unable to make them for themselves. Cloth also reached the Dassanetch through the Kara and the Hamar, but, like the cloth in the Arbore network, it is likely to have originated from the Konso. The supply of cloth reaching the area was too small to have any significant impact upon the mode of dress along the lake.[14]

Exchanges from the Hamar to the Dassanetch were almost exclusively focused on millet, although on occasion the Dassanetch also exchanged small stock for cattle. The dependence of the Hamar on local rainfall for their own crops made shortages endemic. In return the Dassanetch received ironware, clay pots, small stock and honey. The Dassanetch traded some millet and especially small stock with the Kara, for forged iron, clay pots and coffee.[15]

From oral evidence it would appear that trade in Dassanetchland and the surrounding areas was usually conducted by small parties of itinerants. The actual mode of exchange was between individuals with both men and women travelling to seek out trading partners. Having arrived with coffee, cloth or ironware, or driving a few head of small stock, the typical trader was depicted as departing with his donkey fully laden with bags of millet. In point of fact, the millet that was taken away was more likely to have been a small sack made from the skin of a goat and carried on the shoulder of the individual who had received it (See Plate 5.2). The usual practice was for those who sought millet to approach the Dassanetch. Although quite clearly the Dassanetch also went to their neighbors to trade, it was seldom with grain. Rather, it was with stock and tobacco that they went in search of necessities:

> Turkana brought animals and bought my millet. Turkana didn't have food; I didn't go to buy from them. If I wanted to go and buy something from them I took my animals. If I wanted small stock, I gave them my animals, they gave me small stock.[16]

Only for the Dassanetch and their Turkana neighbors to the southwest are there references to trade occuring outside their respective settlements. They especially record their having met each other at the watering points in the no-man's land under Mount Labur. For the Dassanetch who sought to exchange a small bag of tobacco for a sheep or goat, especially of a particular colouring for ritual purposes, this was a ready-made market place. It also proved a more neutral ground for approach since the relations between these two societies were far more nebulous and hostile than those the Dassanetch had with peoples to the north and northeast. However, some trade did take place with the Turkana in Dassanetch settlements.[17]

Outbreaks of hostility were not limited only in relations between the Dassanetch and the Turkana (See Plate 5.3). Forays by warriors, quarrels at watering holes and outright attacks to secure additional grazing were among the circumstances which led to the temporary severing of relations between communities. When this happened and trade was cut off, either exchanges were organized in another direction to circumvent the hostile neighbor or trading ceased until peace was re-established. That such ruptures were not usually lengthy affairs is suggested by one informant's characterization of Dassanetch ties with the Turkana:

> We traded with the Turkana; they brought animals. Their peace is not good. One month it's good, next month they kill people and fighting starts again. Then it stops; they come and trade, trade for millet with the people; give them animals. If the people come back when the month is finished, next month or another [month] people [Dassanetch] follow them [back to Turkana]. People who go there they kill them and the fight begins again, and it's that way up to now.[18]

In addition, a community was seldom dependent on a single source for particular commodities. The Dassanetch were not alone on the lower Omo in producing grain: clay pots could be had from as far away as the Elmolo fishermen, and even spears, one of the region's scarcest articles, could be obtained from many different peoples. The Dassanetch, for example, also obtained spears from the Turkana and other peoples to the west.[19]

In general, while the volume of trade in the lake basin could not by any standards be considered very great, it was more than adequate to supply the various communities present with those items that were necessary or important to their way of life and could not be provided by their particular environment or economic mode. This trade appears neither to have encouraged significant increases in the production of particular commodities nor to have extended greatly the range of their exchange. Even the Arbore and Kara, who were in the most advantageous positions to dominate these networks, do not appear to have developed a specialized class of traders. Instead, trade was carried out merely as an extension of herding and agricultural labors. Later, when long distance trade began to make its way toward Lake Turkana, these indigenous commercial networks still showed no appreciable change.

Salt was widely available through the region so did not feature as a major commodity of exchange (des Avanchers 1859:163; Stigand 1910:236-37). In part this was due to its availability. However, to the northeast, the Oromo used the salt found in local deposits as a medium of exchange with the Konso but there is no evidence that the Konso traded this salt further south or west. In part this was related to the greater value of salt in the east, at Lugh and Bardera, from where Somali caravans journeyed to Konso. This caravan trade from the coastal region did not, however, by the middle decades of the nineteenth century, extend beyond Konso to the west or south, although it did penetrate northwards into the Sidama principalities (Abir 1962:132-34; Sobania 1980:109).

Not until well into the second half of the century did trade goods from the coast, and later the caravans themselves, expand into the interior country of the Boran (Guillain 1857:531-32; Ravenstein 1884:268; Bottego 1895:450; Ferrandi 1903:318-21; Turton 1970:105-11; and Dalleo 1975:37-38). Once in Boran country, however, these Somali caravans were obliged to depend on local inhabitants to dispose of their cloth and other trade goods to the country beyond.[20] Although the Somali did not themselves succeed in penetrating to the actual lands of such people as the Konso and Arbore until the last decades of the century, they appear to have been relatively well-informed about them. The Hamar, Dassanetch and Nyangatom or Turkana ("Semidero") were, for example, identified as "tributaries" of the Arbore (des Avanchers 1859:161-64; Christie 1876:191). By the end of the century these caravans followed an established route and regularly reached as far as the Arbore country at Lake Stefanie. One or two found their way beyond, to as far as the Dassanetch, but in general, they did not trade in the region north and northeast of Lake Turkana where the local trade networks continued to be dominated by the Arbore and the Kara (Vannutelli and Citerni 1899:328-29; von Hohnel 1894,II:187-88; DHT 38, DHT 45).

The traders from the coast brought a wide variety of cloth, brass and copper wire for bracelets and earrings, iron for spears and knives, beads, cowrie shells and tobacco for exchange along the route to the interior. Livestock are notably absent from the items of trade they are said to have brought to the region. Ivory, salt, rhinoceros horn, hippopotamus teeth, ostrich feathers, game skins, domestic stock including horses, and perfumed woods and gum were among the attractions which drew them to the area (Vannutelli and Citerni 1899:344,348,492-93,498; Smith 1896:136; Ferrandi 1903:361).[21] When these caravans halted to trade along this route, individual traders were typically housed in a settlement by a local resident. As well as being the trader's host during his sojourn, this resident, whether Boran or Arbore, also served as broker with the local population. The host provided milk to the trader during the length of his stay, and, if so requested, made baggage animals available for the return journey to the coast. In turn, the trader cemented this partnership by presenting gifts of cloth and various other goods to his host and no doubt favored treatment in trade (Vannutelli and Citerni, 1899:485-86; and Smith 1900:603). Such a welcome to an itinerant trader was not an isolated response but rather a recognized, well grounded, cultural response.

Intra-Societal Bond Partnerships

At the neighborhood level, networks of social relationships frequently overlapped and merged with those of local trade. Exchanges were not solely the result of barter. Throughout the Lake Turkana basin there operated an institutionalized relationship of reciprocity through which commodities were said to have been "freely" given. Among the Dassanetch this relationship was called *bel*, among the Borana *jal*, and in each of the other societies of the area it had its own name. Broadly translated, these terms all mean "friendship"; "Friends, just friends. It is a bond partnership."[22] When mutually recognized between two unrelated men, a bond partnership was created that would henceforth be embodied in the reciprocal exchange of gifts:

> We meet and greet each other. We give each other food and we talk. After we have talked, then we shall ask each other to be friends. If we discuss it and agree to be friends, he will not go back empty-handed from my settlement. Or I will not come back empty-handed from his settlement. We shall give each other [gifts]; or to the person who came to your settlement, you have to give him a goat to take to his home. Then after he takes the goat, what I do is stay here for some months or even a year, and then I will go and see my friend. I will go to his settlement and I will also be given something on coming back to my settlement. Whatever it is, I must come back with something even if it is a cow skin or something else. He is my friend and I will not come back to my settlement empty-handed.[23]

A gift always provided the foundation of these formally contracted friendships.

As emphasized by Mauss in his classic study "L'Essai sur le don", the nature of reciprocity is such that there are the equal obligations to give, to receive, and to repay (Mauss 1966:158-63; *cf.* Sahlins 1972:148-83, *passim*). These three features are always discernible in a description of bond partnerships. The notion of repayment cannot be assumed to restore an economic equilibrium as in a barter situation. In an analysis of pre-industrial economics Firth argued that with reciprocity "the significance of economy is seen to lie in the transactions of which it is composed and therefore in the quality of the relationships which these transactions create, express, sustain and modify" (Firth 1971:4,14-15).

It is precisely in this way that the economics of bond partnership should be viewed in the Lake Turkana basin. The emphasis on repayment is in the actual act of returning and balancing a gift irrespective of the "value" of the goods returned. While ideally the "value" of the return gift should be equal to or greater than the one received, the "worth" of a gift was largely computed on a scale of estimation. Cattle were valued over small stock, cows over oxen, and a proven dam over a heifer, but even two oxen of apparently equal size and worth could be valued differently due to a cultural preference in ritual for a particular color of beast. Irrespective of which partner initiated the friendship, it was through the giving and receiving of gifts that bond partnerships were activated and sustained.

All of the Lake Turkana basin societies recognized differing degrees of quality or strength in the bond partnerships which their members formed. And, although the same pattern was broadly recognizable among the other societies of the region, the Dassanetch provide a valuable illustration because they separately named each of these partnerships (Gulliver 1951:105-6). The Dassanetch distinguished five distinct partnerships (*lil mech*) with each partner in the relationship recognized as a close friend (*bel*). Those bonds that individuals entered into were "friends of lips" (*bel afo*), "friends of gift-giving" (*bel shisho*), "friends of smearing" (*bel uro*), "friends of holding" (*bel kerno*), and "friends of name-giving" (*bel meto*). The bond partnerships of "lips" is of little importance to this discussion. Formed between youngsters in herding camps, it carried no long term rights or obligations.[24] The partnership of "gift-giving" was, like all bonds, made manifest by the presentation of a gift and was often used to evince an already existing line of economic cooperation. Having brought a little coffee to initiate the request to become partners (*bel*), the same individual cemented the relationship a few days later with another gift. The strength of the intended bond was indicated by this second gift. An ox or a heifer intimated a strong partnership and a goat or ox-bell a less important one. After a time the gift receiver visited his partner. Taking along coffee, the receiver now returned a gift. The nature of the economic cooperation these partners engaged in could embody the sharing of herding tasks for example, through the placement of several head of stock in a partner's herd or the loan of a young affine or agnate as additional labor, as well as providing a head of stock for ritual or bridewealth requirements. In theory, to keep this bond active required the continued exchange of gifts, although a bond that had once existed and then lain dormant always held the potential for renewal.[25]

The friends of a "smearing" partnership were usually confined to co-equal members in the age-set system. However, because of the wide variance in age which can exist between Dassanetch age-mates, it would not be unusual for the partners of this bond to be a teenager beginning to herd cattle and an adult herdsman who would assist his young partner in herd management tasks. The bond was publicly declared by smearing the stomach contents of a slaughtered ox on each other's chest, the presenting of a headrest, and the ritual eating of meat. In later life the bond could be strengthened depending on the needs and circumstances of each partner by the periodic giving of gifts.[26]

The partnership of "smearing" had a structurally inherent weakness because it was made between warriors before they entered into the wider realm of community politics as elders. Should these warriors later find it useful to their own positions to maintain their partnership they would normally renew it by forming a new bond of "holding" or "name-giving". All bond partnerships could be and frequently were formed between two previously unrelated herdsmen. By doing so they created a new relationship with all the inherent potential for further expansion of networks. On the other hand, they might find it more advantageous to strengthen a previously established bond relationship by upgrading it, for example, from one of "gift- giving" to a stronger one of "holding" or "name-giving".[27]

Circumcision ceremonies provided the opportunity for the formation of the bond partnership of "holding". At circumcision it was customary that the initiate be held from behind around the arms and chest by a "holder". Prior to the ceremony the "holder" was responsible for providing the initiate with the necessary trappings for the ceremony and on the occasion itself the bond was established and the two became "friends of holding" (*bel kerno*). In the following year, there occurred a prescribed exchange of gifts. Also at this time coffee was drunk and blessings given. Here, as with the bond of "smearing", and, as will be seen, with that of "name-giving", a junior-senior pattern of partnership was established that was often characterized as a child-father relationship: "In the bond partnership of holding, if I myself hold [then] I am the bigger. [If] you are the one who holds him you are big; his father. He is like your child."[28]

"Name-giving" was regarded as the strongest bond of all. A "name-giving" bond was established between a man whose name was given and a new-born boy who received it. Although they were the recognized bond partners (*bel meto*), the bone also clearly represented an undeclared link between the name "giver" and the baby's father, who selected the name for his son: "...that child can be given anything if his father comes and demands it." By placing this partnership in the realm of a father-son tie, the relationship between the partners became more one of kinship than mere partnership. Indeed, in some partnerships the strength of cooperation in these quasi-kinship relationships was perceived as being of the same quality as those of kinship and similar terms of recognition were applied: "If I take his name, this is my father. If he takes my name, I am his father; he is my child".[29]

The formation of bond partnerships thus occurred at different times throughout an individual's life. The design and endurance of each bond was less a matter of affection than of the economic and social needs of the parties at a time of their partnership formation. And although clearly the bond created through being held at circumcision limited that individual to a single partner, the number of bond partnerships which could be formed as the "holder" were not limited. The actual number of bond partners that an individual could form in his lifetime across the entire range of partnership was theoretically without limit. The key factor in these bond partnerships was that the rights between the partners were inherent.

To activate these rights, a degree of proximity between partners was necessary or the bond would be neglected and "disappear". Intra-societal bonds were predominant in the latter part of the nineteenth century, much as they are today, but bond partnerships were not made exclusively between individuals within a particular society. Indeed, there were no restrictions that precluded the formation of a bond partnership with individuals of other societies. As one elder summarized it, "Bond partnerships do not have a particular place."

Inter-Societal Bond Partnerships

The anthropological literature on peoples in the Lake Turkana basin is devoid of any reference to the existence of inter-societal bond partnerships (Gulliver 1951, 1955; Dyson-Hudson 1966; Spencer 1965; 1973; Almagor 1971, 1978). However, among the many societies at the north end of Lake Turkana in the last century, the lack of administrative boundaries between them, their proximity, and the similarity, as much as the diversity, of their economic adaptations made possible, just as it did trade, the formation of bond partnerships that cut across societal boundaries and linked neighboring herdsmen. Bond partnerships grew out of existing trade relationships, the hospitality extended to a neighboring traveler on a visit, and the sharing of a grazing area which brought alien herdsmen into prolonged contact. Regardless of what precipitated the event, proximity was required to inaugurate and keep alive a bond partnership across inter-social boundaries: "A friend (*bel*) is what the people who stay together will make, but people who stay and meet each other only once, how can they make it (*bel*)?"[30]

Tradition avers that amidst the two exchange networks that operated north and northeast of the Omo delta, commodities were "freely" given to friends as often as individuals bartered for what they required:

> The Hamar came and brought small stock and traded for millet with the Dassanetch. The Hamar gave them animals. Others came to see their friends and their friends gave them millet; if he did not have a friend, he would have his small stock to buy the millet.[31]

To the question of what was exchanged for a particular item such as a clay pot, a not uncommon response was, "We are friends", indicating that nothing was exchanged.[32] Between the Hamar, Kara, Dassanetch and to the southwest the Turkana, the most common type of bond partnership that existed was that of "gift-giving".[33]

The inauguration of bond partnerships was also widespread between the Dassanetch and Arbore and their herdsmen neighbors just to the south, the Samburu and Rendille. As the latter were immediate neighbors at the end of the last century, this was both prudent and judicious. For the Samburu, and through them, the Rendille, the Arbore served as another source - although less frequently than did the Dassanetch - from whom they could procure grain and other agricultural products.[34] Here also the most widely shared partnership between neighboring herdsmen was that of "gift-giving". Not only livestock, grain and other agricultural products such as tobacco, gourds and coffee but household and personal objects such as carved milk and fat containers, porridge bowls, sleeping skins, cloth, beads and wild animal hide sandals also passed from friend to friend in the maintenance of active partnerships.[35]

Recognized as "stronger" than that partnership of "gift-giving", the bond partnership of "name-giving" and "holding" were also formed across societal boundaries. The formation of these latter two bonds required both prolonged physical contact and genuine affection between partners, since in establishing such a bond across a societal boundary the individual initiating the bond lost the opportunity to invest it more profitably within his own society. More often than not, these two bonds were used to strengthen an already existing relationship: "...to any other person who is not your friend you will not give his name to your child".[36] Some traditions even suggested that between the Samburu and the Dassanetch the ties became so close that the partnership of "smearing" was taken up, although by elders rather than warriors:

> In this place all of them ate grass. They were very close and then if these elders came and visited us, animals we killed and then we made [partners of] smearing (*bel uro*). The Dassanetch also went; they killed animals and smeared them.[37]

Others, however, claimed that the bond of "smearing", because it was formed between warriors, was too "powerful" and could not be taken "to a far place." "Maybe sometimes if you take it to a far place people will fight and you will go and kill that man you made it [the bond] with; your family would die" because of such unpropitious behavior.[38]
Between all these societies, friends of "name-giving" were established. After giving a son the name of a bond partner,

> ...then your friendship grows to be very pure and (becomes) a very big friendship...you can even give him a camel with milk. It is a strong friendship and means that he is like your son...one of your strongest and best friends. And in case he will come to ask [you] for something, he will not miss it, you will give him.[39]

Unique, however, to those societies that had the ritual of circumcision - the Dassanetch, the Arbore, the Samburu, and the Rendille - was the inter-societal forming by individual herdsmen of the bond partnership of "holding". Like the bond of "name-giving", it was considered a very special partnership, "because the one you hold will be the same as your son..., he will just be your child."[40] And, again, the range of affection and assistance that the formation of these bonds established approached that recognized in close kinship.

The creation of an inter-societal bond partnership, like those within a society, went beyond the casual provision of a gourd of milk to drink, a handful of tobacco to chew, roast meat to eat, or hospitality that a traveler or settlement neighbor could expect as a matter of course. The gift of a head of stock was not an impulsive action but was rather both given and received as a compliment calculated to extend an individual's sphere of supportive relationships. Although unable to garner support in political matters or settlement disputes from those friends who lived in neighboring societies, as would be the case with partners from within his own society, a herdsman's inter-societal partnerships greatly enlarged his knowledge of the region and his options in the economic sphere. As a visitor himself, as well as a receiver of visitors from areas beyond which his own livestock (normally) never ventured, he acquired valuable information regarding neighboring peoples, environmental conditions and trade, and information about the general region as a whole. When confronted with the risks and perils brought on by natural or man-made disasters, such as drought, disease and raids, the herdsman could turn to his bond partners in addition to his kin and affines. When the difficulties of his intra-societal partners coincided with his own, the individual who had invested in partnerships beyond the bounds of his own society continued to have options of assistance open to him.

Pastoral Viability, Cataclysm and Changing Ethnicity

The severity of the crisis created by the disasters of the 1880s and 1890s led the pastoralists of the Eastern Lake Turkana system to draw upon the various relationships that they had long nurtured for just such an occasion. And, because those pressures that existed at the best of times were now magnified, the suble distinctions between the complementary subsistence modes of the region were made sharper. Few people east of Lake Turkana escaped having to deal with one or more of these disasters, although the degree of suffering felt by different societies and individual households within each one was subject to a wide range of factors. The effects of bovine pleuro-pnemonia and rinderpest on the cattle-keeping Samburu and the famine that ensued were devastating. The massive dislocations that followed dominate the tradition of this period:

> Most of the people died of starvation...they didn't have food...so people went and hunted elephant and ate; ate rhinocersos .... A few of them had small stock [sheep and goats] and lived again.... The time of starvation people scattered everywhere, is it not so? Some escaped to the Turkana, some went to the Boran, some went to the Dassanetch and some went to the Elmolo and some were killed by the Rendille while stealing livestock. Some went to the Rendille and [others] became thieves who lived in the bush and stole camels. Some went to the Ndorobo and took roots from the ground.... Most people died of starvation. No matter which person it was, a warrior, a child, a woman...all died.[41]

The Dassanetch were more fortunate, not because they were unaffected but because the individual who lost self-sufficiency in pastoralism could turn to the alternative provided by the grain within his own economic mode. In addition, because the Dassanetch incorporated a fishing group as part of their society, the Dies, they further insured the potential of their members to survive and reacquire access to full status as pastoralists.[42] In this light, the agro-pastoralist pattern was a more easily sustained subsistence mode. As a result, departure from it was a matter of personal choice rather than a necessity. The exclusively cattle or camel pattern offered no such option. The Samburu and Rendille were unable to exist wholly within the framework of their economies and often had no recourse but to migrate.

For those Rendille who lacked sufficient stock, including those simply without access to a viable herd in the first place, the other three economic categories of the regional system - cattle pastoralism, agro-pastoralism and hunting-gathering - all represented possible alternatives. For the displaced Samburu the options were limited to relocation among the agro-pastoralists or the hunter-gatherers. In either situation, an assessment that such migration would only be a temporary affair was not without foundation. Neither pattern precluded options for reacquiring stock. But the destitute camel herder had little probability of rebuilding his herd and migration from cattle to camel pastoralism was normally impossible. Nevertheless, the smallpox epidemic of the 1890s did present such an occasion. Initially the Rendille were better off because the cattle diseases of pleuro-pneumonia and rinderpest did not affect their camels. However, when smallpox struck, the Rendille were among the hardest hit. This set the stage for the unusual situation in which labor was in such short supply in Rendille that their ability to successfully herd their camels threatened the very existence of the productive system. Thus their economy was in the unique position of having to assimilate outsiders at a time when the suffering Samburu had labor to give.

The direction in which an individual or group chose to migrate was determined, if the 1880s and 1890s can be taken as paradigmatic, by the links or pathways that already existed: bond partnerships, affinal relationships, kinship ties and claims of putative kinship. There, beyond the boundary of their original community, the most fortunate found work tending the herds of patrons and remained within the pastoral fold. In return for their labor they were incorporated into families and provided with a head of stock from which they began the process of re-establishing their own herds. The less fortunate existed by some combination of hunting, fishing, planting or gathering and then traded or begged in order to begin the same process of returning to pastoralism.

At one level, then, environmental factors established the range of possible subsistence patterns that could be used to exploit a particular region. This economic matrix of complementary modes lent a degree of stability to the region. This is not meant to imply, however, that only camel pastoralism as practiced by the Rendille, for example, would allow individuals to subsist in that particular area. Rendille pastoralism was (and remains) but a single point on a continuum of possible adaptations that provided an acceptable level of existence. At the same time, however, cattle pastoralism as an adaptation in the niche occupied by the Rendille would not be as efficient. In the pastoral sphere, the environment limited the type and number of animals that a particular niche could support and thereby placed an upper limit on the human population as well.

Just as the environment provided stability to the system from below, ethnicity lent stability from above. In the Eastern Lake Turkana system, ethnicity embodies a value orientation, a shared pattern of normal behavior, that is expressed through a particular social system. The cultural trappings of the system do not in themselves define ethnicity. What they do is maintain a particular system that organizes and regulates those who have access to the means of production. Thus the boundary between one society and another is two-dimensional, in that it is both related to an economic category and to a group of people, whose commitments stem from a way of ordering that category. Therefore, when cataclysmic events led to the migration of individuals and groups across ethnic boundaries, ideological commitments and environmental conditions encouraged their return. At the same time, the commitment to re-enter the world of self-sufficient pastoralism, which necessitated gaining access to the resources of stock and grazing, provided a countervailing force that fostered acculturation and assimilation.

Viewed from the opposite perspective, cataclysmic events resulted in other communities absorbing population, and, as such, they were presented with a potential for expansion. Any major shift in population disturbed the critically balanced relationship between human and stock numbers and the environment. Just as major stock losses caused the migration of human population to counterbalance the relationship, so the disparity created by an increase in either population component also had to be countered: increased stock with additional households and additional herders with increased stock. For example, as a community lost stock to raiders, it at one and the same time had an excess of human beings which the reduced herds could no longer support and was threatened with the possible loss of its peripheral grazing areas which it could no longer control or defend. Thus, successful raiders could by the magnitude of their gains become a conquering army absorbing, along with the captured herds as spoils of war, the former owners of the stock who were being displaced by their losses. The Turkana expansion into the western Lake Turkana basin in the early nineteenth century can be seen in this light, as can the later internecine warfare of the Maasai.[43]

Similarly, potential for expansion also belonged to those communities whose economic differentiation enabled them to provide refuge for dislocated herdsmen. Whether the eventual acquisition of cattle by such refugees led to expansion in order to meet an increased requirement of grazing or to further migration because the grazing potential was too limited, the effects these adjustments engendered were seldom unaccompanied by repercussions elsewhere in the region. Only in terms of this dynamic relationship between ethnic identity and economic differentiation can the continuous reshaping that the societies of the eastern Lake Turkana basin have undergone be recognized.

Imperialism and the End of Reciprocity

The end of the nineteenth century saw disease, drought and enemies successively sweep across the region in cataclysmic proportions. When these had passed, the Samburu found themselves in a considerably reduced grazing area in the process of rebalancing their human population against their remaining but already increasing stock. The Rendille were also endeavoring to strike a balance between the the size of their camel herds and the losses of population they had suffered as a result of smallpox. Only the Dassanetch had increased their population and were in a position of potentially being able to increase their access to stock and grazing.[44] However, a new era was about to dawn in which empires would impose conceptions of law and order that would greatly inhibit the ebb and flow of people characteristic of the earlier pre-colonial period.

Across East Africa, in the early decades of the twentieth century, the traditional flexibility by which pastoralists had survived the changing conditions of their environment ceased to exist. Among the many rules and regulations that came into force in the colonial period, the imposition of grazing boundaries had the greatest impact, as once relatively fluid societal boundaries became crystallized. While the creation of "tribal grazing areas" satisfied the desires of the colonial authorities who saw their primary task as one of achieving administrative order, the policy of "separation" by which it was achieved bred ill-feelings and led to increased hostility between the local peoples. For the Rendille the levying first of tribute and then of tax payments and the restrictions imposed on their movement intensified hostility toward the Boran and Gabbra. The confinement of the Samburu in a newly created district from which the Rendille were excluded undercut the symbiotic ties that they had long enjoyed. The restrictions imposed on contact between the Samburu and the Rendille with the Dassanetch resulted in their mutual isolation and the withering of their trading ties. Effectively cut off from their neighbors to the south, the Dassanetch increasingly looked to the north and became firmly entrenched in the Ethiopian fold.

The artificial boundaries which government so adamantly promulgated brought to a halt the peaceful means of contact and exchange which had for so long bred familiarity between societies. No longer did community elders hold the decision-making powers over whether watering points and grazing grounds were to be shared or fought over with neighboring peoples. No longer could individual herdsmen extend their networks of social relationships across societal boundaries through trading partners, marriage alliances or the formation of bond partnerships. No longer were the inter-societal means of "insurance" available to be used in alleviating localized destabilizing crises. By limiting societies to bounded regions, and thereby creating in each increased need for greater self-reliance, the colonial authorities heightened the ethnic consciousness of each society. In response, cultural and ritual differences were magnified to promote a unique "tribal" identity distinct from that of geographic and cultural neighbors, further driving in the wedge that split long-standing relations of reciprocity between the peoples east of Lake Turkana. The notion never emerged in the first quarter of this century that the limitations and restrictions which were being imposed on these pastoralists might in the long term have a detrimental effect both on their well-being and the environment in which they lived.[45]

Notes

1. The fieldwork upon which this paper is based was conducted in 1975-1977 and 1978-1979 with the permission of the Office of the President, Republic of Kenya. It was supported in part by a School of Oriental and African Studies (University of London) Governing Body Postgraduate Exhibition and a Grant from the British Institute in Eastern Africa.

2. The genesis traditions of the peoples today identifiable in East Africa attest to the existence of these earlier populations. Linguistic and archaeological evidence suggest many more layers of settlement in still earlier periods. See Sobania and Waller (forthcoming); cf. Ehret (1974) and Heine (1974).

3. In a series of simulated models of herd growth, Dahl and Hjort (1976:66) presented a growth rate of 3.4 percent as being that of a "typical" herd, but noted under optimnal conditions there exits a potential to double the size of a herd in six and one-half years. Spencer (1965) recorded an annual increase among the Samburu of 5.6 percent and cited one informant who had actually achieved a growth rate of 14 percent.

4. See, for example, Spencer (1973:132). Comparative evidence suggests that the limits on the Rendille economy are not typical but may be a direct result of their herding techniques and the particular environment they inhabit (Dahl and Hjort 1976:78-86).

5. Social relationships and social values in these pastoral communities are focused on rights and obligations in cattle and/or camels to the virtual exclusion of smallstock, despite the important economic role of the latter.

6. For example, among the Dassanetch the word *dies* means "poor" and is also the name applied to those Dassanetch who have no cattle and form a fishing element within the society (Alamgor 1978:52; Sobania 1988a:47).

7. Today very little is known of these last four peoples who, if they survive at all, do so as subordinated segments of other societies in the region. For observations on these mixed economies as practised in the last years of the nineteenth century, see Cavendish (1898:384-85); Neumann (1966 [1898]):294-95, 303-5, 315; Smith (1900:609); Welby (1901:200); Austin (1902:677-78); and Stigand (1910:236).

8. "If rains rained they [the Hamar] planted millet. If there was no rain they brought small stock to trade for it [millet]. If we were fighting they stayed in their area and ate animals. If rain refused to rain for them they ate the animals": Lockasit (and others) at Nyiomeri on 17 June 1976, Dassanetch Historical Text (hereafter DHT) 35. Transcriptions of historical texts are cited as follows: the name of the informant(s), followed by the number of the interview, and then the date. If an informant is not directly quoted, only the text will be referenced (for example, "also see DHT 14"). Interviews with Boran, Samburu and Rendille informants are cited in the same fashion, but with "BHT" to indicate Boran Historical Text, "SHT" for Samburu Historical Text, and "RHT" for Rendille Historical Text.

9. These names are used contextually to refer to either one segment specifically or to the whole society for which there is no all-encompassing name; "Arbore" appears to be a designation employed only by outsiders. Jensen (1959:385) noted a tradition about two brothers, Marle and Arbore, who quarreled and separated; one went north, the other south and thus the people were divided forever into two groups. Also see DHT 3, 6, 18; SHT 35; and Lydall (1976:394).

10. "Cloth, the Konso had it. Arbore and Konso are closer [to each other]. Konso had it, and then brought it from them. Arbore took it and brought it to me (Dassanetch)." Hasubite and Towota at Bubua on 20 June 1976, DHT 38. Also see interviews, including DHT 30, 36 and 49.

11. Interviews including DHT 23, 25, 27, 30, 36, 38, 49; cf. Cavendish (1898) and Smith (1897).

12. DHT 38.

13. See, for example, DHT 11, 38, 42, 45; E.R.Shackleton, "The Merille or Gelubba", 1932, in Kenya National Archive (KNA)/DC/TURK/2/1.

14. Long multi-pleated skirts of goat skins remain even today the dominant dress of married Dassanetch women, and some of the oldest men alive recall their fathers wrapping a short skirt of goat skin (*tele*) around themselves rather than the cloth men wear today. See, DHT 36, and the photograph in Vannutelli and Citerni (1899:333).

15. "The Kara used to have coffee; coffee we exchanged; coffee they came and traded. Leg irons they brought and leg irons we bought....They also brought clay pots; [for] their pots we exchanged. Those are the things we exchanged with them." Narenyimoi (and others) at Herek on 14 June 1976, DHT 30.

16. Iliwan and Lotimanimoi at Salany on 15 June 1976, DHT 31; and interviews including DHT 25, 38 and 45.

17. Interviews including DHT 5, 7, 21, 36.

18. Hasubite and Towoto at Bubua on 14 February 1976, DHT 21.

19. Throughout much of the nineteenth century, spears competed with bows and arrows as the principal weapon of the herdsmen east of the lake. See DHT 30, 33, 45; and Lamphear (1976:192-93).

20. The extent to which the Boran became involved in this trade is evident in the rise of Boran as the commercial *lingua franca* as far east as Lugh. See Vannutelli and Citerni (1899:82, 355) and Smith (1897:239).

21. Dalleo (1975) includes an attempt to establish the value and volume of this trade.

22. Lokasit (and others) at Salany on 16 June 1976, DHT 35.

23. Silamu at Korr on 30 July 1976, RHT 4; see also RHT 8, DHT 18, 35, 42, 50; SHT 30, 80.

24. Generally based on the exchange or loan of decorative ornaments such as beads, feathers and bells for dancing, or on the sharing of herding tasks, these casually-made partnerships simply disappeared as the participants grew older and their interests changed. Their social value, however, of furnishing experience in the making of bonds which could in no way restrict the child in later life is obvious; Almagor (1978:109) and BHT 2.

25. DHT 18, 35, 42, 50; *cf.* Almagor (1978:109-111).

26. See for example, DHT 15, 38, 42, 50; Almagor (1978:112-14).

27. DHT 42.

28. Iesho at Ilkamerreh on 4 September 1976, DHT 50; Almagor (1978:114-118).

29. Hamgan at Ngurinet on 3 August 1976, RHT 8.

30. Lonyamedo (and others) at Herek on 14 June 1976, DHT 29.

31. Lumerimoi and Gudan at Babua on 13 February 1976, DHT 20. Others brought clay pots or tobacco for their friends; see for example, DHT 18 and 25.

32. *E.g.* Lochaya at Ileret on 6 November 1975, DHT 6.

33. Interviews including DHT 12, 18, 25, 30, 35.

34. Interviews including SHT 2, 3, 34, 35.

35. Interviews including DHT 3, 9, 18, 27, 30, 38, 45. Also, SHT 3, 9, 10, 33, 34; RHT 5, 7, 8.

36. RHT 8.

37. Isetel at Ileret on 24 June 1976, DHT 45; also DHT 38.

38. DHT 31.

39. RHT 8; also SHT 30, 34, 80; DHT 9, 26, 30, 42, 50.

40. Lenarokishu aat Gatab on 10 December 1976, SHT 40; also SHT 34, 80; DHT 26, 29, 38, 42; RHT 8.

41. Lenatitai Barantis (and others) at South Horr on 25 September 1976, SHT 37.

42. Sobania (1988a:41).

43. *Cf.* Lamphear (1988) and Waller (1985).

44. See Sobania (1980) and *Man, Millet and Milk: Shifting Boundaries of Ethnicity in Pre-Colonial Kenya* (forthcoming) for the detailed study of this era of disaster and recovery.

45. See Sobania (1988b), which demonstrates this with respect to the Rendille.

PART FOUR

WARFARE, EXPANSION AND PASTORAL ETHNICITY

6

Movement, Warfare and Ethnicity in the Lower Omo Valley

David Turton

Introduction

In a 1985 article, Richard Waller describes East Africa, before the advent of colonial rule, as

> ....a frontier region where society was fluid, highly adaptable, and capable of absorbing outsiders easily. Labour, rather than land, was the scarce resource. This placed a high premium on the ability of pioneering groups of individuals to contract and manipulate effectively a wide range of kinship and other ties in order to mobilise the social and political resources necessary for colonization....as a result of the need for mobility, there were few barriers to the flow of population from one small-scale unit to another and the definitions of identity tended to be inclusive rather than exclusive (1985:348-49).

If there is anywhere in East Africa where this description may be said still to apply it is the Lower Omo Valley in southwestern Ethiopia. But it is not only the relatively weak exercise of government control which makes this an attractive area for the study of population movement, warfare and ethnic group formation. A second reason is its relatively small size (approximately 20,000 km²); a third is its great ecological diversity, which supports several culturally distinct groups of agro-pastoralists. Fourth, changes in the level of Lake Turkana since the beginning of this century have had a clear impact on the human population (Butzer 1971:131-44; Carr 1977:254-300). Fifth, the people of this area have undergone, since 1971, a period of drought and hunger unprecedented in living memory, an experience which has both emphasised ethnic distinctions and brought into focus processes of movement and adaptation which in 'normal' times are barely visible because of the long time span over which they occur.

This chapter is based upon a limited comparison of the three main ethnic groups in the area, the Dassanetch, Nyangatom and Mursi. I have two objectives. The first is to arrive at some general propositions about population movements, warfare and ethnicity which may prove helpful in extending this comparison to a geographically wider region. The second is to attempt what I believe the first regional study of the peoples of the Lower Omo. I do not claim that my account is either exhaustive or definitive, but I hope it will at least have the merit of provoking others to improve upon it.

Agro-Pastoral Production Systems
in the Lower Omo Valley

The economies of these three peoples are linked by their dependence on the River Omo, and yet the Omo forest and bush, being infested with tsetse flies, does not provide a safe environment for domestic animals. Its importance lies in its potential for agricultural, not pastoral, production. Pastoral exploitation of the Omo, therefore, implies a mixed pastoral and agricultural economy. Assessing the exact contribution to daily subsistence of agriculture in a society in which herding is given supreme cultural importance is, of course, a difficult matter, especially since age, sex and locality specific categories of the population are differentially dependent on these two resources. But this is a matter of great importance in attempting to understand the regional economic system of the Lower Omo and the inter-relations of the groups which make it up (See Map 6.1). Let me begin with the southernmost of these, the Dassanetch.

The Dassanetch

Dassanetch territory is a semi-arid plain lying immediately north of Lake Turkana and including the Omo delta. Mean annual rainfall is about 350 mm (14"), but rainfall varies greatly from year to year in timing, location and amount (Butzer 1971:23-26). More important for the Dassanetch than the erratic local rains is the annual rise and fall of the Omo which is controlled by the heavy rains falling over its highland

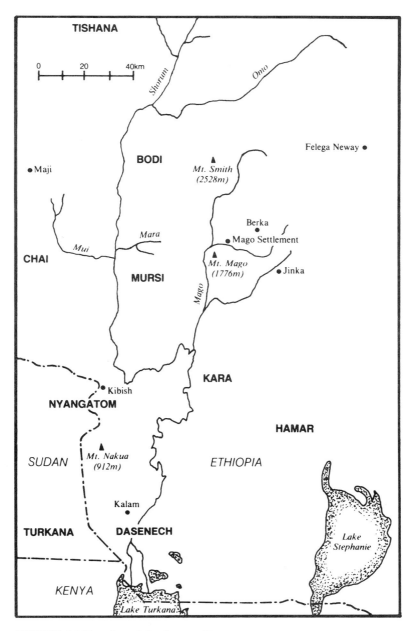

FIGURE 6.1 Peoples of the Lower Omo

catchment area. It starts to rise in May and usually reaches its highest level in August, when it overflows its banks and inundates the surrounding "flats" (Almagor 1978:38). As the river recedes between September and November these flats provide both fertile areas for cultivation and good dry season pasturage. Variation also occurs here, however, not only from year to year (a late flood combined with early local rains can lead to a drastic reduction in crop yield) but also over the longer term. There was a rapid drop in the level of Lake Turkana after the late 1890s, exposing new areas for cultivation and grazing, and a more recent rise during the early 1960s (Butzer 1971:105-124). One consequence of the lowering of the level of Lake Turkana has been the southern advance of forest and woodland along the Omo, which has in turn aided the southward migration of the tsetse fly (Carr 1977:88, 274).

Our two authorities on the Dassanetch, Carr and Almagor, taking their lead from the people's own view of themselves, have focused in their accounts on pastoral activities and values - as is reflected in the titles of their books, *Pastoralism in Crisis* (1977) and *Pastoral Partners* (1978), respectively. But while Carr implies that pastoralism is both ideologically and economically "dominant" for the Dassanetch,[1] Almagor is more ready to recognise their heavy reliance on the production of grain - primarily sorghum but also maize. "Crops and livestock", he writes, "are equally important to subsistence.... The Dassenetch economy...is based on a balance between agriculture and pastoralism" (1978:1). This is borne out by his estimate of the number of livestock per person - three to four cattle and nine to ten small stock. According to available estimates of the theoretical minimum herd size for a "purely pastoral subsistence" (L.H. Brown 1973; Dahl and Hjort 1976), they would need at least double this stock wealth to subsist entirely on the products of their herds. But even these generalizations will not do for the Dassanetch as a whole, for Almagor also makes it clear that the relative contributions made by agriculture and pastoralism to subsistence vary significantly from one area of Dassanetchland to another. He and Carr did most of their work among the Dassanetch of the Inkabelo section, who account for at least a third of the total population[2] and occupy "the largest territory with the greatest diversity of natural resources" (Almagor 1978:51). Statements by both authors about "the Dassanetch" therefore, tend principally to be statements about the Inkabelo section, and this is how the following brief outline of Dassanetch subsistence should be understood.[3]

The Dassanetch are alone among the peoples of the Omo Valley in their total reliance on the Omo flood for cultivation. The availability of large inundated flats, some distance from the river, for cultivation, means that they do not have to rely on rain cultivation to supplement the yield from the narrow strips of floodland along the banks of the river. The latter are planted in early September and give a harvest in late December/early January, while the flats are not dry enough for planting until October/November. This, the main sorghum crop, is harvested in February/March. March is also the month in which the onset of the main rains is expected, an event which can destroy the crop before it is harvested if planting in the flats has had to be delayed by a late flood. So whereas for their neighbours to the north, who rely heavily on rain cultivation, the early and heavy onset of the main rains is a promise of future plenty, for the Dassanetch it is a threat of present hunger. Thus it is precisely in years of poor rainfall, when surrounding peoples are short of rain or literally starving, that the Dassanetch are likely to get a bumper harvest.[4] This is presumably one reason why early travellers were so impressed by the fertility and productivity of Dassanetchland (Austin 1902; Stigand 1910).

Another reason is that the inundated flats (which are more extensive than can be cultivated by the available labour force) provide excellent pasturage during the driest months of the year - November-March. This is a time of plenty, when cultivation and pastoralism are carried out together, largely on the east bank of the Omo. With the onset of the main rains, and as the Omo begins to rise, the cattle are taken across to the west bank and are moved progressively westwards, to "dry" grazing areas as far as the international border. Conditions for cattle herding in Dassanetchland are excellent.

> Cattle are confined to the poor dry west bank pastures for only three to four months of the year, and for at least half of the year green grass is available in addition to high quality supplementary foods - sorghum, maize and bean stalks. However bad the year, livestock are not entirely dependent on rainfall for water since there is always water in the River and the Lake. Salt is also plentifully provided by the Lake and the grass that grows after inundation. Distances between pastures are fairly short and livestock are rarely over-driven and exhausted... these conditions permit a relatively high reproduction rate (Almagor 1978:52).

The inexorable increase in stock number is not, furthermore, significantly checked by disease ("I was assured by the elders that they could not remember any major epidemics in the present century") (Almagor *Ibid.*:53), while Dassanetch expansion is blocked to the west by the international border, to the south by the Turkana, and to the east by the Boran. The resulting problem of how to keep stock numbers within the carrying capacity of available grazing is common, if in a less extreme form, to many East African herders but the Dassanetch have an unusual solution: the regular, ritual slaughtering of surplus animals (Almagor *Ibid.*:52-58).[5]

The unit identifying itself as Dassanetch includes four other sections, which are in various ways marginal or peripheral to the Inkabelo; their numbers are smaller, together making up about half of the total population. They are seen as offshoots from, or accretions to the Inkabelo, and they occupy territory which is ecologically less favoured, in the sense of less diversified, on the outskirts of the Inkabelo "heartland" with which three of them share a common border. These are the Randal (estimated population 1,000) to the north, who are "exclusively pastoral", the Elele (1,500) to the north-west, who "mostly cultivate and fish" and the Naritch (1,800) to the south-west, who "appear to have much the same economy as the Inkabelo". Further to the south-west, around the north-eastern shores of Lake Turkana, are the Inkoria (2,000) who "are mainly pastoralists but also fish and cultivate a little" (*Ibid.*:14) and who do not share a common boundary with the Inkabelo, being separated from them by the territory of the Narich (see also Almagor 1972b:191).

Although "the sections are not mutually dependent for their subsistence" (*loc.cit.*) there is clear evidence that, together, they form a regional system based upon the exploitation of complementary ecological zones. Randal make use of Inkabelo watering and grazing areas on the east bank of the Omo during the dry season, and some Inkabelo send their animals to graze on Randal territory between October and December (Almagor 1972b:199). Although the Elele are mainly agricultural, they do keep some stock and it seems that they are only able to do this by making use of Inkabelo grazing areas, much of their territory being covered by thick tsetse infested bush. Economic inter-dependence is most marked between the Inkabelo and Narich sections. When there is a poor flood the Narich need to make use of riverbank floodland belonging to the Inkabelo and the latter need to graze their animals in Narich territory in the dry season, because the areas available for this purpose on the flooded flats of the east bank is reduced. Economic co-operation between the Inkabelo and the Inkoria does not involve the direct use of each other's resources, which is as one would expect from their geographical separation, but the fact that their harvests come at different times leads to some exchange of sorghum between them. This presumably consists mainly of purchases of sorghum by the Inkoria from the agriculturally better endowed Inkabelo, using cattle and small stock. It seems likely that there is greater economic co-operation between the Inkoria and the Narich, whose territories border each other.

Population movements between the sections are not only seasonal, a point which is of particular importance to the topic of this paper. There is an inflow of population from the Randal to the Inkabelo sections through the "expulsion" (Almagor 1972b:193) of pregnant Randal girls, and there has been a southward movement of Elele into Inkabelo territory, associated with the lowering of the level of Lake Turkana since the late 1890s. This both uncovered a wider area for agricultural and pastoral use in the delta and reduced the agricultural potential of the Omo banks further upstream. Inkabelo and Narich may settle permanently in each other's territory, thereby changing, after the passage of "many years", their section affiliations. Long-term population movement between the Inkabelo and Inkoria sections are not described, but one imagines that they may occur indirectly, through the "intermediary" Narich section. Almagor places considerable emphasis on the institution of bond partnership as a mechanism for bringing about the short-term equalization of the human population and available natural resources. It may be that the key factor by which <u>long-term</u> adjustments in the size of sections are brought about is intermarriage.

> Marriage within the territorial section is subject to far greater restrictions than marriage outside it. Members of the same territorial section may only marry if they belong to the same moiety, but this rule does not apply when a couple belongs to different sections. A man may not marry a wife from the same clan in his own territorial section but he can marry a woman from a clan bearing the same name if she belongs to another territorial section. Inter-territorial section marriages are fairly common. Hence the primary tie linking members of the different territorial sections is one of affinity (Almagor 1972b:192).

The picture that emerges is of a system of contiguous local groups, the distinctive identities of which are based upon the occupation of more or less different ecological zones. Their common identity as Dassanetch is based not only on their sharing a common (Eastern Cushitic) language and various other social institutions (such as an age system) but also on seasonal economic interdependence and on long-term movements of population, mediated by inter-marriage, which seem to have led to a new inflow to the ecologically most favoured Omo delta region. This accords with the view the Dassanetch have of themselves as people "descended from a motley collection of ancestors who came to the Omo from 'far away placed beyond mountains and lakes'". (Almagor 1978:15). I shall return to the question of oral traditions of migration in the second part of this chapter. For the moment I only wish to underline the point that the Dassanetch are an economically heterogeneous collection of local groups between which, not withstanding their distinct territorial borders, there is a constant movement of population, both in the short and the long term. It is a picture which we see repeated when we consider the northern neighbours of the Dassanetch, the Nyangatom.

The Nyangatom

The Nyangatom are one of the "Karimojong cluster" of peoples and speak the same (Eastern Sudanic) language as the Turkana. They have been studied by Serge Tornay who has published a number of articles on various aspects of their social and economic organization (*e.g.* Tornay 1975, 1981, 1982). Unless otherwise stated the following information is taken from Tornay (1981).

There are three ecologically distinct areas of Nyangatom settlement, lying roughly on an east/west line, between the west bank of the Omo and the Moruankipi mountains in the Sudan. The largest concentration of population is in the central or Nakua area along the Kibish River, which here forms the boundary between Ethiopia and the Sudan. This concentration is explained both by the ecological diversity of the Nakua region itself and by its central location in relation to the other two areas of settlement, which further extends the range of resources available to its inhabitants. Tornay calls this the "pastoral region" and its inhabitants the "pastoral Nyangatom", to distinguish them from those who live permanently at the Omo and depend wholly on cultivation. It is among the pastoral Nyangatom that he did most of his work and just as Almagor's and Carr's accounts of the Dassanetch concentrate on the ecologically most diverse territory of the Inkabelo, so Tornay's account of the Nyangatom refers primarily to those based in the Nakua area (*Ibid.*:147).

The Kibish River provides permanent water and areas for flood and rain cultivation along its banks. During the wettest months of the year - approximately between March and June - cultivation and herding can be carried on from the same settlements close to the river, but from July to February there is sufficient grazing in the immediate vicinity of the river to keep only milch animals at the main settlements. The remaining animals are taken progressively further from the river by the young men until, at the height of the dry season (December/January), they are found one hundred or so kilometres to the west, at the foot of the Moruankipi mountains in the Sudan. In September, as the Omo flood recedes, there is a movement, predominantly of women and girls, from Kibish to the west bank of the Omo, where the recently inundated land is prepared for cultivation. Similar preparations also take place along the Kibish at this time, although the flood here is smaller and less reliable than at the Omo

(*Ibid.*:145). Tornay offers no estimate of Nyangatom stock wealth, nor of the size of the contribution made by agriculture to the diet of the "pastoral" Nyangatom. While it seems reasonable to suppose, however, that they depend more heavily on pastoral products than on grain to meet their total energy requirements - simply because their agricultural resources are limited and unreliable - it is evident that cultivation makes a vital contribution to the overall viability of their economy.

Around 1,000 Nyangatom live permanently at the Omo, where the tsetse-infested forest and bush makes cattle herding impossible but where there is a greater agricultural potential than at Kibish. The Omo flood is more extensive and reliable and in a particularly good year they are able to cultivate "swamps" (Almagors's flats) away from the immediate banks of the river (*Ibid.*:146). There are also, presumably, more extensive areas available for rain cultivation in the Omo forest than at Kibish. The existence of this small, permanent population of "agricultural Nyangatom" at the Omo is clearly important for those who are based at Kibish. Tornay speaks of "numerous exchanges" taking place between them, "based on kinship ties, alliances and contractual friendship" (*Ibid.*:146). Items exchanged include dried fish, honey, grain and tobacco from the Omo and meat, butter, hides and small stock from Kibish. It is presumably also the existence of these social ties which makes possible, or at least facilitates, the seasonal occupation of the Omo banks for flood cultivation by the Kibish people. Finally, it seems that the Omo Nyangatom represent a "sloughing off" of surplus population from the predominantly pastoral economy of Kibish since Tornay describes them as "Nyangatom who have lost their livestock" (*Ibid.*:141). There is also a long term movement of Nyangatom from the Kibish area to the Western "transhumance area" in the Sudan, where the bulk of the local population are Toposa. The Toposa and Nyangatom speak mutually intelligible languages and it seems likely that this movement, or drift, is mediated by inter-marriage. Tornay has little to say about it, except that it represents a "trend", partly brought about by "fear of the Dassanetch". Another factor may be population pressure on the fixed agricultural resources at Kibish and the Omo.

During the early 1970s, the Nyangatom were involved in a series of armed clashes with the Dassanetch and the Kara (a small agricultural group living on the east bank of the Omo), which resulted in their losing 400-500 people (around 10 percent of their total population) in a period of five years (Tornay 1979a:111). This represented a dramatic deterioration in Nyangatom-Dassanetch relations since the late 1960s when Almagor and Carr were doing their fieldwork. Almagor has nothing to say about these relations in his monograph, presumably because of his focus on the Inkabelo section, but notes that he "observed no active warfare" during his stay in the area. Carr writes that

> The Nyangatom and the west bank Dassanetch have lived closely for many years now, and although they rarely inter-marry, much economic and social interchange occurs; they also sometimes share a couple of settlement areas ... although the Nyangatom and Dassanetch have for the most part maintained friendly relations, there have been periodic hostile outbreaks (*e.g.* about 1948 and again in 1972)(Carr 1977:10).

When Tornay first arrived in the area, in 1970, Dassanetch and Nyangatom settlements were grouped together at Kibish, the Dassanetch (presumably of the Randal section) watering their cattle at Nyangatom water holes. The first observable signs of friction appeared in 1971, after a disastrously poor harvest had ushered in a period of drought and hunger unprecedented in living memory. By the following year relations had broken down entirely. The Dassanetch withdrew from Kibish and the killings began (Tornay 1979a:104).

The picture of Dassanetch-Nyangatom relations that emerges from this account is of lengthy periods of peaceful co-existence and economic co-operation (not, however, involving significant intermarriage), interspersed with shorter periods of all-out war, precipitated by extreme pressure on ecological resources. Relations between the Nyangatom and their northern neighbours, the Mursi, were also hostile during this period though, being separated by the Omo (the Mursi cultivate on the left bank, opposite Nyangatom cultivation areas), they are not in direct competition for the same resources and the conflict between them remains at the level of retaliatory killings, a few on either side (Tornay 1979a:105). At other times there appears to exist what might be called a watchful peace between Nyangatom and Mursi, with some economic exchange - for example of Mursi pots for grain - between individuals. These contacts are regular and close enough for some Mursi to have learned to understand (if not speak) Nyangatom and, presumably, *vice versa*. In general it seems that whereas the Nyangatom are under pressure from their southern neighbours, the Dassanetch, the Mursi are exerting pressure on their northern neighbours, the Bodi.

The Mursi

The Mursi number about 5,000 and live in an oblong of territory, clearly defined on the west by the Omo and on the east by its tributary, the Mago. They divide themselves into five main territorial sections, the boundaries of which may be thought of as running at right-angles to the Omo. These sections are, from north to south, Mara (the name of a river), Mako (another river), Biogolokare ("red-eyed cattle"), Ariholi ("white ox") and Gongulobibi ("big canoes"). Members of the three northern sections think of themselves as forming a larger unit, named Dola, in opposition to the two southern sections which are not linked by a common name. Since 1969, I have spent a total of about three years living with the Mursi, all but three months of this time in the Mara section, and I have never visited the extreme south of Mursiland.[6] Like Almagor, Carr and Tornay, therefore, I too have carried out most of my fieldwork amongst one group of Mursi whose economic resources and mode of subsistence are not necessarily typical of the society as a whole. Also, like these authors, I worked in an area which, because of its ecological diversity, supports a higher population than in the rest of Mursiland and allows this population to maintain a closer involvement in the pastoral activities that give the whole society its sense of cultural identity. The brief description[7] of subsistence activities that follows must therefore be seen as applying primarily to the Mara section, although I think it also applies, in all important respects, to the three northern sections as a whole.

There are three main subsistence activities: rain-fed cultivation, flood-retreat cultivation, and cattle herding. None of these is sufficient in itself, nor even in combination with the other two, to provide a regular, reliable subsistence, but each makes a vital contribution to the overall viability of the economy. Rain-fed cultivation takes place in clearings along the eastern fringe of the Omo bush belt. If there is a sufficiently heavy and prolonged fall of rain in March or early April, sorghum (the main crop) will ripen in ten weeks and will be ready for harvesting in twelve. There is no shortage of land potentially cultivable by this method, but the unreliability of the rainfall makes it likely that the harvest will be poor or non-existent at least one year in every three. Sorghum is also the main crop cultivated by means of flood-retreat cultivation. Planting takes place along the banks of the Omo as the flood recedes in September and October and the crop is harvested in November and December. This is much more reliable than rain-fed cultivation, since the size of the Omo is controlled by the heavy rains that fall over its highland catchment area, and not by the erratic and light local rainfall. But the potentially cultivable area is confined to small pockets and strips along the banks themselves, there being no flooded flats such as are found further south. Because of its relative reliability, however, flood cultivation provides a vitally important insurance against the failure of the main rain-fed crop.

Cattle are the most valued material possessions of the Mursi, as they are of the Dassanetch and Nyangatom but, in an objective sense, they are less "pastoral" than either of these groups. Having only about one head of cattle per person they would need at least ten times their present cattle wealth to subsist entirely on pastoral products (L.H. Brown 1973; Dahl and Hjort 1976) and I estimate that they depend on cultivation for about three-quarters of their subsistence needs. This still leaves an important contribution to be made by cattle to daily subsistence, particularly to that of young children and unmarried man, but cattle are particularly important to the Mursi as a form of insurance against crop failure. They provide this insurance not, of course, by being consumed directly but by being exchanged for grain - either in Mursiland itself or in the surrounding lowlands (where the localised rainfall may lead to wide variations in crop yields) or, when rainfall in the lowlands is universally poor, in highland villages to the east of the Omo.

I am not sure how to account for their relatively low stockwealth, although part of the explanation must be disease: not so much the more dramatic visitations of such diseases as anthrax and rinderpest, to which their herds are certainly subject but the continuous and growing problem of trypanosomiasis. There are reasons for thinking that the tsetse population becomes more numerous, and the species more dangerous to cattle, from south to north along the Omo. Carr (1977:88) notes that tsetse have migrated southwards along the Omo with the woodland forest advance in that direction, the species in question being the "forest tsetse", *Glossina fuscipes*, which is not, however, a good vector of trypanosomiasis. Along the east bank of the Omo in Mursiland, furthermore, there is a wedge-shaped belt of bushland thicket, narrowest in the south and extending to a width of about fifteen kms in the north, which has probably been developed by a combination of cultivation and overgrazing. This would have allowed entry to the more dangerous "thicket tsetse", *Glossina pallipides*, which is able to penetrate the wooded grasslands east of the Omo by adopting a linear distribution along the numerous seasonal rivers that, in Mursiland but not further south, flow westwards into the Omo (Nash 1969:51). Given the increasingly dangerous nature of this environment to cattle (middle-aged men say that they have "grown up with" the fly), the northern Mursi have only been able to maintain their commitment to a pastoral way of life by the close integration of pastoral and agricultural activities, which is made possible by the ecological diversity of their environment.

The essential difference between the three northern and the two southern sections is, I believe, that the latter (and particularly Gongulobibi) contain a large number of people who have few or no livestock and who therefore live almost exclusively by cultivation and fishing. The above description may therefore be said to apply not so much to the three northern sections, as I suggested earlier, as to the "pastoral Mursi", since these seasonal activities and movements are also engaged in by the "pastoral" members of the two southern sections. The existence of a group of "agricultural" Mursi in the south, where the spreading meander belt of the Omo provides much larger areas for flood cultivation than further north, has been one of the factors allowing the pastoral Mursi, at least two-thirds of whom are members of the three northern sections, to remain actively engaged in cattle herding. Grain from the south has always - or at least until the particularly severe conditions of the past fifteen years - been an important standby when the main harvest fails in the north. Equally, when there is a good rain-fed harvest and a poor flood, members of the southern sections may depend on grain from the north. Inter-section marriages are common and although there is a clear tendency to local endogamy, links of kinship and affinity provide a ready basis for economic co-operation and exchange between north and south.

Mara, with a population of around 2,000, is the largest section, but it is not the historical "centre" of Mursiland, as the Inkabelo section is for the Dassanetch. On the contrary, until the end of the last decade, it was the most recent section to have been formed. In 1979, a group of Mara people, looking for an area of better rainfall after a decade of drought and famine, occupied a new, uninhabited, area fifty miles west of the Omo in the Mago valley (Turton and Turton 1984). This migration has resulted in the formation of a new section, now about 1,000 strong, called Mako (the Mursi name for the River Mago, not to be confused with the other Mako section in Mursiland proper). Although offering the prospect of more reliable rainfed cultivation, the Mago valley is particularly dangerous to cattle, probably because of the presence of *Glossina morsitans*, a species of tsetse that is the most effective vector of trypanosomiasis. As a result, it seems unlikely that the members of the new Mako section will be able to keep an effective foothold in the pastoral economy. The migration may, therefore, be seen as a "sloughing off" process, which has reduced pressure on grazing and agricultural resources in the now numerically depleted Mara section. All this accords with Mursi oral tradition, according to which they entered their present territory from the west bank of the Omo and first occupied that part of it which now forms the two southern sections. This area is consequently thought of as the "stomach" of Mursiland and retains a ritual pre-eminence (most evident in age-set affairs) in relation to the northern sections, which have resulted from a "pioneering" (*cf.* Waller 1985:348-9) northward movement. I shall discuss the nature of this movement in more detail in the next section but must here place it briefly in the context of Mursi relations with two neighbouring groups, the Chai and Bodi.

The Chai (singular Chachi) speak the same language (one of the Didinga-Murle [Tucker and Bryan 1956] or Surma [Bender 1976b] group of languages) as the Mursi and live south and southwest of Maji, close to and probably on both sides of the border between Ethiopia and the Sudan. Mursi-Chai inter-marriage is frequent. Many Chai live in Mursiland with their affines and matrilateral kin, and many Mursi are acknowledged to have a Chachi parent or Chai grandparents. My impression - although I have no statistical evidence to back it up - is that there is a net flow of population into Mursiland from the more marginal (because ecologically less diversified) territory of the Chai. Such a movement would reflect the Mursi tradition that they entered their present territory from the west and it is also borne out by linguistic evidence since phonological differences between Mursi and Chachi suggest that the former has diverged from the latter. This demographic drift has led, I believe, to a growing population in northern Mursiland which has in turn brought the Mursi into competition with their northern neighbours, the Bodi, for pastoral and agricultural resources.

The Bodi number about 3,000 (Fukui 1979:49) and live east of the Omo and north of the Mara. Their language, although closely related to Mursi, is not mutually intelligible with it and the two groups do not inter-marry. Since their subsistence systems are broadly similar they may be said to occupy the same ecological niche, but Bodi country has more sources of permanent water (in addition, that is, to the Omo) and it is therefore better endowed with resources for both grazing and rain-fed agriculture. Mursi-Bodi relations, like those between Nyangatom and Dassanetch, alternate between lengthy periods of peaceful co-existence and shorter periods of all out war. During periods of peace, Mursi of the Mara section have close and regular contact with the southern Bodi. Mursi families may be found living in Bodi settlements on a seasonal or longer-term basis, although I have never come across Bodi families living in Mursi settlements. Similarly, while Mursi may water their cattle at Bodi watering points in the dry season, the opposite does not occur. This peaceful infiltration by Mursi into Bodi territory can quickly become an occasion for resentment and open aggression when environmental conditions deteriorate, which is what happened during the very serious drought of the early 1970s. Between 1971 and 1975, Mursi-Bodi relations were permanently hostile, with no peaceful contact between them. A "no man's land", approximately forty miles deep, opened up between them, across which small raiding parties went regularly to and fro, a favorite tactic being to lie in wait for potential victims beside a path or watering point. There was also at least one much bigger engagement early on in the hostilities, when a large war party of Bodi attacked the Mursi deep in the Omo bush and succeeded in getting away with a large number of cattle (Turton 1979a). After these hostilities had been brought to an end, by peacemaking ceremonies held in 1975, there was no visible difference in the location of the Mursi/Bodi boundary, and although conflict between these groups is clearly related to competition for scarce resources and although it is acknowledged by both sides that the Mursi have, historically, pushed northwards into Bodi territory, the military activity itself is not easily interpreted as a means of acquiring or defending territory (See Plate 6.1). I return to this point in the next section.

Movement, Warfare and Ethnicity

None of the peoples described above think of themselves as the original inhabitants of the territory they now occupy. Their myths of origin and oral traditions are essentially accounts of migrations which brought outsiders into new areas from which they either drove out the existing inhabitants or incorporated them into a new political unit.

This is particularly clear in the case of the Dassanetch who appear to be a fairly recent (*i.e.* since the early nineteenth century) amalgam resulting from the occupation of the Omo delta region by the ancestors of the present Inkabelo section. The latter place their homeland to the west of Lake Turkana from where there did indeed take place a migration during the early nineteenth century associated with both drought and Turkana expansion from the west (Sobania 1980:61-67). The Nyangatom say that they originated from Jie and Dodos country in northeastern Uganda, the Toposa being a western offshoot from the same area. Tornay also dates the arrival of the ancestors of the Nyangatom in the Omo valley to the early nineteenth century and notes that "it is probably Turkana expansion which has forced them to move northward" (1982:140). The Mursi say that, on entering their present territory from the west, they found it occupied by the ancestors of the present Bodi, cattle herding people like themselves, whom they proceeded to displace. But they place their own homeland, *Thaleb*, far to the south east, describing an anti-clockwise migration of five original clans who accumulated other groups on their journey. They describe the people from whom these five clans broke away as *Munubahuli*. (One of the first questions they asked me, when I began my fieldwork amongst them, was whether I had come across the descendants of these people on my journey to the Omo Valley.)

This tradition of a Mursi origin in the south-east is surprising, since all their presently observable cultural and linguistic affiliations are with people living to the west and north of them: the Mursi and Bodi are the easternmost representatives of the Didinga-Murle/Surma-speaking peoples who extend westwards to Murle country in the southern Sudan.

According to Ehret's analysis of the linguistic evidence, furthermore, the speakers of "Proto-Surma", from whom the Chai, Mursi and Bodi languages have developed, were living south and west of the Maji plateau five thousand years ago (1982). Since he also estimates that Mursi began diverging from Tirma (a dialect very similar to, if not identical with, Chai) around one thousand years ago, the split between the mutually unintelligible Mursi and Bodi must have occurred well before that.

> On the whole the Surma peoples have been involved in a remarkably restricted range of population movement over the past five Millennia. Initially centred probably along the west of the Maji highlands, the Surma territory was eventually extended sometime in about the second and/or first Millennium B.C. to include areas up the Omo River to the east of the highlands. Only the Didinga-Murle group since sometime in the last Millennium B.C. have expanded beyond the southwestern Ethiopian fringes (Ehret 1982:23).

Assuming that this interpretation of the evidence is broadly correct, we must conclude that Mursi speakers have been living in the Omo lowlands for at least a thousand years and that it was a movement of population from the west to the east bank of the Omo which was crucially responsible for the creation of the modern Mursi identity. Although the Mursi think of this movement as having occurred at a specific moment in time it is, in a sense, still going on through Chai immigration from the west. As for the tradition of a Mursi homeland to the south-east, whatever historical basis there is for this must lie too far in the past to be recoverable by presently available evidence.

If, as I presume, the distinctive identities of the Dassanetch, Nyangatom, and Mursi are the products rather than the causes of the movements described in their oral traditions, then these traditions are as much attempts to account for present political identities as they are about past events. Much remains of the important task, so ably begun by Sobania, Tornay, Ehret and others, of reconstructing past population movements in this area, but historical reconstruction can only go so far in helping us to understand processes of ethnic group formation. It can tell us that a particular group moved to a particular area at a certain time, and for certain reasons, and that, in this new area, linguistic and cultural differentiation, and the incorporation of the existing peoples, led to the creation of a new political unit. But it cannot tell us much about the details of this process - about, for example, the kind of movement involved. Was it a "soldier ant" migration or a gradual drift? And if the latter, what were the social mechanisms that made it possible? What role did warfare play in the occupation of new territory? What was the mechanism of exchange and domination by which peripheral groups were incorporated? By what means do societies whose "structure" is "process" (Waller 1985:351) or, to put it another way, for whom "existence" comes before "essence", maintain an illusion of permanence in the midst of movement and flux? Attempting to answer these questions is a task for contemporary ethnographic analysis, a task which is made that much easier if, as is still largely the case for the Lower Omo Valley, the processes involved have not been stopped in their tracks by the imposition of rigid administration boundaries.

I think we may tentatively distinguish at least three types of population movement that have played a part in the creation of ethnic identities in the Lower Omo. One is a concerted move by a group that breaks away, at a specific moment, from its parent group due to the pressure of some extreme event. Another is a gradual infiltration of one group by individual members of another, most likely through inter-marriage, resulting in a one-way net flow of population across a geographically stable ethnic boundary. A third is a gradual but concerted *de facto* occupation of territory claimed by another ethnic group, as a result of which the geographical location of the ethnic boundary between them is changed over time. For the sake of convenience I shall call these type A, B and C movements respectively. All these types tend, I think, to be lumped together, both in the oral traditions of the people themselves and in the reconstructions of historians, with greatest prominence being given to type A. Movements of this type are particularly memorable, because of their association with critical historical events, and visible because they take place over a relatively short time. Their attractiveness to historians is that, for the same reasons, they are at least potentially datable. Since these relatively sudden movements certainly do occur, furthermore, they provide a useful format in which the more diffuse, long-term and therefore relatively "unknowable" movements can be encapsulated in oral tradition.

If this last point is correct it complicates the task of historical reconstruction by making it more or less problematic whether a particular population movement, described in oral tradition as though it were of type A, actually did take this form. The task is less complicated, of course, if the time scale is short enough to allow external and independent corroboration of the oral historical account. A case in point is Sobania's discussion of the Dassanetch tradition of migration from a homeland to the west of Lake Turkana. The evidence he presents from both Dassanetch and Turkana oral tradition makes it plausible to suppose that this was indeed a type A movement that occurred in the early years of the nineteenth century following a period of warfare and (probably more important) drought. The Mursi account of their crossing to the west bank of the Omo may also have been a specific historical event, although I have so far been unable to find convincing external corroboration of it. Alternatively, it would be an encapsulation in type A form of a more gradual type C movement, since it is this kind of movement, I believe, which has taken them in recent years further and further into former Bodi territory.

But the Mursi do provide us with our best example from this area of a type A movement in their migration to the Mago Valley (Turton and Turton 1984). This occurred in 1979-1980, when a group from the Mara section deliberately set out to establish a new home for themselves in higher, better watered land, as a direct response to the unprecedented (in living memory) drought and hunger of the previous few years. The attractiveness of the new area, it should be noted, was its agricultural, not its pastoral potential. For although it offers better prospects for rain-fed cultivation than the Omo lowlands, the high tsetse challenge makes it quite unsuitable for cattle herding. The migrants, who now account for about half the former Mara section, are adopting a sedentary and wholly agricultural way of life, although they continue to resist the suggestion that they have given up their commitment to traditional Mursi pastoral values. The Mago Mursi are clearly on their way to acquiring a new ethnic identity as a result of their occupation of an ecological niche that they can only exploit effectively by giving up their foothold in the pastoral economy. Nor do they look upon the Mago valley as a temporary refuge from which they will return in better times to the lowlands, and to a pastoral way of life. Finally, they have moved to an area that, although unoccupied at the time of the migration, was vacated by its former inhabitants, the Bodi, about seventy years ago due to an outbreak of human sleeping sickness.

Once such a group of "pioneers" has successfully established itself in a new area, its members will be added to by the second type of movement - infiltration by individuals seeking access to new economic resources through inter-marriage. This process is well attested by Almagor's account of population movement between Dassanetch territorial sections - the main direction of these movements appearing to be towards the ecologically best endowed Inkabelo section (1972b:203). The movement of Chai into Mursiland is another example. So while type A and type B movements are both ecologically determined, the former is a "revolutionary" response to cataclysmic conditions and the latter a "normal" response to long-term or slowly changing differences in ecological conditions from one area to another. Type C movements, too, fall into the latter category but they differ from type B in that they are not the result of cumulative individual movements across a physically stable boundary. Rather, they are the result of the collective but gradual occupation by one group of another's territory, which causes the boundary between them to move, as it were, across country. It is tempting to describe this in terms of one group "pushing" the other, by force of arms, out of its territory, but the reality is more complex. Its association with periodic armed conflict is certainly another fact which distinguishes this kind of movement from the other two, so that discussion of it raises the general question of the relationship between warfare and population movements. The evidence from the Lower Omo Valley suggests that to see the appropriation by one group of the territory of another as a matter of military superiority would be a great oversimplification.

I shall give two examples of type C movements - of Dassanetch into Nyangatom territory and of Mursi into Bodi territory - and then suggest a tentative interpretation. Tornay considers that there has been taking place in recent years "a slow but certain territorial drift" of Nyangatom in a northerly direction.

> During the 1920s the main settlements of the Nyangatom were located at Leere near Kalam, the Ethiopian police post which is in Dassanetch territory. Nakua or Kibish was a grazing area, used for transhumance from which the Nyangatom, with the help of the Dassanetch, drove away the Turkana. The successive initiation places of the Elephants' age-set illustrates a continuous northward movement of the tribal centre. This centre, located today at Natikar (Kibish), has moved about 40 km northwards during the last fifty years (Tornay 1979a:115-116).

There is a ready explanation for this northward movement of the Nyangatom in the pressure from the Dassanetch for access to new grazing areas and dry season watering points (Almagor 1972b; Tornay 1979a:112-113), but, according to Tornay, it is more a matter of the Dassanetch filling a space left vacant by the Nyangatom than of territorial conquest by direct military action: "it should be emphasised that this move of the Nyangatom towards the north does not seem to be a consequence of Dassanetch hostility" (1979a:114). The fighting is not **followed** by the early occupation of new territory and is not seen to have such a purpose by the participants. During their engagements with the Nyangatom in the early 1970s, the Dassanetch do seem to have inflicted heavier casualties, both in absolute and relative terms, than they suffered themselves but their northern "push" towards Kibish was achieved through peaceful co-operation and co-residence with the Nyangatom over the previous twenty to thirty years (according to Carr there was another period of hostilities "about 1948" [1977:10]). This suggests that the significant fact is population pressure exerted by the Dassanetch (who outnumber the Nyangatom by a ratio of three to one) on Nyangatom resources along their common border. Their numerical superiority does not give the Dassanetch a specifically military advantage, except in the sense that the equalising of deaths on either side, towards which the tit-for-tat of raid and counter-raid seems consciously to aim, will always leave the Nyangatom relatively worse off. What, then, is the role of armed conflict in this kind of movement? The Mursi-Bodi case suggests that the real importance of periodic conflict is that it precipitates the legal ratification of an already achieved territorial advance.

The Mursi are also, without doubt, moving northwards into Bodi territory, a movement which is also accompanied by periodic wars - the most recent of which lasted from 1971 to 1975 (See Plate 6.1). The most obvious explanation of this movement is that the Mursi have "expanded" at the expense of the Bodi through force of arms, but this is not convincing. In this kind of guerilla warfare the Mursi can gain no particular military advantage from their numerical superiority over the Bodi. Each side has equal access to arms and ammunition and each is subject to more or less the same environmental constraints. It cannot be said that the Mursi are more "warlike" than the Bodi, in either their own estimation or that of the Bodi. Mursi pressure on Bodi resources is explained by the inflow of population to the three northern Mursi sections (Dola) which must therefore expand to exist; that is, they do not first exist and then expand; they are expansion. The role of warfare in this process is best revealed, I think, by concentrating not on the hostilities themselves but on the way they are brought to an end.[8]

Peacemaking between the Mursi and Bodi is accomplished by means of two successive ceremonies, one held by each side, at each of which a stock animal is killed in the presence of the other group's representatives. What really matters is not whether one side has lost more men than the other in the conflict but where these two ceremonies are held, since each side is supposed to hold its ceremony in its own territory. At the end of the last war, in 1975, the Mursi held their ceremony at Mara, which had been their *de facto* northern boundary for many years, but at the end of the previous war, in 1952, they held it twenty miles further south. Holding a peacemaking ceremony at a certain place is therefore a way of making (and having acknowledged by the other side's representatives) a claim to *de jure* ownership of territory which was formerly owned only in a *de facto* sense. In this case, it may be said that the "purpose" of the fighting is to give legal ratification to the territorial encroachment which had already taken place, peacefully, before the fighting started. Warfare is not a <u>means</u> of Mursi territorial advance, but part of the retrospective ritual legitimization of it.[9]

The northward movement of the Mursi is not, then, to be seen as a consequence of military success, due to their superior fighting qualities, tactics or strategy. To explain it we have to see it in a broader spatial and temporal context - not in terms of one group "pushing" another, but in terms of several groups and sub-groups which are all involved in, and indeed the products of, a structurally single population movement, going beyond each of them in space and time. The direction of this movement is towards higher, better watered land with greater agricultural potential and its underlying causes are therefore ecological. In this particular corner of the Omo Valley it shows up in the recent migration of Mursi to the Mago Valley (a type A movement), in an inflow of population to northern Mursiland through Chai/Mursi inter-marriage (a type B movement) and in the northward progression of the Mursi/Bodi boundary (a type C movement). We should see all these movements as part of a single process of which the separate identities of the groups involved are by-products. Today's Mursi (or, to be more accurate, today's Dola) are tomorrow's Bodi, and today's Bodi (like the Dola members who have moved "sideways" to the Mago Valley) are tomorrow's highland cultivators. Ethnic identity ("essence") is a product of population movement ("existence").

If, therefore, these groups, like the "subjects" of existentialist philosophy, "make themselves", we are led to ask by what means they maintain a sense of their own separateness and historical permanence. The Mursi case points to the importance of ritual here also for, if peace-making ceremonial defines the changing external boundary of the Mursi political unit, age grade ceremonial (by which local groups of age-mates are promoted from one age grade to another) periodically and retrospectively defines its changing internal divisions. The age organization, by bringing together space and time in a single ritual complex, helps to preserve an illusion of permanence in a society whose "essence" is movement. Age ceremonies define

> ...not only a cyclical series of temporal divisions of the population, based on the physiological aging of individuals, but also a linear series of spatial divisions, based on a continuous northward movement (Turton 1978:124).

As Waller has recently put it, in commenting on the Mursi case, "growth in space is expressed in terms of progress through time" (1985:369).[10]

The northward movement of the Mursi-Bodi, as of the Dassanetch-Nyangatom, boundary is associated with periods of military activity, lasting years rather than months, that must nevertheless be seen as interrupting the "normal" (because extending over longer periods) state of relations between groups. It is now time to look more closely at the nature of these military activities and to ask whether any significant distinctions emerge among the phenomena I have so far referred to by the general term "warfare". The best place to begin is with the people's own distinctions, as expressed in their linguistic categories.

The Dassanetch distinguish three types of armed conflict, according to degree of intensity, by the terms *nyasagsag, hol dim* and *nyakiryam*. These are translated by Almagor as "reciprocal raiding", "escalation", and "all out war" respectively.

> Raiding is typically a small scale, spontaneous and uncoordinated venture. In reciprocal raiding hostilities are governed by certain conventions, namely that the quantities of cattle looted should be reasonable, that casualties should be kept to a minimum ... that the frequency of raids should not be excessive and finally and most important, that each tribe may retaliate similarly. But even if some of the rules are broken... hostility need not escalate into full-scale warfare as long as the injured party receives compensation and is assured that the breach was an exception.... escalation results in a campaign which involves organised recruitment and strategic decision-making processes that extend beyond the limits of a certain locality , so that inter-tribal co-operation ceases and daily social life and economic routines are disrupted (Almagor 1979:122, 126-127).

"All-out-war" is not defined and, indeed, it is difficult to imagine how it might differ from "escalation" as this is defined here, except in degree. All three terms can probably be used to refer to the hostilities themselves - actual armed attacks and engagements - as well as to a state of affairs characterised by the occurrence of these hostilities. This is certainly so of the English word "war". We can speak of a person "going to war", meaning that he is going to take part in a certain kind of activity, and we can also speak of two countries being "in a state of war", meaning that a certain kind of activity characterises the relationship between them. What is common, of course, to all the activities we lump together under the term war in English is that they take place between autonomous political units, the separate political identities of which are partly constituted by these very activities. To put it another way, and speaking logically rather than chronologically, these units do not first "exist" and then go to war with each other. Since war is constitutive of political identity, it is not surprising that the same word should be used to refer both to "actions" and "states" (of affairs). What I want to suggest is that we will make more progress in our search for significant analytical distinctions by focussing on the context of inter-group relations in which warlike activities occur than on the warlike activities themselves. Let me try to illustrate this by returning to Almagor's definition of reciprocal raiding (*nyasagsag*).

This is not so much a definition of a particular kind of <u>activity</u> as of a particular <u>context</u> of inter-group relations - a context which requires that the activities be governed by certain conventions. Almagor is, in fact, describing relations between the Dassanetch and Nyangatom but I suspect that the Dassanetch also use the term *nyasagsag* to describe "small scale, spontaneous and unco-ordinated" raids that they might launch against such groups as the Turkana and Boran. I also suspect that, in this context, the conventional rules which are integral to Almagor's definition either do not apply at all or are less binding. The point about reciprocal raiding between Dassanetch and Nyangatom, as Almagor's account clearly shows, is that its occurrence is seen as a threat to cooperative relations outside and to social order (and therefore to the authority of the elders) inside the group. As for "escalation" between Dassanetch and Nyangatom, this results in a degree of disruption to "normal" social and subsistence activities that cannot be allowed to continue indefinitely. The important distinction which I believe emerges from this is between two kinds of inter-group relationships. In one, military activity represents a potential or actual disruption of "normal", that is peaceful, relations both inside and outside the group. In the other it represents no threat to external relations because these are always hostile and, so far from being a threat to internal order, it is carried out with the encouragement and blessing of the elders.

The same analysis can be applied to the Mursi. Their word *luha* can also be translated as "raid", in the sense of a "small scale, spontaneous and uncoordinated venture", the attack usually being made at night or in the early hours. A large, coordinated and daylight engagement is called *kaman*. The phrase *ba kaman* (*ba* = land/ground) means a state of relations in which raids and counter-raids of both types have become the norm. Mursi-Bodi relations are characterised, like Dassanetch-Nyangatom relations, on the one hand by periods of such intense military activity that normal life is severely (and in the long run unacceptably) restricted and, on the other hand, by longer periods of peaceful coexistence. The occasional *luha* may also occur between Mursi and Bodi during otherwise peaceful periods, but it is the very nature of such periods that these events are quickly damped down by the payment of compensation according to mutually well understood conventions. The difference between a period of peace and a period of war is not that no hostile activities take place during the former, but that they are always of the *luha* variety and they are quickly followed by the payment of compensation. In periods of war these conventions do not apply and large scale engagements of the *kaman* type occur. Both *luha* and *kaman* take place between the Mursi and Hamar, who live far to the southeast, beyond the Mago Valley, but in this case they are terminated neither by the payment of compensation nor by peacemaking ceremonies.

Based on these examples, then, my suggestion is that there is a distinction to be made between inter-group relations that are characterised by alternating periods of war and peace and inter-group relations in which armed conflict constitutes the sum total of interaction. Since, from a purely military point of view, the same activities are involved in both cases, one is led to ask what significance they have, depending on the context of inter-group relations in which they occur. Again, based on these examples and particularly the Mursi-Bodi case, which I know best, I would make the following suggestion. Military activity in the context of alternating periods of war and peace is part of a process by which the ethnic boundaries of groups that are in <u>actual</u> competition for the same natural resources, and therefore in close interaction, are shifted and ritually redefined over time. In the context of permanently hostile relations, military activity is a means by which groups which are in <u>potential</u> competition for the same resources maintain a respectful and geographical distance between themselves. Such groups are separated by an area of unoccupied land, the natural resources of which both can utilise for hunting, honey gathering, and perhaps also for occasional dry season pasturage. Concentration on the military activity itself - trying to distinguish, for example, on the basis of its intensity and the number of people involved, between warfare and raiding - could lead in the wrong direction and even up a blind alley.

Notes

1. She writes that stock raising is their "principal subsistence activity" and the "dominant production branch" (1977: 23;176).

2. Almagor puts the Dassanetch population at 15,000 and that of the Inkabelo section at 7,000 (1978:1, 15). Carr gives 18,000 for the group as a whole and "at least 6,000" for the Inkabelo (1977:9, 100).

3. Unless otherwise stated, all references in the remainder of this section are to Almagor (1978).

4. This was the case in 1984, a year of very poor local rains following an exceptionally high Omo flood, when people were travelling from as far a field as Turmi in Hamar country to the Omo to buy grain from the Dassanetch - a five day round trip to obtain, in some cases, "a couple of kilos" (Brian O'Toole, personal communication).

5. I find it difficult to follow Almagor's argument here, for two reasons. Firstly, if only adult males are slaughtered it is difficult to understand how this could effectively stabilize stock numbers, in the absence of other checks to growth such as disease. Secondly, if ritual slaughter is not consciously employed for this purpose by the Dassanetch, as one supposes it is not, it must be an unconscious adaptation, through natural selection, to environmental constraints. But this argument would seem implausible in view of the fairly recent origin of these constraints. I make this point with some reluctance because no one has contributed more than Almagor to the ethnography of the Lower Omo Valley.

6. Fieldwork was carried out in 1969-70, 1973-74, 1981, 1982, 1983 and 1985. I am grateful to the following bodies for their financial assistance: The Economic and Social Research Council of the United Kingdom; the Area Studies Committee of the University of Manchester; the Central Research Fund of the University of London; the Tweedie Exploration Fellowship Committee of the University of Edinburgh; and the Royal Geographical Society.

7. A fuller description may be found in Turton (1973, 1977).

8. For a fuller account of the argument presented here see Turton (1978, 1979a and 1979b).

9. Rappaport (1967:20) writes that warfare "seems to have defined the border of Tsembaga territory. The Tsembaga as a unit were distinguished from other units by their joint participation in the fighting that defined their borders. This *de facto* association of previously autonomous units then became a *de jure* structure through the synchronization of the rumbin rituals that follow the successful termination of hostilities."

10. It is interesting to note that Tornay uses the location of age-set ceremonies as an index of Nyangatom northward movement. "The successive initiation places of the Elephants' age-set illustrates a continuous northwards movement of the trail centre" (1979a:110).

7

Pastoral Orbits and Deadly Jousts: Factors in the Maasai Expansion

John G. Galaty

Introduction

By mid-nineteenth century, at the peak of their expansion, Maa-speaking peoples occupied East Africa's Rift Valley region from Lake Rudolph in the north to central Tanzania in the south. This enormous territory extended over an area of at least 60,000 square miles more than six hundred miles in length and from seventy-fve to two hundred miles in width. This remarkable expansion[1] occurred during the same period Maasai were refining their highly specialized form of cattle pastoralism and when their age-based social system was taking form. The question this chapter will address is how these three developments were related, to what extent their systems of specialized pastoralism and age organization enabled, resulted from or can help us to better understand the Maasai expansion process.

The history of the Maa/Maasai migration and expansion is too long and complex to enumerate here in detail. On one level, this history is a chronicle of conflict and violence, of groups victorious and groups annhilated, dispersed and assimilated. At a deeper level, these processes of conflict and expansion are manifestations of the evolution of Rift Valley economy and polity, not only of Maasai pastoral society but of a wider regional system of ethnic categories and subsistence forms, including foraging, hunting, agropastoralism and both irrigation and rain-fed cultivation. Maasai (and Maa) expansion was largely at the expense of other pastoralists, even other Maa-speaking groups. But specialized pastoralism, which was consolidated by Maasai as a form of resource allocation and use, a system of labor allocation and production, and a hierarchical pattern of social and economic value, evolved in reciprocal interaction not only with other forms of animal production but with the economic forms of non-pastoral neighbors. The evolution of pastoralism was thus only one part of a wider economic evolution, as the Rift Valley region experienced a "refiguration" towards more productive and specialized pursuits.

We will begin with an account of the stages by which the subdivision and expansion of Eastern Sudanic peoples led to the emergence of Maa-speakers pursuing highly specialized cattle pastoralism, with a complex form of age organization. The chapter will then examine more closely two social and economic processes associated today, and in the historical past, with assertive and specialized pastoralism (widening "pastoral orbits") and well-defined age-sets (age-oriented conflict and "deadly jousts"), in particular that practiced by the Maasai or by groups similar to them in organization. The aim of the chapter is to place ecological aspects of pastoral movement in cultural perspective, investigating through ethnographic analogy the political and economic pressures towards and methods of pastoral expansion experienced in the past.

Maa Expansion and the Evolution of Specialized Pastoralism

The Maasai represent the southernmost extension and highest degree of pastoral specialization of the Eastern Sudanic speaking peoples. Their history, and that of pastoralism in Eastern Africa, involves two dimensions: the first, which begins in the southern Sudan, concerns Eastern Sudanic differentiation and the southward movement of those Eastern Nilotes who developed into the Maa speakers; the second concerns the social and economic evolution of the Rift Valley region of Kenya and Tanzania which was influenced by their arrival and subsequent efflorescence. This early prehistory, beyond the reach of oral tradition, is accessible to us only through combining archaeological findings with historical linguistic reconstruction.

Pastoral Origins and Eastern Sudanic Expansion

Ehret (1982:391) suggests that the linguistic emergence and expansion of Eastern Sudanic peoples 6-7,000 years b.p. involved "the productive advantage of the shift to livestock raising." In the flowering of Eastern Sudanic pastoralism, between 5,500-6,500 b.p., key aspects of intensive cattle pastoralism such as milking and bleeding of animals probably originated and age organization, scarification and extraction of lower incisors (all to become Maasai cultural traits) may well have been developed (Ehret 1974:ii). The first evidence for pastoralism in East Africa proper, probably diffusing southward from the Sudan, appears around Lake Turkana around 5,000 b.p. There, remains of cattle and ovicaprins have been found, together with signs of fishing (David 1982:59) and, over the next two thousand years, signs of plains hunting (Ambrose 1984:227). This Neolithic pastoral (or more properly "pastoro-foraging") complex has been associated with Southern Cushites, who later migrated southward to inhabit the Southern Rift Valley in what is today Kenya and Tanzania.

In the Sudan, the groups ancestral to Western, Southern and Eastern Nilotes emerged after 4,000 b.p., the proto-Eastern Nilotes (ancestral to Maasai) moving just east of the Nile by 3,000 b.p. As the Eastern Nilotes moved southeastward, the Bari and subsequently the Teso-Turkana hived off from the proto-Lotuko-Maa (the latter shortly after 2,500 b.p.), the proto-Lotuko diverging from the Ongamo-Maa in the borderlands sometime after 2,000 b.p. (Vossen 1982:472-3).

Meanwhile, in the wake of neolithic Southern Cushitic herders, a "lowland" Eastern Cushitic presence emerged in the borderland between Ethiopia and Kenya around 3,000 b.p. which later (after 2,000 b.p.) exercised significant cultural influence on Eastern (and Southern) Nilotes prior to their southward migration (Vossen 1984: 474). Directly or indirectly, Maasai derived a number of culturally fundamental prohibitions from the Eastern Cushites, against hunting or eating game and against eating fowl or eggs; Maasai fish-eating taboos and the practice of circumcision and clitoridectomy may also have been acquired from them, or at a later date from Southern Cushites in the south (since these traits are more widely distributed in East Africa than can be explained by the limited Eastern Cushitic contact in the north)(Ehret 1974: 40-42).

For the same period, beginning around 3,000 b.p., three different (archaeological) cultural patterns that combine pastoralism with hunting have been found in or near the central Rift Valley region that later would become the core Maasai homeland. The first, patterned on Southern Nilotic Okiek or "Dorobo" adapations of the present day, involved both incipient pastoralism with (Mau) forest hunting and gathering (and some trade) and cattle pastoralism with plains hunting of medium to large game animals on the Rift Valley floor (Ambrose 1984:220, 223, 231-232). The second, associated with Southern Cushitic pastoralists from northern Kenya, involved the widespread occupation of open wooded grasslands from the Kenya Highlands through Northern Tanzania, the building of stone cairns, and the pursuit of intensive cattle pastoralism and plains hunting (*Ibid.*:227, 230). The third, even now associated with Southern Nilotic (primarily Kalenjin) speakers west of the Rift Valley, involves ovicaprid pastoralism and hunting of the smaller forest game by moorland herders, living in large settlements, and forest cultivators, occupying smaller, temporary sites.[2] The arrival of Southern Cushitic, and subsequently Southern Nilotic, pastoralist-hunters must have dramatically decreased the availability of savanna grasslands for exploitation by their hunting predecessors, who then either developed a more limited economy focused on the forest margins or adopted pastoralism (*Ibid.*:227). Spreading southward, Southern Cushitic savanna (pre-iron age) Neolithic pastoralists - most notably the present-day Iraqw - displaced click speakers (now represented only by the Hadtsa and Sandawe) and came to occupy the Southern Rift Valley by the beginning of the second millenium b.p.[3]

The regional economy of the Rift Valley neolithic must have been rich and complex, with various combinations of pastoralism and hunting - and later some form of grain cultivation - supporting numerous groups between whom material and symbolic exchanges occurred: savanna cattle pastoralism with plains hunting, Rift Valley savanna hunting with some cattle pastoralism, and sedentary Highland small-stock pastoralism with forest hunting. It seems clear that what Lamphear has termed the "old pastoralism" practiced in the Rift Valley region was relatively more sedentary and less specialized than would later be the case, and involved less intensive orbits of pasture use and more varied mixes of animal and crop husbandry and foraging (Lamphear 1985). The economic transformation that followed the entry of pastoralism into East Africa probably involved less sharp symbolic distinctions, in particular between hunting, cultivation and pastoralism, than would obtain following the arrival of the Eastern Nilotic Maa-speaking peoples (Galaty 1982).

The Early Maa and the Old Pastoralism

To what extent was the production of grain and iron associated with, or did it represent necessary conditions for, the evolution of relatively "pure", highly specialized cattle pastoralism in East Africa. We find the first evidence of Iron Age farmers for the period around 2,000 b.p., as the Highland Bantu, later to become the Kikuyu, Kamba, Sonjo or Chagga neighbors of Maasai, began their migrations into East Africa. Regardless of whether limited grain production was already practiced by preceding Southern Cushitic or Southern Nilotic populations, these more intensive highland farmers by serving as reliable partners in the livestock-grain trade may have made possible the practice of more specialized animal husbandry by pastoralists freed from the need to cultivate or forage for their necessary food supplements (Robertshaw and Collett 1983).

The transition to iron-age pastoralism began around 1,400 b.p. in the central Rift Valley, with stone and metal implements coexisting in pastoral technology for another thousand years (Robertshaw and Collett 1983:74; Bower and Nelson 1978:564).[4] It would appear that the Early Pastoral Iron Age in both the Sudan and East Africa was associated both with Nilotic expansion and the development of more intensive and highly specialized pastoralism (Oliver 1982:169). In the Rift Valley, this process is primarily associated with early Ongamo-Maa speakers, whose southward expansion may well have been facilitated by their prior acquisition of early iron technology from Central Sudanic peoples in the southern Sudan. Having diverged from the proto-Lotuko near the borderlands, the Ongamo-Maa interacted first with lowland Eastern Cushites in the north, from whom they may also have derived the institution of low status endogamous blacksmith "castes" (Ehret 1982:35), and subsequently with their Southern Nilotic predecessors in the Rift Valley. From a dispersion point which likely centered on Lake Baringo, the Maa split from the Ongamo (who moved directly to Mount Kilimanjaro) by 1,500 b.p., setting the stage for the Maa expansion (Vossen 1982:71; Ehret 1974:56).

For this period, Vossen observes that:

> ...the early Maa-speaking population, which was then basically a society of cattle and sheep-herders, perfected their nomadic mode of life to such a degree that for one time in their history one may be tempted to call their society the only purely pastoral among the Eastern Nilotes (Vossen 1982: 71).

This process of perfecting highly specialized, semi-nomadic pastoralism must have occurred in the Maa homeland between Lake Baringo and the Laikipia Plateau in the north and the Kaputie Plains east of the Rift Valley, with the lake basin in the center (Ehret 1971:53). Ehret suggests there must have been "early, widespread Maasaian settlement in the area" by 1,000 b.p. (*Ibid.*:54), a time when most cultural attributes associated with Maa social organization, specialized cattle pastoralism and iron technology must have already been acquired.

The Later Maasai and the New Pastoralism

Lamphear has suggested that the "new pastoralism", perfected around 500 years ago, involved the refinement of Late Iron Age technology, the acquisition and spread of more efficient, heat-resistant breeds of East African humped zebu cattle, and perhaps new forms of religious leadership (Lamphear 1985:20-21). In his view, the "old pastoralists" were Sirikwa, a "phenomenon" that may have included both Kalenjiin and early Maasai who participated in a highland-based mixed economy (*Ibid.*:34). The "early Maasai" who, their reconstructed vocabulary suggests, may have practiced both pastoralism and cultivation were "hardly identifiable with modern pastoral Maasai who eschew all cultivation" (Ehret 1971:75, 178). However, a remarkable Chinese record of an early visit to East Africa, written before 863 A.D., supports the presence of specialized pastoralism during the Early Pastoral Iron Age:

> The country of Po-pa-li is in the south-western sea. The people do not know how to grow grain and live on meat only. They are in the habit of sticking needles into the veins of cattle, thus drawing blood, which they drink raw, on having it mixed with milk (Hirth 1910:48).

On the basis of such evidence, it is reasonable to suppose that there were several gradations of specialized to agro-pastoralism being pursued by early Maasai groups, as there are today.

"Early Maasai" practicing agropastoralism may have been signified by the term *Il-umbwa*, by which Maasai refer both to the Southern Nilotic Kipsigis (Sirikwa?) and to the "earliest inhabitants" of Maasailand, who "looked just like Maasai but cultivated" (*eata 'n-gurman*)(Hollis 1905:280-81). Interestingly, Maasai in general (including the Maa-speaking Parakuyo) are called some variant of 'Lumbwa' by their southern neighbors in Tanzania.[5] It may be reasonable to hold that there was an "early Maasai" presence in the southern Rift Valley in close proximity to the earlier Southern Cushites and Southern Nilotes, all associated with the "old pastoralism". However, the nomenclature for Maasai in the west and north stems from the root *en-kop*, signifying 'land' or 'earth'.[6] The earliest written records of Maa speakers, from over a century ago, note that both Wakuafi and Masai "call themselves" *Iloikop* (Krapf 1867:358; des Avanchers 1859:164). Krapf observed that both the 'Kwavi' and Maasai:

> ...live entirely on milk, butter, honey and the meat of black cattle, goats and sheep, and on game which they hunt down; having great distaste for agriculture, believing that the nourishment afforded by cereals enfeebles, and is only suited to the despised tribes of the mountains (Krapf 1867:358-59).

Even today, the hunting/apiary Torrobo, many of whom are bilingual Maa speakers, call Maa-speaking pastoralists in general *'Iloikop'*. Thus, the term *'Iloikop'*, in all its variants, may well have signified not "old" but "new" Maa-speaking pastoralists (*cf.* Jacobs 1968; Lamphear 1985). If so, the "new" pastoralism should be associated primarily with the expansion of later ('frontier') Maa-speakers who were fully pastoral and had already developed the full cultural repertoire associated with Maasai today, initially at the expense of the "old pastoral" Lumbwa.

The later Maa segmentation and expansion out of the Central Rift Valley homeland occurred in three stages, of frontier expansion, internal segmentation and external amalgamation. The first process involved the creation of northern, western and southeastern Maa frontiers through the centrifugal movement out of the central Rift Valley, over a period of several hundred years, of groups who, despite having no closer genealogy one another than with core Maasai, have come to be collectively known as 'Iloikop'.[7] At the northern frontier, the initial 'Kore' expansion followed the split of the "northern Maa" Samburu-Chamus from the pre-Maasai nucleus by the end of the sixteenth century. The Samburu subsequently expanded north and east of the Cherangany Hills in the Baringo Basin (Vossen 1977:214; 1982:74)[8], while the Chamus inhabited the shores of Lake Baringo. In the early nineteenth century, the Chamus hived off (linguistically) from the Samburu, who were subseqeuently expelled with their camel-keeping Rendille allies from west of Lake Turkana by the Turkana. The Samburu, successively defeated by the Ilosegelai and Turkana, later (*c.* 1840) moved out of the Baringo Basin altogether (Anderson 1981:5), moving to the El Barta plains and the region north of Leroghi, where they reportedly had to dislodge the Boran before coming to dominate this 'heartland' (Sobania 1980:82-83, 88-89).

The Laikipiak, forming a branch of "Central Maa" (Heine and Vossen 1979), were the next Maa-speakers to differentiate from the Maa nucleus. A virtual federation of "weak pastoral groups", many of whom are no more than mythical names from the oral tradition (perhaps of residual "old pastoralists"), the Laikipiak came to dominate the Laikipia Plateau (Waller 1978:148-50). The *'Kore'*, as the Samburu and Laikipia were known by their neigbors, dominated northern Kenya, their friends the Rendille, partners in trade the Meru and Dassanetch, enemies the Turkana and Boran.

In western Kenya, local traditions of Maa-speaking *'Kwabuk'* (probably Uasin Gishu and Losegelai, and perhaps Siria) assert that they were instrumental in the defeat and dispersion of the Sirikwa of the Uasin Gishu Plateau (Weatherby 1967:137). Other widespread traditions of Maasai and *'Kwavi'* raiding and intimidation of such western Kenyan groups as Bukusu, Gisu, Elgeyo, Kipsigis, Nandi, Gusii and Luo during the seventeenth and eighteenth centuries doubtless refer to the same Maa groups. Maasai settlements, presumably of ancestral Siria, were present in South Nyanza when the Luo moved southward in the seventeenth century (Ogot 1967:189) and in the Nyando Valley near the Gusii at the end of the eighteenth century (Ochieng 1975:94), and there are reports of Maasai harassing the Kuria in the 19th century (Ogot *op. cit.*:196). Uasin Gishu Maasai were probably instrumental in dividing the Kipsigis from the Nandi (Ochieng 1975:62) and represented the major force inhibiting Nandi expansion until the nineteenth century (Walters 1970:22).[9]

The third great divergence from the Maa nucleus was that of Iloogolala, who inhabited much of the southern Rift Valley and surrounding plateaux from the seventeenth century (Fosbrooke 1948:5; Jacobs 1971:83). It would appear that the southern Maa frontier was constituted by social elements identified by four names, Iloogolala, Ilumbwa, Parakuyo, and Enkang Lema, the latter associated with the area just north of Kilimanjaro and near Moshi (Krapf 1854:5). Since Parakuyo were and are called both Ilumbwa and Iloogolala, who were equally associated with well and dam systems, it is likely that progressive and relatively peaceful amalgamation of these diverse groups occurred during their southward movement, in response to the subsequent expansion of the nuclear Maasai.

No clear-cut linguistic duality underlies the differentiation of the 'core' and the 'peripheral' Maa peoples. The frontier process involved centrifugal migrations, northward, westward, and southeastward, out of the Maa nucleus onto the plateaux adjacent to the Central Rift Valley heartland by practitioners of a "new", more specialized form of pastoralism. These more peripheral 'frontier' Maa came to occupy a common position vis-a-vis the nuclear groups, as culturally and politically 'other' to the those who through a subsequent process of fission and expansion would become the Maasai.

However, the frontier groups themselves evolved through this process, assimilating and accomodating themselves to their predecessors and neighbors, developing pastoral techniques and forms of social life which distinguished them from subsequent Maasai. Occupying plateaux adjacent to the narrowly delimited Rift Valley, they tended to expand laterally, occupying relatively greater areas than did the average central Maasai sections. Also, they were characterized by more intimate forms of contact with non-Maasai groups. The close relation between Samburu and Rendille led to the emergence of the interstitial, bilingual Ariaal, who practice a dual camel/cattle-economy (Spencer 1973; Fratkin 1987). In the nineteenth century, Uasin Gishu developed close relations with Abaluyia groups, who welcomed many as refugees after their defeat by the Purko. And Parakuyo, widely dispersed in Tanzania, live in close, almost symbiotic, relation to cultivators, occupying valleys proximal to fertile hills, engaging in a regional division of labor and trade; indeed, many Parakuyo, though themselves still specialized in animal husbandry, have developed cultivated fields with the labor of agricultural neighbors and today live as minorities in agricultural villages (Beidelman 1963; Rigby 1983; Galaty 1988). Distinct from these peripheral pastoral groups are Maasai sedentary agropastoralists, the Arusha, Kurrman, and Chamus, each of whom is closely linked in history both with peripheral Maa and with cultivating neighbors. The term *Iloikop* may represent either a 'momento' of the past commonality of all later Maa speakers, *vis-a-vis* the southern 'Lumbwa', or a 'sign' of the common experience of frontier expansion. In the latter case, the development by some peripheral Maa groups of patterns of social dispersion and complementary linkages with their neighbors may have led to them being perceived in similar terms by the incipient nuclear or central Maasai, whose expansion would lead to significant conflict with their 'frontier' Maa predecessors.

The Segmentation and Amalgamation of the Central Maasai

Today, the Maasai are divided into numerous autonomous political sections (*Iloshon*) that in the past were affiliated with larger sectional alliances, often identified with their most prominent section. The four major sectional alliances - the Kisongo, Loita, Kaputie and Purko clusters - derived from periods of subdivision and expansion within and out of the Maasai nuclear region, processes which often brought them into conflict with the peripheral 'frontier' groups (See Figure 7.1).

The Kisongo were the first to emerge from the Maasai core, moving to the area west of Mount Meru in northern Tanzania called by their name, the related Sighirari moving to the rich Sanja corridor between Mount Kilimanjaro and Mount Meru. Maasai state that as late as mid-nineteenth century Maasai and 'Kwavi' (or Iloogolala) were peacefully intermingled. Next to emerge were the Purko, associated with the Elementeita-Nakuru lake basin and the adjacent escarpments of the Rift Valley. The Kisongo and Purko came to represent the southern and northern vanguards of the central Maasai, spearheading subsequent expansion and serving as forces of adhesion for later processes of pastoral amalagamation.

Around 1750, before the period of expansion and intense conflict began, the political configuration of the numerous Maasai groups must have included the following: a nucleus of (core) groups in the central Rift Valley, an outer core of groups less closely related to one another than each was to several core sections, two expanding vanguard groups

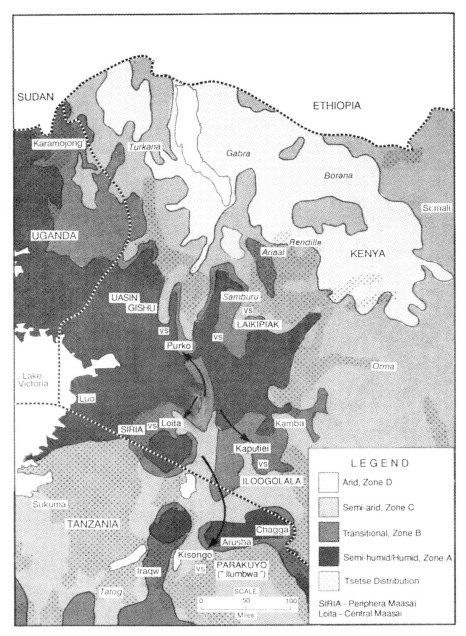

FIGURE 7.1 Rift Valley Ecology and the Expansion of the Central Maasai [*Source*: After OAU (1973) and Pratt and Gwynn (1977)].

PLATE 1.1   The African Humped Zebu, with Maasai Herd-owner

PLATE 1.2   The African Dromedary, Loaded by Gabra Women at a Well

PLATE 1.3   Maasai Meeting in Savanna Landscape

PLATE 1.4   A Tuareg Salt Caravan in Niger

PLATE 2.1   Plow Oxen Near a Tswana Settlement

PLATE 3.1   A Herd of Long-horned Ankole Cattle

PLATE 5.1   Turkana Cattle Watering at Lake Turkana

PLATE 5.2 El Molo with Trade Goods in Eastern Lake Turkana

PLATE 5.3 A Turkana Family

PLATE 6.1   A Speaker Addressing a Meeting in Mursiland during the 1974 Mursi-Bodi War

PLATE 7.1   A Maasai Herder and Herd in Kenya

PLATE 7.2   Maasai Murran with Girls, upon Returning from a Meat Camp

PLATE 7.3   Maasai Murran at the 1975 Ilodikilani *Eunoto* Ceremony

PLATE 8.1　A Moorish Sheikh

PLATE 9.1　Tuareg Sword Dancer in Niger

PLATE 9.2　Fulbe Boys at a Well in Niger

PLATE 10.1   San Hunters in Botswana

PLATE 10.2   San Women and Children in Botswana

projecting south and north in an inner periphery in the process of amalgamating other Maasai, and an outer periphery of frontier groups previously discussed.[10] It is impossible to reconstruct the processes of movement, fission and fusion that accompanied the creation of Maasai sections, but it would appear (by distribution of clans and sub-clans) that sections were in part constituted out of the residues of older groupings (perhaps affiliates of the "old pastoralism"), of peripheral sections, or of groups from the "old Maa" or proto-Maasai core, which assumed the form of descent groups when fragmented and reassimilated.

There were four major fronts, each associated with a sectional alliance, involved in the Maasai expansion, which began at a time the frontier wave was spent. It would appear that the peripheral groups were rebounding from the political and ecological limits of the rangelands at the same time the nuclear Maasai were initiated their own wave of expansion. The ensuing conflict created the systematic chaos we associate with this period of Maasai history.

Jacobs proposes that the Loita expanded from the Rift Valley up the western escarpment to the Loita highlands around 1800, expelling the Iloogolala (Jacobs 1972:83) and pushing the Siria back to the Mara river from the Loita Plains. However, it is reported that Loita expansion into the crater highlands of Tanzania stimulated westward migration of small Bantu hunter-cultivators in mid-eighteenth century (Anacleti 1977). In effect, southwestern frontier Maa were realigned within a loose Loita confederation (which included Siria, Laitayok, Salei and Serenget)(Arhem 1985) as the center moved outward to absorb the periphery.

Krapf observed that "the main strength of the Wakuafi is concentrated...in a country called Kaputie" (1854:9), where the Kaputie Maasai alliance encountered the frontier Iloogolala (*i.e.* 'Kwavi'). Waller reports that there was intermarriage and peaceful relations between the Kaputie and Iloogolala before the former seized control of the Athi river and plains (1978:138). The Matapato, in alliance with the Lodokilani, both allies of Kaputie, drove the Iloogolala out of areas south of the Kapiti Plains that the former now inhabit. And the Loitokitok, a sub-section of Kisongo, drove the Iloogolala out of Amboseli in a "decisive battle" (Western 1983:19). Krapf's informant reported that Enkang' Lema (apparently a sub-section of or allied with Iloogolala), who were "nearly annhilated by the wild Masai", fled to Taveta and to the Pangani River to join the "Barrabuyu" (*i.e.* Parakuyo)(Krapf 1854:4-5). The alliance of the Kaputie, Matapato and Lodokilani, with ties to Loitokitok Kisongo, was forged during the southeastern expansion, during which they (especially Kaputie) assimilated many Iloogolala, others fleeing southward to regroup with, or as, the Parakuyo, who progressively absorbed and became identified with Ilumbwa in southern Maasailand.

Southern Maasailand was dominated in the eighteenth century by the 'Kwavi' (*i.e.* Iloogolala and the Parakuyo), but they were systematically displaced by the Kisongo in the nineteenth century in a series of encounters recalled according to the chronology of Maasai age-sets. In the age of Merishari (*c.* 1811-25)[11], they took the Lake Manyara region from the Southern Nilotic Tatog, and in subsequent ages occupied Engaruka (Kidotu, 1825-39) and the Ngorongoro Crater region (Twati, 1839-53 and Nyangusi I, 1853-67). During the age of Kidoto, Maasai seized the wells and swamps of Naberera and Losogonoi from the 'Kwavi' (Parakuyo), with whom they had previously shared these critical resources. The Kisongo then occupied the right bank of the Pangani and Kibaya (the age of Twati), they clashed with the Nguu and Gogo beyond the southern Maasai frontier (the age of Nyangusi I), and took Talamai and Kiteto in the far south (the age of Laimer, *c.* 1867-81)(Fosbrooke 1948:4-5; 1956:193-95). The Parakuyo were either absorbed by the Kisongo or driven into districts adjacent to the Maasai plains where they have flourished in this century (Rigby 1975), some migrating during the last two decades to southern Tanzania and over the border into northern Zambia, now the southern frontier of Maa speakers (Galaty 1988).

In the north, there were "three successive supremacies" in the nineteenth century, by the Uasin Gishu, Laikipiak and Purko (Weatherby 1967:133). The Uasin Gishu dominated the region west of the Rift Valley before 1840, when they were attacked and defeated by the Laikipiak (Weatherby 1967), perhaps as part of a longer term conflict between Laikipiak and Losegelai, who were aligned with the Uasin Gishu (Waller 1978:151; Sobania 1980:82). The Losegeli were defeated and dispersed by a Purko alliance (known as the 'Enaiposha' Maasai) in the late 1840s (Walters 1970:24) or perhaps a decade or two later (Jacobs 1965:68). Just prior to 1870 (the age of Nyangusi I), the Purko, in alliance with the Laikipiak, decimated the Uasin Gishu, in Thomson's words, "left not a man in the entire land" (Thomson 1885:243). Some Uasin Gishu refugees were absorbed by the Purko while others settled among the Nandi, the Chamus or the Baluyia, whom they served as mercenaries. Uasin Gishu refugees were later moved to Eldama Ravine by the British colonial government and finally to the Trans-Mara where they and their kinsmen, the Moitanik, now live in uneasy proximity to the Siria.

The Laikipiak, who had gained ascendency over the entire Laikipia plateau, apparently "withdrew" from the north in the mid-1870s, "ruled" the Rift Valley at the beginning of the age of Peles (*c.* 1867-81), before coming into conflict with and initially prevailing over the Purko alliance (Sobania 1980:136; Galaty mn). But in the mid-1870s, the Laikipiak were utterly defeated and dispersed by the Left-Hand of the Ilpeles age-set, called Ilaitete or Laimer[12], in a diverse coalition of all four major Maasai alliances (Purko, Kisongo, Loita, and Kaputie) (Thomson 1885:242-43; Jacobs 1965:74-75) forged through the orders of the famous Maasai Oloiboni Mbatiany. The Purko chiefly benefited from this victory, as they subsequently absorbed countless Laikipiak and assumed hegemony over much of the Laikipiak plateau and the northern Rift Valley (Fosbrooke 1956:27). The Purko became the "terror of the northwest" during the age of Iltalala (1881-1896)(Weatherby 1967:141), their power only checked by the subsequent rinderpest and smallpox epidemics of 1889-90 and the onset of British colonialism.

The Maasai expansion resulted in the decimation of virtually all 'frontier' Maa, with the exception of the Samburu in the north and the Parakuyo, who regrouped in the south. During that process, loose alliances were forged around the four strongest Maasai sections, generating the social and political affinities which characterize Maasai society today.

Scenarios of Expansion

In this account, the Maa expansion appears coterminous with a chronology of progressive social differentiation, of a Sudanic people into Eastern Sudanic, Nilotic, Eastern Nilotic, Lotuko-Maa, Ongamo-Maa, Maa, nuclear Maasai, and finally into the constituent sections of the Maasai. 'Segmentation' follows a certain demographic and political logic: the systematic 'fissioning' of social groups followed by their 'fusion' of diverse fragments, producing an emergent order of units roughly balanced through 'complementary opposition' (Sahlins 1964). It is clear that migration and spatial expansion are factors in social differentiation, encouraging the emergence of distinctive linguistic and cultural forms that then in turn establish, signal and reinforce separate identities. However, since more groups wither or are assimilated by others than proliferate and expand, as have the Eastern Sudanic peoples in one epoch and the Maasai in another, differentiation and expansion seems more the exception than the rule. But under what conditions is this process stimulated or even accelerated?

Seen as a dramatic history of characters and scenarios, the Maasai expansion was a prolonged enactment of human aims and motives, shaped by strategies and judgements performed in scenes of enterprise and frustration, ambition and challenge, desperation and conflict, thematically both tragedy and romance. Based on the ethnographic record, two scenarios - of pastoral movement and age set conflict - appear to occur and recur, acted out separately or as successive stages in cycles of encounter and strife, encroachment and expansion.[13] The first process derives from Maasai pursuit of specialized arid-land pastoralism, the second from their participation in a highly elaborated system of age organization; while both of these institutionalized processes are widespread in pastoral eastern Africa, their refinement has been associated with the emergence and southward migration of the Maa peoples and thus are pertinent to the explanation of their expansion.

Expanding Orbits of Pastoralism

The manifest aim of pastoral mobility is to gain competitive access to pasture, water and mineral resources, made scarce through both routine and exceptional episodes of aridity in the pastoral zone. Indeed, pastoralism has been seen by some as an intrinsically expansionist mode of life (Anderson 1974). From a distant perspective and in the long range, the flow of pastoralists and their animals along the dry grasslands of Asia and Africa appears to be a response to ecological factors intrinisic to extensive arid-land animal husbandry: short or long-term imbalances between herd needs and limited water and pasture, brought on by immediate pressures of dry-season or drought. The very origins of pastoralism have been attributed to a prolonged period of aridity in the Saharan and Sudanic zone, making dependence on livestock and mobility necessary. In the short term, the nineteenth century Maasai-Iloikop wars may have been precipitated by competition over the permanent water sources and the more abundant pastures of the central Rift Valley and the wells of the southern Maasai plains (Jacobs 1968; Low 1963:303), a point lent historical weight by the concurrence of warfare with drought, epidemic and plague (Bernsten 1973:119-20). However, it has been pointed out that, from an ecological perspective, expansion can be deduced from "either shortage or superfluity", each of which "could as easily eventuate in foreign aggression, either in search of new cattle, or in search of new pastures" (Low 1963). Among the Nuer, as among the Maasai, cattle raiding is generally associated not with "days of hunger" but with plenty (Evans-Pritchard 1940).[14] 'Abundance theories', in contrast to the more familiar 'scarcity theories', evoke "expanding populations which had a major need for new pastures" (van Zwanenberg 1975:91).

Such general ecological explanations, which seem to account for even contradictory situations, may gain greater credibility when related to historical circumstances or to actual judgements and predicaments of local actors. Movements of people and ripples of culture alike can be usefully situated in the context of the daily and seasonal movements of herds and households in cycles of nomadic and semi-nomadic herding. Households represent the most convincing units of economic action for

Maasai, since the family (*Ol-marei*) is the stock-holding group, with responsibility for allocating labour to the care of domestic animals and rights in the consumption of livestock products. But domestic units function within an ever-widening circle of social and economic relations defined by higher levels of political inclusion. Several families congregate to form a homestead (*Enk-ang'*, lit. 'our place'), within which coordinated herding, labour sharing and food redistribution occurs. The homesteads of a given 'neighbourhood' (*En-kutoto*, lit. 'corner'), within which a political council may be formed, collaborate in allocating local resources, in providing for local defense, in scheduling access to watering points, and in organizing themselves for higher-order meetings, rituals, and combat. In most sections, neighbourhoods are associated with specific sub-sections or locations, within which a corporate age-group (*E-sirit*) is organized and its age-set village (*E-manyatta*) is formed. These serve as loci of influence in allocating, regulating and defending such essential pastoral resources as permanent water sources, salt deposits and dry-season pastures.

Within families, key decisions are made about two processes critical to pastoral production: livestock exchange and nomadic movement. Exchanges begin between houses and families, but their effects - in providing concrete and symbolic form to social ties - are felt within homesteads, neighbourhoods, locations and sections (*Il-oshon*). Exchange leads to the diversification of animal holdings, the consolidating of access to alternative areas of pasturage, and the establishment of networks of social relations marked by flows of people, animals and goods. All types of exchange, including marriage, tend to occur within the section, but some links between allied sections also occur.

In addition to daily herding movements, domestic households conventionally oscillate their residence between wet and dry-season pasture areas, and given the occurrence of two wet and two dry seasons in the year in a bipolar rainfall system, this usually involves at least four moves per year. But the main cattle herd often splits off from the main household several times a year, first to benefit from flushes of grass early in the rains or when showers break the monotony of the dry season, and second to move to distant and isolated highland pastures or to remote grazing in the height of the dry season when home pastures are exhausted.

Routine seasonal moves usually occur within locations or sub-sections. In Keekonyokie section, many inhabitants of Kaputie sub-section (not to be confused with the adjacent Kaputie section) spend the wet season in the table-land pastures behind the Ngong Hills, and move cattle to the top of the escarpment in the height of the dry season.

Inhabitants of Ewuaso location are concentrated near the Ewuaso oon Kedong'i river for the dry season, but move southward into the drier, lower plains of the Rift Valley with the wet season, or onto the sides of the rich but waterless Mount Suswa. Before the Maasai Move of 1905, when the region was vacated by Maasai in favor of British settlement, Keekonyokie occupied the Kinangop Plateau on the south-west slope of the Aberdare Mountains during the hot, dry season (January-March), moving down to the Naivasha plains with the wet season (April-June), where the waters of the lake were available, then using the Kinangop or the Ewuaso region during the cold, dry season (July-September), returning to the Rift Valley plains for the warmer wet season (November-December). But, often, as the dry season advances and grass diminishes, herding orbits become distended and reach beyond the security of the section, as herders desperately drive their herds farther than usual before turning home, or shift to more fertile swamps or grasslands along water courses, where they may come into contact with determined husbandmen from other sections. In this way, members of different sections come into contact with one another, in interstitial zones between home pastures, in regions of critical recourse, where water sources engender unseasonal growth of grass, in distant pastures after localized rains break the dry season, or around long-established water sources to which herds retreat with prolonged drought.

Numerous accounts of intersectional mingling emphasize that herders from diverse sections often congregated without conflict. Sectional alliances also define channels of herding cooperation and access to pasture outside of one's proper section, such as the joint use of Lake Naivasha by Keekonyokie, Damat, and Dalalekutuk sections, a union defining their collective identity as *Enaiposha*. In recent years, Kisongo have been granted by Kaputie use of a river in their territory, signalling cooperation between two related alliances. But sections from alien alliances, and across the center/periphery divide, also were known to mingle peacefully. The Kaputie inhabited the Kapiti Plains together with Iloogolala, and Kisongo jointly used the wells and pastures of the Maasai Plains with 'Kwavi' or Parakuyo. During certain periods, Samburu and Laikipiak lived closely together, the latter also using the waters of the Rift Valley with the Purko. Today, the great Wambere and Usangu swamps in Tanzania are occupied by several pastoral groups, who converge on these final refuges at the height of the dry season (Galaty 1988).

However, in historical perspective, we can see many of these periods of peaceful intercalation of pastoralists as precursor to conflict and preparatory to expansion. And when conflict occurred, it invariable pitted those sections against one another which lacked histories of ritual cooperation and reciprocity, an informal segmentary logic shaping patterns of alliance. Sites of contemporary conflict are well-known and may have witnessed struggle in past epochs. The Ewuaso Ng'iro plains between the Purko and Lodokilani and the Olkejuado River and swamps near the Maparasha Hills between Matapato and Dalalekutuk experience perennial competition today, and we know were loci of struggle between Maasai and Iloogolala. The Kisongo eventually permeated and pushed aside the Parakuyo on the Maasai plains and to the north the Samburu and to the south the Purko, with other allies, ultimately met and decimated the Laikipiak. Even Kisongo and Kaputie, faced with drought and land tenure conflicts (Galaty 1980), clashed over water sources as recently as 1987.

Essential pastoral resources are usually found within the section, or, rather, the sectional territory has come to be defined over time in terms of resources required. In the best of times, these regions overlapped (and today overlap, though land adjudication increasingly eliminates ambiguity), but the parcelling out of rights in water and pasture was in part reckoned according to structural relationships and in part according to power. Herd and household movements tend to occur within a pattern of political relationships, manifested in action and discourse, by which shared exigencies are defined as cooperative, as when Lodokilani and Matapato exchange herders, or competitive, as when Lodokilani and Purko clash (Galaty 1981), or successively cooperative and competitive, as recently between Kisongo and Kaputie.

Most instances just cited are cases of friction at the margin of herding orbits, where members of a more assertive section penetrate the peripheral pastures of another section at the normal extreme of their march, gain implicit rights in those pastures through continued, and often peaceful, use, and finally conflict with and in some cases gain sufficient muster to expel their hosts. Similar processes also occur at the margins of forests and cultivated land, where farmers are inhibited from extending the range of their grazing and tilling. A somewhat different process occurs when pressure leads young herders to pursue long-distance moves to remote and verdant regions, where they often intermingle with other pastoral pioneers, exchanging security for space. Such a site exists today in the Usangu Plains, the southernmost reach of the semi-arid East African corridor, peopled by Parakuyo, Sukuma and Tatog pastoralists and agro-pastoralists (Galaty 1988). The central Rift Valley, between Lakes Baringo and Nakuru, and the southern Rift Valley, in the col between Mount Meru and the Mbulu Highlands, represent locales of pastoral migration and admixture, where diversity was forged into the Maa identity through the events previously described.

Deadly Jousts: Age-set Combat and Expansion

The processes of movement and conflict associated with pastoralism might be called 'economic expansion', since it involves movement to appropriate pastoral resources. A related but conceptually distinct process might be called 'political expansion', which results from conflict engendered by competition between rival age-groups divisions. Although some of the most mortal Maasai combat has occurred in the context of pastoral deprivation, 'need' as a motive rests on an edifice of pride, honour, jealousy and scorn engendered by the structure and ethos of age-sets. Related characteristics of self-reliance and assertiveness have been attributed to herding experience, engrained in the 'pastoral personality' and codified in pastoral culture (Anderson 1974; Edgerton 1971).   Reference has been made to Maasai "qualities of aggressive manliness and individual independence" (Van Zwanenberg 1975:91), and the Maa-speaking Iloikop have been seen as "especially bellicose peoples", "short-tempered and tempestuous" (Jacobs 1978:9)[15]; others speak of the "warlike passions" of the Maasai and their "addiction to the practice of warfare" (Low 1963:303). This psychological profile, although overdrawn, is surely not without some symbolic or behavioral basis (Edgerton 1971), although when seen in the context of age-based political socialization must be tempered by obverse traits, of respect, humility, congeniality, hospitality and obedience, which ideally obtain between age mates or between warriors and their more elderly sponsors.   This personality profile, attributed to successful wielders of regional power, represents less an explanation for than part of the constellation of facts surrounding the practice of warfare, aggression or societal expansion.   However, these values, relevant to the exigencies of pastoral subsistence, do represent internalized motives for action which, under circumstances of age-related or resource-based conflict, are sufficient to stimulate foolish bravery, unmeasured ambition, and self-sacrifice.

Maasai age-groups are constituted over time, a new age-division (*Ol-porror*) being opened every seven years, a successive pair of divisions forming an age-set (*Ol-aji*) on a fourteen year cycle, alternative age-sets forming 'streams' that link older and younger in relations of authority and political affinity (*c.f.* Galaty 1985). In each section, the age-set which has assumed the leading political role as sponsors opens a new age-set for recruitment. At the same time, the sponsors of the previous age-set just leaving 'Moranhood' (*Murrano*, the period of 'warriorhood' following initiation) continues to exercise influence in local meetings. Members of an age-set must respect their sponsors, but routinely experience tension and competition with adjacent age-groups, those immediately preceding and, in time, succeeding them.

Age-sets, with temporal dimensions that ensure decentralized leadership and political turnover, spatially cut across units of residential organization, from neighborhoods to sections. But in structure localized age-set units parallel territorial divisions, beginning with local circumcision groups, neighborhood cohorts, age-set units (*E-sirit*) with organized locational age-set villages (*I-manyat*), and sectional levels of overarching authority, manifested in periodic ritual villages. At the local level, informal leaders emerge, while formally designated 'spokesmen' (*Ilaiguenak*) are appointed to represent locational divisions, one such spokesman serving as age-set leader for the entire section. Thus a structural hierarchy in the age-set system parallels and politically delineates the segments of a territorial section and provides the means for its integration.

Sectional politics involve two dimensions of age-set discussion and negotiation, between successive age-sets in the same locality and between divisions of the same age-group in different localities. Beyond providing order to the process of advising and deciding in councils and conclaves, the culture of the age-set system provides a more pervasive structure for thought and action with regard to selfhood, ethics and morality, collectivity and individuality, and honour, while its social structure lends orientation to seasonal patterns in the use of resources, household movement, collective responses to aggression, or mobilization for expansion. The Maasai age-set system underpins individual clashes, small group raids and collective battle through providing an ethos of assertiveness, a structure for organizing conflict (and its resolution), and a rhythmic entrainment of individual motives to attain honour and livestock wealth, all of which underpin the expansion process.

During the period of 'Moranhood' that follows initiation, young men struggle and form alliances in classic in-group/out-group behavior, in which feelings of animosity and affectionate loyalty are instilled which are intense and lasting. Behavior is maximally restricted during this age-grade period when young men experience great freedom paradoxically combined with intense discipline. The values of bravery, intensity and respect pertinent to this period are apparently situational, applying as they do to the behavior of young initiated men, but the experience of 'warriorhood' casts a cloak of pervasive nostalgia over all subsequent life experiences, so that future action is also measured, if subliminally, against those great days of youthful vigor and self-esteem. Moran perfect the martial and romantic arts in tandem, pursuing training in tracking, shield, spear and bow, and military formation, as well as practicing dance, song and the rhetoric of wooing (See Plate 7.2). These two arts are not arbitrarily juxtaposed, since demonstrations of bravery and daring serve as qualities of attractiveness, and the praise and remonstrations of sweethearts stirs the desire in young men to prove themselves (*c.f.* Spencer 1965). Outbursts of aggressive action born in late-night dances are primarily directed toward cattle raids, but also involve encounters between romantic competitors, perhaps emotionally wrought by exchanges of insults, taunts and challenges, interested in the same cohort of young women.

At this juncture, the structure of political affinities between competitors serves to influence the nature and seriousness of conflict and to calibrate the scale of support marshalled by each side on the occasion of escalation. Within the same neighborhood, young men compete through wrestling and game, and when provoked fight without weapons; between locations, members of different warrior divisions within the same section are expected to actively compete, and upon occasions to break out in serious fighting with non-mortal weapons. Conflict between members of allied sections should be avoided, or kept within these amicable limits, while conflict between non-allied sections of different confederations can quickly become quite serious, with mortal weapons used to deadly ends (Galaty 1981).

In many occasions, insult and encounter between individuals is defined as conflict between age-groups, with escalation ensuing. However, organized age-set villages of different locations and sections were and are formed proximal to one another, for the manifest purpose of joint celebration of ceremonies but at the same time creating an atmosphere of pageantry and challenge once associated with the joust. Despite the efforts of responsible elders, such occasions often resulted in great organized clashes between age-groups, arrayed in long opposing lines with interlocked shields, with the degree of deadliness of projectiles determined by the occasion, the intensity of feeling, and the ability or inability of peacemakers to prevent escalation. Such occasions may have represented a sort of 'training with live amunition', but often was indistinguishable from 'live combat', or led to it.

Conflict between sections, which was earlier depicted as if political entities were actors, can be usefully described as a dynamic political relationship between individual Moran and age-groups. The first European visitor to Maasailand reported having seen in 1883 several age-set villages situated near one another on the approach to Lake Naivasha, apparently inhabited by Kaputie, Enaiposha and Laikipiak. All reports of the extended clash between Maasai-proper and Laikipiak, which led to the demise and assimilation of the latter, emphasize competition between age-groups. Accounts of the defeat of Iloogolala on Oldoinyo Orok (Namanga Hills) emphasize the bravery and ingenuity of Iloogolala

Moran facing overwhelming opposition. The account of Kisongo expansion in Tanzania is a chronicle of advances made by successive age-sets. In short, conflict and expansion represents not simply a struggle over resources but a political process with its own inertia, in which competition between corporate age-groups involves questions of honor and reputation as well as booty, in this case, cattle.

While the ethos of the Moran age-grade provided some of the intrinsic motivation for conflict, age-set organization also provides the means for mobilizing age-set divisions at several orders of scale. The existence of a single age-set across the Maasai sections offers a social and conceptual framework for alliance and conflict, with age-set divisions being amalgamated under circumstances of ceremony and battle *vis-a-vis* other similar age-set aggregations. Age-set ceremonies are still celebrated jointly by several sections, and we know from early colonial evidence that the practice of common rituals celebrated by several sections within sectional alliances was common, an experience on which wider military collaboration was based. Most fronts of Maasai expansion seem to have involved links between sections within a single alliances, but tradition holds that for the Laikipiak war, virtually all central Maasai sections - Purko, Kaputie, Kisongo and Loita clusters - banded together in self-defense. In times of conflict, the members of several successive age-sets - current Moran and junior elders - would mobilize. The Maasai age system thus offered a framework for social and military aggregation, whereby significant 'massing' (Sahlins 1964) could occur across age levels and territory, creating a potent force out of a widely dispersed population.

Such a process of aggregation occurred not only in times of conflict but routinely, as age-set ceremonies were celebrated at the level of locations, sections and clusters. For a given age group, congregating at section-wide ceremonies would occur every few years, cementing ties which would be reinforced during the interim. But since age-sets constitute overlapping cycles, any given section experiences relatively frequent ritual aggregation. The single most important ceremony is *E-unoto*, which occurs in the fourth or fifth year of an age-set cycle, marking the high point of a young Moran's experience, at which time restrictions on sex with initiated women were lifted, opening the age-set to marriageable status (Galaty 1983).

This ordering of the life-cycle by ritual rather than simply individual growth implies that many young men in effect became 'marriageable' at the same time, shortly after celebrating *E-unoto*. But for marriage, a young man should be economically secure in livestock and able soon to establish an independent pastoral household. Although the family herd is formally held by the paternal head of household, the bulk is allocated among the sons of matricentric houses, with larger shares provided for elder and youngest sons. While bridewealth involves a relatively small ritually designated number of livestock (four to six animals), the marriageability of a young man depends in large part on the holdings of his family and the size of his own portion, a measure by which his reliability and future independence can be assessed. A direct connection between marriage and raiding has been drawn, raiding allowing young men to accumulate enough animals to gain sufficient autonomy from their parental homes necessary for marriage and the achievement of full elder status (Tignor 1972). Based on observations by a German traveler through Maasailand at the end of the nineteenth century, Kjekshus comments that

> ...violence is explained as serving the limited economic objective of the moran.... Acquisition of cattle was seen by Fischer as the only motivation for warlike action against other peoples. Young men with modest material demands or those inheriting herds from their fathers would not join in the warfare (Kjekshus 1977:18).

Age organization both defined the time and provided the means whereby the needs of young men could be met through livestock raiding, primarily following *E-unoto*, when marriage was ritually opened for the age-division. The mobilization of age units to carry out smaller raids and the consolidation of the entire age group within the section - and in the past several sectional age groups - through the creation of ritual villages provided the mechanism for collective action. Through age organization the structure of segmentary 'massing' was defined, while through ritual it was enacted. Periods of Maasai expansion are remembered through the age-sets which carried them out, successive waves being set off by the ripple effect of a sequence of ceremonial age-set aggregations.

Maasai Expansion in Cultural Perspective

In the long-run, Maasai expansion appears as an inexorable movement, a southward wave superceded by outward ripples emanating from a Rift Valley epicenter. But each front of expansion involved a historically specific set of encounters and each stage of expansion represented less a punctuated clash than a gradual process, in which armed conflict represented only one of many modes of interaction between Maa-speakers and their counterparts.

Maasai expansion was thus in large part incremental, with herd and household movements to marginal or interstitial areas in search of pasture and water bringing members of different groups and sections into contact; often a period of peaceful admixture of herds and herders would precede a period of friction and armed clashes, concerning, for instance, the order in which herds use wells or the means by which dry season pastures were made available. Serious conflict, however, generally arose through political differences centered on age-set competition, followed by the advance of one group and the retreat or assimilation of another. Definitive expansion is associated less with penetration of new pastures than with either the seizure of livestock after concerted combat or with the seizure of critical water resources, to the exclusion of losers. Thus the two economic and political moments of conflict and expansion, involving shifting pastoral orbits and age-set clashes, occurred simultaneously or in succession. When they were inextricably intertwined, friction over resources was shaped by political realities or age-set conflicts weretriggered by personal jealousies and resentments leading to new economic gains.

The expansion of the Maasai proper involved three noteworthy trends. First was the trend towards political differentiation and segmentation, as Maasai sections evolved within and moved out of the Rift Valley nucleus into an 'inner periphery' adjacent to the dominant frontier groups. Second, the consolidation of political alliances between sections occurred during the expansion onto the Rift Valley highlands, which reconfirmed higher order segmentary relations in some cases and redefined them in others. During this period, the Kaputie, Loita, Kisongo, and Purko clusters emerged that remain salient in the present day. Third, while most expanding Maasai sections assimilated individuals from groups being displaced, either peacefully or after their dispersal and dispossession, the Kisongo and Purko carried out processes of 'amalgamation' distinct in scale and structural significance from the assimilation of outsiders normally practiced by other sections. It is interesting to speculate that this process of pastoral amalgamation might have resulted in the development of a large-scale pastoral polity, had it not been curtailed by the devastations of the last two decades of the nineteenth century and the onset of colonial rule.

In a history of events, the 'frontier' groups were largely dispersed and annhilated as political entities, but in a history of processes, most <u>individuals</u> from those groups survived through affiliating with other sections or groups, their identities evolving over time with their altered circumstances. Some sections were reconstituted in a different form (*i.e.* communities of Iloogolala becoming Kaputie or Parakuyo), some scattered only to reform at a later date (*i.e.* Uasin Gishu, Moitanik), others assimilated by the central Maasai, in particular by Kisongo and Purko (*e.g.* Laikipiak, Ilosegeli). As Waller has pointed out, after such wars, the people followed the livestock into their new kraals (Waller 1978), and today countless loyal Maasai families recall their origins in one of the groups dispersed in the nineteenth century.   But this process of amalgamation also changed both the scale and the nature of the 'section' for the Kisongo and the Purko. In 1916, an average Maasai section was composed of approximately 2,400 people, but the Kisongo numbered 21,000, the Purko 16,500, more than seven times greater in magnitude (Maasai District Records 1916). It is interesting to speculate that if the amalgamation process - halted by the devastation of the Maasai by drought, famine, and disease and by the onset of British colonial control at the end of the nineteenth century - had continued, large Maasai federations of flexible pastoral units may have evolved, consolidated on the basis of sectional alliances, common identity, and ideology, of a coordinated ritual process based on age-sets, and of pastoral resources secured in the past.

Given that the process of Maasai expansion represented both a highly consistent long-term process and one highly dependent on local conditions, to what extent is it possible to identify aspects of their culture, economy, or social organization that lent them a competitive edge over other Rift Valley societies? The Maasai have been distinguished in East Africa by their refinement of a quite specialized form of cattle pastoralism involving high levels of herd mobility, the potential for high rates of herd growth, and an ethos of youthful aggression and cattle raiding. Similarly, Maasai age organization seems unique in having combined autonomous age-set villages, a ceremonial cycle involving age-set aggregation and massing, and constraints on marriage and livestock ownership that motivated young men to seek their fortunes through raiding.   Herd growth often led to disequilibrium between livestock and pasture resources, a condition experienced in the form of seasonal scarcities and asymmetries of wealth between Maasai families that in many cases stimulated pastoral drift and migration. But high levels of pastoral productivity were also necessary to support the extensive system of age-set villages that provided Maasai with effective armed encampments of young men mobilized for defense and aggression. Many of these factors were equally valued by other groups in the region but none proved able to practice them to a comparable degree. Certainly these economic, political, and cultural factors were implicated in the Maasai expansion, but it is difficult to say whether they represent causes or effects of this complex historical process.

It seems clear, however, that the Maasai expansion, tied to highly productive pastoralism, was not simply an outcome of local herd growth in an environment favorable for animal husbandry, nor of periodic pasture insufficiency in a semi-arid zone, because these conditions have and do obtain for numerous other pastoral groups. Rather, what seems distinctive and relevant in the Maasai context was social and political rather than ecological in nature, that is, institutionalized forms of organization and motivation. Territorial sections provided the collective framework for the appropriation and allocation of resources, the securing of regional systems of exchange, and the coordination of larger-scale action and expansion. The age-set system offered a structure for sectional politics, a system of leadership, and a cultural frame of reference. Age-grades and rituals demarcated and engendered motivations common to each stage in the life-cycle and at the same time provided the mechanism and opportunity for amassing warrior units in forms of mobilization that often exceeded local control.

Pastoral expansion is not inevitable, for the history of the East African plains is filled with traces of peoples who failed, and as such were usually eliminated through assimilation. This chapter has suggested that Maasai expansion resulted not just from environmental pressures and opportunities, nor from pastoral character, for surely success in part shapes the ethos of assertiveness and autonomy. Rather, Maasai success involved a convergence of pastoral strategies and age-set organization, which included the inculcation of powerful needs and motivations, and the creation of ritually defined occasions for mustering and massing. But we should be careful not to attribute a linear type of explanation to a long and complicated experience, which involved not only political expansion but also the emergence and refinement of the very factors of specialized pastoralism and age-set organization that may in retrospect seem critical to the expansion process.

Notes

1. While remarkable, Maasai pastoral expansion is not unique. For eastern Africa, one can cite the sixteenth century Oromo expansion (Asmarom 1973; Hultin 1978), the Somali expansion out of the Horn of Africa (G. Lewis 1966), or the nineteenth century Turkana dispersion throughout the northern Rift Valley (Lamphear 1976), for southern Africa the devastating *Mfecane* expansion stimulated by the Zulu (Edgerton 1986), or for West Africa the famous Fulbe expansion eastward across the Sahel.

2. The first culture is known as Eburran Phase 5, for which sites are found for the period between 2,900-1,900 b.p.; the second culture is known as the Savanna Pastoral Neolithic (3,300-1,300 b.p.) and is associated with the earlier Lowland Savanna Pastoral Neolithic (5,200-3,300 b.p.); sites for the third "Elementeitan" culture are found from 2,500-1,300 b.p. (Ambrose 1984; Robertshaw and Collett 1983).

3. The widepsread occupation by Southern Cushites of the Southern Rift Valley in Tanzania is attested by the present distribution of the Iraqw, Burngi and Alagwa in Mbulu and Kondoa, west of the Maasai savanna, and of small pockets of East Rift-speaking hunter-gatherers - the Aramanik and Qwadza - within Maasailand and the neighboring Gogo (Ehret 1974:14). Ehret suggests that Southern Cushites knew grain cultivation as well as stock raising, their principle grain being sorghum (*Ibid.*:7). However, Ambrose points out that contemporary Southern Cushitic farmers in Northern Tanzania cultivate *caudatum* sorghum associated with Sudanic speakers rather than the *durra* sorghum used by virtually all other Afroasiatic speakers in Ethiopia; this would suggest that they were not cultivators during the Neolithic period, since these domestic varieties would have been introduced into the region by Southern Nilotic-speakers at a later date (Ambrose 1984:236).

4. At Dhang Rhial in the Southern Sudan, comparable evidence for an early Pastoral Iron Age has been found for the 1,500-800 b.p. period, speculated to derive ultimately from the far west in Nigeria rather than from the much closer Meroe complex to the north. This early Iron Age in the Sudan is probably associated with Nilotic communities who lived on mounds and herded humpless cattle in relatively constrained systems of transhumance; they surely also practiced some hunting and fishing, and may have cultivated such crops as sorghum (David 1982:54-55).

In East Africa, Early Pastoral Iron Age variants are associated with the (Elementeitan) Southern Nilotes on the western side of the Rift Valley (1,300-1,100 b.p.), with Engaruka in conjunction with specialized irrigation agriculture, and, most importantly, with the Sirikwa, beginning around 1,200 b.p., approximately when it is believed on linguistic grounds that Maa-speakers reached the Central Rift Valley (Ambrose 1982:129, 135, 143-44).

5. Maasai are called *Humha* by the Gogo, *Wahumba* by the Kaguru and Chagga, *Umbe* by the Mbugwe; early maps identify colonies of cultivators as 'Lumbwa' (Wakefield 1870).

6. Maasai are called *Kapkop* by Marakwet, *Ikwopek* by the Kipsigis, *Kwabuk* and *Kipkwop* by Sebei, *Kipchoek* by the Nandi, all variants of *Iloikop*; *Ukapi* by Kamba, *Ukabi* by Kikuyu, *Wakwavi* by Chagga, *Abaikwabi* by the Kuria; all variants of *Kwavi*. For an excellent discussion of the uses and possible derivations of these terms, see Bernsten (1980).

7. The "Iloikop hypothesis" holds that:
...all people who speak Maasai (Olmaa) (are) divided into two distinct ethnic groups - the *Ilmaasai* versus the *Wakwavi* (or *Iloikop*)....This ethnic distinction *Ilmaasai* and *Wakwavi* is based mainly on differences in subsistence practices and dietary attitudes, reinforced by differences in cosmological or religious beliefs and original ethnic origin (Jacobs 1968:21).

The *Iloikop*, who were "semi-pastoralists", have been identified as the present-day Maa-speaking Parakuyo, Arusha, Chamus (Njemps), and Samburu, as well as the now extinct Iloogolala, Uasin Gishu, Losegelai and Laikipiak (Jacobs 1965:112). While the Arusha and Chamus do indeed cultivate, there is no evidence that the other major groups are less pastoral than Maasai, or that they recognized greater affinity with one another than with other Maasai.

8. The Samburu were welded out of three distinct groupings, one from west of Lake Turkana (called *Lebbeyok* by the Pokot, *Ngikuro* by the Turkana), another from the El Barta Plains (*Lorogishu*), and a third from the Laikipia Plateau (*Il-Doigio*)(Anderson 1981:5; Sobania 1980:82).

9. I have assumed here that the Maa-speaking *'Kwabuk'* of western Kenyan tradition were ancestral Uasin Gishu and Siria, and due to the tradition of a Maa presence in the seventeenth century have attributed a 'frontier' expansion to them. However, Vossen's linguistic data concerning the linguistic affinities of the two sections indicate a much later divergence from the Maa nucleus, after the Purko and before other nuclear and 'inner periphery' sections (Vossen 1977). Either these two western Maasai sections retained linguistic contact with the Maasai nucleus after their expansion or reestablished linguistic affinity in this century, or they represent a later expansion at the expense of (and assimilating) an earlier *'Kwabuk'* Maa presence, perhaps of Sirikwa connection.

10. These distinctions presuppose a "concentric" configuration of Maasai sections, based on the relationship between Maasai dialects in Vossen's lexicostatistical studies (Vossen 1988) and on nineteenth century spatial relations between sections. This model differs from an implicit "diametric" model, whereby Maa speakers have been seen as divided into two coequal groups, Maasai and Iloikop (on the distinction between "concentric" and "diametric" models, see Galaty 1977). Within this concentric model, the historical differentiation of sectional dialects can be characterized in terms of their current degrees of divergence from a center or core, in a set of concentric geographical-lexical circles. A 'nucleus' or 'inner core' (least divergent from proto-Maa) includes the Damat, Keekonyokie, Loita and Matapato, arrayed along the central Rift Valley, an 'outer core', in general located on the nearby plateaux, includes the Kaputie, Lodokilani, Dalalekutuk, Salei, Laitayok, Serenget and Siria, the two vanguard groups of the 'inner periphery', the Purko and Kisongo, spreading over the northern and southern reaches, respectively, of the Rift Valley, and the 'frontier' groups, the Iloogolala/Parakuyo, Uasin Gishu (with Moitanik), Ilosegelai, Laikipiak and Samburu, occupying the more distant peripheries.

Regarding orthography, I have generally excluded the gender prefix when naming Maasai groups (Keekonyokie rather than *Il-Keekonyokie*) but have retained the anglicized form for names beginning with a vowel (*e.g.* Lodokilani for *Il-odokilani*).

11. I have followed Fosbrooke's (1956) calculation of nineteenth century Maasai age-sets on the basis of a fourteen year period rather than Jacobs' (1968) reassessment based on a fifteen year period. The historical reality may lie somewhere between but to my knowledge Maasai consciously aim for two successive seven-year age-divisions in an age-set.

12. To my knowledge, Ilaimer represent the only case where the name of the Left-Hand division became identified with the set as a whole.

13. Study among Maasai on which this paper draws was supported by the National Science Foundation (1974-75), the Social Sciences and Humanities Research Council of Canada (1983-90), the Quebec FCAR (1983-89), the International Development Research Centre (1984-87), and McGill University's

Faculty of Graduate Studies and Research. I would like to acknowledge with appreciation the Bureau of Educational Research, now at Kenyatta University, with which I have affiliated during periods of research in Kenya.

14. An exception to this tendency occurs when herds are virtually eliminated by drought or epidemic, as when the 1889-90 devastations led to widespread raiding and the War of Morijo between the Loita and other central Maasai sections.

15. Jacobs, however, adopts a distinctively Maasai point of view by contrasting Maa-speaking *Il-oikop* aggressivity to more pacific Maasai character, the "peaceful pastoralists" (1978), a distinction not supported in this paper. Following from the more modest post-colonial role played by Maasai in Kenya and Tanzania, social historians have appropriately described the extent of trade, intermarriage and positive political interaction between Maasai and their neighbours, as well as the reciprocal rather than one-sided nature of conflict and warfare (Muriuki 1976; Bernsten 1979). This well-grounded argument is taken too far, in my estimation, when used to suggest that the idea of Maasai pre-colonial political dominance resulted from colonial distortions and that Maasai were merely "peaceful pastoralists", one set of actors among many in the complicated ethnic mosaic of the Rift Valley region. Rather than a denial of one of the most well-supported facts in East Africa history, the political and economic dominance of the Rift Valley from Lake Baringo southward to central Tanzania by Maasai speakers, what we need is a framework for interpreting Maasai expansion and exercise of regional power in regional context.

8

Herders, Traders and Clerics: The Impact of Trade, Religion and Warfare on the Evolution of Moorish Society

Abdel Wedoud Ould Cheikh

The Moors make up the majority of the population of contemporary Mauritania and former Spanish Sahara. Farther eastwards, they have populated the areas of Tindouf in Algeria and Azawad in Mali. Prior to the 1970s the mainstay of their nomadic way of life was the husbandry of camels, cattle, sheep and goats. These people, who refer to themselves as *al-biḍān* ("white men"), are politically and socially organized into tribes (*qabā'il*). In the Trarza, Brakna, Adrar and Tagant regions, emirates, established during the seventeenth and eighteenth centuries, amalgamated several tribes under the authority of certain lineages. The emiral and tribal structures were superimposed upon a hierarchy of orders and ranks, namely: warriors (*hassān*), clerics (*zwāya*) tributaries (*lahma* or *aznāga*), praise-singers (*īggāwun*), craftsmen (*m'allmīn*), former slaves (*ḥrāṭīn*) and slaves (*a'bīd*).

According to one hypothesis, these status groups, in particular that of the warrior-clerics, have an ethnic origin, since "Arab" conquerors supposedly subjugated "Berbers". Another interpretation accounts for the distinction between these two dominant groups in terms of a structural duality, a segmentary opposition through which Moorish society, like other acephalus societies, maintained an "ordered anarchy". Yet another explanation of the warrior-cleric antagonism takes the Moorish social order to be the reflection of the tensions and contradictions of its economic infrastructure.

We will briefly reconsider here these various interpretations of events that may have represented a turning point in the establishment of hierarchical political structures in Moorish society. These events are known as *Shurbubba*, a seventeenth century war in the Gibla region (southwestern Mauritania), in which a coalition made up mostly of *hassān* warriors fought against another headed by *zwāya*. This conflict highlights the importance of both trade and Islam in the social organization of Moorish nomadism. After a short discussion of Moorish history before the seventeenth century, our attention will focus upon the Shurbubba War and interpretations of it. Then we will examine hypotheses inspired by functionalism and historical materialism that seek to explain the Moorish social order, with the aim of illuminating key aspects of a system of social organization that essentially hinges upon a nomadic way of life.

From Prehistoric Times to the Gum Era

Long-distance nomadism in the Sahara, in particular among the Moors, developed with the spread of camel-herding across the desert. Although they were domesticated in the Arabian Peninsula about 3000 B.C. (Bulliet 1975; Mason 1984), dromedaries were apparently only brought into North Africa much later, though this argument is not unanimously accepted. Referring to Demougeot's study (1960), Bulliet has reduced arguments about the presence of dromedaries in North Africa to three basic hypotheses. First, some scholars

> ...maintain that the North African camel of purest lineage, the Mehari, a slender graceful riding camel prized by the Tuaregs and other desert tribes, is a separate species descended from a prehistoric camel that is known from fossil evidence to have roamed the then grassy Sahara in the Pleistocene Age (Bulliet 1975: 113).

The second possibility is that the Romans brought camels into North Africa from Syria. Third, in Demougeot's opinion, with which Bulliet agrees, domestic camels may have come into the Sahara "from somewhere in Egypt or the Sudan" (Bulliet 1975:114).

Although fossil remains do prove that camels were living in Africa before the presumed date of their domestication in Arabia, there are serious objections to the hypothesis that they were domesticated in

Africa. Bulliet has emphasized that differences between the Asiatic and African varieties (number of teeth, color, distance between neck and hump, *etc.*), which undoubtedly resulted from local selection, are not sufficient to define these varieties as separate species. Furthermore, since the rare cave drawings of camels are relatively recent, the hypothesis that dromedaries were reintroduced into Africa after domestication in the Near East cannot be dismissed. This hypothesis is supported by the spread of saddles known as "South Arabian" and North Arabian" across the Sahara (Monod 1967). The Moorish men's saddle (*ŗāḥla*) is a variant of the North Arabian; it is probably of more recent date than its counterpart among the Tuareg (the *terik* and *tahyast*).

Although the extent of Arabic influence on the jargon of camel husbandry (Trancart 1941; Leriche 1952; Monteil 1952; Le Borgne 1953) argues in favor of recent Arab-Moslem influence on Moorish camel-herding, the historical evidence indicates that, nonetheless, a camel-based economy had developed in the Western Sahara prior to the arrival of the Arabs.[1] The Tiris area on the border between Mauritania and former Spanish Sahara is considered not only to be the historical center of the Moorish homeland but also to have been especially suited for raising camels.[2]

The spread of Islam along Berber-controlled routes across the Sahara after the ninth century might have been a factor in the southward expansion of tribes involved in the caravan trade. In the western Sahara, there were two main periods of trade: the "age of salt" during which the north-south trans-Saharan trade developed, based on the mobility of pastoralists and the spread of Islam across northwestern Africa; and the "age of gum" during which, from the fifteenth century onwards, maritime trade developed as Europeans set up posts along the Atlantic coast.

Cultural and commercial relations between North Africa and Saharan and sub-Saharan Africa grew significantly after being established on a regular basis when Moslem armies overran North Africa between 661 and 708 A.D. The basic commodities in these transactions were salt and gold. For a long time the saltworks at Teghaza-Taoudenni provided most of the salt exchanged in the *Bilād al-Sudān*. In the distant past, salt from Kidyit aj-Jill might also have been supplied to markets in the West African Sahel and the Sudan (McDougall 1980). Other products from the Sahara and North Africa were an appreciable part of this trade: fine cloths, copper, animals (especially horses), cowries, pearls, perfume, paper, manuscripts and "luxury" foodstuffs (wheat, barley and dried fruit, raisins as well as dates and figs), for consumption in particular by the colonies of North African and by Middle Eastern merchants. Gold was the initial export from the south to the north, followed by slaves, cereals (especially millet), ivory and spices (Mauny 1961; Devisse 1972).

The size and relative constancy of this trade over the centuries - in spite of the insecurity endemic to the regions crossed - necessitated organized mining and food production, harvesting, storage and commercial trade at both ends of each caravan route. At each end, specialized trading groups came into being, notedly the Wangara in the south. Trade was surely also a factor in political centralization, both in the north (the Sharif monarchies) and in the south (the Sahelian empires and Berber principalities).

The trans-Saharan trade also permanently affected the nomadic peoples through whose lands caravans passed (Lewicki 1974; Mauny 1961; Devisse 1972). The groups strongest in arms or dominant in politics drew revenue from the caravans. Furthermore, tribes or their social fractions became involved in the transport and commercial sale of goods.

To appreciate the impact of caravans upon Moorish nomads, we must recall that there were two major netrworks of north-south trade routes that crossed the western and central Sahara before the fifteenth century (Mauny 1961; Devisse 1972): one linked Ouargla and Ghadames to Tadmakka and Gao, whereas the other, centered in the north around Sijilmassa and Aghmāt, ended in the south along the Senegal River and near Timbuktu. This western network, which is of particular interest here, was divided into two routes: one ran from Sijilmassa through Taghaza to the Niger River, the other from the Dar'a Wādī and Sijilmassa to the western Sudan, linked to an trading itinerary along the Atlantic Coast at Nūl-Āwlīl. The latter, "one of the principal Saharan routes of all times" (Mauny 1961:427), included the itineraries described by al-Bakrī (1964:309) between Tāmdālt, Āwdāghust and Dar'a Wādī. Although the stations along this route have not yet been satisfactorily identified, we do know that after a certain period (about the chronology, see Ould Cheikh 1985:62-87), the Mauritanian towns of Wadān, Shingīti, Tishīt and Walāta were among them. In spite of the changing fortunes of these two principal networks of trade, the above-mentioned routes, which had been established from the eleventh century onwards, were still more or less the same during the sixteenth century, insofar as we can judge, given the scarcity of our later information on the Western Sahara between the twelfth and seventeenth centuries.

One of the outstanding events during these "dark ages" of western Saharan history was the infiltration of the Arab Banī hassān tribes south of the Sāgya al-Hamra, beginning in the early fourteenth century. By the late seventeenth century, it appears that these newcomers wielded political power throughout the region bounded by the Senegal River, Sāgya al-Hamra, the meridian of Timbuktu and the Atlantic Ocean. The hierarchy and culture of present-day Moorish society still bears the marks of this hegemony. Since the seventeenth century, the Arabic dialect (*al-hassāniyya* or *klām al-biḍān*), spoken by the Banī hassān, has more or less displaced Berber languages (*klām aznāga*). Owing to both the hegemony of the *hassān* and the ideological predominance of Islamic values, genealogies were "Arabized" by being accomodated to the patrilineal requirements of the Arab model; the genealogical system of the Aznāga, the Berber substratum of Moorish society, was characterized by quite different forms of filiation.

The social hierarchy in contemporary Moorish society is thought to have been formed when it came at that time under the domination of Arab tribes. The Moorish social and political order rested upon a combination of tribal and emiral structures, which contained a more or less hereditary and endogamous hierarchy of status groups, dominated by the *hassān* warrior aristocracy. Below the warriors (*hassān*) were situated the *zwāya* or *ṭulba* (the "clerics" whom the French have called "marabouts"), as well as other previously mentioned groups. The Shurbubba War, we would suggest, represented a decisive phase in the establishment laying of these ranks, a crucial moment in the shaping of the hierarchical relationship between *hassān* and *zwāya*.

Shurbubba: The Founding of Moorish Society

Shurbubba or *Sharr Babba* is the name given in southwestern Mauritania to the seventeenth century war between two coalitions, the one comprised mostly of *hassān*, and the other, headed by Imām Nāsir al-Dīn, of *zwāya*. Stewart (1973b:378) has taken these events to be a "founding myth" of the separation of religious and military functions, a mythical charter of *hassān* superiority over the *zwāya*, while Marty (1917: 23; 1921:8) maintained that the Shurbubba War gave form to the ethnic hostility between "hard working" Berbers and "plundering" Arabs. More recently Barry (1972:142-143) has considered this war to be the ideological and military extension of the economic antagonism between trans-Saharan and European commerce.

In fact, little is known about this conflict. There is even doubt about its name. The commonly accepted tradition calls it *Sharr Babba*, which in Hassāniyya means Babba's War (Ahmad 1958:174, 491). The reference is to Babba Wul Aḥmad Wul Āsūr as-Ṣgay'ī, a client of the Tāshbidbīt, a *zwāya* tribe, who refused to pay the *zakāt* he owed to the tax-collectors appointed by Nāṣir al-Dīn. Through the intermediary of his Tāshidbīt masters, he placed himself under the protection of the *hassān* chief, Haddi Wul Ahmad Bin Damān. The tax-collectors' obstinacy was at the origin of the first clashes between the *zwāya* and Haddi's men. In the *Manāgib al-Imām Nāṣir al-Dīn* ("*The Qualities of Imām Nāṣir al-Dīn*"), the first and major Moorish account of the war, Muhammad al-Yadāli al Daymānī (d. 1753) wrote *Shurbubba* and suggested that this word was originally a rallying cry. Imām Nāṣir al-Dīn, whenever he recruited a warrior, made him stand up and said to him, in the Aẓnāga Berber dialect, "Shurbubbīh!" ("Cry out assent!"). Regardless of the etymology, the events to which al-Yadāli referred took place during the second half of the seventeenth century.

Al-Yadāli's account is, of course, strongly tilted toward proving the moral exemplariness of the *zwāya* heroes in this war, in particular of Nāṣir al-Dīn, as the title of this clerical version of events indicates.[3] The account begins with a collection of hagiographic testimonies attributed to persons who lived at the time of the Imam. The latter's extraordinary divinatory powers are abundantly illustrated. Given the eschatological and millenarian feelings that inspired his words and deeds, he resembled a *mahdī*, a latter-day prophet. He preached repentance, made the dead speak, and foresaw events. These powers soon attracted a growing number of admirers who "drank" his words, even his saliva and the water he used for his ablutions. After this preliminary period, which, according to al-Yadāli, lasted three years, Nāṣir al-Dīn had the principal *zwāya* leaders pledge allegiance (*bay'a*) to him. He then established an organization of the state based on Islam, extending clerical influence through religious conquest as far as Jolof, Cayor, Walo and Futa Toro. The movement finally collapsed due, above all, to the *hassān*.

The chronology of these events is not well known. We know neither when this war began nor how long it lasted. The frequently cited period of thirty years (1644-1674), accepted by Marty (1917:60), is based on weak evidence, in fact, upon a verse of poetry attributed to Wālid Wul Khālunā and repeated in al-Mukhtâr W. Djangi's poetic chronicles (Ould Cheikh 1985:836 ff.).

On the basis of local tradition (Ould Cheikh 1985:836-838), the crucial events of the Shurbubba War can be assigned to the approximate period of the 1680s. Ritchie (1968) has confirmed that the *zwāya* were active in 1673. In *The History of Toubenan or the Change of Sovereigns and the Reform of Religion among these Negroes from Its Origin in 1673 till the Current Year of 1677*, one of the two texts that Ritchie has reproduced, Louis Moreau de Chambonneau, a director of the French trading house at Saint Louis, reported on Nāṣir al-Dīn's reform (known in the Gibla as *Toubenan*, probably from the Arabic *tawba*, "to repent" or "repentance") and its effect on nearby black principalities. According to Chambonneau (Ritchie 1968:341), Nāṣir al Dīn died in 1674. This source broadly corroborates al-Yadāli's account with respect both to the clerical party's quarrels with the Negro principalities in the lower and middle Senegal River Valley and to the role of certain leaders in the two rival coalitions.

This historical evidence, however, does not justify interpreting the "marabouts' war" simply as a myth that explains the contemporary social order among the Moors. Although al-Yadāli recounted many miraculous events and regardless of how these affected the sequence of historical events, his writings are not works of pure imagination. After discussing the hypothesis that al-Yadāli created the character of Nāsir al-Dīn, Norris (1969:521) rejected it in view of the historical evidence. Curtin (1971), who has emphasized the effects of Nāsir al-Dīn's movement upon lands as far away as the Futa Jallon, has conjectured a continuity between the themes - *jihad, imām* (becoming *eliman* or *almani*) - that ran through the Shurbubba War and the forms of religious and political agitation that gave rise to the *imamates* of Bundu, Futa Jallon and, a few years later, Futa Toro.[4]

This war, geographically restricted to the Gibla, both heralded a new type of political organization (the emirate) in Moorish society and marked a turning point in the consolidation of the social hierarchy in favor of the "Arabs" (*hassān*). The conflict broke out in a region where European trade had been growing in importance since the first trading posts were established in the mid-fifteenth century.

We shall not dwell upon the ethnic interpretation of the Shurbubba War proposed by Marty, which Hamès (1979) has shown to be essentially ideological in nature. Leaving aside the black peoples living along the lower Senegal who were involved in these events, the ethnic heterogeneity of the two opposing coalitions contradicts Marty's conclusions regarding an ethnic cleavage between "Arabs" and "Berbers". Since this war, and perhaps even beforehand, the claim to "Arab" origins has reflected the prestige of Islam as well as of the Arab conquerors and the determination to signal one's status as much as the assertion of mere ethnic identity. This claim is also an indication of a new form of social and political stratification among Moorish nomads that some scholars have suggested is the direct effect of trade.

In his history of the Walo kingdom, Barry (1972:142-143), discussing the relations between the leader of the *zwāya* coalition and the French in Saint Louis, has commented:

> Nāṣir al-Dīn's profession of faith... covered a much deeper economic reality.... Beyond the difference of religion, what was involved was a reaction of self-defense by the economy based upon trans-Saharan trade against the more and more powerful monopoly over trade at Saint Louis.

This affirmation, which takes the Shurbubba War to be the political and military outcome of the antagonism between two types of trade, between the champions of caravans and of caravels (*zwāya* and *ḥassān* respectively), is based almost exclusively upon Chambonneau's account. But what does this source actually tell us?

Chambonneau, who arrived in Saint Louis on February 18, 1675 in order to head the French establishment that originated there about twenty years earlier, wrote a history of the Toubenan when he returned to Europe in January, 1677, in which he recounted the major events concerning the Shurbubba War and trade through Saint Louis. He maintained that the movement led by Nāṣir al-Dīn was essentially religious in nature. The latter, according to Chambonneau (Ritchie 1968:338-339), sent a mission to the Satigui, the sovereign of the Fulbe in Futa Toro, in order to exhort him to administer his subjects according to the rules laid down by Islam. Chambonneau's text then mentions a mission to Saint Louis by Munīr al-Dīn, Nāṣir al-Dīn's brother and ambassador, an undertaking clearly indicating the latter's intention of maintaining good relations with the French. The emissaries recommended that the French not take sides with established political authorities in the *zwāya* conflict. In spite of their declarations of good will, the French administration refrained from adopting the neutral attitude recommended by the Imam's messengers. De Muchins, the director of the Saint Louis trading house, even imagined taking Nāṣir al-Dīn's brother prisoner or having him assassinated when he received word of the Mahdi's death while the delegation was still in Saint Louis.

The reason that de Muchins accused the Toubenan of harming the Saint Louis trade had less to do with this movement's hostility to European commerce, or with a principled refusal by Nāṣir al-Dīn's party to deal with the French, than with the resulting insecurity rife throughout the Senegal River Valley or, as Chambonneau wrote, with the "upheaval in the kingdoms" (Ritchie 1968:342). In order to end this upheaval, which inhibited trade, the French administration resolutely sided with opponents of the reform. Chambonneau described de Muchins' efforts (which were ultimately successful) to convince the Brak of Walo to break with Nāṣir al-Dīn's movement. Agents from the Saint Louis company traveled along the river and threatened to kill any Wolof who continued to support the Toubenan. Villagers did, in fact, kill many of those who refused to heed this threat. In May and June, 1674, they set out by boat to raid along the river, burning Toubenan villages, killing several men there and bringing back much booty. Is it possible that Nāṣir al-Dīn's prohibition on trade was a security measure following the murderous raid by the French? It might even have been a local initiative, a spontaneous reaction as people fled de Muchins' men.

An episode mentioned by Chambonneau shows that the Shurbubba leader persistently sought - in spite of continuing French hostility and the intensity of clashes during the second quarter of 1675 - to maintain good relations with Saint Louis. The Imam magnanimously had a French clerk set free in spite of proof that he had participated in de Muchins' murderous raids. This gesture was undoubtedly intended to ease tensions so that the Saint Louis traders would resume the payment of "customs" to native rulers, for these "had not been paid at all during the whole time of the Toubenan" (Ritchie 1968: 348). Far from refusing the maritime trade, the "marabouts" tried in every way to profit from it. This question of customs, in particular the traders' persistent refusal to yield to requests from the *zwāya* chiefs, was one more factor that embittered relations between Saint Louis and the clerical party, for the Saint Louis merchants were already troubled by religious conflicts, the activist preaching of Nāṣir al-Dīn and, of course, the insecurity generated by the Shurbubba War.

Saint Louis did not favor any extension of Nāṣir al-Dīn's political and religious movement, which the French establishment resolutely sought to stop. At stake was the economic, political and ideological control over the peoples living in the Senegal River Valley. Chambonneau's text concludes (Ritchie 1968:352-353) by pointing out the disadvantages of Nāṣir al-Dīn's reform in terms of trade:

> (T)he marabouts glorified themselves by fleeing us in order to show their people that they have withdrawn from worldly possessions, that they are motivated uniquely by zeal for the service of God and for His law. Moreover, they scorn us because our religion is different from their superstition, and they make people believe that we deal in captives only in order to eat them. Since they have taken control of the land, not one captive has, till present, boarded our boats ....

Barry has used this conclusion to support his statement that Nāṣir al-Dīn's movement was deeply opposed to the maritime trade. He is right, however, about the economic significance of the river valley for the neighboring Moors, about the complementarity between the riverine peasant economy and Moorish nomadism, and about the importance to Nāṣir al-Dīn and his movement of controlling this area. The severe climatic crisis that struck the region (Ould Cheikh 1985:854-862) certainly revived the interest of Moorish nomads from the Gibla in the cereals and pastures of the nearby lands of Walo, Jolof, Futa Toro and Kayor.

Our knowledge of the Shurbubba War can hardly justify the statement that it represented a reaction by those involved in trans-Saharan trade, which was in crisis, against the menacing European trade. What the "History of the Toubenan" shows is a sharp rivalry between the advocates of reform and the Saint Louis trading houses. This rivalry certainly did not result from the clerics' refusal to trade with the French, nor from their determination to secure a monopoly on Senegalese produce for trans-Saharan trade routes. Rather, the principal issue appears to have been the economic, political and ideological control of the black populations of the river valley.

Saint Louis' support of certain major *hassān* chiefs did not mean - contrary to what Barry has suggested - that the *zwāya* were involved more in the trans-Saharan than the maritime trade, and *vice-versa* for the *hassān*. Let us leave aside the argument about the heterogeneity of the two coalitions. According to Barry (1972:145-146), the *zwāya* controlled Arguin, a trading post that was neither less maritime nor more trans-Saharan than Saint Louis. Presumably, Nāsir al-Dīn's supporters went to war because the establishment at the mouth of the Senegal River thrived to the detriment of Arguin. This hypothesis is, however, unfounded since, according to the available historical evidence (Ould Cheikh 1985), Arguin was under the political control of *hassān* groups towards the middle of the seventeenth century. In support of his hypothesis, Barry has cited a Dutch document[5] according to which Arguin mainly dealt in gum arabic. The gum was harvested by the two *zwāya* tribes, the Tāshumsha and Idaydba, most involved in the Shurbubba War. There was no apparent reason that these two tribes should move against the maritime trade simply because, instead of asking them to sell their gum at a distance of 500 km (Arguin), European traders offered to buy it at places bordering on their lands, an offer that did away with intermediaries and the considerable risks of transportation.

The *zwāya* party, according to Barry, opposed selling slaves to French traders because it was determined to maintain "the level of stocks" in the areas from which it drew them. Even though we might suspect that *zwāya* agitation involved some demagoguery about the issue of slavery, it would be absurd to deny that Islam has laws that fully recognize and regulate slavery. There is no evidence that Nāsir al-Dīn was not being honest whenever he rose up against enslaving the Satigui's Moslem subjects, who were traded for liquor, glass beads and trinkets. Barry (1972:144) has not minced his words:

> By declaring a holy war along the river, the Moors wanted, above all, to eliminate the establishment at Saint Louis and guarantee their supply of foodstuffs and of manpower.

In seventeenth century nomadic society, the use of slaves, integrated as they were into domestic production units, was limited - all the more so during the Shurbubba War, since much livestock probably perished as a result of the climatic crisis, one of the causes of this war. Neither agriculture, which was futile during these years of turmoil and drought, nor the harvests of gum arabic for European trading houses, which according to Barry were voluntarily boycotted, could account for an increasing demand for slaves by the Moorish Gibla.

As for the demand arising from the trans-Saharan trade with North Africa, the Gibla lay more or less outside the major Mauritanian axis (Wādī Dar'a-Wādān-Shingīti-Tishīt-Wālāta-northern Mali). Besides, there is no precise evidence that the *zwāya* from the Gibla, the backbone of Nāṣir al-Dīn's movement, were much involved in this trade. Regardless of their involvement, they were not hindered from becoming the principal and direct beneficiaries of the Atlantic trade, whereas the *hassān* were satisfied with collecting customary duties from European firms. Gum arabic, the major product that the *biḍān* had to offer to Europeans, was harvested almost exclusively by *zwāya* groups. It hardly figured in north-south trade across the Sahara.

The rigid opposition between maritime and trans-Saharan trade, upon which Barry's explanation of the Shurbubba War rests, is an oversimplification (Ould Cheikh 1985). Continuity, specialization and complementarity - not to be overlooked in favor of confrontation and competition - played an appreciable part in the transition from the dominance of trans-Saharan exchange to the hegemony of maritime trade. Even if the slave trade was in a crisis, and even if this was a major factor in the origin and failure of Nāṣir al-Dīn's movement, the complicated interplay of alliances during the Shurbubba War cannot be reduced to a conflict between the sea and the desert, caravans and caravels, warriors and marabouts.

Nonetheless, the converging interests between *hassān* chiefs, who opposed the reform, and the French at Saint Louis, and the *de facto* alliance that they contracted in order to overcome the *zwāya* party, marked a turning point in the evolution of Moorish political structure. According to Moorish traditions, the defeat of Nāṣir al-Dīn's supporters signaled the establishment of an emiral organization under which a *hassān* lineage assumed the political leadership of a set of warrior, clerical and tributary tribes. The customs paid by the European companies, which sought to guarantee the security and continuity of their trade, were an important means of both stabilizing and manipulating a supratribal political authority in the making. This new type of organization, to be discussed later, first came into being among the Trarza and Brakna in southwestern Mauritania, just after the Shurbubba War, and spread in the eighteenth century to the neighboring Adrar and Tagant. In addition to such issues as the extraction of customs duties, the provision of arms by

European companies, and forms of competition that occurred within the warrior aristocracy, the existence of the new type of organization raises the same questions about the relationship between *ḥassān* and *zwāya* as did the Shurbubba War.

Does this opposition, which is ideologically founded upon the religious and military specializations of the two dominant groups in Moorish society, reflect the structural duality of Moorish aristocracy or stratification into a hierarchy? Does it have to do with the differentiation of the relations of production? Or does it correspond to the equilibrium of a segmentary society and thus is a special aspect of the way that the anarchy (in the etymological sense of the word) of Moorish tribes was organized and maintained during the pre-colonial period? Preceding interpretations are far from satisfactory: ethnic interpretations are inconsistent and economic factors prove of limited value.

Inspired by Evans-Pritchard's and Gellner's (1969) functionalist analyses of segmentation, Stewart has sought to apply the principle of complementary opposition to the case at hand. Accordingly, the industrious and pacific nature of the *zwāya* was complementary to *ḥassān* aggressivity; the need for production created the need for protection. In Stewart's words (1973b:63):

> Traditionally Moorish society was directed by two theoretically separate segmentary, patrilineal groupings, each dependent upon the other for its physical or spiritual security. Nobles from the *zwāya* enjoyed a life of greater ease and comfort than did the *ḥassānis*, yet they were in constant need of *ḥassāni* protection. The *ḥassānis*, ... lived a more mobile life, yet were dependent upon the *zwāya* for their water, gum revenues and religious instruction. Strong leadership was in the hands of the *zwāya shaikhs* who exercised, in theory, no temporal authority; temporal authority was the prerogative of the *ḥassāni* chiefs .... In this way the segmentary principles of opposition and complementarity balanced the numerically superior *zwāya* against the *ḥassānis*, the pastoral against the raiding economy, and spiritual against physical protection.

The rather arbitrary nature of this (re)construction - for Moorish society has never been made up of two patrilineal segmentary groupings - proceeds from the same necessity that led Stewart to see the Shurbubba War as a founding myth. His view of Moorish society associates the idea of segmentation with that of an egalitarian tribal society in which the alternating fission and fusion of tribal groups constantly tend to reproduce an anarchic equilibrium that is fundamentally incompatible with the emergence either of autonomous political power or of a system of social stratification capable of explaining this power. Using examples from the history of the Adrar Emirate, Bonte (1979) has discussed the limitations of Stewart's analysis. Contrary to the latter's rather rigid functionalism, he has shown how, in the emirates established since the late seventeenth century, tribal organization and the processes of fission and fusion that it generated, far from permanently blocking the emergence of a centralized political authority, were gradually subordinated to the emerging power of the emirs. Within the warrior aristocracy from which the emirs were recruited, the hierarchical and hierarchizing tendencies of this new source of power were a decisive factor in the ranking of the *hassān* tribes and even a direct cause of their formation and fragmentation.[6] Moreover, these tendencies were a factor in the consolidation of *hassān* political hegemony over all other status groups, and particularly the *zwāya*.

The Shurbubba War is neither the founding myth of *hassān* supremacy nor the mere reflection of the clash of economic interests between clerics and warriors. This episode of Moorish history sheds light upon the political and ideological aspects of the opposition between these two status groups. This opposition involved two sets of political units (tribes) whose conceptual framework came from their system of patrilineal filiation but who were, in terms of status, united through their obedience to the warrior and clerical "codes". The *hassān* wielded political and military power most forcefully through the emirates, even though many tribes, *hassān* as well as *zwāya*, were not under emiral control. The specificity of the *zwāya* lay, above all, in their magical and religious duties. Even if the hierarchical relations between these two groups cannot be deduced from an economic basis, the specific ideological and political attributes the Moorish status system assigned to each of them entered into the system of relations that characterized the production processes of Moorish nomadism and that pertained to the particular economic specialization by which was defined the way each group participated in these processes.

Tribes and Emirates: The Social and Political
Organization of Moorish Nomadism

With regard to Barry's comments about the Shurbubba War, Hamès, on the basis of his conclusions about how the Moorish emirates were affected by capitalist trade, has suggested that the division of the Moorish aristocracy into two groups was related on one hand to the direct exploitation of slave labor by the *zwāya*, and on the other hand to the levy of tribute by the *hassān*:

> To the aristocratic warrior pole correspond, in the main, tributary social relations: warrior lineages extort revenues in kind from tributary lineages that remain owners of their means of production and of their capital in

livestock. To the other, cleric, pole correspond rather social relations of
a slave type: livestock belongs to the cleric lineages who tend to add to
their labor force that of a servile class directly involved in pastoral
production (Hamès 1979:393).

True, the *zwāya* used slave labor more than the *hassān* but this was so
because they were, historically, the principal actors responsible for the
development of the Moorish economy, pastoral (livestock, wells, *etc.*) as
well as agricultural (cereals, dates, *etc.*). This circumstance, along with
the role of the larger *zwāya* population in the production and
commercialization of basic commodities (salt, gum, dates, cereals, and so
forth), has perhaps led Hamès to set up too rigid an opposition between
the prevalence among clerics of slave labor and the predominance among
warriors of tributary relations, from which they drew a substantial part
of their revenues by "managing violence" (raids, levies, *etc.*).

However, slavery was never a *zwāya* monopoly. The clerics never
refrained - whenever the opportunity came up - from levying "revenues"
(they adapted the terminology to the case) upon their *tlāmīd* ("disciples"
but, in fact, wards), more or less with the latter's consent.
Notwithstanding Caille's (1965) comments about the use of slave labor for
harvesting gum arabic, this activity, depending as it does upon the
weather, hardly amounted to enough work to keep hands busy for more
than a few weeks a year. This occasional, seasonal activity was
undertaken by herders who were following their flocks or by farmers
who were idle between two crops. The scraping of gum for harvest fits
into a division of labor that was determined by those structures of
pastoral society already mentioned. This division of labor occurred
within domestic production units in which slaves were first assigned the
tasks of watching over livestock and tilling the soil and later of scraping
gum.

By looking at territorial organization, we can see how relations
between *zwāya* and *hassān* overlapped and were ranked. The apparent
simplicity of what has survived from the precolonial Moorish institution
of land rights should not make us forget the complexity of control over
pastoral lands; owners' and users' rights were bound up with
considerations of status and of personal relations. Wells, for instance,
were usually in the hands of *zwāya* groups. However, even though they
were the principal organizers of the pastoral economy, they were
generally subject to *hassān* groups who could, owing to their weapons,
guarantee for themselves access to forage and water even when their
rights to these resources were not recognized. The *Thulth al-ma* ("third
of the water") clause, evoked at the end of the Shurbubba War, stipulated
that the losers should henceforth offer, in case of need, a third of the

water that they themselves drew from their own wells to the winners and their offspring. Control over the use of pastures was usually stabilized through individual (*ḥurma*; plural: *ḥrum*) or collective (*gavr*; plural: *ágvār*) payments that in principle were part of a contract of protection in a society constantly subject to *razzias*.

Only the emirates (At-Trārza, Brākna, Adrār and Tagnīt) formed in the seventeenth and eighteenth centuries or a few powerful *hassān* tribes (Awlād Mbārak, Awlād Dā'ūd, Awlād An-Násir, Mastūf, *etc.*) strived, in spite of their precarious authority, to give a specific territorial content, often within unclear boundaries, to the political and hierarchical system, the unity of which they guaranteed and expressed. In this case, the levy by emirs of a "tribute of protection" (*ḥurmit tamajārit*) on foreign nomads, a kind of tax that the latter paid to enter the territory and live in (relative) security, was a means both of regulating the use of pastures and of affirming the power of the *hassān* within the territory, because they alone were able to collect this sort of revenue. However, the instability of the emirs, whose personal positions were nearly always precarious, and the uncertainty legitimacy of the ideological and hierarchical foundations of the emirates, when added to the absence of fixed and recognized boundaries, in fact allowed herders freedom of movement restricted only by their networks of alliance and their capacities for self-defense. Problems pertaining to pastoralist spatial mobility appear, then, to be closely related to the political organization of tribes and emirates.

The Moorish tribe (*qabīla*), identified with a common genealogical ancestor, seeks to maintain its original unity through tribal endogamy. Ideally, every man should marry the daughter of his father's brother (*mint al-'amm*) so that all free men within a tribe can say that they are *awlād 'amm* (patrilateral parallel cousins). However this genealogical ideal is a far cry from the reality, because the tribe's hierarchical structure includes persons who are not free men. Tribal endogamy must accommodate the hypergamy - and sometimes endogamy - that characterizes relations between different status groups within the tribe. There is another reason for the disparity between the ideal and reality. The hierarchy that results when free men are ranked with respect to each other (in terms of many factors, such as courage, wealth, knowledge and charisma), which is generally interpreted in genealogical terms, tends to reinforce the system of inequality based on hereditary status. As a function of "birth" within (in particular *zwāya*) tribes, the distinction was made between the pure nucleus (*samīm*) and migrants or foreigners (*'aṣab*), who contracted organic alliances with the tribe with regard to dwelling places, nomadic zones, marriages, *etc.*, thus coming to be considered as members. The former were, of course, usually thought to be "nobler" than and superior to the latter. But, among the prerogatives underlying tribal unity was the sharing - subject to restrictions - of the same territory.

Spatial dispersion did not, however, prevent expression of sentiments of tribal unity, particularly during conflicts with other tribes.[7] A *qabīla* was, first of all, a human group in which certain forms of collective responsibility existed, for which the shared territory and brand (*nār*) on animals were the outer signs. The territory and the brand were also the signs of special alliances between *hassān* and *zwāya* tribes; the former normally used the brand of "their" marabouts. Each *qabīla* had a collective duty to actively protect its members and their possessions; it was also required to make amends for serious offenses, in particular murders, that its members committed outside the tribe. Simplifying matters, we might say that a *qabīla* was a group of people who contributed *diya* to settle a homicide committed by one of them. More than a demographic (tribes ranged from a few score to several thousand or tens of thousands of persons), genealogical or residential unit with well-marked boundaries, a Moorish tribe during precolonial times was a political reality.

The political organization of the emirates was in many ways the outcome of the tribes. Like a tribal chief, an emir, in Stewart's words (1973b:380), "was no more than the first among equals in his own family and tribe, and with his *hassāni* cousins in his region". He was first and foremost the chief of the warriors, both in his tribe and in the emirate. As such he had to protect his subjects against foreign aggression. He also had judicial power, either exercised by himself or through a Moslem judge (*qādi*). Nonetheless, the office of emir differed from a tribal chieftaincy in many respects, notably: (1) authority was exercised not over a single tribe but over a set of *hassān* and *zwāya* tribes; and (2) a certain number of goods and revenues, in particular forms of tribute (*hurma* and *gavr*), were attached to it. Furthermore, the emirs in regions where Europeans traded received yearly presents called "customs". Symbolically, the emir's authority was most noticeable through his power over the emiral camp (*hilla* or *mahsār*), his mobile political capital. In this camp, a war drum (*tbal*) near the emir's tent symbolized his authority over the whole emirate. Among the Trarza, the emir alone - in principle - had the right to wear "the white trousers" (*as-sirwāl labyat*), a special sign of office.

The establishment of the office of emir within a single lineage entailed raising a military force for maintaining the emir's authority lest it dissipate, as so often happened to the chief's authority within a tribe.

This held true even though the office of emir was frequently the object of bloody strife, fanned by opposition within a segmentary society. The holding of this office caused blood to be shed between brothers, between nephews and uncles, between cousins: rival tribes or factions were often moved by kinship to take sides with one of the candidates. Nonetheless, the office of emir, its duties and symbols, generally survived these battles and assassinations. Moreover, factional strife over this source of power was a major factor in the reclassification of the tribes involved in these wars of succession. For instance, weakened *hassān* groups could give up their status in order to become *zwāya*, a practice known as *tawba* or *hijra*; or tributaries could emancipate themselves and become full-fledged warriors. Other noteworthy examples (the A'bīd Ahl 'Utmān in the Adrār and the Awlād ar-Rayyig among the Trarza) are the tribes who had no claim to common genealogy but drew their "tribal" cohesion from their common service as bodyguards or tax-collectors for the emir's family. To simplify, we can say that in all these cases, tribes did not make the emirate but, on the contrary, the latter made the tribes. Far from hindering the emergence of a centralized political authority, the segmentary processes of fission and fusion seemed to have been determined by this emerging source of power.

The tribal modal thus provides a means of presenting quite diverse realities: the reordering of social affiliations according to the political order of the Emirate; and the creation of new groups primarily defined by their political functions or, in the case of Islamic brotherhoods (*ṭuruq*), by religion. As in other cases considered in this volume, the actual features of social groups cannot simply be deduced from the "segmentary" properties attributed to the system of social organization (fission and fusion, the complementary opposition of social segments). Rather, the composition of social groups reflects a continuous process or reorganizing the social order according to diverse economic, political, or religious demands, and, above all in Moorish society, of politically "reclassifying" individuals and groups within the status hierarchy.

These observations bring us back to the question of the status of the *zwāya* and their position with respect to the *hassān*. Comments made above concerning the relations of kinship, segmentation and power within *hassān* groups, from which Emirs were recruited, are relevant here. As previously stated, within a Moorish political and social hierarchy a significant role existed for the *zwāya*, whose power derived from their economic functions and their religious duties. They were involved in the administration and legitimation of the emirates and moslem judges (*quḍḍāt*) were drawn from their numbers. Most importantly, they developed a higher degree of political autonomy, especially through religious brotherhoods. The principal religious leaders (*Shaykh*, plural, *ashakh*) in some respects had as much authority as the emirs (See Plate 8.1). The political hierarchy that resulted from the Shurbubba War, insofar as it still operates within the emirates from the point of view of the *hassān*, is constantly put into question from the point of view of the *zwāya* and their Islamic values. In the name of Islam, the *zwāya* have never recognized the tribute levied by the *hassān* on other Muslims. Even if they accept the established order, renouncing revindication based on the *jihād* (a religious war) and the establishment of Islamic political power in Moorish society (a revindication adopted in the eighteenth and nineteenth centuries in other West African societies), the *zwāya* reinforced their economic and religious power by creating parallel structures of power, in particular, through the brotherhoods.

The brotherhoods (*aṭ-ṭuruq al-ṣufiyya*) are religious organizations centered around the *shaykh*, the master and teacher (*murabbî*), who derived his authority through a chain that led back to the Prophet. For his disciples, he was a guide, an intercessor to be served and obeyed until he led them along the "way" (*ṭariqa*). They could then, after appropriate ceremonies, leave him, being qualified through the title of *shaykh* to lead other persons along the "way". Beyond individual concerns about salvation, the spread of the brotherhoods resulted from complex interactions among geographical and economic factors. Tribal solidarity was an important factor in the decision to join a specific brotherhood. In effect, these brotherhoods were historically associated with tribes: the Idawᶜali were *tijâniyya*; the Kunta, *qadîriyya*, *etc.* In contrast, certain other religious movements were founded on a tribal model, rapidly forming new tribes through assembling quite heterogeneous elements around prestigious shaykhs, the best example being that of Ali Sîdi Mahmud of Assabu, founded at the beginning of the nineteenth century. In all these cases, the major figures[8] in the brotherhoods were very active in developing the caravan trade,[9] digging wells and improving agriculture. The heads of brotherhoods sometimes exercised decisive political influence over the emirates, especially during critical periods of succession, by lending their support to rivals in power or by serving as mediators.

This account of Moorish social organization, viewed through the events of the Shurbubba war, shed light upon what this organization, beyond its ecological and economic bases in the nomadic way of life, owed to trade and to Islam. Moorish organization was not imposed exclusively on the political sphere, for the *zwāya* were even more involved economically in establishing a monopoly in commerce and a leading position in agriculture and herding. The traditional political hierarchy and system of economic specialization persisted throughout the period that followed Shurbubba, and partially endured during the colonial period. The long and difficult process of colonization of Mauritania by France left in place these statutory hierarchies, but also served to give value and emphasis to the economic power of the *zwāya*. The Moorish diaspora, which extended over a large portion of West Africa, establishing a new commercial network and contributing to a new expansion of Islam, raised the tensions and contradictions that had existed in precolonial Moorish society to yet a higher level of intensity.

Notes

1. Ibn Hawqal (de Slane 1842:83-85) wrote in the tenth century about how wealthy in camels the Berbers living in the Mauritanian Adrar were: the Tanbarutān chief sent 200 cameleers, each with 150 camels, against his enemies. According to Al-Bakri (1964:298-299), this same chief was able to rally 160,000 warriors with camel mounts and he sent to his ally, Tarim, a force with 50,000 camels.

2. The exceptional qualities of the Tiris grazing lands have been proclaimed in folk poetry:
> Four thousand camels and a bull
> Four nights and we've been on the move
> No need to test urine on our forearms
> Four years and we're getting rich

The third line refers to the fact that there is no camel trypanosomiasis (*tāburīt*) in the Tiris area; cameleers believe they can detect this sickness by smelling the animal's urine, which they put to dry on their forearms.

3. Like Nāṣir al-Dīn, Muhammad al-Yadāli (n.d) belonged to the Tāshumsha confederation, the spearhead of the *zwāya* coalition, and his father, from the ranks of the Imam, actually took part in clashes. For a brief account of Muhammad al-Yadāli's life, see Norris (1969).

4. The Bundu *imamate* was established by Malik Dauda Sy around 1690, and that of Futa Jallon about 1726 (Malik Sy's brother-in-law played an important role in establishing it). The rule of an *almami* over Futa Toro dates from the late 1780s (Curtin 1971).

5. This document from the Dutch West Indies Company, written in 1670-1671, reads:
> The Chamber of Zealand has Argyn and neighboring places, located near Cape Blanc (20. N) under its administration. This fort, located on a reef in a small bay, has a garrison of 25 men. Trade is in gum arabic and ostrich feathers... The profits are rather good for the Chamber (Barry 1972:146).

6. The making of the A'bīd Ahl 'Uṭmān tribe in the Adrār Emirate and of the Awlād ar-Rgayyig tribe in the Trarza Emirate are the clearest examples of the formation of "artificial" tribes around this new source of power.

7. Border disputes were a frequent cause of war among *zwāya*: for example, in the fifteenth century, between Tandga and Midlish; and in the nineteenth century, between Idaġzaymbu and Taguānit, Idablihsan and Idawa'li, Awlād Abyayri and Idaydba.

8. For the Qadiriyya, S. Sīd al-Mukhtār al-Kuntī (d. 1811) and his son S. Sīdi Muhammad (d. 1826), S. Sidiyya al-Kabīr (d. 1868), S. Muhammad Fādil (d. 1869) and his sons, S. Mā al-'Aynīn (d. 1910) and S. Sa'd Būh (d. 1917). The Tijaniyya was propagated over Moorish lands principally by S. Muhamd al-Hāfit (d. 1831).

9. Regarding the economic organization of Ash-Shaykh Sidiyya, a *zwāya*, and his political influence, see Stewart (1973a) and Ould Cheikh (1982, 1985).

PART FIVE

HIERARCHY AND INEQUALITY IN REGIONAL SYSTEMS

9

Herders, Hunters and Smiths: Mobile Populations in the History of Kanem

Edouard Conte

Sovereignty, Conversion and Modes of Livelihood in the Wider Chad Basin

The emergence of the Kanemi polity often has been attributed to the sole initiative of Saharan herders. The belief, implicit in certain Arabic chronicles,[1] that pastoralists were endowed with an exceptional "instinctive" dynamism in matters of empire-building is only one of the preconceptions veiling the historical role of communities practicing diverse modes of livelihood. Indeed, these writings often convey assumptions concerning "racial" hierarchy and the causal role of Islam in the process of state formation which, rather than being critically scrutinized, have tended to be taken somewhat for granted. "Pastoralism" frequently has been viewed as a concomitant to "white" dominion over "black" agriculturalists, a postulate only too reminiscent of certain "Hamitic" theories. Certain scholars, notably under the influence of diffusionism, have not always subjected these biases to adequate criticism.

Arabic documents concerning the history of Kanem can thus hardly be

222   *Edouard Conte*

regarded as neutral. They came to us from Muslim chroniclers serving Muslim rulers and forcefully convey the perception that an organic relationship existed between Islam, sovereignty and legitimacy. Each modern historian in turn tends to over-emphasize the formal aspects of government, dynastic continuity and imperial authority. Correspondingly, there has been a tendency to exorcise the memory of non-islamized, mobile populations of hunters and smiths who acted out of sight of scribes but were nevertheless very much a part of Kanem history.

Our main concern in this study is to contribute to a better understanding of the long-term interrelations between the different modes of livelihood developed by the peoples of Kanem. In particular, the historical role of pastoralism might be profitably reassessed by considering its bearing on the broader dynamics of Saharan-Sahelian socio-economic relations in this region. This presupposes a close examination of patterns of subordination affecting the largely hereditary socio-professional categories into which Kanemi society has long been divided. The barriers separating these categories are hierarchically expressed, in both genealogical and economic terms. Modes of livelihood, ranging from exclusive pastoralism to various combinations of herding, farming, smelting and hunting, even today reflect deep-rooted historical cleavages, as do corresponding marriage prohibitions and methods of tribute extortion between them. The present study will consider these phenomena in the light of recent archaeological, ethnographic and historical research, with the aim of supplementing and enhancing analyses of developments in the strictly political domain based on Arabic sources.

Some preliminary remarks on language distribution should help to situate in geographical and cultural terms the vast area to be examined (See Figure 9.1).[2] The centers of gravity of the main language areas today found between northern Chad and Borno have shifted southwestward in the course of the last millennium. This pattern is thought to reflect the successive emergence and decline of a "Zaghawa" polity (*c.* eighth to tenth centuries), Kanem (tenth to thirteenth centuries) and Borno (thirteenth to twentieth centuries). It is widely accepted that the Nilo-Saharan domain expanded southward with the progression of Saharan herders, culturally affiliated to today's Tubu (or Teda) and Zaghawa (or Beri), who still are represented, respectively, in the Tibesti and Ennedi massifs of North Chad. These pastoralists are credited with having established a certain ascendancy over Sahelian agro-pastoralists and agriculturalists belonging to the Chadic-speaking peoples. This vast process encouraged the emergence of Kanembu and Kanuri, two intimately related tongues of the Nilo-Saharan group, and favored the wide acceptance of these languages among Chadic-speakers. The latter continue to be represented by the Hausa and the descendants of those peoples globally designated as the "Sao", to whose presumptive cultural heirs one may reckon the Kotoko (or Makari) of the northern banks of the river Shari and the insular Buduma of Lake Chad. The Kuri of Lake Chad's southeastern periphery recently adopted Kanembu but were also originally Chadic-speakers.

The incursion and partial settlement of Arabic-speaking groups in greater Kanem appears from a linguistic point of view almost incidental to the southwestward extension of Nilo-Saharan languages. This is not to deny, however, that Arabs have long mingled with peoples of Nilo-Saharan and Chadic linguistic affiliations. Among Arab settlers, one encounters the so-called Shuwa of Lake Chad's southern shores, whose ancestors are purported to have arrived in these lands as early as the fourteenth century. The Tunjur "Arabs", according to Trimingham (1962:139), "were probably Nubians, who through contact with Arabs had become Arabic-speaking". They invaded Kanem from Waday in the seventeenth century and are still present in southeast Kanem. Finally, different communities of Arab camel herders from Libya nomadize in northern Kanem. The Awlad Sliman, who played a politically decisive role in the mid-nineteenth century,[3] are the best known of these groups.

In historical terms, we are very poorly informed about the relations which may or may not have prevailed between the Zaghawa, whose zone of influence during the ninth century was centered to the north-east of Lake Chad, possibly around the Jurab lowlands, and the so-called Duguwa dynasty believed to have reigned over Kanem as early as the eighth or the ninth century (Lange 1977). The history of the central Chad basin is sometimes too exclusively equated with the saga of the Muslim successors of the Duguwa, the Magemi Sefawa, who ruled Kanem and then Borno from the end of the eleventh century to the middle of the nineteenth century. Until recently, research dealing with the peoples of this vast realm has tended to juxtapose an "imperial zone" and an ever-shrinking non-Muslim culture area populated by groups subsumed under the blanket term "Sao". To the north, west, and, for a time, east of Lake Chad, purportedly devout rulers of pastoral extraction are seen as having maintained military control over large expanses of the central Sahara and Sudan, notwithstanding chronic strife among royal lines (Lange 1982), would-be successors or usurpers (Lange 1989). To the south, in contrast, political centralization was initially limited in scope to the Kotoko-type city-state "predestined" to be assimilated politically and religiously into the Muslim "dynastic" society of Kanem and Borno.[4] This perspective rests on the credence granted to an irreversible, early southwestward

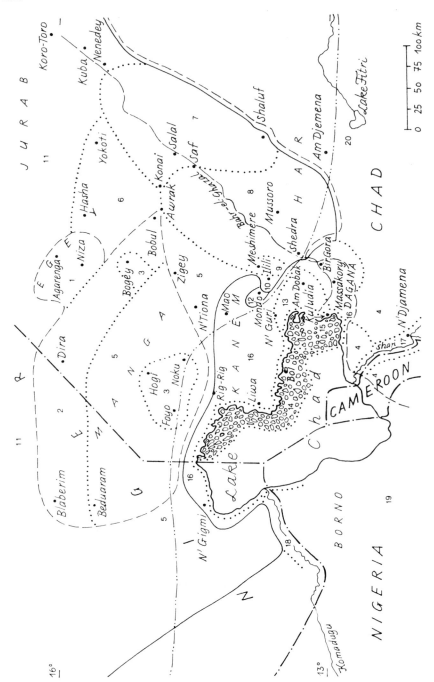

progression of Islam, largely borne by conquering pastoralists.

Mohammed's doctrine here emerges as a political catalyst instrumental to the consolidation of large-scale state formations. Religion appears to operate as a stabilizing influence, counterbalancing the inherently "anarchistic" quality of "dynamic" nomadic cultures. Such integratory and expansionary processes are presumed to have brought in their wake the full or partial sedentarization of sizeable sections of those pastoral groups credited with key roles in Kanemi history.

More credibility is today lent to the hypothesis of a progressive integration of the so-called Sao populations into the Kanemi and Bornoan polities than to earlier theories postulating their outright decimation.[5] In a interestingly provocative article concerning the Arabs, the Kotoko and the originally Central Sudanic - but of a late Arabic - speaking Babalia of the Shari delta, Décobert (1982) goes as far as to invert prior propositions; he interprets the emergence of "Sao" identity and a belated development of the walled city-state and defensive mounds in this area as <u>responses</u> to the arrival of Arab pastoralists south of Lake Chad rather than as long-standing traits of local "pagan" culture engaged in a rear-guard, albeit perseverant, action against "inevitable" Islamic expansion fostered by Kanem and Borno. In the course of this specific encounter, it was the Shuwa Arabs rather than the Chadic-speaking peoples south of Lake Chad who changed their mode of livelihood! Settling at such southerly latitudes implied abandoning camel-breeding and converting to semi-sedentary bovine husbandry combined with seasonal agriculture,[6] Lange (1989), adopting a broader perspective, tends to interpret Sao identity as an ideological construct invoked by the rulers of Borno and their chroniclers in the struggle to consolidate their empire.

In the light of these analyses, we are led to question the validity of the often uncritically accepted pastoralist-cultivator-artisan/hunter hierarchy (regularly stated in this order) upon which many facets of the historiography and ethnography of the wider Chad basin repose. Recent

---

FIGURE 9.1 The Peoples of Kanem [N.B. This map was drawn by G. Wittner (Frobenius-Institut, Frankfurt am Main, Germany) on the basis of Le Rouvreur (1962:63)].

    State boundary
    Southern limit of Teda-Daza habitat
-------- Northern limit of Arab habitat
    Northern limit of Fulani habitat
.... Approximate inter-group boundaries

1. "New" 'Awl⁻ᵃd Slim⁻ᵃn Arabs
2. "Old" 'Awl⁻ᵃd Slim⁻ᵃn Arabs
3. Hasa'una Arabs
4. Semi-sedentary Shuwa Arabs
5. Daza of Manga
6. Jagada
7. Kesherda
8. Kreda
9. Ankorda
10. Warda
11. Teda
12. Tunjur "Arabs"
13. Duu
14. Buduma
15. Kuri
16. Kanembu
17. Kotoko
18. Mober
19. Kanuri
20. Bulala

archaeological and ethnographic evidence suggest that the Sao debate has turned away attention from at least two other issues of importance to the history of Kanem-Borno:

(1) The extremely recent character of conversion to Islam:

Pastoral populations who contributed to the formation of the Kanem polity, such as the Teda, their Daza cousins of the South and the Zaghawa themselves, extensively resisted conversion to Islam until centuries <u>after</u> the empire's apogee. And non-pastoral but mobile hunters constituted a further core of resistance to in-depth penetration of Islam in the central Chad basin <u>into the twentieth century</u>.

(2) The development of metallurgy:

It is questionable whether Kanem could have existed as a state without an indigenous iron industry. Swords, armor and luxury metal goods may well have been imported from North Africa in exchange for slaves, but local smelters and smiths assumed a basic function in the simultaneous development of agriculture and arms production upon which the polity was tightly dependent. In dealing with these issues, we will be lead to reconsider the manner in which the Islamic/non-Islamic and the nomadic/sedentary distinctions have been used in interpreting processes of state formation in Kanem and Borno.

The conversion of the Magemi Sefawa rulers of Kanem by the end of the eleventh century and of the cadet branch of this dynasty known as the Bulala by the forteenth century may be seen as having contributed to the extension of those Sahelian zones subjected to systematic slave-raiding. It also may be argued, however, that Islam was not a precondition for this practice. The Zaghawa, the Duguwa and the early Bulala all were equally dependent on the sale of "infidels", non-Muslims. Later, believers and non-believers, sedentaries and nomads, often allied to perpetuate this lucrative trade. The ongoing southward expansion of slave-raiding may be seen as linked to the southwestward displacement of poles of sovereignty from Borku/Jurab to Kanem and thence to Borno and beyond. The process of conversion to Islam, in contrast, only came to affect large sectors of the population of a shifting imperial core with a time lag of as much as several centuries.

In this perspective, the "Sao" myth (*cf.* Migeod 1923; and Lange 1989) may be read as a reflection of the progressive subordination of cultures of the Chad basin in which hunters and agro-pastoralists were ritually and economically bound together with pastoralists, both black and Arab, sedentary and nomadic, Muslim and non-Muslim. North of Lake Chad, in Kanem proper, the systematic extortion of harvests by herders and the concomitant multiplication of servile farming communities in oases or on the southern reaches of grazing zones favored the development of bovine as opposed to cameline husbandry. Hunters and metallurgists were in the process subjected to a variety of forms of social segregation. Crucial though their role was in the early history of Kanem, they were over time politically, maritally and ritually relegated to the interstices and margins of imperial society: for them, conversion to Islam, the abandoning of migratory patterns, and the ever more exclusive recourse to sedentary agriculture was tantamount to vassalization (*cf.* Conte 1986).

Before confronting these hypotheses with available sources, it is important to underline how shorter- and longer-term climatic and environmental variations have operated to affect the degree of potential complementarity of the different modes of livelihood which have co-existed in Kanem.

Harsh Environmental Fluctuations
in a Unique Ecological Haven

Kanem proper extends from the northeastern shores of Lake Chad to the southern confines of the Sahara. The region is today bounded by the Niger-Chad border to the west, and the Chadian Bahr el-Ghazal to the east. Along a north-south axis of barely 250 km traversing the center of Lake Chad, one passes from a Sudano-Sahelian environment (12 -13 N. Lat.), through the Sudano-Saharan belt (*c.* 14 N. Lat.) and quickly reaches the Sahara itself which, in Kanem, now descends as far south as 15 30′ N. Lat. Lake Chad is located between approximately 12 20′ and 14 10′ N. Lat. This situates it, under "normal" pluviometrical conditions, between the 240 mm and the 500 mm isohyets. The austere, undulating Kanemi landscape is tempered during the summer rainy season by the furtive appearance of steppic grasses, which transform the country into an immense green pasture. In spite of the apparent aridity which prevails during the greater part of the year, Kanem constitutes a unique ecological haven in relation to neighboring Sahelian areas at comparable latitudes. The watershed is often easily accessible from the bottom of the interdunary depressions, known as *b'la* in the tongue of the Kanembu who probably number over 100,000 and form the dominant ethnic group of the region. When *b'la* are not rendered sterile by temporary or permanent natronization, they may be irrigated and can furnish two or more annual crops of cereals (millet, wheat, maize) or vegetables. This produce complements the millet cultivated during the rainy season around dune-top villages, which today have an average population of only some sixty inhabitants. All conditions thus are fulfilled to enable the flourishing of an agro-pastoral economy dependent neither on monoculture nor on a single yearly cereal harvest. Historically, it is in no way surprising that Kanem has afforded refuge to pastoral and hunter populations of more northerly origins.

From the southern shore of Lake Chad, mainly inhabited by semi-sedentary agro-pastoral Shuwa Arabs, to the southern fringes of the Sahara, home to the Awlad Sliman camel nomads of Fezzani origin, one encounters an astounding variety of pastoral and agricultural activities. These intermesh to form what surely may be regarded as one of the most complex and delicately balanced economic complexes of Sahelian Africa. The Buduma, while practicing millet cultivation in their lacustral habitat, lead their cattle from one uninhabited island to another to benefit optimally from seasonal grass as well as more permanent shoreline pasture. The riverine Kuri, culturally and linguistically closer to the Kanembu, also possess substantial herds but place as much or more weight on the intensive cultivation of the rich, seasonally dried-up or dammed-off channels and inlets of their marshy archipelago. The southern Kanembu of the mainland hill country are sometimes less expert but nevertheless prosperous herders whose stock graze within a restricted radius around their villages. The latter shift site from decade to decade in response to soil exhaustion on sandy dune-tops and localized salinization of *b'la*. Progressing northward, one encounters a steppe which, before reaching Mao, the political center of Kanem, gives way to the Bir Lure plateau, formed by a stable, grassless duneland. *B'la* become fewer, shallower, and drier. The countryside is marked only by some oval depressions in which scant desert shrubs contrast with an otherwise dismally naked landscape. The area surrounding Mao is characterized by the alternation of dunes 30 to 60 m high and vales situated at almost regular intervals of 3 to 6 km. The latter sometimes harbor extensive palm groves. Dry farming loses progressively in importance in relation to both bovine and ovine husbandry, thus rendering *b'la* cultivation even more crucial than in the south. Here begins the domain of the Daza and Teda pastoralists whose habitat extends as far north as Fezzan.

In spite of its relative clemency, the Kanemi environment periodically reserves harsh crises for cultivators and pastoralists alike. The flooding of Lake Chad from 1954 to 1956, for example, corresponded to a period of high rainfall that favored farmers from south to north. At the same time, it is believed to have caused 25 to 30 percent losses among the herds of the Buduma (Bouquet 1974:87). In contrast, from 1960 to 1975-1980, the depth of Lake Chad decreased to such an extent that vast areas of the lacustral periphery presenting an extremely low declivity became dry. The surface of Lake Chad shrunk from *c.* 24,000 sq km to only 8,000 sq km over this period! The desiccation of such broad expanses of sediment-rich shoreland inevitably entails an economic upheaval, the effects of which, notably with regard to movements of the labor force, reach far beyond the lake's immediate periphery. Somewhat paradoxically, drought thus may allow the production of local grain surpluses in rich dried-out areas precisely when most parts of Kanem are suffering from severe food shortages. Long dry cycles also entail a lesser and more painstaking access to underground water. They equally render many seasonally inundated *b'la* in more northerly parts of Kanem periodically uncultivable. For pastoralists, this determines southward moves of greater or lesser amplitude, in search of water and pasture, at just those times when the resources of more sedentary Kanemi are most strained.

Shorter and longer-term drought cycles, as well as the permanent danger of pasture saturation in densely populated agricultural areas, serve to modify the agro-pastoral balance in Kanem for periods of variable duration. Barth (1965 [1857] II:248), for instance, observed long-distance transhumance associated with intensive bovine herding during his visit to northwestern Kanem, in 1851, at the beginning of a four-decade period of high rainfall. Quoting oral sources, Le Rouvreur (1962:92) relates that at the time of the French conquest in 1899 - after ten years of rapid decrease in precipitation and, admittedly, two decades of civil strife - Kanem was on the contrary almost empty of cattle. Before the 1969-1973 drought, the Kanem and Lake *préfectures*, with a combined population of some 323,000, were thought to supply pasture to approximately 1,370,000 cattle, 900,000 sheep and goats, 80,000 donkeys, 62,000 camels and 25,000 horses.[7] During the 1969-1973 catastrophe, cattle mortality is estimated to have ranged from an average of 25 percent on the southern shore of Lake Chad to as much as 90 percent in certain areas of North Kanem!

The comparison of these modern accounts illustrate the interrelatedness of variations in rainfall and herd wealth. There is no reason to believe that comparable fluctuations had been foreign to the wider Chad basin during earlier periods. Over the centuries, hydrological changes also have had important effects on population movements and settlement patterns, as well as on the degree of complementarity between different economic pursuits. Maley (1976) has documented a period of persistent high water stands in Lake Chad from *c.* 800 A.D. to *c.* 1400 A.D. Interestingly, this period broadly covers the lifespan of the Kanem state. After significant lows in the mid-fifteenth and late sixteenth centuries, the lake's surface level again remained exceptionally high from *c.* 1625 to *c.* 1750. Its dramatic decrease at the end of this period was probably related to the drought conditions in Tibesti to which oral traditions attribute the important southward movements toward the Bahr el-Ghazal of Teda and Daza pastoralists. This southwest-northeast oriented, sometimes partially flooded, depression extends over 500 km from Lake Chad's southeastern tip to the Jurab lowlands, south of Borku. For centuries, this axis represented a major migratory corridor offering ample of variable resources in water, arable lands and trees to pastoralists, agriculturalists, hunters and metallurgists alike. Since the early 1700s, however, drastic reductions in water level have affected Lake Chad about twice a century. These oscillations have had a negative effect on the watershed in North Kanem, in the Jurab, and along the Bahr el-Ghazal. They also influenced Lake Fitri, which was in one period much larger and possibly linked to Lake Chad.

Do these hydrological variations denote a long-term trend towards desiccation of the northern Chad basin? Nicholson (1981:35), in an analysis of Saharan climates centered on the water level of Lake Chad, considers

> ...that there has been no steady trend toward increased aridity in the Sahel throughout the past centuries or even within the present century, but instead numerous episodes of wetter or dried conditions.

Following Maley (1976), Nicholson (1981:37) nonetheless concedes that "the present normal stand of Lake Chad ... is lower than at any other period since about 3,5000 B.P.". This situation follows a span of two centuries during which highs in water levels globally do not compensate for lows.

Such a process may be deemed "transitory" in terms of climate history. Yet, in human and environmental terms, it is to be feared that desiccation, deforestation, and desertification have wrought irreversible damage. The hunter who no longer finds game to hunt, the smith who finds only dry wells on his route, have all seen their modes of livelihood rendered sufficiently precarious as to become non-viable in many areas. In South Kanem, successive droughts and deforestation have even come to affect the riverain groves and inlets of Lake Chad, threatening at times to reduce what was once an inland "sea" to no more than a squalid marsh. Even a longer-term wet period would not necessarily result in the restoration of those conditions of flora and fauna that once allowed the development of an historically most singular set of relationships and inter-dependencies linking the herders, hunters, and smiths of Kanem.

Kanem the Crossroads, the Empire, the Fief

The term Kanem is first recorded in a text of al-Yaqubi, dated 872 A.D., where it designates a place described as the home of the Zaghawa (Cuoq 1975:52). However, it is impossible to say when the name Kanembu may have come to denote a culturally distinguishable people rather than a very heterogenous population sharing a most broadly defined territory. Furthermore, relatively scant Arabic-language sources yield hardly a clue as to the economic structure of this early central African polity. Contemporary historical studies, mainly preoccupied, as were the chroniclers of old, with dynastic continuity, likewise grant little consideration to this theme. One is left to wonder how a political entity of such considerable importance could have come to be without an indigenous metal industry capable of furnishing agricultural implements, tools and weapons. Taking up this query, recent archaeological research suggests that the development of an agro-pastoral economy in wider Kanem was not unrelated to the extension of iron production during the second half of the first millennium A.D. (Coppens 1969; and Treinen-Claustre 1982). A significant smelting capacity may be considered to have been a precondition for the maintenance of military forces capable of ensuring both the large-scale acquisition of captives in Sahelian areas and the control of trade routes essential to their marketing as slaves in Arab-dominated North and Northeast Africa.

Treinen-Claustre's excavations in the Koro-Toro area at the Bahr el-Ghazal's northern extremity indicate that from the fifth to the tenth centuries A.D. (Middle Iron Age), that is during the formative period of the Kanem polity, there occurred a considerable development of iron production. This industry is attributable to groups with fixed points of settlement who drew their subsistence in a wider or lesser radius from hunting, fishing <u>and</u> animal husbandry. For this epoch, mortars and recipients testify to the use of grains but there is no conclusive proof available for cereal cultivation, as opposed to extensive gleaning in areas where seed-bearing grasses were seasonally plentiful (Treinen-Claustre 1982:178-181).

Data attesting to the practice of agriculture are more abundant for the Late Iron Age (eleventh to sixteenth centuries). This phase seems to correspond to a substantial reduction in metal production determined by the exhaustion of wood resources in a drier climatic situation (Treinen-Claustre 1982:181-183). Unfortunately, no systematic archaeological investigations along the southern Bahr el-Ghazal or in Kanem proper have been carried out. Only such research could indicate if the relative desiccation of more northerly areas studied by Treinen-Claustre corresponded to an expansion of iron production closer to Lake Chad, in the more humid core zone of the Kanem polity. Evidence does suggest, however, that the close social and ritual proximity of hunters and smiths observable in modern Kanem could reflect a very long-standing economic tradition in the northeastern Chad basin. It further appears from Treinen-Claustre's results that the development of metal production in Jurab and along the northern Bahr el-Ghazal was associated with intense animal husbandry among hunter-smiths.

For the more southerly reaches of the Chad basin, Lebeuf (1969) underlines the determining role of hunter groups from North Kanem, the region east of Lake Chad and the Mandara mountains (today North Cameroon), with a knowledge of iron production, in founding what he chooses to term the Sao culture (*cf.* Forkl 1983). Under this label he includes all pre-Islamic groups settled on the southern periphery of Lake Chad. Lebeuf hypothesizes the dispersal of the "Sao" following their "final defeat" by Idris Alawma of Borno during the sixteenth century but does not come to any conclusion regarding their subsequent position in the Kanem-Borno polity (*cf.* Lange 1989). This is to neglect in particular the importance of non-Islamic hunter-smiths all around Lake Chad into the nineteenth century.

According to indications furnished by older blacksmiths in Central and South Kanem in 1973, ore extraction and smelting continued to prosper there, labor-intensive though these activities were, until the end of the pre-colonial period. It has been a commonplace belief that Kanem is practically devoid of mineral resources. Indeed, no iron ore of the quality of that to be found in Enedi, in the northeast of Chad, whence Kanemi smiths claim to originate, nor is it available in Waday, to the east of Kanem near the present-day Sudan. Nonetheless, the ferruginous soil accessible from 0 to -2.5 m at certain *b'la* bottoms in Central Kanem contains a sufficient proportion of iron oxide to allow, granted adequate wood supplies, successful if painstaking reduction. Analyses of soil samples taken in 1974 at Koro *b'la*, 65 km west of Mao, sustain this assertion.[8] Kanemi smiths affirmed that comparable ore was obtained at numerous other sites in Kanem.[9] Smelting, as any traveler may observe, was common along the southern Bahr el-Ghazal, notably around Shedra. To the south of Lake Chad, the Haddad (Arab affiliated smiths) reduced iron-rich nodules collected on the surface.

To show that iron was produced a century ago in what was, for a period, the heartland of the Kanemi polity of course has no value *per se* in demonstrating the historical continuity of smelting in this region. Nonetheless, it is important to observe that founders did use locally obtained ores. This fact has been surprisingly neglected until now and would in itself warrant serious archaeological investigation of mining and smelting sites in central Kanem and along the southern Bahr el-Ghazal. Where possible, systematic datings of smelting activities at a multiplicity of known locations might indicate whether and when local resources would have been drawn upon to satisfy specific military and economic requirements. Here lies one of the few lateral roads presently open for the further exploration of Kanemi history beyond the isolated episodes known to us through written sources.

Lange's interpretation of the dynastic history of early Kanem is of particular interest in that it postulates a certain continuity of "smith" tradition from pre-Islamic times to the present (Lange 1977:151-154). This author considers that the pre-Islamic rulers of Kanem, the Banu Duku of the *Diwan Salatin Bornu* (Lange 1977), believed to have attained their apogee between the end of the tenth and the later eleventh century, may be identified with the Zaghawa of Saharan pastoral tradition, whom chroniclers cite as the predecessors of the Islamic Sefawa dynasty. Lange is understandably tempted to view the present-day Duu (or Dogoa), whom Nachtigal refers to as the Danoa and portrays as the "oldest" inhabitants of Kanem, as the heirs of the Banu Duku (Arabic) or Duguwa (Kanuri, equivalent of Duu). These interesting hypotheses regarding the genesis of the Kanem state would stand to gain by more clearly distinguishing ancient dynastic names from contemporary designations of socio-professional categories. Ethnographic data could prove to be of interest in this regard.

Before further considering Lange's analysis, attention must be drawn to a major ambiguity which has arisen in European literature due to the hasty assimilation, in both colloquial and scholarly usage, of the Kanembu term *Duu* and the Arabic *Haddad*. Indeed, in both literary and Chadian Arabic *haddad* (plur. *haddadin*) signified blacksmith(s). In the latter dialect the term is extended to designate, as a group or as individuals, all craftsmen and their kin. Especially when applied to Kanembu neighbors, the denomination even covers hunters and many non-craftsmen descended from or related to the former. In this acceptation the singular becomes *haddadi* and the plural *haddad*. The Kanembu, in contrast, make both a linguistic and social distinction between blacksmiths qua craftsmen (*kagelma*) and members of "smith" groups of *duu* (also pronounced *dugu* or *dughu*, plur. *duguwa* or *duua*), who are mainly of hunter (*m'barama*) heritage. *Haddadi* better renders the term *Duu* and hence may not be translated *a priori* as "blacksmith".

This having been said, we may return to Lange's reading of the *Diwan Salatin Bornu*. By way of conclusion, Lange (1977:152): (1) retains a "mythical or historical" connection between the Dogoa/Haddad and the Banu Duku; (2) postulates a relationship between the Banu Duku and the Zaghawa; and (3) is inclined to link the latter to the Middle Iron Age, demonstrating the existence of metallurgy at this period in the Koro Toro area, which led Coppens (1969) to speak of a *"culture haddadienne"*. Lange (1977:153) comes to define the Zaghawa neither as a nomadic people nor as a blacksmith caste but rather as an "allogenous group which dominated Kanem and, by extension, all the inhabitants of the state of

Kanem" or, as he writes elsewhere (Lange 1978:513), a "dominant aristocracy". He believes that the "people who brought iron directly or indirectly to Kanem stimulated the foundation of the state" of the same name (Lange 1977:153).

This period of Kanemi history is assumed to have ended when the Kanemi sovereign Hummey, himself described as a Berber married to a Tubu, and, hence, possibly a non-Muslim woman, converted to Islam in 1075 A.D. Thus would have been founded the Beni Hummey dynasty. The rulers of this line enhanced their genealogy by claiming descent from the Himyarite Arab Sayf ibn Dhi Yazan, whence stem the designations Yazani and Sefawa. Lange thinks that Islam was consolidated and disseminated widely during the reign of Kunama Dibalami but notes that an all too rapid islamization cannot have been in the interest of a pastoral nobility whose main source of external revenue is presumed to have been derived from the sale of "pagan" captives transported north through Tubu country over desert routes, then firmly under Kanemi control. Lange (1978:512) is of the opinion that, following the dynastic conversion, Duguwa subjects were defined as a primary source of slaves for the free (*kambe*) Muslim population, whereas the Zaghawa aristocracy, equally irreducible in its resistance to Islam (Lange 1978:505, quoting al-Idrisi), was forced to return to a nomadic life-style in Kanem's Saharan periphery. The loss of status of Duguwa subjects may have facilitated taking captives from their midst but, as oral traditions underline, this must not have entailed their statutory enslavement within the framework of the them prevalent system of social stratification.

During the twelfth century, a deep rivalry developed between the ruling Magemi, to which the Sefawa belonged, and a junior branch known as the Bulala. Trimingham (1962) interprets this struggle for supremacy as a "pagan reaction to the islamizing tendencies of the Saifi house". Under the pressure of this conflict, the Kanemi court transferred its seat to Borno during the first half of the thirteenth century. The establishment of Bulala dominion over Kanem ensued during the second half of the 14th century (*cf.* Lange 1982:316). Idris Katagarmabe (r. 1502-1526) finally wrested Kanem back under his line's command by defeating the Bulala prince Dunama in one of several expeditions to the province narrated by Ibn Furtua.[10] The Bulala officially became tributary to Borno but in practice remained independent for several decades more, namely until their final defeat by the Tunjur, who entered Kanem after a heavy undoing at the hands of the founder of the Waday sultanate, ʿAbd el-Karim, *c.* 1630 (*cf.* Lavers 1980:199). The invaders inflicted a resounding blow on the Bulala, whose rulers fled east and reestablished themselves among the Central-Sudanic speaking Kuka around Lake Fitri.

The Tunjur subsequently tried to take control of Mao but their strength did not prove sufficient to usurp the function of governor of Kanem. The Bornoans blocked this attempt by sending an army to Kanem under the command of Mageni, Dala Afuno, who became the first viceroy of Kanem. The descendants of Dala, known as the Dalatoa, have administered Kanem, at least nominally, ever since.

The chain of events surrounding the Bulala debacle of the seventeenth century and the subsequent rebalancing of the political situation in favor of Borno have remained embedded in Kanemi oral tradition to date. Oral sources concur in depicting the period following the Bornoan reconquest as one of endemic unrest. This time of turmoil is associated with internal and external population movements, as well as with a major realignment of internal poles of sovereignty and subordination. Few groups resident in Kanem today can trace their aristocratic lines further back than this "breaking point" in historical memory.

For the historian of Kanem, the seventeenth and eighteenth centuries remain largely impenetrable due to the lack of written sources. Oral traditions,[11] however, do offer important insights concerning social and political organization under Dalatoa rule. In the following section, we will examine Kanemi social stratification in the light of these traditions. The redefinition of Duu status indeed appears just as central to our understanding of this "dark" period of Kanemi history as it is to that of dynastic change and islamization in early Kanem.

Hierarchy and Subordination in Kanem

In its widest acceptation "Kanembu", literally derived from the Tedaga "people-of-the-south", means anyone belonging to the people of Kanem and whose mother tongue is Kanembu. In current contemporary usage, the term may be restricted to those groups of Kanemi freemen whose claim to being distant descendants of Sefawa affiliated elements, or their marriageable allies or successors, notably Tubu or Bornoan, is socially recognized. Among freemen (*kambe*), a major distinction is drawn between the "people-of-the-spear", or cattle-owning Kanembu pastoralists of "noble" descent in the widest sense, and the "people-of-the-bow", or Duu of hunter or smith origin for whom cattle ownership was for centuries forbidden. The two social categories are separated by a rigorous marriage barrier.[12]

Until the beginning of the twentieth century, Kanembu society was crosscut by three important cleavages, which distinguished Kanembu from Duu, freemen from slaves, and masters from dependents. These partially overlapping lines of division entailed a certain number of "paradoxes" which differentiated the stratification system of this agro-pastoral society from those of its more exclusively pastoral neighbors. Contrary to Lange's (1978:512) understanding, both Kanembu and Duu were and remain freemen and thus, in principle, could both acquire captives. Slaves in turn were born into the servile class or forced into it through capture. They could, however, be emancipated from their hereditary status. Slave women could marry into both the Kanembu and Duu strata, thus determining the thenceforth free status of their offspring.

The free dependent class was defined principally in terms of its tightly restricted access to land and cattle and the variety of tributary obligations it had toward land-controlling lineages. On the one hand, it included most members of the Duu category, due to their dubious Islamic credentials and former alliance with the evicted Bulala. On the other hand, it included a majority of those Kanembu farmers known as *maskin* (from the Arabic "poor") who, by virtue of a complex and exploitative fiscal system (*cf.* Conte 1984), could not freely dispose of the product of their own labor. All Kanembu could in theory own cattle but many could never hope in practice to achieve such a goal.

In this markedly inegalitarian situation, forced stratum endogamy and the geographical dispersion of dependent workers (slaves, Duu and Kanembu *maskin*) by the nobility served to maintain and accentuate social, spatial and economic segregation between dominated groups, as well as between dominated and dominant groups. Cattle owners and beneficiaries of tributary revenues were free to manipulate those rank and status differences that existed within the bounds of their own stratum through a variety of marriage strategies. Successful unions served to favor access to both land and herds while consolidating or extending control over dependent labor. Inversely, where politically and economically motivated marriages were attempted within dependent groups of either stratum, they involved little transfer of land access rights or cattle beyond the village cluster.

Analogous relationships of subordination prevailed on the ethnically mixed fringes of Kanembu society, in regions where both agricultural and pastoral activities could prosper. These areas include the riverain lowlands, North Kanemi *b'la*, palm groves on the desert marches and, to the east, parts of the Bahr el-Ghazal depression. Among neighboring Daza and Arabs, somewhat different relationships often obtained between professional specialization and social stratification:

(1) In Shuwa communities, the Haddad category included only Arab-affiliated smiths to the exclusion of hunters and non-craftsmen. Many forms of hunting ritually associated with "paganism" were practiced, in principle, by non-Arabs only and in particular by the Kotoko. Genealogical distinctions were drawn between persons reputed to be of

"pure" Arab extraction and those of ethnically mixed origins (*cf.* Décobert 1982), yet all Arab-affiliated men had access to both agricultural and grazing lands.

(2) Among northern Daza pastoralists, the Daza/Aza differentiation was comparable in some respects to the Kanembu/Duu discrimination. The subordinate Aza category grouped together both hunters and artisans, who were "discouraged" from forming herds. Smiths tended to remain close to their pastoralist patrons whereas hunters often formed autonomous, mobile communities.

In both the Haddad and Aza cases, marriage between smiths and non-smiths was barred but this interdiction applied only to actual artisans. In contrast, among the Kanembu, there prevailed a ritual and political alliance between groups of smith and hunter origin with far wider implications. The composite Duu category represented a considerable proportion of the population of Kanem. This category, to which the Kanembu relegated *kagelma* (smiths) and *m'barama* (hunters), increasingly became dependent on sedentary agriculture. Duu groups, subordinate though they were in many respects to the Dalatoa and their allies, indeed had vested land rights recognized as prior to those of the Kanembu nobility whose wealth was of largely pastoral origin. The Duu of South Kanem were by all accounts the "masters of the earth", just as the hunters in their midst were "masters of the bush". The rigorous enforcement of the marriage and cattle barriers by the Kanembu nobility contributed both to the perpetuation and transformation of Duu identity. These systematic measures of social and economic exclusion founded a stratification system legitimated largely in terms of profession and mode of livelihood. As oral traditions make clear, these criteria masked a political distinction that until the final retreat of the Bulala nobility from South Kanem had been formulated in "dynastic" terms.

These succinct observations concerning the specificity of the Kanemi system of social stratification, in relation to that of their Arab and Daza neighbors, bring us to reconsider the purported historical relationship between the Duguwa and present-day "smiths" (Lange 1977). Today, all smiths doubtless are considered Duu but only a minority of Duu are smiths. Nachtigal's (Duu) Danoa, rather than being described as the "oldest inhabitants of Kanem", might be better portrayed as the successors of those certainly diverse groups that remained attached to Kanem's oldest mode of livelihood, namely hunting and gathering. "Danoa" is used no longer as a group denomination in South Kanem, yet "Dana" still is recognized by older traditionists as the apical ancestor of the politically autonomous Duu in this area: he was "the first hunter who came from the north". In local Arabic and Dazaga, *dana* jointly designates the bow

Band arrow. The Aza *dana* of North Kanem are the counterparts of the Duu *m'barama* of South Kanem and the Kerebina,[13] west and south of Lake Chad. Presuming that the Zaghawa actually were a dominant pastoral aristocracy who achieved political preeminence in Kanem during the last centuries of the first millennium, they could hardly have avoided using as grazing lands those expanses familiar as hunting grounds to the forefathers of the Duu and the Aza, whatever their appellations may then have been. Archaeological evidence (Treinen-Claustre) suggests that mobile pastoralists and hunters well may have migrated and grazed between settlements of smiths dependent on hunting and gathering or agriculture as well as on more sedentary animal husbandry. Kanemi smiths of Duu affiliations all claim northeastern origins (Borku, Enedi, *etc.*) that link them to the contemporary domain of the pastoral Tubu and Zaghawa. Notwithstanding, it would be risky to assimilate the "original" Zaghawa and the Duguwa, only then to establish a direct filiation between the Duguwa and the Danoa. Granted the scantiness of written sources, the demonstrability of such a link will long remain a matter of speculation. The more approachable question posed by the Arabic chronicles is: did the conversion of Humey entail wide and rapid acceptance of Islam among the communities of greater Kanem?

This does not appear to have been the case among the ancestors of the Duu. They claim to have <u>always</u> been freemen, though not always Muslim freemen (*cf.* Barth [1965 {1858-1859},II:608]). The islamization of many Duu occurred in the late nineteenth or even twentieth century. Even today, some Duu admit to a recent or superficial conversion. The same holds for many Tubu. Briggs (1960:188), with reference to Lyon (1821:251), observes that "as late as 1820 most of ... (the Tubu) were still pagan while other authors say that the Islamization of Tibesti did not get underway until about 1880". The same holds, by their own account, for the Buduma and for numerous Kuri. Thus, one cannot speak reasonably of a "residual" population of "infidels" on the margins of a pious dynastic society. Idris Alawma may well have "reconquered" Kanem from the Bulala pastoralists, who were allied intimately with many Duu and Tubu, he did not succeed fully in converting them. Those who refused his creed were often members of mobile groups of hunters (Duu) or herders (Tubu, Buduma). They lived either in the lacustrine haven, then densely forested enclaves on the mainland or in the desertic peripheries of the "state", which Borno, according to its own chronicler, Ibn Furtua, only subordinated thanks to considerable bloodshed, not only south and west of Lake Chad among so-called "Sao" but equally between the lake's northern shores and the Sahara.

Following the Bornoan and Tunjur invasions of central Kanem, the distribution of territorial fiefs and associated tributary prerogatives among the ruling lines of major patronymic groups meant that the epithet "agro-pastoral" could only be applied to the majority of Kanemi with major reservations: in this land, there were, as there still are today, those who owned herds and those who tended them, those who stocked millet and those who tilled the land. After the Bulala withdrawal to Lake Fitri, many formerly powerful southern Kanembu groups and their Duu allies found themselves assigned to the latter of these categories. In Kanem, pastoralism, and by extension the accumulation of cattle, was controlled henceforth by a dominant class of largely pro-Bornoan noble affiliation, defined principally by its direct access to agricultural and other tributary revenues. For centuries, the aristocracy strived to increase its access to tribute by reinforcing the territorial and hereditary aspects of its administrative system and by accentuating the sedentarization of its subjects in a province extending from the shores of Lake Chad to the edge of the desert. It is hardly a hazard of geography that Mao, the capital of the *alifa* of Kanem since the mid-seventeenth century, is located precisely on the line of demarcation separating the agro-pastoral areas of South Kanem adapted to extensive (dune) and intensive (*b'la*) grain cultivation and the wide spaces of North Kanem more exclusively dedicated to large-scale animal husbandry. Yet, this location and the political and economic strategy it denotes could be put to advantage only at the risk of exacerbating strategic vulnerability *vis-à-vis* Saharan pastoralists.

During the nineteenth century, a hierarchy asserted itself in wider Kanem among groups of differing degrees and types of pastoral specialization. The internal stratification of Kanembu society was determined to a great extent by the balance of forces prevailing at any given time between the semi-nomadic pastoralists of North Kanem and the sedentary herd-owning aristocrats of Central and South Kanem. By the end of the century, northern pastoralists superceded the successive tutelary states of Kanem (Borno and Waday) as real lords of the land and largely subordinated the Dalatoa and their allies.[14] The Hasa'una and Awlad Sliman, for example, arrived in Kanem from Tripolitania and Fezzan after their 1842 defeat at the hands of the Turks. They were soon in a position to demand vast quantities of grain or hundreds of cattle (*cf.* Nachtigal (1979-1889,III:279) from the bitterly divided "rulers" of Kanem. The sedentary agro-pastoralists of South Kanem in turn were the systematic prey both of their own "noble" landlords and those nomads to whom their masters could refuse no levy. Surplus extraction rather than Islam emerges as the crucial factor in this equation.[15]

The Inversion of the Agro-Pastoral Hierarchy under Colonial Rule

After the French conquest of 1899, the goals of the Kanembu aristocracy evolved until they were, by and large, compatible with the objectives of the occupiers. The colonial administration established a limited number of internally centralized "grands sultanats", destined to be the pillars of a viable Chad colony. In the case of Kanem, the French sought to devise a "counterweight" to a rather overwhelming British Bornu. It was hoped that this creation would likewise reduce the influence of the Arab and Teda-Daza populations of Kanem's northern confines, who were suspect of sympathies with the Sanusiya. The protectorate treaty of 1899, linking the Kanembu Dalatoa to the French Republic, was rendered effective by the French victory of 1902 over the Sanusiya at Bir Alali (North Kanem). The conjunction of these two factors largely contributed to breaking the dependence relationship which had obtained between the sedentaries of Kanem, reduced to serfdom, and the Fezzani Arabs who, alone or with confederates from Borno or Waday, had vassalized the impotent *alifa* and their nobles. Major socio-economic changes followed this abrupt shift in patterns of subordination.

A widely "pacified" Kanem quickly became, after two decades of civil war (1880-1899), the home of vast herds. As of 1903, the French promoted the extension of farming beyond the immediate periphery of large villages, where the population had tended to concentrate in order to better ensure its security in the face of frequent raids. That the state of utter dependency of sedentary Kanemi pastoralists and cultivators was brought to an unexpected and abrupt end was put to advantage by the still agile Kanembu nobility, who sought to maintain and indeed reinforce its exploitation of farmer tributaries in spite of certain fiscal "reforms" imposed by the French.

Cattle taxation constituted on of the most notable innovations of the colonial administration. Until 1899, herds were considered "plunderable" rather than "taxable". Modest though they were, the new taxes proved difficult to collect. They went against the interests of both large cattle owners and those of their dependents for whom the acquisition of a few animals, as well as the cattle "trade" with Borno, represented an irreplaceable trump in the struggle to improve their economic conditions. An implicit but durable alliance in matters of tax evasion soon emerged between these two categories of cattle owners. Nonetheless, herd taxes mainly disadvantaged small herders. Those who disposed of numerous animals were free to fulfill their obligations whenever they saw fit, thanks to ground levies received from agricultural dependents. Their herds thus tended to remain intact. Poorer agro-pastoralists had to acquit what cattle tax they failed to evade through the intermediary of the very

Kanembu herd-owning notables who were entrusted with fiscal functions by the French. Such an ambiguous system could only contribute to limiting cattle accumulation by the poor. This inequality was and is often compounded by erratic variations in cattle and grain prices related to climatic vicissitudes.

When millet and other staple grains are plentiful or only locally relatively rare, cattle, though only "semi-durable", offer the potential for longer-term saving. At the end of the dry season or during periods of moderate scarcity of rain and food, people holding surplus staples may advantageously convert them into cattle. During prolonged droughts, however, millet continues to rise in price beyond the time when cattle begin to lose value due to their diminishing transportability, milk-giving capacity, and reproductive potential. The following examples will give an idea of variations in the rate of convertibility of millet and cattle. In 1957, a plentiful year, one *koro* (a unit of approximately 2.5 kg of grain) of millet was sold for 40 francs C.F.A., while a cow varied between 4,000 and 6,000 francs C.F.A. in price (Le Rouvreur 1962:103). In 1973, a drought year, a *koro* of millet was sold for as much as 250 francs C.F.A. whereas many untransportable cows were being "given away" for as little as 500 francs C.F.A. (personal observation). The convertibility ratio of cows and millet into cash thus varied in these two instances from 1:2 to 1:100 - 1:150, respectively.

Within the context of a perduring Kanembu system of social stratification, such fluctuations operate, globally speaking, to the detriment of dependents. The smaller the herd and the lower the social status of the herder, the more difficult it can become to protect animals against drought. Those *maskin* who leave their villages in search of pasture risk not fulfilling their tributary and fiscal obligations and seeing their yearly renewable rights of access to land lapse in consequence. After a period of aridity, many poor cattle-holders are forced to fall back on exclusive millet cultivation and, in extreme cases, must put themselves into debt to obtain seed millet. It is only with much toil that they may hope to reconstitute the nucleus of a family herd. Inversely, tribute recipients are free to stock grain when cereals are plentiful and cattle is marketable at high prices. In addition, they have privileged access to grazing lands and water. Thanks to their accumulated wealth, they may hire herdsmen to drive their cattle out of danger before the animals are exhausted by drought conditions. Thus, large herd-owners rarely lose all their animals at once. Since they benefit from a greater capacity than their dependents to ensure timely conversion of cattle into grain and grain into cash, or *vice versa*, it is easier for them to reconstitute their herds once a drought has passed. In addition, tributary revenues guarantee the automatic replenishment of their depleted grain reserves when rains return. In some periods of climatic hardship, cattle husbandry may appear to be only a secondary resource in relation to agriculture, yet the socio-political regulation of these complementary activities constantly contributes to enforcing class boundaries.

The establishment of French rule signified that the cattle accumulated by the Kanembu nobility ceased to be passed on in large part to the Arabs of North Kanem or the representatives of Waday. As the Kanem *sultanat* was systematically divided into *cantons* placed under the administration of nobles, the still mobile elements of the population, including hunters, smiths and some northern pastoralists, found it increasingly difficult to avoid integrating themselves into the new territorial structure. Secure access to land remained subordinated to hereditary membership in a local patronymic group. Residence at one's place of origin could thus ensure access to arable ground, pasture and water resources and keep tributary obligations to a minimum. The only other option available was become a *metayer*, subject to levies equivalent to half the harvested produce in addition to a variety of other taxes, including those demanded by the colonial administration. The landless and the mobile, such as ex-slaves and former hunters or smelters,[16] tended to increase the ranks of dependent cultivators. The prerogatives of certain powerful land-controlling groups were increasingly reinforced in relation to the pre-colonial period through the attribution of *canton*-chieftaincies. In reaction to this sudden reinvigoration of Dalatoa power, many dependent cultivators left Central Kanem for Dagana and the southern Bahr el-Ghazal, then principally inhabited by Daza Kesherda herders, semi-sedentary Arabs, and Duu hunters. The objective of these migrants was clear: to reduce their dependence on the nobility. They colonized vacant grounds previously too insecure for settlement, where fiscal prerogatives were as yet less clearly established than was the case further to the north. Foremost, they set out to acquire herds.

These trends are reflected in marriage strategies.[17] Noblemen rarely migrated when choosing a spouse, preoccupied as they were to maintain their hold over the irrigated lands under their control. Aristocratic women, however, began to chose husbands from agnatic groups other than their own but from the same land-controlling class. The agnates of these women chose a limited number of spouses among free commoners, with the intention of reducing the martial isolation of the nobility. At the same time, fearing loss of status, they persistently refused to let their kinswomen marry hypergamously. Thus were formed new networks of inter-*canton* marriage exchange, by which pre-colonial patterns of alliance were accomodated to the existence of hereditary territorial chieftaincies imposed by the occupying French.

In both endogamic strata, there occurred a marked increase in marriages outside of one's patronymic group, which was in contradiction to traditional preferences for close-kin and locally endogamous unions. Yet the strong development of this tendency over the decades in no way led to a breaking down of the strict marriage barriers separating Duu and non-Duu. One is not faced here with a simple anachronism that could be explained away as a "residual" effect of a "caste mentality", of dynastic strife opposing the distant heirs of the Bornoan and Bulala parties or, indeed, of the "Zaghawa" and "Duguwa" heritages. The rule of endogamy still impedes the matrimonial and political unification of the dependent class and thus remains a central element in preserving the Kanembu system of social stratification.

Restrictions on hypergamy by the land-controlling Kanembu and the widening of networks of marital exchange, within the limits of stratum boundaries, were accompanied by a series of measures favoring an increased concentration of agricultural surplus in the hands of a restricted number of aristocrats. The traditional auction procedure known as *bumtu* was implemented so as to transfer lineage-vested land titles to the highest individual bidders (Conte 1984). Rights over irrigated fields were thus alienated to the detriment of hereditary land chiefs of commoner status and of the village communities they represented. This trend favored a notable increase in land rents at the expense of the very small farmers who first tilled and made fertile virgin lands. It compounded the dependency of those forced to seek temporary rights of land access to irrigated plots or riverine mud banks controlled by notables. To complete this panoply of exactions, customary ground and head-taxes forbidden under colonial and subsequently national law continued to be extracted under the auspices of "religious alms" in a fashion totally incompatible with *sharia* norms.

Thanks to such procedures, the aristocracy was able to increase its herds and limit cattle accumulation among the dependent class. Noble Kanembu cattle owners rapidly achieved a clear and lasting economic advantage over the semi-nomadic and nomadic pastoralists of North Kanem. The latter found themselves subject to the good will of their former sedentary tributaries when, during periods of drought, they were forced to request grazing and watering rights in South Kanem. This reversal under colonial rule of long-standing patterns of dependency should be taken into consideration when trying to understand why certain Chadian governments thought it appropriate to "close their eyes" to the continued exploitation of farmers and small herders alike in Kanem. It is conceivable that the correspondingly benevolent attitude of

Kanembu aristocrats toward successive N'Djaména regimes contributed to ensuring the non-engagement of "their" province in the course of the civil conflict (*cf.* Buijtenhuijs 1978) that has plagued so many other regions of Chad since 1965. Both parties had an interest in keeping in check the potentially "restless" pastoralists of North Kanem.

Notes

1. The history of early Kanem is known only through a small number of Arabic texts: *cf*. Barth 1965 (1857-59); Cuoq 1975; Lange 1977, 1980, 1987); and Hopkins & Levitzon 1981. The major source is the anonymous "Chronicle of the kings of Borno" (*Diwan salatin Bornu*), which has been translated into French and analyzed by Lange (1977).

2. *Cf*. Lukas 1936; and Newman 1977.

3. A detailed ethnographic panorama of North Chad is presented by Le Rouvreur (1962). The human geography of Lake Chad's northeastern periphery, including that of Buduma and Kuri country is dealt with by Bouquet (1974). The Teda-Daza world has been studied by Chapelle (1957) and Baroin (1985). Conte (1983, 1986) considers Kanembu social and political organization, whereas Zeltner (1970) and Hagenbucher-Sacripanti (1977, 1979) are concerned with Arab populations north and south of Lake Chad.

4. *Cf*. Urvoy 1949; and Lebeuf and Masson Detourbet 1950.

5. *Cf*. Migeod 1923-1924; Cohen 1962; Connah 1981:37-38 & 235-240; Décobert 1982; Forkl 1983; Lange 1989.

6. The very term Shuwa connotes this transition (*cf*. Zeltner 1970 and Hagenbucher-Sacripanti 1977). Reduced in range though Shuwa migrations are (some ten to eighty km), the principle of yearly movements is, to date, scrupulously maintained, along with the continued use of all the symbolically laden elements of material culture typical of <u>mobile</u> Arab herders of the eastern Sahel (*cf*. Conte and Hagenbucher-Sacripanti 1977, particularly the map supplement).

7. 1969 Livestock distribution figures quoted by Decalo (1977:75) give 1,000,000 cattle for Kanem *préfecture* and 250,000 for the Lake *préfecture*. Bouquet (1974:119) gives Chadian veterinary service estimates of 1,100,000 bovines for Kanem and 270,000 for the Lake (year unspecified) which tally with figures advanced by the World Bank (1974), cited here.

8. At Koro, furnace bases as well as slag deposits testify to quite intensive iron smelting. Samples reveal an iron content of 25 to 30 percent in some easily accessible soil layers. It is doubtful whether furnaces could have produced more than one to two kg of usable iron per load. After smelting, iron nodules could be (painstakingly) separated from the mass of slag. Further research may determine if the slag was then reduced to facilitate the extraction of its remaining metal content. "New" iron was mixed with "old" iron (worn agricultural implements, broken weapons, *etc.*). An apparently low level of metal production in relation to population size could thus have proved adequate to meet the demand for new tools, arms, harnesses, amulets, *etc.*

9. According to Kanemi smiths, these include Dine (sixteen km WSW of Noku), Federke (fourteen km WSW of Noku), Gene (twenty-four km NW of Noku), Ule (seventeen km SSE of Noku), Mun (seventeen km NW of Zigey), Bir Am Haddid (twenty km NW of Zigey), Bir Diuli (twenty-one km NW of N'tiona), Wur (nineteen km E of N'tiona), Yuno (twelve km NNE of Mao) and Koro (sixty-five km W of Mao). Other non-located sites inclurde Borku (Kanem), Kufe, Lela, Nunuti, Seycheri and Yeyli.

Chevalier (1904:402) indicates that Kanemi metallurgists extracted ore in Chitati (North Kanem) in the region to the NW of Bir Alali.

10. Ibn Furtua's *Hadha al-kitab huwa min sha'n sultan Idris Alawma* (Kano n.d.), first translated into English by Palmer (1926), has recently been retranslated and commented on by Lange (1987).

11. The historical observations recorded by Barth (1965 [1857-59]), Nachtigal (1979 [1879-1889]), Landeroin (1911) and Carbou (1912) were compared in the course of anthropological fieldwork (1973-1974) with the testimony of Kanemi oral tradition specialists from a variety of descent groups.

12. The nature and implications of this matrimonial barrier are considered in Conte (1983, 1986); see also Nachtigal (1879-1889) and Carbou (1912).

13. The Kanuri *kerbina* is synonymous with the term *kindira*, today used in South Kanem to honor old hunter-diviner-healers of repute, as well as to designate "sorcerers". The Kerebina (see Nachtigal 1879-1889,III:400-404, 428-429, 542; and Carbou 1912,I:18) are rightly or wrongly considered to be distant dispersed heirs of the "Sao" peoples. During the 1870s they still made their living from hunting. Until a few years ago, it was a tradition for certain Duu hunters of southeast Kanem (*m'barama*) to go and visit the Kerebina south of the Shari delta, from Lake Chad as far as Mandara (Cameroon). As youths, they had been sent to these southerly regions for long initiatory periods, during which they perfected their abilities at tracking, trapping, arms fabrication and poison making, as well as their knowledge of plants, healing, divination and other techniques.

14. The only South Kanemi group to have held its own in the face of Arab and Wadayan raiders or of Dalatoa pillaging their own subjects (*cf.* Landeroin 1911:384; and Carbou 1912,I:32) were the Duu Danoa of the Bari district (*cf.* Barth 1965 [1857-1859],II:608; and Nachtigal 1879-1889,III:331). This success often is attributed to their expert use of poisoned arrows but one should not underestimate the strategic value of their mobility, which gave them an advantage over other subordinate communities of South Kanem. The Danoa hunted far to the south and southeast and were only fully sedentarized during the colonial period.

15. A former French administrator, Le Rouvreur (1962:87), remarked with regard to Kanem: "Silos are of a curious kind. A large pit is dug in the sand, at the edge of the village. The bottom of the pit receives a layer of husks and it is then filled with grain. The opening is then sealed off with a mat and (a layer of) sand." The invisibility of Kanemi granaries, as opposed to the above-ground silos used by Arabs south of Lake Chad, hardly comes as a surprise.

16. The decrease or even disappearance of many species of game during the twentieth century (including the elephant on Lake Chad's periphery) led many hunters to sedentarize and concentrate more exclusively to agriculture. Furthermore, the importation of European products, such as scrap metal and cloth, albeit in small quantities, quickly resulted in the economic dissolution of weaver and metallurgist associations among the Duu.

17. The following statements are based on the analysis of a corpus of 1,600 marriage histories recorded by the author among the Duu Rea and neighboring Kanembu groups (Conte 1983, 1986).

10

Pastoro-Foragers to "Bushmen": Transformations in Kalahari Relations of Property, Production and Labor

Edwin Wilmsen

Images of "Bushmen"

Unlike all other native peoples of southern Africa, none of those called "Bushmen" (the majority, but not all, of whom speak San languages)[1] have been able, in this century, to accumulate sufficient capital to maintain significant herds of cattle of their own. Why is this so? What accounts for the existence in modern southern African states of peoples who appear to many outsiders to have practiced until recently an aboriginal foraging economy?[2] Why are there peoples in the twentieth century who could conceivably be labelled *"Bush*men"?

At the same time, in this century in Botswana and Namibia, a significant majority of peoples so labelled have pursued a substantially pastoralist way of life in symbiosis with, employed by, or enserfed to Bantu speaking cattle owners, primarily Batswana and Herero. As we shall see, this is equally true of earlier centuries with the modification that some proportion of San speakers themselves owned herds of respectable size. And all "Bushmen foragers", no matter how far into the center of the Kalahari they may have been found at any particular moment, were in those previous centuries - and remain now - enmeshed through kinship and material production networks in the dominant

248

pastoralist economies of the region. Despite this, during this century, no contemporary San herders have been able to establish livestock-based domestic economies independent of Bantu pastoralists until this decade, when a few are managing to do so. None have yet been able to enter into commodity production of cattle for readily available commercial markets now dominated by Tswana and Herero producers. What are the reasons for this state of affairs?

In the prevailing paradigm of anthropology applied to the Kalahari, that of evolutionary ecology, these have been non-questions, never asked, without answers. This is because the distinction drawn by Levi-Strauss (1958) between peoples prior to history and those in history has fundamentally informed all anthropological approaches to San speaking "foragers". Ethnographers of these peoples have assumed that they were quintessential aboriginal foragers whose way of life had changed little for millennia. Both geographic isolation and cultural conservatism were invoked to account for this static condition. It was asserted, without investigation, that neither African agropastoralist nor any other external influence had impinged significantly on their isolation until the middle third of this century. As a consequence, San were declared to be socially and culturally uninterested in and unprepared for participation in independent pastoral economies. Oddly, at the same time, they were acknowledged to be seasoned herdsmen for others.

More than anything else, that evolutionist paradigm with those premises has raised San from public obscurity; through it, the "Kalahari Bushmen" have captured the imagination of the world. So strong has been the appeal that Wobst (1978) laments with justified consternation that a "Bushman" model has come to dominate anthropological constructions not only of modern but of prehistoric foragers as well. This, indeed, has come to pass. But the image upon which that model is itself constructed was drawn from the intersection of theories of cultural ecology and of cultural evolution where a notion was conceived about the life of hunters-in-a-world-of-hunters prior to the intervention of domesticated modes of production.

Anthropologists have projected this image ahistorically onto a present conceived to have, for Bushmen hunters (now called foragers), an essentially synchronic, shallow past. To paraphrase Cohn's (1980:199) words: a place has been posited where natives are authentic, untouched, and aboriginal; where it is possible to deny the central historical fact that the peoples studied are constituted in the historically significant colonial situation; where it is thought possible to affirm instead that these peoples are somehow out of time and history. Historians, for their part, paint a similarly synchronic image into the first chapters of their books and they insert that image incrementally - unchanged - at points along their otherwise progressive narratives.   A practice to which Vansina (1985) responds eloquently:

> The time should be long past that hunter-gatherers ... are seen as living witnesses to primordial conditions of life, as 'roots of heaven,' ... unfortunately, this image still lingers [and] has made it almost impossible it seems to shake off the old premises.

Wolf (1982), in the same vein, massively documents the fallacy underlying any such notion of peoples without history.

My purpose here is to shake loose, if not off, from the San at least some of those old premises.[3]   The questions that opened this essay are central to a more satisfactory assessment than we now have of the proper place of "Bushmen" in the anthropological lexicon of cultural categories. More urgently, answers to these questions are essential elements in current efforts to gain equity for those of southern Africa's peoples who have been too long relegated to that subordinating category.

San Pastoro-Foragers

For these answers, we must dig into the archaeology of the Kalahari to gain a view of the precapitalist economic formations of the region and into archival records to follow the transformation of these precapitalist forms under colonial domination.   In the course of this exegesis, it will be shown that peoples called "Bushmen" actively played significant roles in the economic and political history of the region; by no means were all such peoples always stockless foragers.   It will also become clear that "Bushmen" is an invented category the referents and designees of which change in concert with altering regional circumstances.   A recently completed work (Wilmsen 1989d) extensively documents the evidence upon which the foregoing assertions are based; much of the following argument is also condensed from that work and from an earlier essay (Wilmsen 1983).

Passarge (1907) set the tone for ethnographic reporting of San when he divided "Das Leben der Buschmänner in früheren Zeiten" (Bushman life in earlier times) from that "in der Jetztzeit" (in the present).   His observational present was 1896-98 and featured Zhu (the !Kung San of ethnography) as husbandmen of cattle and goats, associates (subordinate) of Tswana and Herero, and - in immediately preceding decades - participants in mercantile trade, as well as foragers of wild resources. His earlier time, by which he meant later precolonial time, was the same, with husbandry, external contact, and trade subtracted while foraging was extrapolated to fill the void.   Modern authors - Marshall (1976), Lee (1979), Tanaka (1980), Silberbauer (1981) - follow that precedent.   They report the presence of peoples and activities extraneous to their purpose, then set them aside to be reintroduced later in the narrative, if at all, only to emphasize the distance of San from other peoples and their attendant influences.

I shall not detain readers with a descriptive reiteration of San foraging activities; anyone not familiar with these and wishing to gain such familiarity may turn to the above mentioned ethnographies, even perhaps to Passarge for whom not many allowances due to the passage of time need be made in this regard (See Plate 10.1).

But I will summarize, in order to emphasize, the conditions of husbandry and association that encompassed San economic and social relations at the time the observations were made upon which those modern classic ethnographies of these peoples are based. First, Government of Botswana veterinary service records for anthrax and bucillosis inoculation show that during the 1950s and early 1960s about 10,000 cattle were kept in the CaeCae-Qangwa valleys. This number fell, due to drought and outbreaks of foot-and-mouth disease, to about 6,000 in the late 1960s but had rebounded by 1974. The area in which these animals were kept is about fifth km by sixty km, 3,000 sq km, in size which indicates a stocking rate of about two to three head per sq km. Similar stocking rates are maintained in the rest of Ngamiland where water is obtainable, hence, where people live. Quantitative statements of this kind cannot be projected into earlier decades much less into previous centuries, but evidence to be presented later in this essay will support the proposition that significant numbers of cattle have been kept in the region for a very long time.

During the 1960s and 1970s, 99 percent of the cattle in the CaeCae-Qangwa area were owned by Batswana and Herero. The first accurate figures we have for Zhu stock ownership are provided by Lee (1979:411) for the period 1967-69. At this time, 27 percent of the 151 adult male Zhu in his sample acknowledged ownership of 102 head among themselves for an average of 2.5 head per owning household. Ownership of donkeys and goats was, respectively, 20 percent and 55 percent higher. Furthermore, Lee (1979:409) tells us "that many [of these] men had owned cattle and goats in the past." In addition, every one of these men was then, or had recently been, actively engaged in the care of cattle for others (Wilmsen 1982).

Records for the other areas where San were observed at about mid-century are far less informative. Tanaka (1980:50-51) tells us that in the central Kalahari some Gcwi owned goats and donkeys, but he gives no further information and seems to think that these were more or less whimsical acquisitions. At the same time, he finds that the Gcwi are "parasitic ... on the field and dairy products of the [Ba]Kgalagadi for a good deal of their food". Silberbauer is silent on the matter, while Marshall (1976:61) dismisses it with a footnote saying that many Zhu "expressed the wish to have cattle".

With respect to association with Bantu speakers, Lee (1979:53) again provides the only manageable data; these are revealing. Of the rather stable population of about 900 persons who lived in the CaeCae-Qangwa area during the 1960s and 1970s, 43 percent to 49 percent were Tswana and Herero. Put another way, only slightly more than half of the inhabitants of the area were Zhu "Bushmen" during the period under consideration. We have already heard from Tanaka that Gcwi rely substantially on Bakgalagadi coresidents, whatever their relative numbers which are not given, who are not otherwise mentioned. Again, Silberbauer has nothing to say. Marshall (1976:58-59) equivocates, mentioning only a few non-San pastoralist families while citing several police actions to remove others in enforcement of imposed bureaucratic policies regarding land allocation among native groups.

Now, this brief recitation of economic holdings and group associations should give us pause. If fewer than half the inhabitants (Bantu) of an area are able to control 99 percent of the most valuable commodity (cattle) in the area and the other, proportionally greater, part of the inhabitants (San) remain dependent upon them for substantial parts of their livelihood - through employment, servitude, symbiotic exchange, "parasitism", or whatever - while investing meager resources to gain a small share in that valuable commodity and expressing a wish to increase that share but being unable to do so in significant measure, then, something is going on in the environment that transcends ecology and supersedes evolution.

The structure of this complex situation lies in the historically realized and transformed social relations of production of the groups involved along with their associated means of production. To adequately define these groups and the relations among them, it is necessary to analyze them in their historic and social contexts, and further, to analyze shifts in these contexts as they altered relations among the groups. An analysis of the history of property relations and of the place of labor in the political economy of the region is the essential first step in this project.[4]

The Prehistory of Property Relations

Let us, then, turn our attention to that history of property relations, first to that part revealed by archaeology. Review of the recent prehistory of the Kalahari adds significant dimensions to our understanding of the variety of circumstances in which its present inhabitants exist. Roughly two thousand years ago, Iron Age pastoralists began to occupy the Kalahari as part of the wide-ranging penetration of pastoralist economies into southern Africa. Domestic animals and grains along with metallurgy, which together formed the basis of these economies, were introduced below the Okavango-Zambezi river systems at this time.

During the first centuries A.D., the northern margin of the Kalahari was actively part of a wider sphere extending into Angola, Zaire, and Zambia where relatively small communities of Bantu and Khoisan speakers intermingled. Economic and linguistic - and, therefore, social - transfers appear to have flown freely among those communities with the result that pastoral economies became well established in the Kalahari (Denbow and Wilmsen 1986). By A.D. 500, such economies were entrenched throughout southern Africa all the way to the Cape itself.

This Iron Age system grew rapidly during the next 500 years. In eastern Botswana, a three-tiered hierarchy of settlements developed with a few primary centers dominating surrounding secondary and tertiary sites (Denbow 1984). The pastoral economic form of the system was mature and pervasive. A measure of the size of herds that were kept is provided by kraal dung deposits which were burned and thus preserved through vitrification. At the primary centers, such as Toutswe, these deposits reach diameters of 100 m and depths of 150 cm; such deposits are also found at tertiary sites but in much smaller size. Conversely, hunted animal remains far outnumber those of domesticates in the small locations while at the central nodes these proportions are reversed. Metal is scarce and exotic goods are absent at the smaller locations where stone tools predominate. Abundant metal tools and ornaments along with glass beads and sea shells attest to the hierarchically dominant status of the large central nodes. These beads and shells were luxury items obtained through exchange networks that reached Arab importers on the east coast of the continent. It seems evident that immigrant pastoralists quickly dominated the indigenous foraging systems of the eastern Kalahari and incorporated them hegemonically into an expanded political economy in which hunting and herding were pursued at all hierarchical levels.

The history of pastoralism in the western sandveld Kalahari has a similar chronology although it differs in a number of significant social and economic details. The essential Iron Age elements, cattle-sheep-goat pastoralism, cultivation of grains, and metallurgy, are present here from the sixth century onward (Denbow and Wilmsen 1983). Glass beads and sea shells found at three sites extend the transcontinental trade established for the eastern region far into the west by A.D. 800; at least one site, Nqoma, seems to have been an important entrepot through which exports and imports were channelled. River mussel shell, fish bones, and a distinctive stone material delineate the more local, intraregional trade networks between Okavango and sandveld communities. An important contrast is that these western sites do not display the complex hierarchical structure found in the east. Another is that ceramic styles are not homogeneous; variants often associated elsewhere with Khoisan and others with Bantu are found in the same sites, often in direct association. This suggests that their makers engaged in a more mutually balanced interaction than did their eastern counterparts. It appears that pastoralist penetration into the western Kalahari was on a smaller scale than in the east and that different mechanisms of political economic interaction were at work here.

The entire range of Kalahari environments was incorporated into these Early Iron Age systems, form the riverine and hardveld ecosystems far out into the sandveld (Wilmsen 1978). This is not really surprising; the region is more properly described as savannah rather than desert and provides superb pasturage if not overstocked. It should not be overlooked, moreover, in light of the importance of interregional trade, that pasturage was not the only resource sought at this time; commodities for exchange were equally important.

As trade with the east coast grew in scale, however, the nearer peoples on the Zimbabwe highlands organized trading networks to their own benefit. The routes to the ocean from the west were truncated beginning in the eleventh century by the developing trader states (first K2 then Mapungubwe), followed in the thirteenth through the fifteenth centuries by Great Zimbabwe. The seventeenth and eighteenth century Rozvi kings at Khami and Dhlodhlo were powerful enough to prevent Portuguese usurpation of this interior trade to the coast. The Kalahari was reduced to a producer status in this process. Ceramic and metal using agropastoralist economies continued to function in the Kalahari, now under the shadow of Zimbabwean states; a series of sites from the twelfth to fifteenth century documents this period. None contain external trade items.

Production and Trade in the Nineteenth Century

Large numbers of exotic items, primarily glass beads, reappear in the Kalahari at the beginning of the eighteenth century. Their source was now the Atlantic coast trade into Kongo-Angola established by the Portuguese; this was the beginning of European penetration of the region. A colonial trade boom in the nineteenth century, based on ivory, feathers, and cattle, brought a wide variety of Europeans with their quest for wealth, their goods of many kinds, and their force of arms into the region and transformed its economy and society once again. The first written records show that Europeans entered an already flourishing precolonial trade in which San were major producers. Livingstone (1912:113, 116), in 1850, recorded that a very large number of ostriches were killed annually by Bushmen who traded the feathers of these birds to the Ndabele. A few years later, Chapman (1971 (1868):143) wrote in his diary that Bushmen who accompanied his expeditions urged him to shoot ostriches so that they could obtain more black feathers for that trade, a request with which he readily complied since he wanted the white feathers which then had an inflated value on the European market.

These reports are from the eastern Kalahari. In the west, in Namibia, Galton (1971 (1853):172), also in 1850, observed the active trade among Ovambo, Herero, and San in which beads , shells, iron and copper implements, salt, cattle, and many other goods were constantly moving from source to consumer. European items were quickly incorporated into this precolonial trade (Birmingham 1981:38). Brink (Mossop 1947:51) had already noticed on the Orange River in 1761 the presence of Portuguese glass beads transferred so far south from their Kongo-Angolan entry into Africa through the agency of San, Tswana, Nama, and Herero middlemen. Okihiro (1976:187-189) summarizes similar networks from the east coast where Portuguese had now replaced Arabs as the agents of transmission in the overseas trade.

In 1836, Alexander (1967 (1838):297) recorded trade in metals, ornaments, and livestock between interior peoples in central Namibia and Portuguese north of the Cunene on the Angolan coast. Not long after, Oswell (1900,II:230, 245), who along with Livingstone was the first European to reach the river systems on the northern edge of the Kalahari, reported that many people there were dressed in European cloth and clothing. In 1855, the Canadian trader, Green (1857: 535-539), found that gunpowder was in such abundant supply in the region that it was not hoarded but traded freely among native groups. Earlier, in 1853, Andersson (1854:5, 31) published advice to traders saying that beads were so common that they had little value in the Ngami trade. By that time, Lazlo Magyar and Mambari, following ancient salt trade routes, had been active among the Angolan !Kung for two decades; we can be sure that these people relayed this trade southward to their Zhu kinsmen in Ngami-Namibia.

The scope of that involvement by San was great. Hahn (Mauch *et al.* 1866-67:285-286) gave fifth to sixty tons as his lowest estimate of copper ore produced by Bushmen at Tsumeb mines; he also remarks that these producers would allow no one else to see the diggings. In the same report, he continues with observations of the salt trade - also controlled at the same time by Bushmen - which he says was if anything more valuable that the trade in copper. The routes of this trade were probably as old as the Iron Age and had functioned in the transfer of pastoralism and metallurgy into the western Kalahari from where they splayed out northward into Angola, Zambia, and beyond and were the avenues along which the European goods had already made their way southward as far as the Orange River.

These observations by the first Europeans to enter the region offer convincing evidence that the San were engaged in interregional trade before any whites arrived there. It is evident that these first Europeans penetrated an already existing trade network relaying goods between the interior and the Mozambique, Cape, Namibian, and Angolan coasts (Parsons 1977:118).

It was this long-standing trade that the emerging Tswana states attempted to control while simultaneously acquiring control over the rapidly developing European trade. In the process their suzerainty over the reduced classes, especially peoples such as San, was solidified as they tightened their grip on indigenous trade. Parsons (1977:118) summarizes early records showing that before the 1850s the Tswana hunted little of the ivory which they sold to Europeans but bought it from Bushmen with a fraction of the non-productive goods, such as beads, they received in the trade. Tshekedi, Chief of the Bangwato in 1935 testified to the London Missionary Society:

> There was in those times no question of overlordship of one people over another..at that time we had no strength by which we could force them to become our servants.

The powerful new means of production, guns and horses, introduced in this trade were retained by the Tswana for themselves who were aided thereby in subjugating other peoples - principally San and Bakgalagadi - and in appropriating the surplus product of these peoples' labor for their own profit (Nangati 1982:142, 244).

No part of the region was ignored in the search for ivory. Serton (1954:133, 177) records that traders regularly visited such supposedly remote places as the NyaeNyae-Dobe area and established trading camps there. Robert Lewis, who traded in this area for three decades beginning in 1863, left his name at Lewisfontein by which Qangwa was known on maps until 1965. His exploits and Herero name along with those of other hunter-traders as well as the Boer Dorstland Trekkers, who spent three years in the area at the end of the 1870s, are remembered vividly by current residents of the area. But these were all latecomers. Portuguese beads are found in archaeological components at Tsodilo, Xaro on the Okavango, and the Kgwebe Hills where they were brought in the eighteenth century trade along the ancient routes noted above. It is upon just this area that Marshall (1976) and Lee (1979) build their claim that San were isolated and immune from outside influence and thus retained an aboriginal foraging life.

But, far from being isolated, San were primary producers heavily involved in interregional trade. Chapman estimated that 15,000 to 20,000 pounds of ivory was exported annually from Ngami-Namibia during the 1860s. That rate of production was maintained until the 1880s. In the eastern Kalahari, the average annual production was estimated to be about 80,000 during this period (Chapman 1971 (1868):186, 211; Estherhuyse 1968:13; Parsons 1977:121). The numbers of elephants killed by the best white hunters are known and from these it is clear that at most only half of this annual ivory production could have been shot by Europeans; the actual proportion was almost surely much less. The remainder must have been produced by native hunters, many of whom were San. Consequently, for about three decades these "Bushmen" hunters must have killed every year approximately 300 elephants in Ngami-Namibia and four times that many in the east in order to produce their share of the exported ivory. Their control of the copper and salt trade has already been noted. In addition, "Bushmen" produced the bulk of ostrich feathers and game skins that were exported in great quantity from the region.

The result of all this activity was that European traders were constantly in contact with the producers of sought after items - ivory, feathers, hides, and cattle. This ivory-feather trade vanished at the end of the 1880s when the elephants were hunted out and feathers went out of fashion in Europe. A minor economic boom brought about by construction of Cecil Rhodes' railway from the Cape to Bulawayo briefly, in the late 1880s and early 1890s, stimulated an export of cattle from Angola and Ngami-Namibia (Clarence-Smith and Moorsom 1975:374). Consequently, cattle and their accompanying cowhand jobs passed through many communities along the old trade routes across the Kalahari to the line of rail. The pastoral production upon which this export was based had already been contributing heavily to the Atlantic and Cape trade for more than half a century. Its roots lie in the later precolonial development of Iron Age pastoralism in the region to which we must now return our attention.

We may reasonably infer that large herds were kept in the western Kalahari in the seventeenth and eighteenth centuries because Bangologa pastoralists are known to have been in the Lake Ngami area by 1700 and Herero may have been there as well as in the rest of the northwestern Kalahari much earlier (A. Campbell 1982:130-131). Dated archaeological sites in the Tsodilo Hills, at CaeCae, and in Namibia (Fig. 10.1) argue strongly that pastoralism had been continuously a principal form of economy in the region since its introduction.

Cattle from these interior pastoralist economies began to enter the European Atlantic trade before the beginning of the nineteenth century. Alexander's report of that trade has been mentioned; in addition, in the 1790s American whalers supplied themselves on the Namibian coast and a little later one captain is recorded to have anticipated buying two or three thousand head for their hides from interior tribes (Kienetz 1977:556). Cape traders were established at Walfish Bay in 1841-2. During the next decade, prodigious numbers of cattle must have been obtained; at times, 350 ships with 6,000 crew are recorded to have been fed on interior beef (Kienetz 1977:557-558). During the 1860s and 1870s, 10,000 or more head were sent every year to the Cape from Ngami-Namibia alone.

The Nama chiefs, Jonker Afrikaner and Amraal Lambert, were the principal suppliers of these cattle. To obtain sufficient stock, they raided from their bases near Windhoek and Gobabis northward and eastward into Ngamiland where their targets were mainly Herero and Tswana herds. But San were also victims. The missionary, Tindall (1959:34, 118), reported in 1843 that Bushman smallstock was taken and that Nama had been the agents of dispossession of these people.

There is evidence to make us confident that this state of affairs had not always existed. Vedder (1938:138-139) records that about 100 years earlier, San were able to confiscate Herero herds. Wikar (Mossop 1935:29-79) describes several cattle keeping San along the Orange River at about that time. In 1791, van Reenan (Mossop 1935:305) noted that it was Nama access to European trade that turned the balance against Bergdamara and Bushmen, and deprived them of their livestock.

Nevertheless, the missionary, Irle (1906:158), wrote that some Bushmen had smallstock in the 1860s, while at the same time, Andersson both was told of (1861:187) and saw (State Archive Service n.d.:124) Bushmen cattle in the NyaeNyae area. In the east, Livingstone (1912:65, 119; Schapera 1961:161, 241) often commented on Bushman livestock - cattle as well as goats - and of the ability of these people as herdsmen; by 1869, they had been entirely dispossessed.

Insofar as its strength could sustain interregional economies, the mini-boom brought about by the construction of Rhodes' rail collapsed in 1896, coincident with the onset of rinderpest which wiped out 75 percent of the cattle and remaining wild ungulates of southern Africa. Both the native and the European economies of the Namib-Kalahari, which had fused into an interdependent if not a unitary formation, became correspondingly moribund. As suddenly as it had been set in the 1850s, the commercial scene dissolved in the 1890s. The Kalahari had been sucked clean of commoditizable wild animals as if by a vacuum cleaner, but it was only selectively destroyed and people could manage reasonably well on the bushman diet of nuts and berries left to them as San are recorded by anthropologists to have done in this century.

Labor Relations Transformed: San as Pastoral Serfs

What could not be overcome was the fact that they now had relatively little to offer in trade and less with which to buy from traders. The surplus native product of the region had been exhausted, and nothing had been introduced to replace it. Neither the economy nor the material requirements of the people were as they had been a century before. Except for a few cattlepost jobs, San labor, just recently valued highly if rewarded lowly, had become virtually worthless in a now non-existent market.

It was not only the conditions of production that changed during the nineteenth century period of mercantile capitalism. The social relations of labor were also transformed. The means by which this was accomplished was instituted by Kgari, Chief of the Bangwato in about 1826, who is credited with rationalizing incipient socio-economic stratification present in Ngwato political structure. He did this in order to bring more firmly under his control the spectacularly increased numbers of peoples subject to him and, more to the point, their equally spectacularly increased productive potential. This system, the *kgamelo* (milk jug) system, greatly enhanced the class ranking inherent in Tswana social structure and increased the power of the local elites by giving them direct economic and administrative control over the lower classes in their assigned sphere of responsibility. In 1847, this system was instituted by Batawana in Ngamiland.

Cattle were crucial in this system because they were lent out in patronage by elites to poorer clients under obligatory conditions, called *mafisa*, in which a client's assets were mortgaged against the safety of his patron's property and of his support of the patron's interests. It was clearly to the advantage of administrators to gain control of all cattle in their districts, for they then held not only the intrinsic value of the animals but also their far higher mortgage value by means of which the allegiance of subordinates was assured (Parsons 1974:648).

Those San and other non-Tswana who owned cattle were quickly dispossessed of their herds in this process, and many were reduced to landless servant status (Schapera 1970:89; Parsons 1974:648; Okihiro 1976:135-137). This latter group was transformed into an underclass called *malata* (serf) in Sengwato and *batlhanka* (servant) in Setawana. Although most San were ultimately disenfranchised in this manner, a substantial number were incorporated into Tswana polities (Ncgoncgo

1982:29). It was that San majority relegated to the status of serf that later, in the playing out of the colonial process, became pauperized "Bushmen".

A different process unfolded in the west. There, Nama *kommandos* continued to raid pretty much at will, but after quickly extracting the current crop of ivory and animals from an area, they withdrew to their home bases (Lau 1982). It was only at these bases that Nama exercised anything like political control over other peoples. It is, fortunately, beyond the scope of this essay to attempt to analyze why the course of history was different here than in the east. But Okihiro's (1976:189) observation is cogent: European incursions, from an early moment, destroyed local polities and substituted raiding rather than trading as the dominant form of economic activity. As Ncgoncgo (1982:166) remarks, raiding became necessary for survival. Those who were raided, as those enserfed, were placed in double jeopardy. Not only was the surplus product of their labor expropriated, but their access to newly acquired necessities - both outlets for their products (their only means of accumulating exchange value) and sources of supply for their import needs - was channelled through these same dominant exploitative powers. Their growing dependence on these powers was assured.

With the collapse of hunting, a hunter's life was no longer worth as much as it had been - not to himself, now left with only a slim subsistence supplement, not to centers of accumulation, where emphasis shifted from quick tributary extraction to longer-term sustained production. In practical terms, this meant cattle were now unchallenged by ivory as the central source of wealth in the Kalahari region.

The *kgamelo* system was well suited to the tributary extraction of capital value when, as in hunting, the means of production remained largely with subordinated ranks. In herding, however, the means of production remained in the hands of herd owners, even of absentee owners. In 1875, Khama, Chief of the Bangwato, saw this and moved to bring the new relations of production under his direct control (Parsons 1974: 653). He restructured the *kgamelo* system to bring about in effect the capitalization of labor and land. Part of his reform reassigned cattle of the tribal herd to commoners and vassals, thus bypassing the lower elite administrators and centralizing authority more firmly in the chief.

Khama also nominally freed serfs, ostensibly giving them the right to dispose of their labor in their own interests. This was illusory. In fact, the conditions in which serfs found themselves had deteriorated. In the economic reality of the time, there were very limited opportunities for freed serf labor. As primary producers during the years of mercantile hunting, hunters had retained some bargaining power in the disposal of their product. This power had declined as state capital consolidated its strength and hunting became less remunerative. Hunting and gathering were by no means abandoned. These continued to supply substantial increments to consumption budgets of both foragers and pastoralists, but in the depressed economy and reduced environment of the post-mercantile period, could satisfy little more than immediate domestic requirements. Now, as obligatory herders, former hunters were completely at the mercy of their masters.

A simple imperative difference between forces of production of ivory and of beef underlies that condition: it requires fewer herders to manage one hundred cattle than it does hunters to kill one elephant. Consequently, a cattle owner needs to engage fewer herders than must a merchant hunter, reducing thereby the lateral spread of economic opportunities. The inequalities inherent in the conversion for the underclass whose labor formerly secured the ivory and then secured the herds is readily apparent. There were substantially fewer places for herders than there had been for hunters, even in the expanding cattle economy. With few exceptions, all San who had not been absorbed as Tswana - those who thus were no longer Bushmen - were reduced to the status of a propertyless class.

San as a Regional Underclass

It is readily apparent why members of that underclass, who were mainly San, should compete for the few available positions. The system had quite suddenly alienated San labor from the land more thoroughly than had been possible before and had, thereby, created a captive surplus labor pool with essentially only a single outlet. Those San who could capture a cattlepost position obtained a measure of security in the system - at the bottom of the heap, but in it. Those whose labor was not immediately needed (and it must be noted that these were not only San) were now without direct means to participate in regional economies.

Some turned to raiding. Raiding in the nineteenth century was a response to unequal trade relations and was a means to transfer exchange value in a distorted market system. Successful raiders could expect a viable, if unfair, return for their efforts. Now, in the first decades of the twentieth century, there was no longer raiding of large herds for value but only small scale stock theft for immediate meals. The transition was brought about by the utter exclusion of the reduced classes from legitimate economic channels.

Others were relegated to the more inaccessible and difficult zones of the Kalahari, where they fell deeper and deeper into foraging which had become a condition of poverty in the overall structure of society. They, thus, became a secondary labor pool, maintained at no expense to the controlling classes, who could draw upon this underclass at will to free their own members for cash earning opportunities, education, and "the lifestyle of the 'new elite' that spanned Southern Africa" (Parsons 1977:136).

In his investigation of the servile conditions under which San lived in Botswana in the 1930s, Tagart (1933:7) saw the core of the matter clearly:

> The fact is that there is little opportunity for any natives to obtain paid employment ... in the protectorate. It is probably not going too far to say that this has been the most potent factor in perpetuating the servile condition of the Masarwa, and remains the greatest obstacle in the way of their emancipation ... and until greater opportunity for independent employment presents itself, it is difficult to see how the Masarwa can be helped to emerge from the condition of apathy and dependence into which they have lapsed.

The escape valve from empty local markets for Tswana labor was migration to South Africa, principally to the mines. Schapera (1947:38-39) estimated that, in 1938-1940, 28 percent of all adult male Batswana were away on migrant labor; that proportion rose to 46 percent during World War II when about 10,000 men from the Protectorate served in the British army. In contrast, only forty-two San men from eastern Botswana were registered as being on the mines in 1936 (Botswana National Archives 1938). Tswana would have been unable to avail themselves of migrant employment without a supplementary labor pool from which to replace absent labor at cattleposts and fields. The conditions of migratory work made it necessary for Tswana laborers to retain an agropastoral base at their villages where their families remained and the costs of social production were met (Parson 1981:240). San, prevented from going to the mines in proportionate numbers, supplied the bulk of the required labor supplement.

The foraging that "Bushmen" were now forced to practice was subsistence foraging, no longer the fully formed pastoro-foraging it had been at the beginning of the nineteenth century. Still less was it the pre-pastoral foraging of earlier millennia, which this twentieth century form resembled only in the skills and techniques required to extract resources from the environment. It was now a partial economic formation incapable of supplying all the needs of those in it. The only means to obtain those unfulfilled needs were embedded in the social relations of production dominated by pastoralists who exercised exclusive political and social control over all levels of the structure.

Those doubly dispossessed "Bushmen", foraging unseen in the veld, were entirely dependent upon their kin at the cattleposts to pass on to them what snippets they might of their acquired needs: tobacco, coffee/tea, sugar, cloth, metal implements and utensils; the list is long. Those cattlepost kin were themselves entirely dependent on their pastoral masters who did not overly extend themselves to supply those needs. It is true that a tiny fraction of San managed to retain small livestock holdings through the earlier decades of this century. A somewhat larger number are now building up substantial herds. For these people, the possession of cattle enhances access to other forms of wealth, and even higher rates of return from hunting due to their ability to acquire superior hunting equipment, underscoring the advantage accruing to even marginal livestock holdings (Wilmsen 1989a).

Nonetheless, during the entire course of the last one hundred years, both forms of "Bushmen", those who foraged and those who herded, have been effectively alienated from managing property in their own interests. The end result of this colonial process made San peoples appear to be traditionally landless and created the squatters' communities that are mentioned, only to be discounted as aberrant, in every ethnography of these peoples (See Plate 10.2).

Notes

1. The term, Bushman, has been derogatory since its introduction in the seventeenth century; I use it in quotation marks in irony to emphasize its inappropriateness. The term, San, now in vogue does not alter the referent because the peoples so labelled are spoken of in terms indistinguishable from those employed earlier when those people were called Bushmen. I use San when I wish to designate a large, rather loosely defined set of peoples who speak any Khoisan language except Nama. Whenever possible, I use the terms which particular groups apply to themselves.

2. Jack Parson first posed this question to me in this form and started thereby the thinking that led to this paper; I am happy to acknowledge this debt to so fine a scholar.

3. A recent discussion of these premises and the critique that I and others have of them may be found in an article by Solway and Lee (1990) and in the commentary published along with it.

4. See also Wilmsen 1982, 1989a, and 1989b.

PART SIX

CONCLUSION

11

The Current Realities
of African Pastoralists

John G. Galaty and Pierre Bonte

How can the perspectives put forward in this volume guide us in assessing the current realities of African pastoralists and in evaluating policies devised to address their needs? In the *Introduction*, we discussed how the myths of pastoralism, although not completely unfounded, have proven inadequate to account for its cultural and economic complexities. In light of our revised historical and anthropological understanding, we will examine here the significance of pastoralism in Africa today, outline trends in the current conditions of pastoralists, review how in relevant regions of the continent they have been affected by recent political and economic changes, and consider what more adequate vision of African pastoralists is appropriate in assessing their predicaments and in devising policies which will influence their future.

The Significance of Pastoralism in Africa Today
If we ask what significance pastoralism and pastoralists have in Africa today, our answer will differ with the context. To put the question in geographical perspective, we might point out that the arid regions of Africa primarily dedicated to pastoralism represent one twelfth of the

land in the entire world, a figure which does not include somewhat less
arid regions where pastoralists predominate. However, these eight
million square kilometers represents land of very low carrying capacity
with an extremely sparse population. In demographic terms, Africa
contains well over half of the total world's pastoral population, but this
total still represents only twenty-two million people, nine million of
which are agro-pastoralists (Jahnke 1982).

Because much of the data on rural African population is
impressionistic and reflects a rapidly changing situation, available
demographic figures should only be seen to represent certain general
trends, towards population increase in rapidly diversifying pastoral
communities and decline in the number actually involved in herding,
especially in the more arid lands. The number of occupants of Maasai
districts in Kenya and Tanzania has increased dramatically, with growth
many times over of the Maasai community in this century and significant
in-migration during the last twenty years. However in Mauritania,
between two censuses carried out fifteen years apart, the pastoral and
nomadic segment of the country's population was cut by more than half,
with the remainder scattered among a great number of disparate
communities.

However, the importance of African pastoralists cannot be assessed
simply in terms of their relatively small numbers, spread out over a vast
expanse of marginal land, especially in comparison with the dense
population of Africa's agricultural regions and cities. Rather, the role
pastoral communities have played in African history and continue to play
in contemporary life rests on three major political and economic factors.
The first is the geopolitical significance of the enormous arid and semi-
arid areas they control, the second the ever-growing importance of
livestock production in feeding a continent undergoing rapid population
growth, and the third the growing international awareness of the
ecological fragility of the African arid zone and the problem of its
sustainable habitation. Before reviewing how these factors apply to
recent and current conditions in the major pastoral regions of Africa, we
would like to reflect on more general trends.

It would not be inaccurate to describe the dismal vision of the "new
pastoralism" (Hogg 1986),[1] a legacy of thirty years of ecological
devastation and impoverishment, as a mirror image of the myth of
pastoralism discussed in the Introduction. In that deeply ingrained
system of ideas, it is held that the value attributed to livestock by
nomadic pastoralists is either non-economic or subsistence-oriented, that
their relation to nature is harmonious, and that they are highly
autonomous, mobile and egalitarian. These myths, which are neither

adequate nor completely false, have been less refuted than overtaken by events. The major trends in pastoralism today are towards increasing commercialization and commoditization of livestock values; greater conflict with nature through drought and rangeland degradation; diminished autonomy through greater dependency on local markets, encapsulation by regional administration and entanglement in civil conflict; decreased mobility, through land enclosure and sedentarization; and increasing social differentiation and inequalities in wealth and degrees of economic security. As the discussion that follows will show, these trends are not independent but represent a complex result of changing conditions of life in Africa's arid and semi-arid lands, most of them out of the control of the herders so profoundly affected.

Drought, Degradation and Disruption

Through fifteen years of almost continuous below average rainfall and food shortage, there has been steady decline in the natural and social conditions of the pastoral way of life. The last decade witnessed large scale population movements involving many pastoralists, of whom the fortunate found refuge in urban areas at best and famine camps at worst; this phenomenom continues unabated. Degradation of the natural environment has been appreciable and in certain cases probably irreversible: in some Sahelian areas, for instance, desertification is taking place at the rate of ten km per year (Copans 1975)[2]. Where, in addition to climatic decline, political instability or upheaval is experienced - as has been recently the case for different reasons in Ethiopia and Uganda - famine has decimated an entire generation of those herders who have failed to gain access to international famine relief programs. In refugee camps or urban slums the social relations which were the core of pastoral society are being torn apart. Yet, dismal as the state of the refugee is, the most pressing problem for many pastoralists is immediate survival, often secured through settlement near sites of cultivation, through urban migration and temporary wage labor, or through procuring international assistance. All too often, destitute pastoralists have relocated near food aid transport networks and distribution centers, further undermining local economic systems and skewing patterns of habitation. Whatever our ethical stance is on the difficult questions of international relief, it is clear that international emergency assistance involves the paradox of providing for the survival of individuals while disrupting the reproduction of the social values and institutions, not to mention productive networks, on which those individuals depend (Turton 1977). Forced settlement, the breakdown of the traditional framework of day-to-day social relations, and subjugation of pastoralists to external political and economic interests has only accelerated these negative transformations.

Commercialization, Development and Inequality

It is in this context that the processes of increased commercialization of rangeland, the creation of ranches and the implementation of pastoral development projects should be seen (Sandford 1983; Simpson and Evangelou 1984; Hogg 1988). Given the urban-rural interdependence, growing urban populations have come to represent progressive increase in regional demand for meat, and thus the commercial value of livestock and, indirectly, of rangeland. Many nations have formed large-scale commercial ranches on some of their best rangeland, whether owned or managed by individuals, cooperatives, companies or the state, thus further diminishing the grasslands available to small-holding transhumant herders. At the same time, pastoralists have also become increasingly involved in the marketing of livestock, and development programs have been implemented with the help of bilateral and multilateral aid agencies which encourage greater commercialization of pastoral production through creating herding units or development organizations provided with ranching infrastructure. While these efforts have usually failed in their own terms (Galaty et. al. 1981), they form part of a complex of forces leading to the commoditization of land and labor in the pastoral sector, with many herders losing access to the factors of livestock production, in particular pasture and animals, on which their subsistence and livelihood depends.

At worst, transfers of herd and range ownership in many arid regions threaten to reduce resident pastoralists to the status of contract herders or salaried workers for commercial ranchers or absentee urban stockowners (Copans 1975). The process of rangeland enclosure and privitization is encouraged as a device for simultaneously strengthening conservation practices and stimulating higher levels of range productivity, perhaps incommensurate goals. In fact it often results in the creation of ecologically non-viable units of husbandry and accelerates economic differentials between large- and small-scale pastoralists and between rural and urban herdowners.

Mobility and Sedentarization

In response to their diminished access to resources, pastoralists often experience countervailing pressures, on the one hand towards settlement and on the other hand towards movement, in peripatetic and often pathetic pursuit of grass, water and security, quite different from normal migratory and transhumant patterns. Two apparently opposite but actually complementary processes of new migration are presently at work in the arid lands. In response to progressive encroachment on the rangelands by dry-land cultivation, irrigated agriculture, or commercial ranching, all indirect outcomes of population pressure and economic transformations in more highly productive and fertile regions, pastoralists have been driven out of prime pasture into even more marginal areas for herding, further stimulating environmental decline. Another rational and socially coherent response of pastoralists to declining quality of resources, for both people and their herds, has been migration to areas where climatic conditions are more favorable and where the maintenance and rebuilding of herds is possible. In West Africa, among the pastoral Fulani, in Tanzania among the pastoral Parakuyo, and in Ethiopia by the Oromo, to mention a few cases, large-scale movement into agricultural interstices or to forest frontiers have occurred, stimulating problems of regional integration, ethnic tensions, and friction between pastoral and farming communities.

Dependency and Politics

Drought and its aftermath has also revealed that African pastoralists will experience decreasing autonomy, with greater future dependency on outside sources of food and increasing vulnerability to political control and conflict. Most pastoralists have always required outside food supplements, but local networks of trade and exchange have been largely replaced today by shops, regulated markets and famine relief which pull pastoralists into their unreliable orbits. In most cases, prominent pastoral societies are divided between several neighboring states - one outcome of the logic underpinning the imperialist subdivision of Africa into colonies which were formed around enclaves of agricultural, mineral or commercial resources separated by regions of lower value and productivity: rangeland and savanna. Although the Tuareg and the Fulani occupied coherent environmental zones, they were dispersed among more than five nations. Ethnic Somalis were politically allocated among five colonial entities, while the Maasai and Oromo were each divided between two. With national frontiers transecting rangelands remote from capital cities and concentrations of population, it was virtually inevitable that conflicts between states would involve their pastoral populations, and that weak control over the more remote areas and the movement of pastoralists across boundaries would become factors in their alienation from state authority. The convergence of decolonization and the consolidation of a global geopolitical environment dominated by contending superpowers has given even greater emphasis and attention to conflict in the African arid zone.

Within emergent African states, pastoralists have usually found themselves a minority, and even in the ethnically rather homogeneous states of Mauritania and Somalia, members of the pastoralist majority still find themselves at odds with the state. Often demographically marginal and subjected to the power of larger ethnic groups over which they once exercised political and cultural hegemony, pastoralists now face the consequences of their political decline, even while struggling to regain some of their past privilege. The Tuareg in Mali, and more recently in Niger, have found themselves involved in open or latent conflict with the central political authorities, and where these conflicts coincide with sensitive international problems, as they do in Chad and Ethiopia, warfare is all too often the result. In a different context, successive Sudanese governments have been faced for several decades with both active and passive resistance by Nilotic (agro) pastoralists of the south, most noteworthy the Dinka and the Nuer, to their domination by Arabic-speaking, Islamic northerners (Johnson 1988b).

In these examples of regional African conflict, it may be tempting to perceive inherent aggression in the pastoralists who are involved. It is true for instance that in the struggle with the Moroccan state, POLISARIO troops have drawn upon their knowledge of desert warfare, now utilizing Land Rovers much as they previously did the more traditional camels of their deadly *gazu* raids against outlying adversaries. But in actual fact we should focus on the geo-political and geo-economic stakes involved in regions such as the Sahara or the Horn of Africa, currently the most militarily volatile areas in Africa, if we are to understand the underlying dynamics of these conflicts. For geographical reasons, regional conflicts such as those which have opposed Algeria and Morocco, Libya and Chad, or Ethiopia and Somalia often involve rangelands critical to pastoralists. When armed conflict does break out, pastoralists have often found themselves thrown to the forefront of an international scene where political relations have - until recently with the end of the Cold War - often been dictated by the displaced rationale of super-power confrontation.

For the countries involved geopolitical interests clearly take precedence over the needs and interests of pastoral populations. Difficulties in finding satisfactory economic policies, the present decline in the conditions of both the natural and social environment, and the frequent impossibility for local meat production to compete with capital-intensive international food markets, contributes to feelings of impotence, impatience or disinterest by government and pastoralist alike, leaving solutions through migration or conflict as the only perceived political alternatives. These processes clearly contribute to the escalation of interethnic conflict, especially when linked to the international political arena.

We have described here certain general trends in the conditions of pastoral life, ones that differ sharply with the myths conventionally held regarding pastoralism. Despite great regional variation, the processes associated with drought and famine, land subdivision and degradation, social stratification, migration and sedentarization, political conflict and warfare occur throughout the pastoral regions of Africa, from the Sahel to the Horn of Africa, and southward from Eastern and Interlacustrine to Southern Africa. Now we will describe the experiences of political and economic change particular to the four key pastoral areas, and the regional applicability of the geopolitical, economic and environmental factors in terms of which the wider continental significance of African pastoralism can be defined.

A Zone of Turbulence: The Sahara and Sahel

The drier regions of West Africa are particularly fraught with political and military conflict involving pastoral and nomadic populations. The yearly cycle of transhumance carries these herders into the heart of the arid zone during the wet season and into more verdant areas during the dry season, where they come into contact with sedentary farming communities (Lewis 1978). Sahelian pastoralists are organized in large political units, culturally and linguistically differentiated from their southerly neighbors who were often dominated in the past by warlord aristocracies typical of emirates or tribal confederacies. One of the main sources of present day conflict lies in the emergence of turbulent pastoral minorities in proximity to borders inherited from the colonial era. In Chad, the north/south axis involves overt or latent conflict between an agricultural majority in control of the southern part of the country and Tubu pastoralists to the north. The situation is similar in Niger and Mali, each with Tuareg pastoral minorities, where pre-colonial patterns of domination have been reversed and previously dominant pastoralists have been politically marginalized due to their low levels of schooling, declining economic role and localization in the more arid and less productive north, away from the political power centers of the more fertile south.

The evolution of conflict between nomads and the state has varied from one country to the next. In Mali, confrontation arose early after independence in armed conflict between the Tuareg and government forces, followed by a period of severe repression which, in conjunction with the drought which soon prevailed, led to the political eclipse of the pastoral community. In Niger, similar conflict remains covert but the situation has steadily deteriorated since the most recent coup d'etat. In 1990, armed conflict broke out anew in these two countries, between Tuareg and the local government. As in Chad, where conflict between pastoralists and the state and pastoralists as been, as it were, deferred, or at least redirected, by the more violent north/south civil war which has transpired, external influences have aggravated conflicts between many other African states and their pastoral minorities. In Mauritania, which is almost unique in Africa, having representatives of a pastoral majority in control of the state apparatus, this conflict has taken an unexpected turn. The *Haratin,* ex-slaves who are agriculturalists, have begun to voice political grievances related to their rights in land which has remained the property of their ex-masters. While these ex-slaves represent a significant political force, they remain assimilated to their old Beydan Arabic-speaking pastoral masters, in contradistinction to the *Halpularen* or Soninke agriculturalists of the Senegal River valley, who retain an identity distinct from that of their pastoral overlords. The recent pursuit of development projects within the agricultural zones of the Senegal River stimulated serious conflict between riverine cultivators and dominant Arabic-speakers that resulted in the massive expulsion of Moors from Senegal and of *Halpularen* from Mauritania.

The economic decline of these Saharan pastoral groups only began with the recent drought of the early 1970s. In contrast to the Fulbe, they had a long tradition of pastoralism geared to market exchange, based on their successful development of commercial meat production aimed at coastal markets. Control over this very profitable trade was and remains in the hands of specialized merchants, who conspicuously occupy the region's border areas. The bite of commercialization has had its effect on local systems of pastoral production. Camels have been replaced by cattle and sheep, for which urban consumer demand is greater, and pastures not used previously by cattle are now being exploited on a marginal hit and run basis.

The achievements of pastoral development policies in the region are few. Apart from a few experimental cattle ranches the main thrust has been to provide basic veterinary services, which have succeeded in reducing the incidence of epizootics. Stemming from the major stated national development goal of increasing overall rangeland productivity, innovations in hydraulic development have been introduced to enable pasture areas formerly inaccessible to pastoral production because of lack of water to be better exploited. Questionable technical choices or political considerations - *i.e.* every pastoral community wants its own well - have often led to a detrimental increase in pressure on pastoral ecosystems as a result of indiscriminate water development. In this relatively fragile natural environment, these policies, and the generalized growth of pastoral production associated with the favorable climatic conditions of the 1960s, has resulted in the aggravation of overgrazing and increased ecological disequilibrium.

This disequilibrium is also related to large-scale population movement, the causes of which can in the end can be linked to the more general trend towards population growth in Third World countries. New migration patterns were initiated during the course of the colonial period and encouraged thereafter by the undermining of political regulation of land use by dominant pastoral groups in each area. Pastoral authority was replaced by other "administrative" means of spatial control, implemented by agencies whose logic was foreign. Two patterns of migratory movement can be distinguished. The first pattern, which can be found in all the countries of the Sahara-Sahel interface (with the exception of Chad), consists of the steady northward migration of Fulani pastoralists into more arid areas where productive exploitation was already nearing rangeland carrying capacity. The second form of migration involves demographic pressure of expanding agricultural communities from the south and the encroachment on northern rangelands by subjugated groups of agriculturalists, who, having been integrated into Sahelian pastoral societies, now represent a large proportion of their population. In most countries, governments have tried but failed to slow down the process of rangeland encroachment by setting geographical limits to agriculture. The continued presence of settlements in these agriculturally marginal areas have further added to environmental pressure.

As early as 1973, the great drought had become the direct cause of widespread famine and generalized exodus of pastoralists from the arid zone in search of food. In successive waves, which occurred with each acute phase of the drought, pastoralists congregated in informal settlements at the proximity of urban areas. This process was particularly dramatic in Mauritania, for which the 1979 census revealed that only 300,000 people remained active in pastoralism; today this figure might be as low 100,000, although many have not left the pastoral sector altogether. The conditions under which these impoverished herders continue to tend their remaining herds and flocks are made even more difficult by their concentration around administrative settlements and permanent water holes, where famine relief is usually distributed. The decline of the total herd has only been slowed down through massive transfers of livestock to new urban owners, who maintain the necessary mobility required for the survival of herds and flocks only through hiring male herders from the severely affected segment of the Mauritanian pastoral sector. To varying degrees the same situation can also be observed in the other Sahelian countries. Endemic political problems of drought and chronic economic depression of the region have tended to affect pastoralists more than other groups. The drought, by resulting in the marginalization of herders and the weakening of Sahelian governments, has given a new dimension to the tensions created by borders inherited from colonialism, especially when this problem is projected onto the international political arena. These often arbitrary frontiers, derived from contingent historical circumstances, were already the objects of political tension at independence. Morocco for instance has always claimed that Mauritania merely represents its Saharan hinterland and so supported internal strife in the newly independent Mauritanian state. Algeria and Morocco have been opposed in what has been appropriately dubbed "the war of sand" over control of extensive territory in the Sahara. These conflicts were quite obviously related to that region's mineral wealth potential and to French foreign policy attempts, in the context of the Algerian war of independence, to foster the creation of a Saharan client state.

The 1960s was a period of relative economic prosperity devoted to institution-building in the Sahelian region, during which these geopolitical problems remained dormant, only to resurface in a more acute form in the 1970s. Following the fall of the government in Chad, Tubu pastoralists became central actors in the ongoing armed struggle, fueled by periodic French and Libyan interventions that respectively stimulated a series of successive political upheavals. If one does not take into account minor military incidents between Mali and Mauritania, on the one hand, and Mali and Burkina Fasso (formerly Upper Volta), on the other, the other major military episode in the region took place in 1975 at the time of Spanish decolonization, when Moroccan and Mauritanian claims to the Spanish Sahara led to the creation of the Algerian-backed POLISARIO movement. With their first-hand knowledge of the terrain and lessons learned from a prior episode of armed struggle (ironically backed by Morocco in the 1950s), during which they had suffered heavy losses at the hand of the joint Franco-Spanish *Ecouvillon* military operation, POLISARIO lost no time in evacuating its civilians towards the east. It subsequently inflicted heavy losses on Moroccan and Mauritanian troops, resulting in 1978 in the withdrawal of the latter from the conflict. However, the war between the POLISARIO and Morocco continues, despite discussion of a referendum on the ultimate affiliation of the region. In this case, foreign intervention took the form of direct military assistance (in the case of France) or of political support for the local protagonists by the superpowers from both the western and eastern blocs. Military operations in both Chad and Mauritania have greatly hampered and at times has even caused the complete disappearance of pastoralism, and, where animal husbandry has continued, have exacerbated veterinary health problems where normal government extension services have proven impossible to provide, including the resurgence of dangers related to locust invasion.

After a period when international relief programs have been a dominant feature wherever permitted by military and environmental conditions, efforts aimed at salvaging pastoral production and renewing pastoral populations have begun to emerge. For instance an integrated research program has been undertaken by the countries of the region, in collaboration with the International Livestock Centre for Africa (ILCA), on improved methods of animal breeding and management. Following the positive experience of Niger, development programs centered on the active involvement of pastoralists in the management of herder associations have been initiated, with some initial signs of success (Swift 1984).

The Horn of Conflict:
Revolution, Secession and Irredentism in Ethiopia and Somalia

The primarily Cushitic-speaking pastoralists of the Horn of Africa have been profoundly influenced by the Ethiopian state, founded long ago by the Semitic-speaking and Christian Amhara. The ancient and enduring presence of an independent African state in the Ethiopian highlands, only colonized by the Italians for a short period before the Second World War, lends the history of and current developments in the region certain unique qualities. In part made possible through the delicate colonial balance of power, the Amhara expansion occured during the colonial partition of Africa, achieving its maximum under Menelik II (1889-1911), under whom the Italians were rebuffed and the influence of the Ethiopian state extended to the south and south-east over diverse pastoral and agro-pastoral peoples, most prominently Oromo and Somali, into the hinterland where the border with British East Africa was eventually established (Barber 1968; Almagor 1986).[3] When the coastal zone was subdivided between Italy (Eritrea and Italian Somaliland), France (Djibouti) and Great Britain (British Somaliland), the Amhara Empire was in effect recognized and consolidated, the more so by its ultimate occupation by the Italians. After the Italian defeat in the Second World War, the Ethiopian Empire was reconfirmed in its present boundaries, after a brief flirtation of the British Foreign Office under Ernest Bevin with the notion of a Greater Somalia, which included Eritrea, later annexed by Ethiopia. Thus was founded an autochthonous, non-colonized imperial state, its frontier secured through a series of bloody ethnic conflicts (Donham and James 1986).

Eritrea, inhabited by numerous nomadic pastoral commmunities organized on the basis of Islamic tribes (Beja, Tigre, Afar, Saho, *etc.*), experienced Italian colonization from the end of the nineteenth century and, following the Second World War, was first federated to (1952) and then annexed (1962) by Ethiopia. A guerilla conflict ensued between Ethiopia and Eritrea, the latter being Muslim receiving Arab support. After gaining independence in 1962, and uniting the former British and Italian colonial territories, Somalia sought to reclaim the areas occupied by ethnic Somalis in north-eastern Kenya, the French Territory of the Afars and the Issas, otherwise known as Djibouti, and the Ogaden region of Ethiopia. Following the long "shifta" war of the 1960s against northern Somali insurgency, a legacy of ethnic animosity remains in Kenya; periodic civil unrest and recurrent smuggling near the Kenya-Somali border led to a brutal suppression in the mid-1980s of Somali communities in the region, and in 1990 the forced registration of all ethnic Somalis resident in Kenya and the expulsion of many to Somalia.

The cumbersome bureaucracy and the quasi-feudal system of imperial Ethiopia, under the Emperor Haille Sellasie, was unable to cope with the changing world, especially given the great African drought and famine of the 1970s that precipitated in Ethiopia a major political crisis. In 1974, the government and subsequently the monarchy foundered with the radicalization of urban centres and the military, followed by the creation of a Marxist-Leninist military regime, directed by the "DERG", which under the authority of Mengistu Haile Mariam liquidated the aristocracy, nationalized rural lands, initiated agrarian reform, created neighborhood cooperatives (*Kebele*) and established the state on a Soviet model. However, the central Government, preoccupied with establishing itself in urban areas, progressively lost influence over the more peripheral and non-Amharic areas and has had little actual impact on the organization of pastoralism in the rangelands of the south and east. By 1977, the weakness of the Ethiopian state resulted in a series of political crises involving conflict between the government and diverse ethnic and provincial interests throughout the Horn of Africa.

The Eritrean conflict has steadily heightened, despite conflict between the two major guerilla movements, the ELP (Eritrean Liberation Party) and the EPLF (Eritrean People's Liberation Front), each of which rests on a different ethnic and political base and whose support from Arab countries was for divergent aims. This resistance involved pastoral and nomadic populations, the urban inhabitants of the city of Asmara and cultivators of the highlands near Tigre. In the latter province, guerilla resistance was subsequently initiated by those within the Tigrean People's Liberation Front (TPLF), opposed to the regime in Addis Ababa. In 1977, after the Eritrean liberation movement fell just short of occupying the entire province, an Ethiopian counter-offensive in 1978 pushing their opponents back to their sanctuaries near the border with Sudan. A period of murderous skirmishes was followed by a new Eritrean offensive in 1984, which, however, coincided with a drought that decimated the region, ultimately driving them northward to seek refuge in the Sudanese border areas.

In Somalia, the military regime of Siad Barre also adopted a socialist model, which, however, had little concrete relevance for the country's pastoral and nomadic majority. In 1977, the Western Somali Liberation Front (WSLF), in conjunction with Somali troops and assisted by the Oromo Liberation Front (OLF), which also had irredentist and secessionist aims, attempted to seize control of the Ogaden region of Ethiopia. The Ogaden represents a quite important pasture area for the Darood Somali, who tend to dominate the independent Somali state. After a period of initial success, the Ethiopians, with the aid of Cuban troops and the support of the Soviet bloc (the U.S.S.R. having finally made a choice between its two allies in the region), defeated the Somalis. Ethiopian repression following a new Somali offensive in 1980 provoked an exodus of around 750,000 refugees from the Ethiopian Ogaden into Somalia. Failing to establish autonomy *vis-a-vis* Mogadishu, the national Somali movement, which recruits from among the Issaq tribes of the north, opposed both the central government and the Marxist-Leninist Somali Democratic Front. This conflict led to a progressive weakening of the Somali regime, which then sought outside support by turning towards the West and in November, 1984 coming to an accord with Kenya, formally abandoning its irredentist claims. As the political and economic crisis bred increasing conflict, the country became polarized between Issas in the north and the central government, with support limited to the south. By early 1991, the northern rebellion had spread to insurgents in the central region, who placed the capital, with the President and entrenched government supporters, under siege. The fall of Mogadishu led to widespread civil disorder and the dissolution of central authority. Although the south remained under the control of the former government, the capital was occupied by one group of insurgents, the north by another, with the latter declaring independence.

Other movements, more modest in aims and ambitions, have emerged out of pastoral and agro-pastoral populations within the Ethiopian Empire. Out of the loose congeries of Oromo-spreaking groups, who together represent around forty percent of the total Ethiopian population, emerged the Oromo Liberation Front (OLF), a politically and ideologically somewhat obscure group; the Afar Liberation Front (ALF) in Djibouti is directed by Sultan Ali Mirah Aupere, formerly representative of the Afar National Liberation Movement.

Outside the political and military machinations that seem endemic to Ethiopia, pastoral populations occupying the more distant frontiers and administered in indirect fashion have only recently overcome the centrifugal tendencies of colonialism, under which their ancient ties with the Amhara state were weakened, and have now begun to exercise influence of their own. Apart from more agriculturally-oriented groups of Oromo, who though related to pastoral "Galla" (i.e. Borana) are strongly "Amharaized" and now often Islamicized, these pastoral populations are less numerous than the agricultural Amhara of the Ethiopian highlands and gain global significance primarily through their strategic location, their military value and their geopolitical role in the "great game" for influence and control over the Horn of Africa, strategically located between the Arabian Peninsula and the Red Sea, that has been played by the great powers since the nineteenth century. To the military and political difficulties just described must be added an ongoing economic and ecological crisis in the region, stimulated in part by drought and in part by the effects of agrarian reform, which has disrupted patterns of agricultural production through stimulating excessive clearing and tilling by freed peasants, undermining regional food redistribution, and discouraging surplus production and marketing through inadequate price incentives and coercive appropriation of crops by the state. A more recent episode of drought and famine occurred in 1984, which has also devastated the neighboring countries of Sudan and Somalia, claiming over 200,000 lives and resulting in heated discussion in the Western World about the means by which the Ethiopian government has distributed international aid. These dramatic events led the government, under catastrophic and improvised conditions, to create resettlement villages in the more humid, agriculturally-rich but disease-ridden south-west, to which people of the dry north - from areas involved in insurgency - were forced to move, provoking speculation about the motives of Ethiopia in dealing with the human problems of the north through a policy of displacement. In the spring of 1990, with the dramatic shift in the economic and international policies of its patron, the Soviet Union, and increasingly grave threats to its own power, the Ethiopian Government proposed far-reaching measures to "liberalize" the national economy, including freer markets for agricultural produce, a diminished role for local cooperatives and greater security of land tenure for peasants.[4] In May, 1991, Mengistu fled Addis Ababa in the face of rapid military advances by the Ethiopian People's Liberation Front (EPLF)[5], a Tigrean-led coalition, which, with Western concurrence, subsequently occupied the capital to maintain civil order. On July 1st, the provisional EPRDF government convened a broad-based meeting of parties, except for the former ruling Worker's Party of Ethiopia (WPE), to establish a transitional government and arrange for subsequent multi-party elections, a move favorable to future political stability in the region.

Plains of Change: Ranching, Development and Stratification
in Eastern and Southern Africa

The region south of the Horn of Africa has also suffered the impact of drought and political upheaval, but not on the scale experienced to the north. Rather, the major processes affecting pastoral populations of this area have followed from increased influence of government, progressive growth and expansion of arid land populations, growing demand for meat and subsequent increase in the commercialization of livestock, and the implementation of arid and semi-arid land development programs. The ambivalence of pastoralists towards state intervention is ubiquitous, as are tensions between them and their agricultural neighbors, but these attitudes now occur from positions of relative pastoral weakness and vulnerability. The perennial struggle to achieve an adequate subsistence has recently been heightened through competition for land and evolution in forms of land tenure, with the state intervening to alter the relation between pastoralists and their resources. Privileged access to land for commercial ranching or farming is currently laying down the basis for class formation and stratification in pastoral populations, a process stimulated and made possible by state intervention.

Several national boundary regions have become sites of conflict and instability, due both to the weakness of state power in and competition over interstitial areas. Little remembered in the wake of the Somali/Ethiopian Ogaden war is the secessionist "*shifta*" movement of ethnic Somali in northeast Kenya during the 1960s, or its brief resurgence in the 1970s with episodes occuring as late as 1984, which made pastoral homesteads so vulnerable to government efforts - ultimately successful - at pacification. The Kenyan/Ethiopian border has long been a locus of instability, with peoples of southern Ethiopia having had access to arms and have thus achieved leverage over northern Kenyan populations who were kept relatively unarmed. The four corners region of the Ethiopian-Sudan-Ugandan-Kenyan border has been known for its absence of effective security since the early days of colonialism, and in actuality took on its marginal and interstitial status in large part because of being maximally distant from the four centers of economic and political power around which the four states were formed. With the fall of Amin in Uganda, the dispersion of automatic weapons throughout the four-corners region heightened regional insecurity, giving pastoral groups such as the Karamojong' the means of achieving rapid and effective stockraiding, but equally making each vulnerable to the others (Cartrell 1988). Raiding and counter-raiding between the Kenyan Turkana and such groups as the Pokot of Kenya, Dassanetch of Ethiopia, Karamojong of Uganda, and the Dodoth of Sudan, has increased in recent years, both stimulated by the drought and exacerbating the effects of drought by reducing the range each group in its own insecurity is able to exploit (Fukui and Turton 1977). Thus, the drought of the mid-1970s and mid-1980s created conditions of widepread raiding by *Ngoroka* bandits, with the result that frontier pasture areas were abandoned, thus even further hastening pastoral collapse in this region, remote from most established networks of international relief (Hogg 1988).

Insecurity is only one factor in the tendency of pastoralists to make less effective use of available grazing resources in the drier regions. The growth of famine relief camps and spontaneous settlements around wells, rivers, roads, and trading centers has led to effective sedentarization of populations, despite their lack of a significant non-pastoral base of subsistence and the frequent futility of practicing local dry-land cultivation. The camel-keeping Rendille and Gabra of Northern Kenya are now largely gathered together in large permanent settlements, with herds being tended by young men who shift in temporary campments (O'Leary 1985). Unfortunately, the aim of sedentarization has become a feature of government policy in most nations of the area, due to ill-considered beliefs that nomadic pastoral practice is the primary cause of range degradation. All too often, the difficulty experienced by government in providing services to mobile and widely dispersed populations is equated with pastoralist resistance to development, leading to attempts to concentrate pastoralists in sedentary villages where they can both be provided social services and put under administrative control (Galaty 1989). In Tanzania, pastoral villages were created into which herding communities were gathered under the threat of military force. When this concentration led to overgrazing of the village proximity and underuse of more distant pastures, the village plan was modified for pastoralists through being extended over a several mile area (Ndagala 1984). Today, with more liberal domestic policies being adopted in Tanzania, pastoralists as well as peasants trickle back to their former lands as political pressure is lessened, with the village maintained as a unit of political organization and a locus of services, rather than as a mandatory and uniform residential site (Parkipuny 1988).

However, most sedentarization processes are indirect, unintentionally facilitated, for instance, at locales of famine relief; nonetheless, precipitous settlement often leads to decline in pastoral productivity and health, especially without the investment of significant national resources for aid or infrastructure. Each of the Saharan-Sahelian droughts have reached the Horn of Africa and have extended southward down the semi-arid Rift Valley plains and plateaux of East Africa. Famine relief has become customary in northern Kenya, and, in part due to greater international awareness, hunger has been checked short of the catastrophes experienced elsewhere. But the boom and bust cycle of herd growth is common, with, for example, sixty percent of their cattle herds having being lost to Maasai in 1962, again in 1974-75, and yet again in 1984, with herds increasing to pre-drought levels or more before the next devastation. This process is not simply due to normal patterns of herd management on commonly-held land (Allan 1965), as the "tragedy of commons" argument maintains (Hardin 1968; Hopcraft 1981), but to several factors that render pastoralism today less resilient in the face of drought than in times past, due to loss of land and labor and increased commercialization of livestock production (Galaty 1988b)

Through most of the nineteenth century, eastern Africa was largely dominated by pastoralists who controlled the extensive rangelands that stretched between the few loci of highly productive highland agriculture. The successive blows of animal and human epidemic and drought in the 1880s decimated herds and pastoral communities alike, altering forever the balance of power between pastoralists and agriculturalists, the former often seeking refuge with the latter, as in the case of Maasai who fled to the Kikuyu (Spear 1981). The successive arrival of European explorers, missionaries and colonists coincided with this period of vulnerability. Many Maasai settled near the first British military garrison near Ngong in the interior of the East African Protectorate, later Kenya Colony, which afforded them protection against Kikuyu and opportunity to rebuild herds through serving as irregulars on early colonial pacification raids. This Maasai-British "alliance" (Waller 1976) was instrumental in shaping later colonial policy towards them and towards other pastoral communities as well.

The British perceived the Maasai as the greatest potential threat to their control over the East African Protectorate and thus gave them greater administrative latitude. However, the Maasai-occupied land along the railway, built in 1902, was seen as economically and strategically vital to colonial and, more importantly, settler interests. In the first Maasai Move of 1905, land in the Rift Valley was allocated to white colonists, some in huge parcels, while the Maasai were split between two reserves, south and north of the railway line. It took only a few years for the colonists to cast their eyes on the rich northern Laikipia reserve, and subsequently (in 1911 - with much political clamor and controversy) the former treaty was broken and a new treaty signed with the Maasai, who were ultimately moved to a single expanded southern reserve. While Maasai suffered the loss of the greatest amount and proportion of land taken for White Settlement, they gained a formal treaty and a rights over a formally designated reserve, which, while confirming their land rights, had the effect of isolating them from incursion and change from the outside. Other pastoral areas of northern Kenya, though lacking treaty status, became closed districts for security reasons. Thus, during the colonial period, pastoral communities were allowed to flourish relatively autonomously within the limits of district boundaries, direct administration and civil control, but experienced few developments in education, pastoral infrastructure or industry, although livestock trade, often mediated by Somali middlemen, was slowly established (Turton 1970).

The colonial appropriation for European settlement of the central Rift Valley and the Laikipia plateau in Kenya established a pattern of pastoral dispossession that continues in less overt form today. National Parks and Game Reserves, mines, state farms, trading centers, and commercial ranches, currently exploit a large proportion of the pastoral plains of East Africa. The Group Ranch program in Kenya was initiated in order both to establish land security for pastoralists and increase commercial meat production, but in reality has achieved neither (Galaty 1980, 1988b; Grandin 1986). Similarly, Tanzanian ranching associations and then pastoral villages have failed to create a viable mode of pastoral organization to supplant the Maasai system of political and economic regulation, and have actually served to disrupt adapative patterns of resource allocation and use (Parkipuny 1988). At present, the semi-arid Maasai regions are in the process of being subdivided into family holdings in Kenya or parcelled out for diverse national uses in Tanzania, each case rationalized as involving an increase in the productivity of land dedicated to national use (*c.f.* Simpson and Evangelou 1984).

It is doubtful, however, that family ranch holdings could prove ecologically viable across the entire pastoral society, especially given that private ranches in Kenya have in part thrived through use of the common lands of the reserves during the colonial period and group holdings in the post-independent era (Galaty 1988b). Similarly, the nucleation of the pastoral process, combined with increased access to education and the occurrence of outmigration, dramatically decreases the potential of pastoral households to cooperate in the allocation of labor, leading some households to experience decline while others hire outside labor (Sperling 1985b). In comparative perspective, we are far from experiencing the creation of a reservoir of landless and stockless pastoralists in the arid lands, but trends towards population growth, land loss, and decreased family livestock holdings are disquieting (Sperling and Galaty 1990).

While governments exercise pressure on pastoralists to adopt commercial strategies, they too often ignore the fact that pastoralists are and have been throughout the century profoundly involved in livestock marketing, developing networks of livestock trade throughout the pastoral areas and using formal and informal markets and auctions for animal transactions (Little 1987). The Dinka supply cattle for northward trade with the Khartoum market, the Beja and Somali serve as agents in the huge livestock trade between eastern Africa and the Arabian Peninsula that has grown out of the oil economy, and the Maasai represent the single largest suppliers of meat to the Nairobi market (Evangelou 1984). In general, returns on the livestock trade are frugally reinvested in herds, a rational economic practice only disconcerting to proponents of destocking. Yet increased commercialization, by pastoralists or ranchers alike, does not appear to represent the unilateral pursuit of capitalist animal production, even by those whose access to land, labor, and capital has increased, due to their use of a market rational. Rather, pastoralists tend towards dual management of herds, both for subsistence milk production and herd reproduction and for fattening and commercial sale of steers, as they straddle production systems in a shrewd diversification of their interests and investments.

While most development projects in pastoral areas involve investment in veterinary care, stocking programs, and water development, they often have minimal secondary impact (except for control of livestock diseases through innoculation), partly because insufficient resources were invested to stimulate radical change. It is ironic that, given the difficulties facing Sudan's pastoral population (Haaland 1980), perhaps the most ambitious development project in Africa today is the Jonglei canal in southern Sudan which, if and when completed, will probably have a profoundly negative impact on pastoralists living not only along the banks of the Upper Nile but in the wider area effected by the changes in hydrology that the canal will bring. The canal will dramatically shrink the current floodplain in its immediate vicinity, with a massive reduction of up to fifty percent if the Bahr al-Jabal returns to its pre-1961 levels. The line of the canal also intervenes between permanent Nuer and Dinka settlements and dry-season, river-fed pastures, which will make access to a large area of the reduced pasturage more difficult. Rapid flow of the canal may drain the water table towards it, thus reducing effective use of pastures even farther to the east. Planning for the Jonglei has always emphasized the irrigation needs of people far to the north, a fact that has made the canal project a contentious issue in north/south Sudan politics and a major factor in the current renewal of the Sudanese civil war (Johnson 1988b; 1988c).

In Botswana and Kenya, despite land enclosure, privatized title and access to markets and credit, a ranching bourgeoisie has not in fact developed, despite the emergence of a social and political elite who, dependent on government, has in general not fulfilled the economic role of their class position (Aronson 1980). In the Tribal Grazing Lands Policy

(TGLP) of Botswana, effective control over huge areas of rangeland has been gained through rights in boreholes granted to individuals with links to government deemed "progressive" (Worby 1984). At the same time, pastoralists (Tswana) and pastoro-foragers (San) have been legally dispossessed, theoretically squatting on rangeland at the behest of the new owner, whether company or individual (Worby 1988). As family ranch-holdings in Kenya are sold following rangeland subdivision and privatization, as has previously been the case and is today occurring at an accelerating pace (Galaty 1988b), pastoralists without pasture may become a social reality.

But much of the pressure on rangelands is indirect, resulting from growing population, progressive encroachment by cultivators into higher potential grazing lands, and the expansion of commercial wheat production, rather than from the direct appropriation and nationalization of pastoral lands and the sort of forced sedentarization that occurred in the history of Iran or Mongolia. In this sense, land allocation programs have at best served to consolidate pastoral land rights. Most rangelands have little potential for forms of exploitation other than livestock production, so the critical question becomes the relation of herders to range resources as they progressively commercialize their production strategies, as has become the trend throughout the area.

Plateau of Upheaval: Intralacustrine Revolt and Revolution

Rwanda and Burundi, the foremost among the Intralacustrine kingdoms, are also the only ones whose former boundaries coincide with the frontiers of their colonial states and current independent nations. Other kingdoms such as Bunyoro and Nkore were integrated into the larger territorial structure of Uganda with which their evolution has been intertwined, including the well-known political and economic difficulties of that country (Beattie 1964). We will focus here on the recent situation in Rwanda and Burundi, formerly colonies of Germany, placed under Belgium mandate after the First World War. Under colonization, the client relations that formed the basis of their systems of kingship, itself symbolically represented by the hierarchical circulation of cattle, were transformed and solidified in the form of an ethnic opposition - in the eyes of colonial officials, the population concerned, and ethnologists - between Tutsi herders, "Hamitic" and dominating, and Hutu cultivators, Bantu and dominated. The evolution of tenurial relations increasingly controlled by aristocratic Tutsi and of the political prerogatives reserved for them, such as access to colonial schools, tended to reinforce this opposition between the two groups just when the moment of Independence erupted. However, the consequences of Independence for these similar nations proved radically different.

Rwanda experienced a virtual Hutu revolution, against the Tutsi and against the Mwami royalty. The initial expression of Bahutu opposition to the independence party, APROSOMA, occurred in the violence of 1957, followed by anti-Tutsi jacquerie; by the end of 1959 the country experienced fire and blood, in which the Mwami Vjutara III and his successor Nigala V were killed. At the creation of the republic, in January, 1961, the country was further polarized by the Parmehutu Hutu Emancipation party, which exiled principal Tutsi leaders and the Mwami. Violence did not end at independence, in July, 1962, but escalated into a virtual anti-Tutsi pogram by the beginning of 1964. Continuing ethnic and economic difficulties (the country has 5.9 million inhabitants, with the highest population density in rural Africa at 225 persons per square kilometer) provided the backdrop for the military *coup d'etat* of July, 1973, by General Jukenal Habyarimana who, although a Hutu, pursued a policy of ethnic reconcilation oriented towards issues of economic development and of halting ecological degradation.

In Burundi, the independence movement was organized around the UPROMA of Prince Louis Rwagasore, the son of the Mwami, who won the elections of September, 1961, which preceded 1962 independence, only to be assassinated two weeks later. Ethnic divisions were rapidly worsened by the actions and policies of the Mwami Mwambutsa IV. Several attempted Hutu *coups d'etat* were suppressed before the military-based Colonel Micombero of the Tutsi minority came to power in November, 1966. A veritable civil war - with definite links to the Congolese insurrection - began in 1972, involving the systematic elimination of between 50-100,00 Hutu, virtually the entire Hutu elite. These bloody events and economic difficulties, exacerbated by the corruption of the regime, stimulated another military *coup d'etat* directed by Colonel J.B. Bageze in November, 1976. Since then, the political situation has stabilized, marked only by continuing conflict between the state and the Catholic Church, which is accused of favoring the Hutu people. Ethnic tensions between Hutu and Tutsi lie, however, just under the surface, erupting periodically in explosions of violence, such as occurred in 1988. The economic difficulties of the country, which has 4.5 million inhabitants and a population density of 163 persons per square kilometer, are similar to those experienced in Rwanda.

What are the reasons for this divergence between the two countries, Rwanda, which experienced a Hutu revolution, and Burundi, where a Hutu revolt was mercilessly suppressed by the Tutsi, who continued to exercise power? Economic domination by the Tutsi, even though accentuated by colonialism, cannot provide a total explanation. In Rwanda, the identification of royalty with the Tutsi created a "hegemonic" situation, such that egalitarian revendication by the Hutu peasantry could only by expressed through a simultaneous reversal of both royalty and the Tutsi order. In Burundi, this identification was less absolute and the Tutsi/Hutu distinction less coincident with the hierarchical social order. The *baganwa* bureaucratic class was better able to negotiate with modern political realities, offering hope for peasant revendication greater than that offered by Hutu revendication. Paradoxically, over the decades of colonialism, mechanisms of stratification and aristocratic domination, which previously had produced the "ethnic" distinction between herders and cultivators, ultimately represented the stimulus for social change, violent as it was.

Conclusion

This book has developed the influence of the "pastoral factor" on African history and society, through mediating the great caravan and trade routes, underpinning the establishment of pre-colonial states, controlling vast regions of savannah, shaping systems of social and political hierarchy, and stimulating migration and expansionary conflicts that have reshaped Africa's political configurations. In each region of Africa, pastoral groups such as the Fulani, the Moors, and the Tuareg of West Africa, the Somali and the Oromo of the Horn of Africa, the Nuer, Dinka, and Bedouin of the Sudan, the Tutsi and Bahima of the Interlacustrine area, the Maasai and Turkana of East Africa, and the Zulu and Tswana of Southern Africa, stand with the creators of sedentary polities and states as major determinants of Africa's history. The roles played by livestock in enhancing mobility, in generating, storing and expressing economic value, in facilitating exchange, in creating political ties (both lateral and hierarchical), in securing subsistence in the arduous dry lands, in generating dynamic social structure, and in shaping the autonomous and independent character of herders, contributed to the formation of dynamic and influential societies.

Directly or indirectly, the volume has set forth notions concerning five aspects of pastoral life: its concept of *Value*, its relation to *Nature*, its degree of *Autonomy*, its practice of *Mobility*, and its degree of *Equality*. In Chapter 1, the *Introduction*, we presented the somewhat romanticized "myths of pastoralism", an integrated model that characterized pastoralists as: asserting the cultural and subsistence value of livestock; being in harmony with nature; being highly autonomous; being highly mobile and expansionary; and being universally egalitarian. We then set forth, in a critical manner, a "dynamic perspective" on these aspects of pastoralism, suggesting that historical and anthropological evidence supported a more complex view of pastoralists: as attributing to livestock various economically and culturally rational forms of value; as interacting in a dynamic way with nature (high labor needs, with both conservationist and environmentally destructive practices); with only relatively autonomous forms of household production. depending on regional systems of resource allocation and exchange; with expansion representing not simple pastoral predation but the reallocation of regional population across resources through migration, often involving reciprocity and negotiation; and as politically characterized by stratified as well as egalitarian organization, with the ideology of pastoral equality often combined with notions of the inequality of non-pastoralists. Finally, in this chapter, we presented "current trends in African pastoralism", towards: commercialization of livestock production; greater antagonism with nature and degradation of the environment; increased dependency and regional insecurity; diminished mobility and increasing sedentarization; and greater inequality of access to resources and stratification of wealth.

One might be tempted to see these three quite different visions of the African pastoralism (mythological images, retrospective complexities, prospective trends) as representing slices in time of rapidly evolving systems: an original state of affairs, with growing complexity, and, most recently, the inevitable experience of development. We would prefer, however, to present the three visions as coexisting dimensions of pastoralism, each portraying a segment of a continuum as well as an aspect of the complexities of individual experience. The "reality" occurs across these three dimensions of experience, between which pastoralists move in thought and practice, motivated by complex needs and aims, making contextualized attributions and judgements on the basis of contradictory values, weighing what was and might be against what is. In short, something about the internal tenacity and continuity of pastoral culture and economy would elude us if we were to accept the somewhat dismal "trends" as the only current reality, ignoring the "myths" which still influence pastoral practice and the "dynamic perspectives" on regional relations, which persist despite the sweeping forces of Market, State and Ecology.

What lessons can be drawn from this volume for the development of policy regarding pastoralists in Africa? The "trends" described above represent not only what is actually happening but also the results of planning, from the "mainstream" perspective on arid land development (Sandford 1983), based on policies subject to the following critical commentary. First, while the process of commercialization of pastoral production has resulted in significant economic benefits, to pastoralists and their nations, there are ecological costs to accelerating the pace of production in ecologically fragile semi-arid and arid lands, and there are social costs as the subsistence base of herders is further undermined (Sandford 1983); many pastoralists are sensibly turning to "semi-commercialization", by dividing their herds between market and home production. Second, the view that the environmental problems of the arid lands require a strategy of economic diversification has much to commend it, but not if nonpastoral pursuits (*i.e.* irrigation agriculture, trade) are supported as alternatives to strengthening animal husbandry (Hogg 1986); the economic future of the arid lands by necessity lies in animal husbandry, and while diversification will and should occur, appreciable flows of labor out of the herding enterprise can only have further negative affects on rangeland degradation. Thirdly, the related viewpoint that the economic and ecological predicaments of the arid lands derive from nomadic land use is short-sighted, since the most efficient and productive use of rangeland resources, in terms of labor, nutrition and the environment, is through continuing mobility; sedentarization, the policy of most African governments, may serve to centralize control of and services for pastoralists but is disastrous in most other respects (Galaty 1989). Fourthly, while in today's complex world no community is completely autonomous, pastoral management and decision-making is most effective at the local-level, where high levels of indigenous knowledge, interest, and commitment coincide. Loss of pastoral autonomy has come about not only through encapsulation by the state but through the spread of regional conflict and insecurity, which directly threaten herders' livelihood and indirectly curtails their judicious use of pastures and access to markets. Given the agricultural (and livestock) policies and the inability to avoid or resolve civil conflicts of many governments in countries such as Chad or Ethiopia, it is unreasonable to attribute conditions of famine and environmental degradation to the resulting practices of pastoralists (lower levels of production and marketing, concentration of livestock around settlements, less mobility). And, fifthly, growing herder inequality, often taken to be a "cost" of development, is undesireable for several reasons: (a) the undue accumulation of pasture and livestock resources often reflects the exercise of political power rather than the outcome of economic growth and investment, thus represents a "braking" rather than an "accelerator" effect; (b) while there are often economies of scale to be gained through increasing herd sizes, there are also losses in productivity due to less diligent and personal management, often the case when the pastoral elite is increasingly "absentee" (Little 1987); (c) while few benefits are gained by increased social stratification in rangeland communities, there are definite social, economic, and human costs of generating an impoverished class of herders out of pastoralists who are able and willing to work autonomously and productively.

The nature and requirements of colonial and independent states almost inevitably marginalized pastoral polities and reduced their regional influence, even in those countries where they formed the ethnic basis for the state. Divided between nations, deposed from positions of regional domination, stripped of ethnic arrogance and cultural supremacy, and experiencing the erosion of claims on the extensive lands on which a resilient animal-based economy depends, African pastoralists have been rendered increasingly vulnerable to the internal challenges of growing population, encroachment of non-pastoralists, sedentarization, commercialized animal husbandry, and the complex challenges of development. Yet the most pervasive and dramatic threat to the life of pastoralists and pastoralism is that of rangeland ecological collapse, initiated by the multiple factors of drought, political loss of high quality resources followed by ecological marginalization, undue commercialization of already weak subsistence bases, regional conflict and insecurity, undesireable sedentarization, and inappropriate economic stratification. The outcomes of herd loss, famine, and the creation of refugees, fleeing to relief camps, small towns and urban peripheries, present familiar and still appalling images to the world. Yet the future of Africa's arid lands and their human populations will continue to rest on a pastoral base. The major questions of today concern the means by which the livelihood and the social existence of pastoral peoples can be secured and enhanced, given the myths and predicaments of their past and current realities.

Notes

1. Hogg's description of the "new pastoralism", characterized by increasing impoverishment, vulnerability to drought and food insufficiency, and diversified activities (1986), should be distinguished from Lamphear's notion that the "new pastoralism" (1985) emerged historically with the refinement of specialized husbandry, improved iron implements, acquisition of the zebu and novel forms of social organization (see Galaty in this volume).

2. However, recent satellite measurements indicate that what appeared as a consistent trend towards expansion of the Sahara, from 8.8 to 10.1 million square kilometers between 1980-1984, may simply reflect dramatic annual fluctuations; from 1983 to 1984, the area of the Sahara actually shrunk by 730,000 square kilometers (*Science*, Vol. 253, 19 July, 1991).

3. In the south-east, this expansion brought an Islamic majority under Christian domination, as in the occupation of the Islamic city of Harar in 1887, while in the south it resulted in the subjugation of small primarily non-Islamic kingdoms, as well as dynamic Oromo groups, e.g. the Macha, Borana and Guji.

4. While these tentative changes may have stimulated increases in highland cultivation and crops marketed in late 1990, Ethiopia faces yet another grim drought and potential famine in its dry, low-lying conflict-fraught areas, without the assurance of a strong international response to its plight.

5. The EPLF is a broad-based pan-ethnic coalition which officially includes the TPLF, the Ethiopian People's Democratic Movement (EPDM), the Oromo People's Democrative Organisation (OPDO) and the Ethiopian Democratic Officer's Revolutionary Movement, with affiliation or contact with several other local liberation groups. However broad-based in conception, the TPLF provides the leadership and over 80% of the fighters for the EPLF (*Africa Confidential* 32 (11), 31 May, 1991).

Bibliography

Abadie, M.
   1927 *La colonie du Niger*. Paris: Societe d'Editions Geographiques, Maritimes et Coloniales.
Abir, M.
   1970 Southern Ethiopia. In *Pre-Colonial Trade in Africa*. R. Gray and D. Birmingham, eds. London: Oxford University Press.
Adamu, Mahdi and A.H.M. Kirk-Greene, eds.
   1986 *Pastoralists of the West African Savanna*. Manchester University Press.
Ahmad, B. al-Amin
   1958 *Al-Wasit fi tarajim udaba Sinqit*. Le Caire and Casablanca: al-Hanji.
Alexander, J.
   1967 [1838] *An Expedition of Discovery into the Interior of Africa, through the hitherto Undescribed Countries of the Great Namaquas, Boschmans, and the Hill Damaras*. Cape Town: Struik (Facsimile reprint of 1838 original).
Al-Bakri
   1964 *Al-Mugrib fi dikr bilad Ifriqiyya wa-l-Magrib*. (Translation: de Slane.) Paris: Maisonneuve.
Allan, J.A., ed.
   1981 *The Sahara: Ecological Change and Early Economic History*. Cambridge: Middle East and North African Studies Press.
Allan, W.
   1965 *The African Husbandmen*. New York: Barnes and Noble.
Almagor, U.
   1971 *The Social Organization of the Dassanetch of the Lower Omo*. Ph.D. dissertation, University of Manchester.
   1972a Name-Oxen and Ox-Names Among the Dassanetch of Southwest Ethiopia. *Paideuma* 18:79-96.
   1972b Tribal Sections, Territory and Myth: Dassanetch Responses to Variable Ecological Conditions. *Asian and African Studies* 8:185-206.
   1978 *Pastoral Partners: Affinity and Bond Partnership among the Dassanetch of South-West Ethiopia*. Manchester University Press.

Almagor, U. (cont.)
  1979 Raiders and Elders: A Confrontation of Generations among the Dassanetch. In *Warfare among East African Herders*. Katsuyoshi Fukui and David Turton, eds. pp. 119-145. Senri Ethnological Studies No. 3, Osaka: National Museum of Ethnology.
  1986 Institutionalizing a Fringe Periphery: Dassenetch-Amhara Relations. In *The Southern Marches of Imperial Ethiopia*. Donald Donham and Wendy James, eds. Cambridge University Press.
Alverson, Hoyt
  1978 *Mind in the Heart of Darkness*. New Haven: Yale University Press.
Ambrose, S.
  1984 The Introduction of Pastoral Adaptations to the Highlands of East Africa. In *From Hunters to Farmers: Considerations of the Causes and Consequences of Food Production in Africa*. J. Clark and S. Brandt, eds. pp. 212-239. Berkeley: University of California Press.
Anacleti, A.O.
  1977 Serengeti: It's People and Their Environment. *Tanzania Notes and Records* 81-82:23-34.
Anderson, D.
  1981 Some Thoughts on the Nineteenth Century History of the Il Chamus of Baringo District. Paper No. 149. University of Nairobi: Institute of African Studies.
Anderson, Perry
  1974 The Nomadic Mode of Production. In *Passages from Antiquity to Feudalism*, NLB: 217-228.
Andersson, C.
  1854 A Journey to Lake Ngami, and an Itinerary of the Routes Leading to it from the West Coast. *South African Commercial Advertiser and Cape Town Mail*, 22 May.
  1861 *The Okavango River: a Narrative of Travel, Exploration, and Adventure*. New York: Harper.
Appadurai, Arjun, ed.
  1986 *The Social Life of Things: Commodities in Cultural Perspective*. Cambridge: Cambridge University Press.
Arhem, Kaj
  1985 *Pastoral Man in the Garden of Eden: the Maasai of the Ngorongoro Conservation Area, Tanzania*. Uppsala: Research Reports in Cultural Anthropology.
Arnal, J.P. and M. Garcia
  1973 *Survey of Animal Losses in the Nigerien Pastoral Zone*. Niamey: Communaute Economique du Betail et de la Viande.
Aronson, D.
  1980 Kinsmen and Comrades: Towards a Class Analysis of the Somali Pastoral Sector. *Nomadic Peoples* 7:14-22.
Arrighi, Giovanni
  1979 Peripheralization of Southern Africa, I: Changes in Production Processes. *Review* 3:161-91.

Asad, T.
1979 Equality in Nomadic Social Systems? Notes Toward the Dissolution of an Anthropological Category. In *Production Pastorale et Société*, édité par l'Equipe Ecologie et Anthropologie des Société Pastorale, Paris. Cambridge et Paris: Cambridge University Press; Editions de la Maison des Sciences de l'Homme: 419-428.

Asmarom, Legesse
1973 *Gada: Three Approaches to the Study of African Society*. New York: Free Press.

Austin, H.H.
1902 A Journey from Omdurman to Mombasa. *Geographical Journal* 19:669-690.

des Avanchers, Leon
1859 Esquisse Geographique des Pays Oromo ou Galla, des Pays Soomali, et de la Cote Orientale d'Afrique. *Bulletin de la Société de Geographie* 17:153-170.

Azarya, V.
1978 *Aristocrats Facing Change: The Fulbe in Guinea, Nigeria and Cameroon*. University of Chicago Press.

Bacon, C.R.K.
1917 *The Lau Nuers*. Khartoum (mimeo).

Bader, F.
1978 De protéger à razzier au néolithique indo-européen. Phraséologie, étymologie, civilisation. *Bulletin de la Société de Linguistique de Paris*, 73(1): 103-219.

Baier, Stephen.
1976 Economic History and Development: Drought and the Sahelian Economies of Niger. *African Economic Development*, Spring.
1980 *An Economic History of Central Niger*. Oxford: Clarendon Press.

Baier, Stephen and Paul Lovejoy
1976 The Desert-edge Economy of the Central Sudan. In *The Politics of Natural Disaster: the Case of the Sahel Drought*. Michael Glantz, ed. New York: Praeger.
1977 The Tuareg of the Central Sudan: Gradations in Servility at the Desert-Edge (Niger and Nigeria). In *Slavery in Africa: Historical and Anthropological Perspectives*. Suzzane Miers and Igor Kopytoff, eds. Madison: University of Wisconsin Press.

Bala, U.
1979 *Pastoralists and the Sokoto Jihad: Reflections on a Concept of Colonialist Historiography*. Paper presented to the Seminar on the Pastoralists of the West African Savannah. Zaria: Ahmadu Bello University.

Barber, J.
1968 *Imperial Frontier*. Nairobi: East African Publishing House.

Baroin, C.
1985 *Anarchie et Cohésion Sociale chez les Toubou: Les Daza Keserda (Niger)*. Cambridge and Paris: Cambridge University Press, Editions de la Maison des Sciences de l'Homme.

Barrow, John
1806 *A Voyage to Cochinchina*. London: Cadell and Davies.

Barry, Boubacar
 1972 *Le Royaume du Waalo*. Paris: Maspero.
Barth, F.
 1967 Capital, Investment and the Social Structure of a Pastoral Nomad Group
  in South Persia. In *Capital, Saving and Credit in Peasant Societies*. R. Firth and
  B.S. Yamey, eds. London: G. Allen and Unwin.
Barth, H.
 1965 [1857] *Travels and Discoveries in North and Central Africa, 1849-1855*. 3 vol.
  London: F. Cass. (Originally published in 1857, in German, Gotha: J. Perthes;
  in English, New York: Harper and Row)
Baxter, P.
 1954 *The Social Organization of the Boran of Northern Kenya*. Ph.D. dissertation,
  Oxford University.
Beattie, J.H.M.
 1957 Nyoro Kinship. *Africa* 27 (4):317-339.
 1964 Bunyoro, an African Feodality? *Journal of African History* 5:25-35.
 1968 Aspects of Nyoro Symbolism. *Africa* 38:413-442.
 1971 *The Nyoro State*. Oxford University Press.
Beidelman, T.O.
 1960 The Baraguyu. *Tanganyika Notes and Records* 55:245-278.
Bender, M.L.
 1976a Nilo-Saharan Overview. In M.L. Bender, ed. pp. 439-383.
Bender, M.L. ed.
 1976b *The Non-Semitic Languages of Ethiopia*. East Lansing: Michigan State
  University Press.
Bennett, J.W.
 1984 *Political Ecology and Development Projects Affecting Pastoralist Peoples in East
  Africa*. Land Tenure Center, Research Paper No. 80.
 1988 The Political Ecology and Economic Development of Migratory Pastoralist
  Societies of Eastern Africa. In *Power and Poverty: Development and
  Development Projects in the Third World*. D. Attwood, T. Bruneau, and J.
  Galaty, eds. pp. 31-60. Boulder: Westview Press.
Benveniste, E.
 1969 *Le vocabulaire des institutions indo-européennes*. 2 Vols. Paris: Ed. de Minuit.
Bernsten, J.
 1973 *Maasai and Iloikop: Ritual Experts and Their Followers*. M.A. thesis (History),
  University of Wisconsin, Madison.
 1979 Maasai Age-Sets and Prophetic Leadership: 1850-1910. *Africa* 49(2):134-146.
 1980 The Enemy is Us: Eponomy in the Historiography of the Maasai. *History
  in Africa* 7:1-20.
Bernus, Edmond
 1974 Possibilité et Limites de la Politique d'Hydraulique Pastorale dans le
  Sahel Nigerien. *Cahiers ORSTOM*, Série Sciences Humaine, 11(2):119-126.
 1981 *Touaregs Nigeriens: Unité Culturelle et Diversité Regionale d'un Peuple Pasteur*.
  Paris: Memories ORSTOM No. 94.

Bernus, S.
1969 *Particularismes ethniques en milieu urbain: l'example de Niamey.* Mémoire de l'institut d'ethnologie No.1. Paris: Musée de l'Homme.
Birmingham, David
1981 *Central Africa to 1870.* Cambridge and New York: Cambridge University Press.
Black-Michaud, J.
1975 *Cohesive Force: Land in the Mediterranean and the Middle East.* Oxford: Blackwell.
Bonfiglioli, A.M.
1988 *Dudal. Histoire de famille et histoire de troupeau chez un groupe Wodaabe du Niger.* Cambridge: Cambridge University Press; Paris: Editions de la Maison de Sciences de l'Homme.
Bonte, Pierre
1975a Cattle for God: An Attempt at a Marxist Analysis of the Religion of East African Herdsmen. *Social Compass* (Louvain) 22 (3-4):381-396.
1975b La Civilisation Nomade. *La Recherche* (Paris) 53:129-142.
1978a Pastoral Production, Territorial Organization and Kinship in Segmentary Lineage Societies. In *Social and Ecological Systems.* P. Burnham and R.F. Allen, eds. ASA 18. pp. 203-226. London: Academic Press.
1978b Non-Stratified Social Formations among Pastoral Nomads. In *The Evolution of Social Systems.* J. Friedman and M.J. Rowlands, eds. pp. 173-200. London: Duckworth.
1979 Segmentarité et Pouvoir chez les Eleveurs Nomades Sahariens: Elements d'une Problematique. In *Production Pastorale et Société.* Equipe Ecologie et Anthropologie des Sociétés Pastorales, ed. pp. 171-199. Cambridge et Paris: Cambridge University Press, Editions de la Maison des Sciences de l'Homme.
1981a Ecological and Economic Factors in the Determination of Pastoral Specialisation. *Journal of Asian and African Studies.* 16(1-2):33-49.
1981b Marxist Theory and Anthropological Analysis: The Study of Nomadic Pastoralist Societies. In *The Anthropology of Precapitalist Societies.* J.S. Kahn and J. Llobera, eds. pp. 22-56. London: MacMillan Press.
1984a Le Bétail Produit les Hommes. Sacrifice, Valeur et Fétichisme du bétail en Afrique de l'Est. *Uomo* (Rome) 9(1-2):121-147.
1984b *Tribus, Factions, Etat: Les Conflits de Succession dans l'Emirat de l'Adrar.* [Mimeograph]
1984c L'Emirat de l'Adrar après le Conquête Coloniel et le Dissidence de l'Emir Sidi Ahmed. *Journel des Africanistes* (Paris) 54 (2):5-30.
Bonte, P. and D. Becquemont
Forthcoming. *Pratiques et Sens: Essais pour une Theorie Anthropologique de la Valeur.* Paris.
1979 Travail, Valeur, Besoins et Conscience Aliènée: Le Cas des Eleveurs d'Afrique de l'Est. Comment les hommes font leur histoire. *La Pensée* (Paris) 207:98-121.

Bonte, P., A. Bourgeot, J.P. Digard and C. Lefébure
   1980 Pastoral Economies and Societies. In *Tropical Grazing Land and Ecosystems.*
      pp. 260-303. Paris: UNESCO, Natural Resources Research.
Botswana National Archives
   1938 S360/1 Joyce, Marsarwa Report.
Botte, R., F. Dreyfus, M. Le Pape and C. Vidal
   1969 Les Relations Personnelles de Subordination dans les Sociétés
      Interlacustres de l'Afrique Centrale. *Cahiers d'Etudes Africaines* IX (3) 35:350-
      401.
Bottego, V.
   1895 *Viaggi di Scoperta nel Cuore dell'Africa: Il Giuba Esploratoro.* Rome.
Bouquet, C.
   1974 *Iles et Rives du Sud-Kanem (Tchad): Etude de Geographie Regionale.* Travaux
      et Documents de Geographie Tropicale, No. 13. Talence: Centre d'Etudes de
      Geographie Tropicale du C.N.R.S.
Bower, J. and C. Nelson
   1978 Early Pottery and Pastoral Cultures of the Central Rift Valley, Kenya. *Man*
      (N.S.) 13: 554-66.
Brainard, J.M.
   1981 *Herders to Farmers: The Effects of Settlement on the Demography of*
      the Turkana Population of Kenya. Ph.D. Dissertation. State University of New
      York at Binghamton.
Brandstrom, J., J. Hultin and J. Lindstrom
   1979 *Aspects of Agropastoralism in East Africa.* Research Report No. 51. Uppsala:
      The Scandinavian Institute of African Studies.
Breutz, Paul L.
   1956 *The Tribes of Mafeking District.* Pretoria: Department of Native Affairs.
Briggs, L.C.
   1960 *Tribes of the Sahara.* Cambridge, Mass.: Harvard University Press.
Brock, L.
   1984 *The Tomejirt - Kinship and Social History in a Tuareg Community.* Ph.D.
      Dissertation, Columbia University, New York.
Brown, J. Tom
   1926 *Among the Bantu Nomads.* Philadelphia: J.B. Lippincott Co.
   1931 *Secwana Dictionary.* Tiger Kloof: The London Missionary Society.
Brown, L.H.
   1973 The Biology of Pastoral Man as a Factor in Conservation. *Biological*
      Conservation 3:93-100.
Brun, Thierry
   1975 Manifestations Nutritionelles et Medicales de la Famine. In *Sécheresses et*
      Famines du Sahel, Vol. I. Jean Copans, ed. Paris: Francois Maspero.
Buijtenhuijs, R.
   1978 *Le Frolinat et les Révoltes Populaire du Tchad, 1965-1976.* La Haye
      and Paris: Mouton.
Bulliet, R.W.
   1975 *The Camel and the Wheel.* Cambridge, Mass.: Harvard University
      Press.

Bundy, Colin
1977 The Transkei Peasantry, c. 1890-1914. In *The Roots of Rural Poverty in Central and Southern Africa*. R. Palmer & N. Parsons, eds. pp. 201-20. London: Heinemann.
1979 *The Rise and Fall of the South African Peasantry*. London: Heinemann.
Burchell, William J.
1822-4 *Travels in the Interior of Southern Africa*. 2 volumes. London: Longman.
Butzer, K.W.
1971 *Recent History of an Ethiopian Delta: The Omo River and the Level of Lake Rudolf*. University of Chicago, Dept. of Geography, Research Paper No. 136.
Caille, R.
1965 *Journal d'un Voyage a Tombouctou et Djenne dans l'Afrique Centrale*. 2 Vols. Paris: Anthropos.
Campbell, A.
1982 Notes on the Prehistoric Background to 1840. In Hitchcock and Smith. pp. 13-22.
Campbell, John
1813 *Travels in South Africa*. London: Black, Parry. [Reprint, 1974. Cape Town: Struik.]
1822 *Travels in South Africa... Being a Narrative of a Second Journey*. 2 volumes. London: Westley.
Carbou, H.
1912 La Région du Tchad et du Ouadai. Algiers (City) University, Faculté des Lettres et Sciences Humaine Publications. *Bulletin de Correspondance Africaine*, 47-48. 2 vols. Paris: Leroux.
Carr, C.J.
1977 *Pastoralism in Crisis: The Dasanetch and their Ethiopian Lands*. University of Chicago, Department of Geography, Research Paper no. 180.
Carter, P.L., and Flight, C.
1972 A Report on the Fauna from the Site of Ntereso and Uintempo Roak Shelter Six in Ghana: with Evidence for the Practice of Animal Husbandry during the Second Millenium, B.C. *Man (N.S.)* 7 (2): 277-282.
Casalis, Eugene
1861 *The Basutos; or, Twenty-Three Years in South Africa*. London: James Nisbet.
Cassaneli, L.V.
1982 *The Shaping of Somali Society: Reconstructing the History of a Pastoral People, 1600-1900*. Philadelphia: University of Pennsylvania Press.
Cavendish, H.S.H.
1898 Through Somaliland and Around the South of Lake Rudolph. *Geographical Journal* 11: 372-396.
Chapelle, J.
1957 *Nomades Noirs du Sahara*. Paris: Plon.
Chapman, James
1971 [1868] *Travels in the Interior of Africa, 1849-1863*. (Ed. by E. C. Tabler.) Cape Town: A.A. Balkema. (Originally published 1868, London: Bell and Daldy.)

Chevalier, A.
  1907 *Mission Chari-Lac Tchad, 1902-1904, L'Afrique Centrale Française: Récit de Voyage de la Mission*. Paris: Challamel.
Chrétien, Jean Pierre
  1974 Echanges et Hierarchies dans le Royaume des Grands Lacs de l'Est Africain. *Annales* (Paris) 29 (6):1327-1337.
  1983 *Histoire Rurale de l'Afrique des Grands Lacs: Guide de Recherches*. Travaux du Centre de Recherches Africaine (Universite de Paris I), no. 1. Paris: AFERA.
Christie, J.
  1876 *Cholera Epidemics in East Africa*. London: Macmillan & Company.
Clapperton, H.
  1966 [1829] *Journal of a Second Expedition into the Interior of Africa*. 2 vols. London: Cass. (Facsimile, originally published 1829, Philadelphia: Carey, Lea and Carey.)
Clarence-Smith, W. and R. Moorsom
  1975 Underdevelopment and Class Formation in Ovamboland, 1845-1915. *Journal of African History* 16:365-381.
Clifford, James
  1988 On Ethnographic Authority. In *The Predicaments of Culture*. Cambridge: Harvard University Press: pp. 21-54.
Clutton-Brock, J. ed.
  1989 *The Walking Larder: Patterns of Domestication, Pastoralism and Predation*. London: Unwin Hywan.
Cohen, R.
  1962 The Just-so So? A Spurious Tribal Grouping in Western Sudanic History. *Man* 62:153-54.
Cohn, B.
  1980 History and Anthropology: the State of Play. *Comparative Studies in Society and History* 22:198-221.
Collins, Robert O.
  1983 *Shadows in the Grass: Britain in the Southern Sudan, 1918-1935*. New Haven: Yale University Press.
Colloque, Bujumbara
  1981 *La Civilisation Ancienne des Peuples des Grands Lacs*. Paris: Karthala.
Comaroff, Jean
  1974 *Barolong Cosmology: A Study of Religious Pluralism in a Tswana Town*. Ph.D. Dissertation, University of London.
  1985 *Body of Power, Spirit of Resistance*. University of Chicago Press.
Comaroff, Jean and John L. Comaroff
  1989 The Colonization of Consciousness in South Africa. *Economy and Society*, 18:267-296.
  n.d. *From Revelation to Revolution*. [Forthcoming].
Comaroff, John L.
  1973 *Competition for Office and Political Processes among the Barolong boo Ratshidi*. Ph.D. Dissertation, University of London.

Comaroff, John L. (cont.)

1980 Bridewealth and the Control of Ambiguity in a Tswana Chiefdom. In *The Meaning of Marriage Payments*. J.L. Comaroff, ed. pp. 161-96. London: Academic Press.

1987 *Sui Genderis*: Feminism, Kinship Theory, and Structural "Domains." In *Gender and Kinship*. J. Collier and S. Yanagisako, eds. pp. 53-85.

n.d. *Class, Culture and the Rise of Capitalism in an African Chiefdom*. [In preparation].

Comaroff, John L., & Jean Comaroff

1981 The Management of Marriage in a Tswana Chiefdom. In *Essays on African Marriage in Southern Africa*. E.J. Krige & J.L. Comaroff, eds. pp. 29-49. Cape Town: Juta.

1987 The Madman and the Migrant: Work and Labor in the Historical Consciousness of a South African People. *American Ethnologist*, 14:191-209.

Comaroff, John L., & Simon A. Roberts

1981 *Rules and Processes*. University of Chicago Press.

Comité Information Sahel

1974 *Qui se Nourrit de la Famine en Afrique? Le Donier Politique de le Famine au Sahel*. Paris: Maspero.

Conant, F.P.

1980 Thorns Paired, Sharply Recurved: Cultural Controls and Rangeland Quality in East Africa. *Anthropology and Desertification*. London, England: Academic Press.

Connah, G.

1981 *Three Thousand Years in Africa: Man and his Environment in the Lake Chad Region of Nigeria*. Cambridge University Press.

Conte, E.

1983 *Marriage Patterns, Political Change and the Perpetuation of Social Inequality in South Kanem (Chad)*. Paris: Office de la Recherche Scientifique et Technique Outre-Mer (ORSTOM).

1984 Taxation et Tribut: Considerations sur l'Accumulation Inégale dans une Société Agropastorale. *Paideuma* 30:103-121.

1986 La Dynamique de l'Alliance chez les Anciens Chasseurs Sédentarisés Duu Rea du Sud-Kanem. *Paideuma* 32:129-161.

Conte, E. and F. Hagenbucher-Sacrpanti

1977 Habitation et Vie Quotidienne chez les Arabes de la Rive Sud du Lac Tchad. *Cahiers de l'O.R.S.T.O.M.*, Série Sciences Humaines, 14(3):289-323.

Copans, J., ed.

1975 *Sécheresses et Famines au Sahel*. Paris: Maspero.

Coppens, J.

1969 Les Cultures Protohistoriques et Historiques du Djourab. *Actes du premier colloque international d'archeologie africaine* (1966), pp.234-241. Fort-Lamy: I.N.T.S.H.

Coriat, P.

1991a Transfer of Barr Gaweir to Zeraf Valley District [1926]. In *Governing the Nuer: Documents in Nuer History and Ethnography 1922-31*. D.H. Johnson, ed. Oxford: JASO.

Coriat, P. (cont.)
   1991b Settlement of Ol Dinka - Goweir Nuer Boundary Dispute [1925]. In *Ibid.*
Coupez, A. et M. d'Hertefelt
   1964   *La Royauté Sacrée de l'Ancien Rwanda: Texte Traduction et Commentaire de son Rituel.* Tervuren, Belges: Annales (Musée Royal de l'Afrique Centrale), Sciences Humaines No. 52.
Cuoq, J.M.
   1975 *Recueil des Sources Arabes Concernant l'Afrique Occidentale du VIIe au XVIe siècle (Bilad al-Sudan).* Paris: Editions du C.N.R.S.
Curry, John and Martha Starr
   1984 Farmers and Agropastoralists (in Central Niger). In Swift, ed.
Curtin, P.
   1971 Jihad in West Africa. *Journal of African History* 12:11-24.
Dahl, Gudrun
   1979 *Suffering Grass: Subsistence and Society of Waso Borana.* Stockholm Studies in Social Anthropology, No. 8. University of Stockholm, Dept. of Social Anthropology.
Dahl, Gudrun and Anders Hjort
   1976 *Having Herds: Pastoral Herd Growth and Household Economy.* Stockholm Studies in Social Anthropology, No. 2. University of Stockholm, Dept. of Social Anthropology.
   1979 *Pastoral Change and the Role of Drought.* SAREC Report R2. Stockholm.
Dalleo, P.T.
   1975 *Trade and Pastoralism: Economic Factors in the History of the Somali of Northeastern Kenya, 1892-1948.* Ph.D. dissertation, Syracuse University.
David, K.
   1982 Prehistory and Historical Linguistics in Central Africa: Points of Contact. In *The Archaeological and Linguistic Reconstruction of African History.* C. Ehret and M. Posnansky, eds. pp. 78-95. Berkeley, Los Angeles and London: University of California Press.
Decalo, S.
   1977 *Historical Dictionary of Chad.* Metuchen, N.J. and London: The Scarecrow Press.
Decobert, C.
   1982 Le Conseil des Anciens: Islamisation et Arabisation dans le Bassin Tchadien. *Annales* (Paris) 37(4):754-782.
Demougeot, E.
   1960 Le Chameau et l'Afrique du Nord Romaine. *Annales* (Paris) 15(2):209-247.
Denbow, J.
   1984 Prehistoric Herders and Foragers of the Kalahari: the Evidence for 1500 Years of Interaction. In *Past and Present in Hunter Gatherer Studies.* C. Schrire, ed. pp. 175-194. Orlando: Academic Press.
Denbow, J. and Wilmsen, E.
   1983 Iron Age Pastoralist Settlements in Botswana. *South African Journal of Science* 79:405-408.
   1986 The Advent and Course of Pastoralism in the Kalahari. *Science* 234:1509-1515.

Devisse, J.
1972 Routes de Commerce et Echanges en Afrique Occidentale: Essai sur le Commerce Medieval du XIe au XIVe Siecles. *Revue d'Histoire Economique et Sociale* 50:42-73, 357-397.

Dickey, James
1982 *Distribution of Livestock Populations in Sahelian Countries: Trends in the 1970s.* USAID/Bamako: unpublished report.

Donham, D. and W. James, ed.
1986 *The Southern Marches of Imperial Ethiopia: Essays in History and Social Anthropology.* Cambridge University Press.

Doornbos, Martin
1978 *Not All the King's Men: Inequality as a Political Instrument in Ankole, Uganda.* The Hague: Mouton.

Dumas-Champion, Francoise
1983 *Les Masa du Tchad: Betail et Societe.* Cambridge and Paris: Cambridge University Press, Editions de la Maison des Sciences de l'Homme.

Dupire, M.
1962 *Peuls Nomades; Etude Descriptive des Wodaabe du Sahel Nigerien.* Paris: Institut d'Ethnologie.
1970 *Organisation Sociale des Peul.* Paris: Plon.
1975 Exploitation du Sol, Communautés Résidentielles et Organisation Lignagere des Pasteurs Wodaabe. In *Pastoralism in Tropical Africa.* T. Monod, ed. Oxford University Press.
1981 Réflexions sur l'Ethnicité Peul. In *Itinérances en Pays Peul et Ailleurs.* Mélanges à la Memoire de P.F. Lacroix. Paris: Société des Africanistes.

Dusengeyezu, M.E.
1978 *L'Importance de la Vache dans les Relations Socio-économiques du Rwanda Precolonial.* [Mimeograph.] Butare (Rwanda): I.P.N.

Dyson-Hudson, Neville
1966 *Karimojong Politics.* Oxford: Clarendon Press.
1980 Strategies of Resource Exploitation among East-African Savanna Pastoralists. In *Human Ecology in Savanna Environments.* D. Harris ed. London: Academic Press.

Dyson-Hudson, Neville and Rada
1982 The Structure of East African Herds and the Future of East African Herders. *Development and Change* 13:213-238.

Dyson-Hudson, Rada and T. McCabe
1985 *South Turkana Nomadism: Coping with an Unpredictably Varying Environment.* New Haven: Human Relations Area Files, Inc. HRAFlex Books, Ethnography Series.

Echard, N., ed
1983 *Metallurgies Africaines.* Paris: Societe des Africanistes.

Eddy, Edward D.
1980 *L'Utilisation de la Terre et de la Main-d'oeuvre à l'Interieur des Exploitations Agricoles Integrées de la Zone Pastorale Nigerienne.* Ann Arbor: Center for Research on Economic Development, University of Michigan.

Edgerton, R.
   1971 *The Individual in Cultural Adaptation*. Berkeley: University of California
      Press.
   1988 *Like Lions They Fought: The Zulu Wars and the last Black Empire in South
      Africa*. N.Y.: The Free Press.
Ehret, Christopher
   1971 *Southern Nilotic History: Linguistic Approaches to the Study of the Past*.
      Evanston: Northwestern University Press.
   1974 *Ethiopians and East Africa*. Nairobi: East African Publishing House.
   1982 Population Movement and Culture Contact in the Southern Sudan c. 3,000
      BC to AD 1,000: A Preliminary Linguistic Overview. In *Culture History in the
      Southern Sudan*. John Mack and Peter Robertshaw, eds. pp. 19-48. Nairobi:
      British Institute in Eastern Africa, Memoir No. 8.
Elam, Y.
   1973 *The Social and Sexual Roles of Hima Women: A Study of Nomadic Cattle
      Breeders in Nyabushozi County, Ankole, Uganda*. Manchester University Press.
Eliot, Sir C.
   1905 Preface In *The Masai: Their Language and Folklore*. A.C. Hollis. Westport,
      Ct.: Negro Universities Press.
Elsammani, Mohamed Osman and Farouk Mohamed Elamin.
   1978 *The Impact of the Extension of the Jonglei Canal on the Area from
      Kongor to Bor*. Khartoum.
Epstein, H.
   1971 *The Origin of Domestic Animals in Africa*. 2 volumes. New York, London
      & Munich: Africana Publishing Corporation.
Esterhuyse, J.
   1968 *South West Africa, 1880-1894: The Establishment of German Authority in South
      West Africa*. Cape Town: Struik.
Evangelou, P.
   1984 Cattle Marketing Efficiency in Kenya's Maasailand. In *Livestock
      Development in Subsaharan Africa: Constraints, Prospects, Policy*. J.R. Simpson
      and P. Evangelou, eds. pp. 123-141. Boulder, Colo.: Westview Press.
Evans-Pritchard, Edward E.
   1940 *The Nuer: a Description of the Modes of Livelihood and the Political Institutions
      of a Nilotic People*. Oxford: Clarendon Press.
Ferguson, James
   1985 The Bovine Mystique. *Man (N.S.)* 20:647-674.
   1988 Cultural Exchange: New Developments in the Anthropology of
      Commodities. *Cultural Anthropology* 3:488-513.
Ferrandi, U.
   1903 *Seconda Spedizione Bottego: Lugh Emporio Commerciale*. Rome.
Fielder, Robin J.
   1973 The Role of Cattle in the Ila Economy. *African Social Research* 15:327-361.
Firth, Raymond
   1967 Themes in Economic Anthropology: A General Comment. In *Themes in
      Economic Anthropology*. R. Firth, ed. London: Tavistock Publications.

Ford, J.
1971 *The Role of Trypanosomiasis in African Ecology.* Oxford: Claredon Press.

Ford, J. and K.M. Katondo
1973 *The Distribution of Tsetse Flies in Africa, 1973.* Nairobi: Interafrican Bureau of Animal Resources (Map Series).

Forkl, H.
1983 *Die Beziehungen der zentral-sudanesischen Reiche Bornu, Mandara und Bagirmi sowie der Kotoko-Staaten zu ihren südlichen Nachbarn unter besonderer Berüchsichtingung des Sao-Problems.* München.

Fosbrooke, H.A.
1948 An Administrative Survey of the Masai Social System. *Tanganyika Notes and Records* 26:1-50.
1956 The Masai Age-Group System as a Guide to Tribal Chronology. *African Studies* 15:188-206.

Fratkin, Elliot
1986 Stability and Resilience in East African Pastoralism: The Rendille and the Ariaal of Northern Kenya. *Human Ecology* 14(3):269-286.
1987 Age-sets, Households, and the Organization of Pastoral Production: The Ariaal, Samburu, and Rendille of Northern Kenya. *Research in Economic Anthropology,* Vol. 8:295-314.

Fuglestad, F.
1983 *A History of Niger (1850-1960).* Cambridge University Press.

Fukui, K.
1979 Cattle Colour Symbolism and Inter-tribal Homicide among the Bodi. In *Warfare among East African Herders.* Katsuyoshi Fukui and David Turton, eds. pp. 147-177. Senri Ethnological Studies No. 3, National Museum of Ethnology, Osaka.

Galaty, John G.
1977 *In the Pastoral Image: The Dialectic of Maasai Identity.* Ph.D. dissertation, University of Chicago.
1980 The Maasai Group Ranch: Politics and Development in an African Pastoral Society. In P. Salzman, ed., *When Nomads Settle.* N.Y.: Praeger.
1981 Models and Metaphors: On the Semiotics of Maasai Segmentary Systems. In *The Structure of Folk Models.* L. Holy and M. Stuchlik, eds. pp. 63-92. A.S.A. Monograph No. 20. London and New York: Academic Press.
1982a Being 'Maasai'; Being 'People-of-Cattle': Ethnic Shifters in East Africa. *American Ethnologist* 9(1):1-20.
1983 Ceremony and Society: the Poetics of Maasai Ritual. *Man (N.S.)* 18:361-82.
1984 Cultural Perspectives on Nomadic Pastoral Societies. *Nomadic Peoples* 16:15-29.
1985 Aînesse, Cyclicité et Rites dans l'Organisation des Ages Maasai. In *Age, Pouvoir et Société en Afrique Noire.* M. Abélès & C. Collard, eds. pp. 287-316. Paris: Editions Karthala, Montréal: Presses de l'Université de Montreal.
1986 East African Hunters and Pastoralists in a Regional Perspective: an 'Ethnoanthropological' Approach. *Sprache und Geschichte in Afrika* 7.1:105-131.

Galaty, John G. (cont.)

1988a Pastoral and Agro-Pastoral migration in Tanzania: Factors of Economy, Ecology and Demography in Cultural Perspective. In *Power and Autonomy: Anthropological Studies and Critiques of Development*. J.R. Bowen & J.W. Bennett, eds. pp. 163-183. Monograph in Economic Anthropology 5, Washington D.C.: University Press of America.

1988b Scale, Politics and Cooperation in Organizations for East African Development. In *Cooperatives and Rural Development*. D. Attwood and B.S. Baviskar, eds. pp. 282-308. Delhi: Oxford University Press.

1989 Pastoralisme, Sédentarisation et Etat in Africa de l'Est. Etats et Société Nomades, *Politique Africaine* 34:39-50.

Galaty, John G., Aronson, D., Salzman, P., and A. Chouinard, eds.

1981 *The Future of Pastoral Peoples*. Proceedings of a Conference held in Nairobi, Kenya, 4-8 August, 1980. Ottawa: International Development Research Center.

Galaty, J.G. and D. Doherty

1989 Big Man, Rich Man, Poor Man, Thief; Raider, Trader, Artisan, Chief: Maasai Economic Types and Pastoral Strategies in Social Change. Working Papers in East African Pastoral Systems, McGill University, Department of Anthropology.

Galaty, J.G. and D. Johnson, eds.

1990 *The World of Pastoralism: Herding Systems in Comparative Perspective*. New York and London: Guilford Press and Belhaven Press.

Galton, F.

1971 [1853] *The Narrative of an Explorer in Tropical South Africa*. London: J. Murray. (Facsimile reproduction of 1853 original.)

Gartrell, B.

1988 Prelude to Disaster: The Case of Karamoja. In *The Ecology of Survival: Case Studies from Northeast African History*. D.H. Johnson and D.M. Anderson, eds. London/Boulder: Lester Crook Academic Publishing/Westview Press.

Gauthier-Pilters, H. and A. Innis Dagg

1981 *The Camel: Its Evolution, Ecology, Behavior and Relationship to Man*. University of Chicago Press.

Gellner, E.

1969 *Saints of the Atlas*. London: Weidenfeld & Nicholson.

Gifford, D., G. Isaac, and C. Nelson

1980 Evidence for Predation and Pastoralism at Prolonged Drift: A Pastoral Neolithic Site in Kenya. *Azania* 15:57-108.

Goldschmidt, Walter R.

1972 The Operations of a Sebei Capitalist: A Contribution to Economic Anthropology. *Ethnology*. 9:187-201.

1974 The Economics of Brideprice among the Sebei and in East Africa. *Ethnology* 13 (4):311-31.

1976 *The Culture and Behavior of the Sebei*. Berkeley and Los Angeles: University of California Press.

Goody, J., ed.

1958 *The Development Cycle in Domestic Groups.* Cambridge University Press.

1971 *Technology, Tradition and the State.* Oxford University Press.

Grandin, B.

1986 Land Tenure, Subdivision, and Residential Change in a Maasai Group Ranch. *Development Anthropology Network* 4(2):9-13.

Gray, Robert F.

1960 Sonjo Bride-price and the Question of African "Wife-purchase". *American Anthropologist* 62:34-57.

Green, F.

1857 Narratives of an Expedition to the Northwest of Lake Ngami, Extending to the Capital of Debabe's Territory, via Souka River, hitherto an Unexplored Portion of Africa. *Eastern Province Monthly Magazine* 1:535-539.

Gregory, Christopher A.

1982 *Gifts and Commodities.* London: Academic Press.

Grove, Richard.

1989 Scottish Missionaries, Evangelical Discourses and the Origins of Conservation Thinking in Southern Africa 1820-1900. *Journal of Southern African Studies* 15:163-187.

Guilaine, J.

1976 *Premiers Bergers et Paysans de l'Occident Méditerranéen.* Paris: Mouton.

Guillain, M.

1857 *Documents sur l'Histoire, La Geographie et le Commerce de l'Afrique Orientale.* Paris: Bertrand.

Guillaume, Henri

1974 *Les Nomades Interrompus: Introduction a l'Etude du Canton Twareg d'Imanan.* Niamey: Institut de Recherches en Sciences Humaines, Etudes Nigeriennes No. 35.

Gulbrandsen, Ornulf

1986 *To Marry or Not to Marry: Marital Strategies and Sexual Relations in a Tswana Society.*

1987 *Privilege and Responsibility.* Bergen: Department of Anthropology, University of Bergen.

Gulliver, P.H.

1951 *A Preliminary Survey of the Turkana.* Communications from the School of African Studies, University of Cape Town (NS) No. 26.

1955 *Family Herds: A Study of Two Pastoral Tribes in East Africa, The Jie and the Turkana.* London: Routledge and Kegan Paul.

Haaland, Gunner, ed.

1980 *Problems of Savannah Development: the Sudan Case.* Bergen: Department of Social Anthropology, Occasional Papers No. 19.

Hagenbucher-Sacripanti, F.

1977 Les Arabes dits "Suwa" du Nord-Cameroun. *Cahiers do l'ORSTOM*, Série Sciences Humaines, 14(3):223-249.

1979 Note sur les alliances et les marques de bétail chez les Arabes du Nord-Kanem (Tchad). *Cahiers de l'ORSTOM*, Série Sciences Humaines, XIV, 3, 351-380.

Hamès, C.
  1979 L'Evolution des Emirats Maures sous l'Effet du Capitalisme Marchand Européen. In *Production Pastorale et Société*. Equipe Ecologie et Anthropologie des Sociétés Pastorales, ed. pp. 375-398. Cambridge and Paris: Cambridge University Press, Editions de la Maison des Sciences de l'Homme.
Hardin, G.
  1968 The Tragedy of the Commons. *Science* 162:1243-1248.
Hardin, G. and J. Baden, eds.
  1977 *Managing the Commons*. San Fransisco: W.H. Freeman.
Heine, B.
  1974 Notes on the Yaaku Language (Kenya). *Afrika und Ubersee* 58:27-61, 119-138.
Heine, Bernd and R. Vossen
  1979 The Kore of Lamu - a contribution to Maa dialectology. *Afrika und Ubersee* 62, 4:271-288.
Herskovits, M.J.
  1926 The Cattle Complex in East Africa. *American Anthropologist* 28:230-272, 361-388, 494-528, 633-664.
d'Hertefelt, Marcel
  1962 Le Rwanda. In *Les anciens royaumes de la zone Interlacustre Meridionale Rwanda, Burundi, Buha*. Par A. Trouwborst, M. D'Hertefelt, J. Scherer. Tervuren: Musée royale de l'afrique centrale.
de Heusch, L.
  1966 *Le Rwanda et la Civilisation Interlacustre: Etudes d'Anthropologie Historique et Structurale*. Université Libre de Bruxelles, Institut d'Ethnologie.
Hiskett, M.
  1973 *The Sword of Truth: the Life and Times of the Shehu Usuman dan Fodio*. London: Oxford University Press.
Hitchcock, R.
  1985 Water, Land and Livestock: The Evolution of Tenure and Administration Patterns in Grazing Areas of Botswana. In *The Evolution of Modern Botswana: Politics and Rural Development in Southern Africa*. L.A. Picard, ed. London: Rex Collings. (Reprinted in Galaty and Johnson, 1990).
Hitchcock, R. and M. Smith, eds.
  1982 *Settlement in Botswana*. Marshalltown.
Hogg, R.
  1986 The New Pastoralism: Poverty and Dependency in Northern Kenya. *Africa* 56(3):319-33.
  1988 Changing Perceptions of Pastoral Development: A Case Study from Turkana District, Kenya. In *Anthropology of Development and Change in East Africa*. D. Brokensha and P. Little, eds. pp. 183-99. Boulder: Westview Press.
Holl, A.
  1986 *Economie et Société Neolithique sur le Dher Tichitt*. Paris: Editions Recherche sur les Civilisations (Memoire No. 68).
Hollis, A.C.
  1905 (1970) *The Maasai: Their Language and Folklore*. Westport, Ct.: Negro Universities Press.

Holub, Emil
  1881 *Seven Years in South Africa*. 2 volumes. (Translated by E.E. Frewer.) London: Sampson Low.
Hopcraft, P.
  1981 Economic Institutions and Pastoral Resource Management: Considerations for a Development Strategy. In J. Galaty, *et. al.*, ed. pp. 224-243.
Hopen, C.E.
  1958 *The Pastoral Fulbe Family in Gwandu*. London: Oxford University Press.
Hopkins, A.
  1973 *An Economic History of West Africa*. London: Longman.
Hopkins, J. and N. Levitzon
  1981 *Corpus of Early Arabic Sources for West African History*. Cambridge: Cambridge University Press.
Howell, P., M. Lock, and S. Cobb, eds.
  1988 *The Jonglei Canal: Impact and Opportunity*. Cambridge University Press.
Hugot, H.J.
  1974 *Le Sahara Avant le Désert*. Paris: Hesperider.
Hultin, J.
  1975 Social Structure, Ideology and Expansion: The Case of the Oromo of Ethiopia. *Ethnos* 1-4: 273-284. (Reprinted in *The Long Journey: Essays on History, Descent and Land among the Macha Oromo*, Doctoral Thesis, Department of Anthropology, Uppsala University (1987).)
Hunter, Monica
  1936 *Reaction to Conquest*. London: Oxford University Press.
Hurst, H.E.
  1920 *Short Report on Nile Gauge Readings and Discharges*. Cairo: Government Press.
Hutchison, Sharon E.
  1988 *The Nuer in Crisis: Coping with Money, War and the State*. Ph.D. Dissertation, University of Chicago.
Ibn Khaldûn
  1967 *The Maqaddimah*. Princeton University Press (English translation: F. Rosenthal).
Irle, J.
  1906 *Die Herero; ein Beitrag zur Landes-, Volks-, & Missionskunde*. Gutersloh: C. Bertelsmann.
Issoufou, Kouada
  n.d. *Chronological Price Data in Niger, Upper Volta, Mali and Senegal*. Niamey: unpublished report to the Niger Range and Livestock Project.
Jacobs, Alan
  1965 *The Traditional Political Organization of the Pastoral Maasai*. Ph.D. Dissertation, Oxford University.
  1968 A Chronology of the Pastoral Maasai. In *Hadith* 1. Bethwell A. Ogot, ed. pp. 10-31. Nairobi: East African Publishing House.
  1972 The Discovery and Oral History of Narosura. *Azania* 7:79-87.

Jacobs, Alan (cont.)

1979 Maasai Inter-Tribal Relations: Belligerant Herdsmen or Peaceable Pastoralists? In *Warfare Among East African Herders*. K. Fukui and D. Turton, eds. pp. 33-52. Senri Ethnological Studies No. 3. Osaka: National Museum of Ethnology.

Jahnke, Hans

1982 *Livestock Productions Systems and Livestock Development in Tropical Africa*. Kiel: Kieler Wissenschaftsverlag Vauk.

Jensen, A.E.

1959 *Altvölker Süd-Athiopiens*. Stuttgart: Kohlhammer. [JIT] Jonglei Investigation Team.

1948 *Report on the Jonglei Scheme*. Third Interim Report. Khartoum.

1954 *The Equatorial Nile Project and its Effects on the Anglo-Egyptian Sudan*. 4 Volumes. Khartoum.

Johnson, Douglas H.

1979 Colonial Policy and Prophets: the 'Nuer Settlement', 1929-1930. *Journal of the Anthropological Society of Oxford* 10:1-20.

1980 *History and Prophecy among the Nuer of the Southern Sudan*. Ph.D. Dissertation, University of California, Los Angeles.

1981 The Fighting Nuer: Primary Sources and the Origins of a Stereotype. *Africa* 51: 508-27.

1982a Tribal Boundaries and Border Wars: Nuer-Dinka Relations in the Sobat and Zaraf Valleys c. 1860-1976. *Journal of African History* 23: 183-203.

1982b Evans-Pritchard, the Nuer and the Sudan Political Service. *African Affairs* 81: 231-46.

1985 C.A. Willis and the "Cult of Deng": A Falsification of the Ethnographic Record. *History in Africa* 12: 131-50.

1986a On the Nilotic Frontier: Imperial Ethiopia in the Southern Sudan, 1898-1936. In *The Southern Marches of Imperial Ethiopia: Essays in History and Social Anthropology*. D. Donham and W. James, eds. Cambridge University Press.

1986b The Historical Approach to the Study of Societies and their Environment in the Eastern Upper Nile Plains. *Cahiers d'Etudes Africaines* 101-2, 26:131-44.

1986c Judicial Regulations and Administrative Control: Customary Law and the Nuer, 1898-1954. *Journal of African History* 27:59-78.

1988a Adaptation to Floods in the Jonglei Area: An Historical Analysis. In *The Ecology of Survival: Case Studies from Northeast African History*. D.H. Johnson and D.M. Anderson, eds. London: Lester Crook Academic Publishing; Boulder: Westview Press.

1988b Environment and the History of the Jonglei Area. In *The Jonglei Canal: Impact and Opportunity*. P.Howell, M. Lock, and S. Cobb, eds. Cambridge: Cambridge University Press.

1988c *The Southern Sudan*. London: Minority Rights Group, Report no. 78.

Forthcoming *Nuer Prophets: A History of Prophecy from the Upper Nile*. Oxford University Press.

Johnson, Douglas. H. and David M. Anderson, eds.

1988 *The Ecology of Survival: Case Studies from Northeast African History*. London: Lester Crook Academic Publishing; Boulder: Westview Press.

Johnston, H.A.S.

1967 *The Fulani Empire of Sokoto.* London.

Johnston, R.T.

1934 *Handing Over Report on Bor & Duk District.* National Records Office, Khartoum, UNP 1/51/3.

[JSERT] Jonglei Socio-Economic Research Team

1976 *An Interim Report.* Khartoum.

Kagame, A.

1947 Un Poeme du Rwanda. *Africa* 17 (1):41-46.

1951 *La Poesie Dynastique au Rwanda.* Bruxelles: Institut Royal Colonial Belge, Section des Sciences Morales et Politiques.

1961 *L'Histoire des Armées Bovines dans l'Ancien Rwanda.* Bruxelles: Academie Royale des Sciences d'Outre Mer.

Karugire, Samwiri Rubaraza

1971 *A History of the Kingdom of Nkore in Western Uganda to 1896.* Oxford: Clarendon Press.

Katoke, I.K.

1975 *The Karagwe Kingdom.* Nairobi: East African Publishing House.

Kelly, Raymond C.

1985 *The Nuer Conquest: The Structure and Development of an Expansionist System.* Ann Arbor: University of Michigan Press.

Kenya, Government of

1916 *Maasai District Records.*

Kienetz, A.

1977 The Key Role of the Orlam Migrations in the Early Europeanization of South-West Africa (Namibia). *The International Journal of African Historical Studies* 10:553-572.

Kinsman, Margaret

n.d. *Notes on the Southern Tswana Social Formation.* Unpublished paper read to the Africa Seminar, University of Cape Town, 1980.

1983 'Beasts of Burden': The Subordination of Southern Tswana Women, *ca.* 1800-1840. *Journal of Southern African Studies* 10:39-54.

Kjekshus, H.

1977 *Ecology Control and Economic Development in East African History.* London: Heinemann Press.

Kluckholm, R.

1962 The Konso Economy of Southern Ethiopia. In *Markets in Africa.* P. Bohannan and G. Dalton, eds. pp. 411, 415-51. Evanston: Northwestern University Press.

Kopytoff, Igor

1987 *The African Frontier: The Reproduction of Traditional African Societies.* Bloomington: Indiana University Press.

Krapf, J.Ludwig

1867 *Travels, Researches and Missionary Labours during Eighteen Years Residence in Eastern Africa.* London: Trubner and Co.

1854 *Vocabulary of the Engutuk Eloikob or Of the Language of the Wakuafi-Nation in the Interior of Equatorial Africa.* Tübingen: L.F. Fues.

Kratz, Corinne
  1981 Are the Okiek Really Maasai? Or Kipsigis? Or Kikuyu? *Cahiers d'Etudes Africaines* 79(20):355-368.
  1986 Ethnic Interaction, Economic Diversification and Language Use. *Sprache und Geschichte in Afrika* 7(2):189-226.
Krige, Eileen J.
  1981 Lovedu Marriage and Social Change. In *Essays on African Marriage in Southern Africa*. E.J. Krige and J.L. Comaroff, eds. pp.148-157. Cape Town: Juta.
Kuper, Adam
  1982 *Wives for Cattle*. London & Boston: Routledge & Kegan Paul.
Lamphear, J.E.
  1976 *The Traditional History of the Jie of Uganda*. London: Oxford University Press.
  1985 The Persistence of Hunting and Gathering in a 'Pastoral' World. International Symposium: African Hunter-Gatherers, Institut für Afrikanistik, Universität zu Köln, 3-5 January.
  1988 The People of the Grey Bull: the Origin and the Expansion of the Turkana. *Journal of African History*, 29:41-56.
Landeroin, M.A.
  1911 Notice Historique. In *Documents Scientifiques de la Mission Tilho (1906-1909)*, Vol. 2. J. Tilho, ed. pp. 341-417. Paris: Imprimerie Nationale.
Lange, D.
  1977 *Le Diwan des Sultans du (Kanem-) Bornu: Chronologie et Histoire d'un Royaume Africain (de la Fin du Xe Siecle jusqu'à 1808)*. Wiesbaden: Steiner.
  1978 Progrès de l'Islam et Changement Politique au Kanem du XIe au XIIIe siècle: un Essay d'Interpretation. *Journal of African History* 19(4):495-513.
  1980 La région du Lac Tchad d'après la géographie d'Ibn Sacid: textes et cartes. *Annales islamologiques* 16:149-181.
  1982 L'Eviction des Sefuwa du Kanem et l'Origine des Bulala. *Journal of African History* 23(3):315-331.
  1987 *A Sudanic Chronicle: The Expeditions of Idris Alauma (1564-1576) According to the Account of Ahmad b. Furtu*. Stuttgart: Steiner.
  1989 Préliminaires pour une histoire des Sao. *Journal of African History* 30:189-210.
Last, M.
  1967 *The Sokoto Caliphate*. London: Longman (1st publication).
Lau, B.
  1982 *The Emergence of Kommando Politics in Namaland, Southern Namibia: 1800-1870*. Unpublished M.A. thesis, University of Cape Town.
Lavers, J.E.
  1980 Kanem and Borno to 1808. In *The Groundwork of Nigerian History*. O. Ikime, ed. pp. 187-210. Ibadan: The Historical Society of Nigeria.
Lebeuf, J.P.
  1969 Essai de Chronologie Sao. *Acts du premier colloque international d'archeologie africaine* (1966), pp.234-241. Fort-Lamy: I.N.T.S.H.

Lebeuf, J.P. and A. Masson Detourbet
1950 *La Civilisation du Tchad*. Paris: Payot.
Le Borgne, C.
1953 Vocabulaire Technique du Chameau en Mauritanie. *Bulletin de l'Institut Francais d'Afrique Noire* [IFAN] (Dakar) 15:292-380.
Le Rouvreur, A.
1962 *Saheliens et Sahariens du Tchad*. Paris: Berger-Levrault.
Lee, Richard B.
1979 *The !Kung San: Men, Women, and Work in a Foraging Society*. Cambridge and New York: Cambridge University Press.
Legesse, Asmaron
1973 *Gada: Three Approaches to the Study of African Society*. New York: The Free Press.
Leriche, C.
1952 Vocabulaire du Chameau en Mauritanie, *Bulletin de l'Institute Francais d'Afrique Noire* [IFAN] (Dakar) 14:984-995.
Lévi-Strauss, C.
1958 *Structural Anthropology*. New York: Basic Books.
Lewicki, T.
1974 *West African Foods in the Middle Ages*. Cambridge University Press.
Lewis, B.A.
n.d. *Beir Notes*. B.A. Lewis Papers, Institute of Social Anthropology, Oxford.
Lewis, H.S.
1966 The Origins of the Galla and Somali. *Journal of African History* 7 (1):27-46.
Lewis, I.M.
1961 *A Pastoral Democracy: A Study of Pastoralism and Politics among the Northern Somali of the Horn of Africa*. London: Oxford University Press.
Lewis, J.V.D.
1978 *Descendents and Crops. Two Poles of Production in a Malian Peasant Village*. Ph.D. Dissertation. Yale University.
Lichtenstein, Henry (M.H.C.)
1928-30 *Travels in Southern Africa, in the Years 1803, 1804, 1805, and 1806*, 2 Vols. Translated from the 1812-15 editions by A. Plumptre. Cape Town: The Van Riebeeck Society.
1973 *Foundation of the Cape (1811) and About the Bechuanas (1807)*. (Translated and edited by O.H. Spohr.) Cape Town: A.A. Balkema.
Lienhardt, Godfrey
1961 *Divinity and Experience*. Oxford: Clarendon Press.
Little, Peter D.
1983 *From Household to Region: The Marketing/Production Interface among the Il Chamus of Northern Kenya*. Ph.D. Dissertation, Indiana University.
1985 Social Differentiation and Pastoralist Sedentarization in Northern Kenya. *Africa* 55 (3):244-261.
1987 Domestic production and regional markets in northern Kenya. *American Ethnologist* 14 (2):295-308.

Livingstone, David
  1912 [1857 and 1858] *Missionary Travels and Researches in South Africa.* London:
        J. Murray (Originally published in 1857, London: J. Murray; in 1858, New
        York: Harper & Bros.)
London Missionary Society
  1935 *Report of an Enquiry by the South Africa District Committee.* Alice.
Louis, Suchet
  1982 *Technical Report on Animal Production in the Pastoral Zone of Niger. Niamey*:
        unpublished report to the Niger Range and Livestock Project.
Lovejoy, Paul E.
  1983 *Transformations in Slavery: A History of Slavery in Africa.* New York:
        Cambridge University Press.
  1986 *Salt of the Desert Sun: A History of Salt Production and Trade in the Central
        Sudan.* New York: Cambridge University Press.
Lovejoy, Paul E. ed.
  1986 *Africans in Bondage: Studies in Slavery and the Slave Trade.* Madison: African
        Studies Program.
Low, D.A.
  1963 The Northern Interior, 1840-1844. In *History of East Africa.* Roland Oliver
        and G. Mathew, eds. London: Oxford University Press.
Lukas, J.
  1936 The Linguistic Situation in the Lake Chad Area in Central Africa. *Africa*
        9:332-49.
Lukyn-Williams, F.
  1938 Hima Cattle. *Uganda Journal* 6 (1):17-42 and 6 (2):87-117.
Lydall, J.
  1976 Hamer. In M.L. Bender, ed.
Lyon, G.F.
  1821 *A Narrative of Travels in Northern Africa in the Years 1818, 1819 and 1820.*
        London: Murray.
Mackenzie, John
  1871 *Ten Years North of the Orange River.* Edinburgh: Edmonston & Douglas.
Mair, Lucy
  1985 Correspondence: The Cattle Complex. *Man (N.S.)* 20:743.
Makinon, Marty and Edgar Ariza-Nino
  1980 *The Market for Livestock from the Central Niger Zone.* Ann Arbor: Center for
        Research on Economic Development, University of Michigan.
Maley, J.
  1976 Les Variations du Lac Tchad depuis un Millenaire: Consequences
        Paleoclimatiques. In *Paleoecology of Africa,* 9. E.M. van Zinderen Bakker, ed.
        pp. 44-47.
Maliki, Angelo Bonfiglioli
  1982 *Introduction to the History of the Wodaabe.* Niamey: Niger Range and
        Livestock Project, Discussion Paper No. 3.
Maquet, J.J.
  1954 *Systeme des Relations Sociales dans le Rwanda Ancien.* Volume 1. Tervuren:
        Annales (Musée Royale de Congo Belge).

Maquet, J.J. (cont.)
1961 Une Hypothese pour l'Etude des Feodalites Africaines. *Cahiers d'Etudes Africaines* 2:292-314.

Marshall, Lorna
1976 *The !Kung of Nyae Nyae.* Harvard University Press.

Marty, P.
1917 *L'Emirat des Trarza.* Paris: Leroux.

Marx, Karl
1967 *Capital: A Critique of Political Economy,* 3 volumes. New York: International Publishers.

Mason, I.L.
1984a Origin, Evolution and Distribution of Domestic Camels. In *The Camelid, An All-purpose Animal.* W. Ross Cockrill, ed. pp. 16-36. Uppsala: Scandinavian Institute of African Studies.
1984b *Evolution of Domesticated Animals.* London and New York: Longman.

Mason, I.L. and J.P. Maule
1960 *The Indigenous Livestock of Eastern and Southern Africa.* Technical Communications Commonwealth Bureau Animal Breeding and Genetics 14:1-151. Farnham Royal England: Commonwealth Agricultural Bureau.

Matthews, Zachariah K.
n.d. *Fieldwork Reports.* Botswana National Archives.

Mauch, Karl, Hugo Hahn, and Richard Brenner
1866-67 Neueste Deutsche Forschungen in Süd-Afrika. *Petermann's Geographische Mitteilungen* 13:281-298.

Mauny, R.
1961 *Tableau Geographique de l'Ouest Africain au Moyen Age.* Dakar: Institute Francais d'Afrique Noire.

Mauss, Marcel
1954 (1966) Essai sur le Don: Forme et Raison de l'Echange dans les Societes Archaiques. In *Sociologie et Anthropologie.* Paris: Presses Universitaires de France (*The Gift.* Translated by I. Cunnison. London: Cohen & West).

Mefit-Babtie Srl.
1983 *Development Studies in the Jonglei Canal Area.* Final Report. Volume 1: Summary. Glasgow, Khartoum & Rome: Technical Assistance Contract for Range Ecology Survey, Livestock investigations and Water Supply.

McDougall, A.E.
1980 *The Ijil Salt Industry: Its Role in the Pre-colonial Economy of the Western Sudan.* Ph.D. Dissertation, University of Birmingham.

McBurney, C.B.M.
1967 *The Hama Fteah (Cyrenaica).* Cambridge University Press.

Migeod, F.W.G.
1923-24 The Ancient So People of Bornu. *Journal of African History* 23:19-29.

Moffat, Robert
1842 *Missionary Labours and Scenes in Southern Africa.* London: Snow.

Monod, J.
1967 Notes sur le Harnachement Chamelier. *Bulletin de l'Institute Francais d'Afrique Noire* [IFAN] (Dakar) 29:234-306.

Monod, T., ed
1976 *Pastoralism in Tropical Africa*. London: International African Institute.
Monteil, P.L.
1893 *De Saint-Louis à Tripoli par le Lac Tchad*. Paris: Alcan.
Monteil, Vincent
1952 *Essai sur le Chameau au Sahara Occidental*. Saint Louis (Senegal): Institut Francais d'Afrique Noire [IFAN].
Moraes-Farias, P.F. de
1970 *The Trig Lemtuni (XIth - XIIth C): a Trade Route?* Seminar on Muslim and non-Muslim in Africa. London. [Mimeograph]
Mossop, E.E., ed.
1935 *The Journal of Hendrik Jakob Wikar (1779) with an English Translation by A.W. van der Horst, and The Journals of Jacobus Coetse Jansz (1760) and Willem van Reenan (1791) with an English Translation by Dr. E.E. Mossop*. Cape Town: The Van Riebeeck Society.
1947 *The Journals of Brinck and Rhenius*. Cape Town: The Van Riebeeck Society.
Muhammad, Al-Yadali
n.d. *Manaqib al-imam Nasir al-Din*, Manuscrit arabe, collection personelle (Ould Cheikh).
Munn, Nancy
1977 The Spatiotemporal Transformation of Gawa Canoes. *Journal de la Société des Oceanistes* 33:39-53.
1986 *The Fame of Gawa*. Cambridge & New York: Cambridge University Press.
Muriuki, Godfrey
1974A *History of the Kikuyu 1500-1900*. Nairobi: Oxford University Press.
Murray, Colin
1980 Kinship: Continuity and Change. In *Transformations on the Highveld: The Tswana and Southern Sotho*. C. Murray and W.F. Lye, eds. pp.106-121. Cape Town: David Phillip.
1981 *Families Divided: The Impact of Migrant Labor in Lesotho*. New York: Cambridge University Press.
Mworoha, E.
1977 *Peuples et Rois de l'Afrique des Lacs. Le Burundi et les Royaumes Voisins au XIXe siecle*. Dakar.
Nachtigal, G.
1979 [1889] *Sahara und Sudan*. Berlin: Weidmannsche Buchhandlung & Leipzig, Brockhaus. (Also published in English, translation by Fisher and Fisher, London: Hurst.)
Nangati, F.
1982 Early Capitalist Penetration: the Impact of Precolonial Trade in Kweneng (1840-1876). In Hitchcock and Smith. pp. 140-147.
Nash, T.A.M.
1969 *Africa's Bane: The Tsetse Fly*. London, Collins.
Ncgoncgo, L.
1982 Impact of the *Difaqane* on Tswana States. In Hitchcock and Smith. pp. 161-171.

Neumann, A.H.
  1966 [1898] *Elephant Hunting in East Equatorial Africa*. 2nd ed. New York: Abercrombie and Fitch. (Originally published 1898, London: R, Ward)
Newcomer, Peter J.
  1972 The Nuer are Dinka: an Essay on Origins and Environmental Determinism. *Man (N.S.)* 7:5-11.
  1973 The Nuer and the Dinka. *Man (N.S.)* 8:307-308.
Newman, P.
  1977 Chadic Classification and Reconstructions. *Afroasiatic Linguistics* 5:1-42.
Nicolas, G.
  1981 La Conversion Ethnique des Peuls du Nigeria. In *Itinérances en Pays Peul et Ailleurs*. Melanges a la Memoire de P.F. Lacroix. Paris: Société des Africanistes.
Nicholson, S.
  1981 Saharan Climates in Historic Times. In *Ecological Change and Early Economic History*. J.A. Allan, ed. London: Menas Press.
Norris, H.T.
  1969 Znaga Islam during the Seventeenth and Eighteenth Century. *SOAS (School of Oriental and African Studies, University of London) Bulletin* 32:496-526.
Ochieng, W.R.
  1975 *An Outline History of the Rift Valley of Kenya, up to A.D. 1900*. Nairobi: East African Literature Bureau.
Ogot, B.A.
  1967 *History of the Southern Luo, Vol. 1: Migration and Settlement 1500-1900*. Nairobi: East African Publishing House.
Okihiro, G.
  1976 *Hunters, Herders, Cultivators, and Traders: Interaction and Change in the Kgalagadi, Nineteenth Century*. Unpublished Ph.D. Dissertation, University of California, Los Angeles.
O'Leary, Michael F.
  1985 *The Economics of Pastoralism in Northern Kenya: The Rendille and the Gabra*. Integrated Project in Arid Lands (IPAL) Technical Report Number F-3. Nairobi: UNESCO.
Oliver, R.
  1983 The Nilotic Contribution to Bantu Africa. In *Nilotic Studies*, Pt. Two. R. Vossen and M. Bechaus-Gerst, eds. Berlin: Dietrich Reimer Verlag.
Oswell, W.
  1900 *William Cotton Oswell, Hunter and Explorer*. 2 vols. London: Heinemann.
Ould Cheikh, A.W.
  1985 *Nomadisme, Islam et Pouvoir Politique dans la Société Maure Precoloniale*. These de Doctorat, Universite de Paris (V).
Ould Cheikh, Abdel Wedoud and Pierre Bonte
  1982 Production Pastorale et Production Marchande dans la Société Maure. In *Contemporary Nomadic and Pastoral Peoples: Africa and Latin America*. Philip Carl Salzman, ed. Studies in Third World Societies, No. 17. pp. 31-56. Williamsburg, Va: Dept. of Anthropology, College of William and Mary.

Pages, C.
   1933 *Un Royaume Hamite au Centre de l'Afrique*. Institut Royale Colonial Belge, Section des Sciences Morales et Politiques. Bruxelles: Falk.
Palmer, H.R.
   1926 *History of the First Twelve Years of the Reign of Mai Idriss Aloma of Bornu (1571-1583). By his Imam, Ahmed ibn Furtua, together with the "Diwan of the Sultans of Bornu" and "Girgam of the Magumi"*. Lagos: Government Printer.
Palmer, Robin and Neil Q. Parsons, eds.
   1977 *The Roots of Rural Poverty in Central and Southern Africa*. London: Heinemann.
Parkipuny, N.S. Ole
   1988 The Ngorongoro Crater Issue: The Point of View of the Indigenous Maasai Community of Ngorongoro. International Congress on Nature Management and Sustainable Development, University of Groningen, 6-9 December, 1988.
Parson, Jack
   1981 Cattle, Class, and State in Rural Botswana. *Journal of Southern African Studies* 7:236-255.
   1984 *Botswana: Liberal Democracy and the Labor Reserve in Southern Africa*. Boulder: Westview Press.
Parsons, Neil
   1974 The Economic History of Khama's Country in Southern Africa. *African Social Research* 18:643-675.
   1977 The Economic History of Khama's Country in Botswana, 1844-1930. In *The Roots of Rural Poverty in Central and Southern Africa*. Robin Palmer and Neil Parsons, eds. pp. 113-143. Perspectives on Southern Africa No. 25. Berkeley: University of California Press.
Passarge, S.
   1907 *Die Buschmänner der Kalahari*. Berlin: D. Reimer (E. Vohsen).
Payne, W.J.A. and Farouk Mohamed Elamin
   1977 *An Interim Report on the Dinka Livestock Industry in the Jonglei Area*. UNDP, Economic and Social Research Council, the Executive Organ for Development Projects in the Jonglei Area. Technical Report No. 5. Khartoum.
Peters, Pauline
   1983 *Cattlemen, Borehole Syndicates, and Privatization in the Kgatleng District of Botswana: an Anthropological History of the Transformation of the Commons*. Ph.D. Dissertation, Boston University.
Philip, John
   1828 *Researches in South Africa: Illustrating the Civil, Moral, and Religious Condition of the Native Tribes*, 2 Volumes. London: James Duncan. [Reprinted, 1969. New York: Negro Universities Press].
Population Census Office
   1962 *First Population Census of Sudan 1955/1956*. Final Report. Vol. III. Khartoum: Ministry for Social Affairs.
Posnansky, M.
   1966 Kingship, Archeology and Historical Myth. *Uganda Journal* 30 (1):1-12.

Pratt, D.J. and M.D. Gwynne
 1977 *Rangeland management and ecology in East Africa*. London: Hodder and Stoughton.
Raikes, P.
 1981 *Livestock Development and Policy in East Africa*. Uppsala: The Scandinavian Institute of African Studies.
Ranger, Terence
 1978 Growing from the Roots: Reflections on Peasant Research in Central and Southern Africa. *Journal of Southern African Studies* 5:99-133.
Rappaport, R.A.
 1967 *Pigs for the Ancestors*. New Haven: Yale University Press.
Ravenstein, E.G.
 1884 Somal and Galla Land; Embodying Information Collected by the Rev. Thomas Wakefield. *Proceedings of the Royal Geographical Society* 6:255-273.
Reed, L.V.
 1932 Note on some Fulani Tribes and Customs. *Africa* 5(4):422-454.
Rigby, P.
 1985 *Persistent Pastoralists: Nomadic Societies in Transition*. London: Zed Books Ltd.
Ritchie, C.A.
 1968 Deux Textes sur le Senegal (1673-1677). *Bulletin de l'Institut Francais d'Afrique Noire* [IFAN] (Dakar) 30:289-353.
Robertshaw, P., and D. Collett
 1983a A New Framework for the Study of Early Pastoral Communities in East Africa. *Journal of African History* 24:289-301.
 1983b The Identification of Pastoral Peoples in the Archaeological Record: an Example from East Africa. *World Archaeology* 15 (1):67-78.
 In Press The Beginnings of Food-Production in South-Western Kenya. In *Food, Metals and Towns in Early African History*. T. Shaw, et. al. London: Allen and Unwin Ltd.
Roe, Emery
 1980 Development of Livestock, Agriculture and Water Supplies in Botswana Before Independence. Cornell University, Rural Development Committee, Occasional Paper No. 10.
Roscoe, John
 1923 Uganda and some of its problems. *Journal of African Society* 22(80-87): 96-108, 218-225.
Rwabukumba, J. and V. Mudandagizi
 1974 Les Formes Historiques de la Dependance Personnelles dans l'Etat Rwandais. *Cahiers d'Etudes Africaines* 14 (53):6-25.
Sacks, Karen
 1979 Causality and Chance on the Upper Nile. *American Ethnologist* 6:437-48.
Sahlins, Marshall D.
 1961 The Segmentary Lineage: an Organization of Predatory Expansion. *American Anthropologist* 63:322-345.
 1972 *Stone Age Economics*. Chicago: Aldine-Atherton, Inc.
 1976 *Culture and Practical Reason*. University of Chicago Press.

Salvadori

1951 *Rapport sur le recensement du 3e groupe nomade; Tahoua.*

Salzman, P.C.

1967 Political Organization among Nomadic Peoples. *Proceedings of the American Philosophical Society* 111:115-31.

Sandford, S.

1983 *Management of Pastoral Development in the Third World.* Chichester, West Sussex, and New York: John Wiley and Son.

Sandilands, Alexander

1953 *Introduction to Tswana.* Tiger Kloof: The London Missionary Society.

Sankan, S.S.

1971 *The Maasai.* Nairobi: East African Literature Bureau.

Sansom, Basil

1974 Traditional Economic Systems. In *The Bantu-speaking Peoples of Southern Africa.* W.D. Hammond-Tooke, ed. pp. 135-176. London & Boston: Routledge & Kegan Paul.

1976 A Signal Transaction and its Currency. In *Transaction and Meaning.* B. Kapferer, ed. pp. 143-161. Philadelphia: ISHI.

Schapera, I.

1933 Economic Conditions in a Bechuanaland Reserve. *South African Journal of Science* 30:633-55.

1934 The Old Bantu Culture. In *Western Civilization and the Natives of South Africa.* I. Schapera, ed. pp.3-36. London: Oxford University Press.

1938 *A Handbook of Tswana Law and Custom.* London: Oxford University Press.

1943 *Native Land Tenure in the Bechuanaland Protectorate.* Alice: Lovedale Press.

1947 *Migrant Labour and Tribal Life.* London: Oxford University Press.

1953 *The Tswana.* London: International African Institute.

1970 *Tribal Innovators: Tswana Cheifs and Social Change, 1795-1940.* London: Athlone Press.

1971a *Rainmaking Rites of Tswana Tribes.* Leiden: Afrika-Studiecentrum.

1971b *Married Life in an African Tribe.* Harmondsworth: Penguin.

Schapera, I., ed.

1961 *David Livingstone's Missionary Correspondence, 1841-1856.* Berkeley: University of California Press.

Schapera, Isaac and A.J.H. Goodwin

1937 Work and Wealth. In *The Bantu-Speaking Tribes of South Africa.* I. Schapera, ed. pp. 131-71. Cape Town: Routledge.

Schlee, Günther

1985 Interethnic clan identities among Cushitic speaking pastoralists. *Africa* 55 (1):17-23.

1989 *Identities on the Move: Clanship and Pastoralism in Northern Kenya.* Manchester and New York: Manchester University Press.

Schneider, Harold K.

1964 Economics in East African Aboriginal Societies. In *Economic Transition in Africa.* M.J. Herskovits & M. Harwitz, eds. pp. 53-75. Evanston: Northwestern University Press.

1979 *Livestock and Equality in East Africa.* Bloomington: Indiana Univ. Press.

Schrire, C.
1980 An Inquiry into the Evolutionary Status and Apparent Identity of San Hunter-Gatherers. *Human Ecology* 8(1):9-32.
Sere De Rivières, E.
1965 *Histoire du Niger*. Paris: Berger-Levrault.
Serton, P., ed.
1954 *The Narrative and Journal of Gerald McKiernan in South West Africa, 1874-1879*. Cape Town.
Shackleton, E.R.
1932 The Merille or Gelubba. Kenya National Archives DC/TURK/2/1.
Shaw, T.
1981 The Late Stone Age in West Africa. In *The Sahara Ecological Change and Early Economic History*, J.A. Allan. Middle East and North African Studies Press, Cambridge.
Shillington, Kevin
1982 The Impact of the Diamond Discoveries on the Kimberley Hinterland. In *Industrialization and Social Change in South Africa*. S. Marks & R. Rathbone, eds. pp. 99-118. London: Longman.
1985 *The Colonisation of the Southern Tswana, 1870-1900*. Johannesburg: Ravan Press.
Silberbauer, G.
1981 *Hunter and Habitat in the Central Kalahari Desert*. Cambridge and New York: Cambridge University Press.
Simpson, J.R. and P. Evangelou, eds.
1984 *Livestock Development in Subsaharan Africa*. Boulder: Westview Press.
de Slane, W.M.
1842 *Description de l'Afrique*. Paris: Imprimerie Royale.
Smaldone, J.
1977 *Warfare in the Sokoto Caliphate: Historical and Sociological Perspectives*. Cambridge University Press.
Smith, A.B.
1974 A Preliminary Report of Excavations at Karkarichinkat, Nord and Karkarichinkat, Sud, Tilemsi Valley, Republic of Mali, Spring, 1972. *West African Journal of Archaeology* 4:33-55.
Smith, A. Donaldson
1896 Expedition Through Somaliland to Lake Rudolf. *Geographical Journal* 8: 120-137.
1897 *Through Unknown African Countries*. London: Arnold.
1900 An Expedition Between Lake Rudolf and the Nile. *Geographical Journal* 16: 600-625.
Smith, Andrew
1939 *The Diary of Dr. Andrew Smith, 1834-1836*. Edited by P.R. Kirby. Cape Town: The Van Riebeeck Society.
Sobania, Neal
1980 *The Historical Tradition of the Peoples of the Eastern Lake Turkana Basin. c. 1840-1925*. Ph.D. Dissertation, School of Oriental and African Studies, University of London.

Sobania, Neal (cont.)

   1988a Fisherman Herders: Subsistence, Survival and Cultural Change in
   Northern Kenya. *Journal of African History* 29:27-39.

   1988b Pastoralist Migration and Colonial Policy: A Case Study from Northern
   Kenya. In D. Johnson and D. Anderson, eds. pp. 219-39.

Sobania, N. and R. Waller

   Forthcoming. *Oral History and the End of Time.*

Solomon, Edward S.

   1855 *Two Lectures on the Native Tribes of the Interior.* Cape Town: Saul
   Solomon.

Solway, Jaqueline S. and Richard B. Lee

   1990 Foragers Genuine or Spurious? Situating the Kalahari San in
   History. *Current Anthropology* 31:109-146.

[SDIT] Southern Development Investigation Team

   1954 *Natural Resources and Development Potential in the Southern Provinces of the
   Sudan.* Khartoum.

Southall, Aiden

   1976 Nuer and Dinka are People: Ecology, Ethnicity and Logical Possibility.
   Man (N.S.) 11:463-491.

Spear, T.

   1981 *Kenya's Past: An Introduction to Historical Method in Africa.* London:
   Longman.

Spencer, Paul

   1965 *The Samburu: A Study of Gerontocracy in a Nomadic Tribe.* London:
   Routledge & Kegan Paul.

   1973 *Nomads in Alliance: Symbiosis and Growth among the Rendille and Samburu
   of Kenya.* London: Oxford University Press.

   1988 *The Maasai of Matapato.* Bloomington: Indiana University Press.

Sperling, Louise

   1985a The Introduction of Camels into a Lowland Samburu Area. In
   Significance and Prospects of Camel Pastoralism in Kenya. S.E. Migot-Adholla,
   ed. University of Nairobi, Institute for Development Studies, Occasional
   Paper No. 45.

   1985b Labour Recruitment Among East African Herders: The Samburu of
   Kenya. *Labour, Capital and Society* 18(1):68-86.

   1987 Wage Employment among Samburu Pastoralists of Northcentral Kenya.
   Research in Economic Anthropology 9:167-190.

Sperling, Louise and Galaty, John G.

   1990 Cattle, Culture and Economy: Dynamics in East African Pastoralism. In
   J. Galaty and D. Johnson, eds. New York: Guilford Press.

Starr, Martha A.

   1984 Animal Numbers, Distribution, Drought Losses and Recovery in Central
   Niger. Niamey: unpublished report to the Niger Range and Livestock
   Project. State Archive Service, Windhoek

   n.d. D2.8-A30. The Andersson Papers. Microfilm. A(83)1.

Steinhart, E.I.
1967 Vassal and Fief in Three Lacustrine Kingdoms. *Cahiers d'Etudes Africaines* 7 (4):606-623.
Stenning, D.J.
1958 Household Viability among the Pastoral Fulani. In *The Developmental Cycle in Domestic Groups*. J. Goody ed. Cambridge University Press.
1959 *Savannah Nomads: A Study of the Wodaabe Pastoral Fulani of Western Bornu Province*. London: Oxford University Press.
Stewart, C.C.
1973a *Islam and Social Order in Mauritania*. Oxford: Clarendon Press.
1973b Political Authority and Social Stratification in Mauritania. In *Arabs and Berbers*. Ernest Gellner and Charles Micaud, eds. pp. 375-393. London: Duckworth.
Stigand, Chauncy Hugh
1910 *To Abyssinia, Through an Unknown Land*. London: Seeley and Co. and Philadelphia: J.B. Lippincott.
Stiles, Daniel
1983 More on Camels and Desertification. *Nomadic Peoples* 14:47-49.
Sutter, John
1982 Commercial Strategies of the Wodaabe Nomads of Tanout Arrondissement, Niger. Niamey: Niger Range and Livestock Project, Discussion Paper No. 18.
Swift, Jeremy
1977 Sahelian Pastoralists: Underdevelopment, Desertification, and Famine. *Annual Review of Anthropology* 6:457-478.
1979 West African Pastoral Production Systems. Livestock Production and Marketing in the Entente States of West Africa. Working Paper No. 3. Ann Arbor: Center for Research on Economic Development. University of Michigan.
Swift, Jeremy, ed.
1984 *Pastoral Development in Central Niger: Final Report of the Niger Range and Livestock Project*. Niamey: unpublished report to the Ministry of Rural Development and USAID.
Tagart, E.
1933 *Report on the Conditions Existing among the Masarwa*. Pretoria: Government Printer.
Talbot, L.
1972 Ecological Consequences of Rangeland Development in Maasailand, East Africa. In *The Careless Technology: Ecology and International Development*. Farvar, M.T. and Milton, J.P. ed. Garden City, N.J.: Natural History Press.
Taussig, Michael T.
1980 *The Devil and Commodity Fetishism in South America*. Chapel Hill: University of North Carolina Press.
Tanaka, J.
1980 *The San: Hunter-Gatherers of the Kalahari, a Study in Ecological Anthropology*. (Translated by David W. Hughes). University of Tokyo Press.

Thomson, Joseph
1968 [1885] *Through Masai Land, A Journey of Exploration among the Snowclad Volcanic Mountains and Strange Tribes of Eastern Equatorial Africa*. London: Frank Cass & Co., 1968. (Originally published 1885, London: Sampson Low, Marston, Searle and Rivington.)

Tignor, R.L.
1972 The Maasai Warriors: Pattern Maintenance and Violence in Colonial Kenya. *Journal of African History* 12:271-90.

Tindall, Benjamin Arthur
1959 *The Journal of Joseph Tindall, Missionary in South West Africa, 1839-55*. Cape Town: Van Riebeeck Society.

Thomson, J.
1981 *Analysis of Pastoral Zone Institutions*. Unpublished report to the Niger Range and Livestock, Niamey.

Torry, W.
1977 Labour Requirements among the Gabra. ILCA Conference on Pastoralism in Kenya, Nairobi, Kenya.

Tornay, S.
1975 *Recensement Nyangatom*. Nanterre: Laboratoire d'Ethnologie et de Sociologie Comparative, Université de Paris (X).
1979a Armed Conflicts in the Lower Omo Valley, 1970-76: An Analysis from within Nyangatom Society. In *Warfare among East African Herders*. Katsuyoshi Fukui and David Turton, eds. pp. 97-117. Senri Ethnological Studies No. 3, National Museum of Ethnology, Osaka.
1979b Generations, Classes d'Ages et Superstructures: à propos de l'Etude d'une Ethnie du Cercle Karimojong (Afrique Orientale). In *Pastoral Production and Society*. L'Equipe Ecologie et Anthropologie des Sociétés Pastorales, eds. pp. 307-327. Cambridge University Press.
1981 The Nyangatom: An Outline of their Ecology and Social Organisation. In *Peoples and Cultures of the Ethio-Sudan Borderlands*. M.L. Bender, ed. pp. 137-178. East Lansing: Michigan State University African Studies Center.
1982 Archeologie, Ethno-Historie, Ethnographie: Trois Facons de Reconstruire le Temps In *Culture History in the Southern Sudan: Archaeology, Linguistics and Ethnohistory*. John Mack and Peter Robertshaw, eds. pp. 131-148. Nairobi: British Institute in Eastern Africa, Memoir No. 8.

Trancart, A.
1941 Note sur le Vocabulaire Camelin en Haute Mauritanie. *Bulletin de l'Institut Francais d'Afrique Noire* [IFAN] (Dakar) 3(1-4):45-52.

Treinen-Claustre, F.
1982 *Sahara et Sahel à l'Age du Fer: Borkou, Tchad*. Paris: Société des Africainistes.

Trimingham, J.S.
1962 *A History of Islam in West Africa*. London: Oxford University Press.

Trouwborst, A., M. d'Hertefelt and J.H. Scherer
1962 *Les Anciens Royaumes de la Zone Interlacustre Meridionale: Rwanda, Burundi, Buha*. Volume 6. Tervuren: Musée Royal de l'Afrique Centrale.

Tucker, A.N. and M.A. Bryan
1956 *The Non-Bantu Languages of North-Eastern Africa*. Oxford University Press.

Turner, Terence
n.d. Marx's Concept of Structure and the Structure of Marx's Model of Capitalist Production: An Anthropological Re-reading of *Capital*. [Manuscript]

Turton, David
1973 *The Social Organization of the Mursi*. Ph.D. Dissertation, London School of Economics.
1977 Response to Drought: The Mursi of South West Ethiopia. In *Human Ecology in the Tropics*. J.P. Garlick and R.W.J. Keay, eds. pp. 165-192. London: Taylor and Francis (Reprinted in *Disasters* 1: 1979)
1978 Territorial Organization and Age among the Mursi. In *Age, Generation and Time: Some Features of East African Age Organizations*. P.T.W. Baxter and U. Almagor, eds. pp. 95-133. London: C. Hurst.
1979a War, Peace and Mursi Identity. In *Warfare among East African Herders*. Kaysuyoshi Fukui and David Turton, eds. pp. 179-210. Senri Ethnological Studies No. 3. Osaka: National Museum of Ethnology.
1979b A Journey Made Them: Territorial Segmentation and Ethnic Identity among the Mursi, In *Segmentary Lineage Systems Reconsidered*. L. Holy, ed. pp. 119-143. The Queen's University Papers in Social Anthropology, vol. 4. Dept. of Social Anthropology, The Queen's University of Belfast.

Turton, D. and P. Turton
1984 Spontaneous Resettlement after Drought: An Ethiopian Example. *Disasters* 8: 178-189.

Turton, E.R.
1970 *The Pastoral Tribes of Northern Kenya 1800-1916*. Ph.D. Dissertation, University of London.

Urvoy, Y.
1949 *Histoire de l'Empire du Bornou*. Memoire de l'Institut Francais de l'Afrique Noire [IFAN], No. 7. Paris: Larose.

Usuman Dan Fodio
1979 *Le Livre de la Lumiere des Coeurs (Nur al-albab)*. (Traduction M. Lagarde.) Etudes Arabes. 2 trim. n. 52.
1980 Ne Kitab al-Farq, Ali Merad, ed. *Islamochristiana* 6:179-209.

van Zwanenberg, R. and A. King
1975 *An Economic History of Kenya and Uganda 1800-1970*. Atlantic Highlands, N.J.: Humanity Press.

Vannutelli, L. and C. Citerni
1899 *Secondo Spedizione Bottego: L'Omo Viaggio D'Esplorazione nell'Africa Orientale*. Milano: Ulrico Hoepli Editoe.

Vansina, J.
1985 Hunter-Gatherers of Equatorial Africa in Historical Perspective. In *Sprache und Geschichte in Afrika* 7. F. Rottland and R. Vossen, eds. pp. 431-446. Hamburg.

Vedder, Heinrich
1938 *South West Africa in Early Times; Being the Story of South West Africa up to the Date of Maharero's Death in 1890*. London: Oxford University Press.

Vidal, C.
   1974 Economie de la societe feodale Rwandaise. *Cahiers d'Etudes Africaines,* 14(53):52-73.
von Hohnel, Ludwig
   1894 *Discovery of Lake Rudolf and Stefanie.* 2 vols. London: Longmans Green.
Vossen, R.
   1977 *Eine wortgeographische untersuchung zur Territorialgeschichte der Maa-sprechenden Bevölkerung Ostafrikas.* M.A. thesis, University of Cologne.
   1982 *The Eastern Nilotes: Linguistic and Historical Reconstructions.* Kölner Beiträge zur Afrikanistik, 9. Band, Berlin: Dietrich Reimer Verlag.
   1988 *Towards a Comparative Study of the Maa Dialects of Kenya and Tanzania.* Nilo-Saharan Linguistic Analyses and Documentation, Vol. 2. Helmut Buske Verlag Hamburg.
Waller, R.D.
   1976 The Maasai and the British 1895-1905: the Origins of an Alliance. *Journal of African History* 17(4):529-53.
   1978 *The Lords of East Africa: the Maasai in the Mid-Nineteenth Century, c. 1840-1885.* Ph.D. Dissertation, Darwin College, Cambridge University.
   1985 Ecology, Migration and Expansion in East Africa. *African Affairs* 84:347-370.
Walter, B.
   1970 *Territorial Expansion of the Nandi of Kenya, 1500-1905.* Papers in International Studies, Africa Series No. 9. Athens, Ohio: Ohio University Center for International Studies.
Weatherby, J.M.
   1967 Nineteenth Century Wars in Western Kenya. *Azania* 2:133-144.
Wellby, Montagu Sinclair
   1901 *Twixt Sirdar and Menelik; an Account of a Year's Expedition from Zeila to Cairo through Unknown Abyssinia.* London and New York: Harper and Bros.
Were, Gideon S. and M.A. Ogutu
   1978 *Essays on the History of Southern-Central Africa.* Nairobi: Kenya Literature Bureau.
Western, D.
   1983 *A Wildlife Guide and A Natural History of Amboseli.* Nairobi: General Printers Ltd.
White, Cynthia
   1984 *The Wodaabe.* In Swift, ed.
Willoughby, W.C.
   1928 *The Soul of the Bantu.* New York: Doubleday, Doran & Co.
   1909 Notes on the Initiation Ceremonies of the Becwana. *Journal of the Royal Anthropological Institute* 39:228-245.
Wilmsen, E.
   1978 Prehistoric and Historic Antecedents of an Ngamiland Community. *Botswana Notes and Records* 10:5-18.
   1982 Migration Patterns of Remote Area Dwellers. In *Migration in Botswana: Patterns, Causes, and Consequences.* C. Kerven, ed. pp. 337-376. Central Statistics Office. Gaborone.

Wilmsen, E. (cont.)
1983 The Ecology of Illusion: Anthropological Foraging in the Kalahari. *Reviews in Anthropology* 10:9-20.
1989a *Land Filled with Flies: A Political Economy of the Kalahari.* Chicago: University of Chicago Press.
1989b Those Who Have Each Other: San Relations to Land. In *We Are Here: The Politics of Aboriginal Land Tenure.* E. Wilmsen, ed. pp. 43-67. Berkeley, Los Angeles and London: Univ. of California Press.
Wilson, P.T. and K. Wagenaar
1982 *An Introductory Survey of Livestock Population Demography and Reproductive Performance in the Area of the Niger Range and Livestock Project.* Bamako: International Livestock Center for Africa.
Winder, J.
1946-7 *Notes & Queries.* Sudan Archive. University of Durham. 541/9.
Winter, J.C.
1977 Maasai shield patterns: A documentary source for political history, In J.G. Mohlig, G. Rottland and B. Heine, eds., *Zur Sprachgeschichte und Ethnohistorie in Afrika*, Berlin: Neue Beiträge Afrikanistischer Forschungen:324-347.
Winter, Michael
1984 The Twareg. In Swift, ed.
Wobst, M.
1978 The Archaeoethnology of Hunter-Gatherers or the Tyranny of Ethnography in Archaeology. *American Antiquity* 43:303-309.
Wolf, Eric
1982 *Europe and the People without History.* Berkeley: University of California Press.
Worby, Eric
1984 *The Politics of Dispossession: Livestock Policy and Property Relations in Botswana.* MA thesis, Department of Anthropology, McGill University.
1988 Livestock Policy and Development Ideology in Botswana. In *Power and Poverty: Development and Development Projects in the Third World.* D. Attwood, T. Bruneau and J. Galaty, eds. pp. 155-180. Boulder: Westview Press.
World Bank
1974 *Chad: Development Potential and Constraints.* Washington, D.C.
Zeltner, J.C.
1970 Histoire des Theses sur les Rives du lac Tchad. *Annales de l'université d'abidjan*, Série F, Tome 2, 2:108-237.
1980 *Pages d'histoire du Kanem. Pays tchadien.* Paris: L'Harmattan.

Index